Visualizing Law in the Age of the Digital Baroque

Visualizing Law in the Age of the Digital Baroque explores the profound impact that visual digital technologies are having on the practice and theory of law. Today, lawyers, judges, and lay jurors face a vast array of visual evidence and visual argument. From videos documenting crimes and accidents to computer displays of their digital simulation, increasingly, the search for fact-based justice inside the courtroom is becoming an offshoot of visual meaning making. But when law migrates to the screen it lives there as other images do, motivating belief and judgment on the basis of visual delight and unconscious fantasies and desires as well as actualities. Law as image also shares broader cultural anxieties concerning not only the truth of the image but also the mimetic capacity itself, the human ability to represent reality. What is real, and what is simulation? This is the hallmark of the baroque, when dreams fold into dreams, like immersion in a seemingly endless matrix of digital appearances. When fact-based justice recedes, laws proliferate within a field of uncertainty. Left unchecked, this condition of ontological and ethical uneasiness threatens the legitimacy of law's claim to power. *Visualizing Law in the Age of the Digital Baroque* offers a jurisprudential paradigm that is equal to the challenge that current cultural conditions present.

Richard K. Sherwin is Professor of Law and Director of the Visual Persuasion Project at New York Law School, and author of *When Law Goes Pop: the Vanishing Line between Law and Popular Culture.* His research includes law and culture studies, law and film, law and humanities, rhetorical studies, visual litigation and litigation public relations.

Discourses of Law

Series editors: Peter Goodrich, Michel Rosenfeld and Arthur Jacobson
Benjamin N. Cardozo School of Law

This successful and exciting series seeks to publish the most innovative scholarship at the intersection of law, philosophy and social theory. The books published in the series are distinctive by virtue of exploring the boundaries of legal thought. The work that the series seeks to promote is marked most strongly by the drive to open up new perspectives on the relation between law and other disciplines. The series is also unique in its commitment to international and comparative perspectives upon an increasingly global legal order. Of particular interest in a contemporary context, the series has concentrated upon the introduction and translation of continental traditions of theory and law.

The impetus for the series came from the paradoxical merger and confrontation of East and West. Globalization and the internationalization of the rule of law have had dramatic and often unforeseen and ironic consequences. An understanding of differing legal cultures, particularly different patterns of legal thought, can contribute, often strongly and starkly, to an appreciation if not always a resolution of international legal disputes. The rule of law is tied to social and philosophical underpinnings that the series seeks to excoriate and illuminate.

Titles in the series:

Nietzsche and Legal Theory: Half-Written Laws
Edited by Peter Goodrich and Mariana Valverde

Law, Orientalism, and Postcolonialism: The Jurisdiction of the Lotus Eaters
Piyel Haldar

Endowed: Regulating the Male Sexed Body
Michael Thomson

The Identity of the Constitutional Subject: Selfhood, Citizenship, Culture, and Community
Michel Rosenfeld

The Land is the Source of the Law: A Dialogic Encounter with Indigenous Jurisprudence
C. F. Black

Shakespearean Genealogies of Power: A Whispering of Nothing in Hamlet, Richard II, Julius Caesar, Macbeth, The Merchant of Venice, and The Winter's Tale
Anselm Haverkamp

Forthcoming:

Novel Judgments: Legal Theory as Fiction
William Macneil

Crime Scenes: Forensics and Aesthetics
Rebecca Scott Bray

Sex, Culpability and the Defence of Provocation
Danielle Tyson

The Rule of Reason in European Constitutionalism and Citizenship
Yuri Borgmann-Prebil

The publishers gratefully acknowledge the support of the Jacob Burns Institute for Advanced Legal Studies of the Benjamin N. Cardozo School of Law to the series *Discourses of Law*.

Visualizing Law in the Age of the Digital Baroque

Arabesques and Entanglements

Richard K. Sherwin

Routledge
Taylor & Francis Group
LONDON AND NEW YORK

First published 2011
by Routledge
4 Park Square, Milton Park, Abingdon, Oxon OX14 4RN
605 Third Avenue, New York, NY 10017

Routledge is an imprint of the Taylor & Francis Group, an informa business

British Library Cataloguing in Publication Data
A catalogue record for this book is available from the British Library

Library of Congress Cataloging in Publication Data
Sherwin, Richard K.
Visualizing law in the age of the digital baroque : arabesques and entanglements/Richard K. Sherwin.
p. cm.
Includes bibliographical references and index.
1. Law—Philosophy. I. Title.
K230.S535A38 2011
340′.1—dc22

2010048526

ISBN: 978-0-415-61290-6 (hbk)
ISBN: 978-0-415-61293-7 (pbk)
ISBN: 978-0-203-81586-1 (ebk)

Typeset in Minion
by RefineCatch Limited, Bungay, Suffolk

Contents

To my parents, Erma and Stanley Sherwin

List of Illustrations

Acknowledgements

During the years of this book's gestation, I have benefited from the generosity of numerous friends and colleagues. It gives me great pleasure to acknowledge in particular Peter Goodrich, Austin Sarat, Jennifer Deger, Marie Rudden, Dani Celemajeur, Alison Young, Peter Rush, Andrew Kenyon, Amy Adler, James Elkins, Richard Schechner, Desmond Manderson, Francis Mootz, Frank Munger, Michael Perlin, David Johnson, Beth Noveck, Dan Hunter and James Grimmelmann. I am very grateful to Laura Marks for sharing some of her extremely interesting work on enfoldment and infinity prior to its publication. Needless to say, what I have made of others' efforts in my behalf remains my responsibility alone. I also wish to express my thanks to Dean Richard Matasar of New York Law School for his intellectual and material support over the years. Nicholas Tambone, NYLS class of '12, provided first-rate assistance in the final stages of the book's preparation. Naomi Allen and Alexzia Plummer provided all manner of technical assistance, for which I am also most grateful. Finally, my heartfelt thanks to my children, David and Ellie, and to my wife Gilda for their unwavering support and their sustaining love.

An earlier version of part of Chapter 3 has been published as "Law's Screen Life" in A. Sarat (ed.) *Imagining Legality*, Tuscaloosa, AL: 2011; Chapter 4 is adapted from an earlier version that appeared in *Law on the Screen*, edited by Austin Sarat, Lawrence Douglas, and Martha Merrill Umphrey © 2005 by the Board of Trustees of the Leland Stanford Jr University, all rights reserved; by permission of the publisher, www.sup.org.

CHAPTER 1

Introduction

Tell me where is fancy bred,
Or in the heart, or in the head?
It is engendered in the eye.
(William Shakespeare[1])

You're living in a dream world, Neo.
(*The Matrix*[2])

O God, show us things as they are.
(Sufi prayer[3])

This is a book about law and visual culture. It poses the question, what happens when the search for truth and fact-based justice is increasingly driven by visual evidence and visual argument inside the courtroom? The answer takes us beyond the pragmatic concerns of lawyers and judges facing new interactive, audiovisual technologies of persuasion. The shape and texture of the legal imagination itself – how we think and feel and deliberate about truth and justice – are undergoing radical change.

When I refer to "visual culture" in these pages, I have in mind David Morgan's description of the field: "what images, acts of seeing, and attendant intellectual, emotional, and perceptual sensibilities do to build, maintain, or transform the worlds in which people live."[4] When we study visual culture we are not only analyzing and interpreting images, but also "ways of seeing (or gazes) that configure the agents, practices, conceptualities, and institutions that put images to work."[5] Styles of imagining the world have been known to shift along with significant changes in technology, culture, and socio-economic conditions. For example, Benedict Anderson has observed that during the nineteenth century the technologies of "navigation, astronomy, horology, surveying, photography, and print" gave rise to a manner of imagining a world in which the particular came to be viewed as a fungible representative in a series, as if everyone and everything wore a serial number.[6] Today the technologies of digital imaging, interactive computing, and instant access to an almost infinite flow of information online are likewise giving rise to new communities, institutions, and practices, including the communities, institutions, and practices of law. In a visual culture law, too, operates visually. In contemporary legal practice, lawyers, judges, and lay jurors face a vast array of visual evidence and visual argument. From videos documenting injuries, crimes, and accidents, or advocating the mitigation or enhancement of sentences in criminal cases, to computer displays of all manner of digital graphics and re-enactments, the search for fact-based justice inside the courtroom is increasingly becoming an offshoot of visual meaning making.

Visual meaning making is different from the way we make meanings in words alone. Visual meanings are written in the body, so to speak. We respond to images quickly, holistically, and affectively – the same way we perceive the world at large. Vision is a complex physiological, cultural, and cognitive response to visual stimuli. It depends on a variety of cues. Implicit meanings – often the offspring of emotional and mnemonic associations to what we see on the screen – tend to remain hidden from conscious reckoning. Images quickly activate patterns of seeing and feeling that we have internalized from a lifetime of watching. So when law lives as an image on the screen it lives there as other images do. That is to say, it motivates belief and judgment on the basis of visual delight and unconscious fantasies and desires as well as actualities – all within the discrete aesthetic code in which a given visual medium operates.

In short, analyzing and interpreting the visual culture of law requires that we understand the peculiar logic of the media that produce it, and the kind of visual world those productions help to create. This is not the world of strict linear logic, deductive reasoning, and rational volition that legal positivists, rational choice theorists, and behavioral economists tend to favor. Law has always been a matter of effective storytelling as well as logic, and now *visual* storytelling must be added to the lawyer's (scholar's and law teacher's) cultural toolkit. Thus it falls upon us to ask: How does visual culture alter the legal mind, and with what consequences for the practice and theory of law? That is the subject of this book.

How do we know the truth of what we see on the screen? What warrants our belief in images? When does the image add a living reality (of feelings and impressions) which words alone may not convey, and when does it divert judgment and belief through an intensification of irrational fantasies and desires? When law marries visual culture their joint offspring requires new academic partners, including media and cultural studies, art history, cognitive psychology, psychoanalysis, and neuroscience. In short, jurists need to cultivate a new visual literacy so that they may understand better how images work, the better to cultivate competencies in visual communication, cross-examination, and judgment. That objective is one of the core goals of this book. But it is not the only one.

If law is to be treated as a part of contemporary visual culture, and of that need there can be no doubt, it is not enough to consider the way in which law partakes in the various aesthetic, cognitive, and cultural codes that different visual media deploy. Law also shares in the various normative aspirations and afflictions that are bound up in the culture at large. For this reason, we must also be attentive to cultural conditions. What does it mean to aspire to visual eloquence, for example? How do we recognize and capture it in contemporary cultural terms? Moving to the other end of the spectrum, what anxieties, what loss of confidence in the reliability of visual representation afflicts the visual legal imagination? Addressing these highs and lows represents the second core objective of this book.

Writing about visual eloquence is not an easy undertaking. In what follows, I shall seek to retrieve a category that I believe can help. I call it the visual sublime. There is something uncanny in the excess of meaning that some images convey. The poignant dignity of a victim wrongfully harmed, the implicit malice of one who has perpetrated (or is about to perpetrate) an act of violence, the collapse of time in the visual and aural synthesis of various pieces of visual evidence presented at trial – these legal examples, together with a host of other illustrations of the visual sublime will be explored in these pages. There are times when images move us with an uncanny power, a sense of presence that cannot be easily explained. But there are also times when visual images convey a very different kind of reality, perhaps something that may not be reality at all. This is the image as mere sensation or digital simulacrum, the image as aesthetic delight or flight of fancy, the image as progenitor of irrational desire. These forms of vision are also now part of the legal landscape.

They are a part of what it means when we say law lives as an image on the screen as other images do.

And here is where the specter of the baroque comes to the fore. In a time when we can digitally picture just about anything we can imagine it should not prove surprising that doubts may arise concerning the truth of what we see. This feeling of doubt, which culminates in a loss of confidence in the faculty of representation itself, lies at the core of baroque culture – both the baroque culture of seventeenth century Europe, and the global digital baroque culture that we are living in today. What is real, and what is imaginary? And how can we be sure of the difference? Baroque visuality is an affliction of vision. It comes about amid a proliferation of visual forms, forms that invite an intensification of feeling as well as a dizzying sense of dislocation and confusion. For the baroque mind, lurking beneath the surface of visual spectacle and delight lies a formidable terror. It takes shape in the thought that perhaps there is nothing else but this, these dancing forms, these infinitely unfolding arabesques. Such was Pascal's horror in the face of the infinite.

The anxiety that accompanies baroque visuality, on the one hand, which is at bottom a fear of the loss of meaning, and the uncanny presence of the visual sublime on the other, frame the contemporary, culture-wide quest for visual competence. The stakes of that search grow weightier when it plays out on the landscape of law, where visual representations are secured by the police power of the state. Law's aspiration to fact-based justice can ill afford the baroque recession of reality inside the courtroom.

In order to counter the uncertainties that afflict the baroque mind, in what follows I seek out those cultural and cognitive resources that may help us to recognize (and display) visual eloquence. Overused categories such as "postmodernism" no longer provide a useful source of insight here. And while the constructivist perspective, and the critical deconstructivist method that illuminates it, remains of value, it is possible to have too much of a good thing. Deconstruction usefully excavates structures of meaning in texts and images. But like that classic Marx Brothers scene from *A Night at the Opera* (1935), in which Chico and Groucho rip away extraneous clauses of a contract until nothing worth saving remains, deconstruction risks excessive critical zeal. Even the inexpressible (perhaps that above all) in text and image alike is worth saving. Ultimately, that act of recuperation and affirmation may well be what deconstruction is for. (After all, didn't Derrida say, deconstruction *is* justice?[7])

Baroque visuality, at any rate, has no difficulty discerning the forms; it's meaning that gives it trouble. Consider in this regard the Wachowski brothers' film, *The Matrix* (1999), which struck a nerve worldwide.

There is something eerily recognizable about Neo's discovery that he is living in a neuro-interactive simulation, a vast computer program called the matrix. It's as if in the film we've stumbled upon a collective fantasy, or shared terror: what we've taken for reality all our lives turns out to be no more than a collective dream. That the quintessentially baroque vision of dreams endlessly enfolding within dreams resonated so powerfully a decade later in Christopher Nolan's film *Inception* (2010) should not be surprising. In these films (and innumerable other contemporary movies, novels, plays, and games on line) the precariousness of our grasp on reality has emerged as a pervasive cultural theme. Bruno Latour calls it "iconoclash." We love the image and we hate it. We are enchanted by its vivid persuasive power, but remain fearful of being seduced and deceived, taken in unawares, like Neo.

One lesson of the digital baroque is that the rationalist assumptions underlying modern jurisprudence are manifestly inadequate to the demands of the times. The Cartesian legacy, with its anti-rhetorical animus and its repudiation of embodied forms of knowing, which is to say, with its dismissal of emotional knowledge and the creative power of the imagination, is ill equipped to cope with the challenges of visual culture. The model of visual jurisprudence that I propose in these pages offers a new approach to legal theory and practice that is more suitable to the actual conditions of contemporary life, including the visual life of the law. Cut off from its figurative, poetic roots, blinded by lack of a pragmatic ethical phenomenology, justice recedes from view. In its place, legal forms endlessly proliferate: guidelines and principles, policies and regulations, rules and metrics – overwhelming in their disparate array. An overabundance of forms and measures leaves us disoriented and uncertain, longing for a way out of the dazzling baroque labyrinth we've made for ourselves.

To meet the challenge of visualizing law in the age of the digital baroque, this book argues for the cultivation of visual literacy and for a renewal of confidence in the world-maintaining power of human inventiveness. Simply put, we need to revitalize the legal imagination. This effort must not only incorporate new insights from neuroscience and cognitive psychology, but also from the humanities, and in particular from the rich rhetorical tradition that flourished before the age of modernity. Inventiveness, eloquence, and the power to give life to social and legal reality in verbal as well as visual figures and images dominated the pre- (and early) modern culture of law.[8] In this book, I advocate greater attentiveness to the properties and virtues of visual eloquence not as ornament ("mere rhetoric"), but as both constitutive and invocative of the real. Visual eloquence takes us beyond ourselves to something other, something that comes to be in the field of attunement that is generated between seer and seen. The authenticity of this kind of visual experience consists in its capacity to animate *mimesis* – not as mere imitation (as Aristotle wrote), but rather as a form of identification.

Visual eloquence invites the viewer to experience the reciprocal nature of mimetic identification, a process in which the viewer identifies what is present in the field of vision and, in that very act of recognition, experiences a renewed sense of identity. This visual experience is not entirely vicarious, which is to say, it is not wholly removed from the real. It allows an experience of the real in its own right. Experience influences our way of knowing and being in the world. This kind of embodied cognition serves as a springboard to integrated judgment. Judgment in this sense is the offshoot of an entangled identity. It reflects both what one knows (and feels) and who one is in relation to others and objects in the world beyond the self. Sensation, by contrast, merely registers a range of physical stimulations or affects. Images that move us simply by simulating the real, perhaps by merely reproducing the effects of authentic experience, lack the authority of mimetic identification. Sensational images may affect us, but they cannot change us, or alter our relationships with others and the world around us. Sensational images leave us as they find us. Judgments made on the basis of sensation alone are quick, thin, and ephemeral. I shall contend that they are unworthy of law's aspiration to fact-based justice.

What constitutes prudent judgment in a predominantly visual society? How do we know we have gotten right the truth and justice claims that visual digital images make in particular cases? These questions make vivid the need for forms of knowledge and discourse that are suitable to the practice, theory, and teaching of law in the digital age. When law shifts away from words alone to encompass visual meaning making, the modern jurist's habitual reliance upon semiotic conventions, deductive and inductive logic, and dispassion in the deliberative process no longer suffice.

There is much work to be done to excavate and reconstruct the habits of heart and mind (of passion and knowledge) in the visual meaning making process. Consider in this regard the traditional Anglo-American common law ideal of adversarial justice. The adversarial system has always expressed a preference for live testimony. The live witness may be tested in court, as tradition has it, by taking an oath to testify truthfully as well as through the clash of cross-examination, and of course based on the fact finder's close scrutiny of the witness's bodily and expressive demeanor during the testimonial process. Today, however, videos, graphics, and digital simulations of all kinds increasingly compete with live testimony. As a result, contemporary triers of fact increasingly find themselves cast in the role of putative *eye witnesses* to electronically mediated events (filmed, remixed, or digitally simulated). But how does the adversarial process test the *decision maker's* reliability as witness to these screened realities?

Law's migration to the screen raises in a new form a very old controversy. It harks back to the ancient Greek debate about rhetoric versus philosophy (what Plato called "dialectic"). Platonic philosophy posits universal Ideal Forms of knowledge, effectively reducing everything else to mere appearances. In this framework, rhetoric becomes mere ornamentation, a matter of stylistic adornment without truth-value. Thus began a long tradition in the West in which truth and appearances, knowledge and persuasion, ethics and aesthetics were split asunder. Recurrent outbreaks of iconoclastic fervor attest to the persistence of this binary opposition. For the iconoclast, false idols (mere appearances) mock hidden realities (invisible truths). Material forms blaspheme against spiritual substance. As Protestant reformer John Calvin put it, "Since God has no similarity to those shapes by means of which people attempt to represent him ... all attempts to represent him are an impudent affront ... to his majesty and glory."[9] At issue here is not only how much truth the image can bear (or bare), but also how much power the image maker should wield. If mimicry is a form of mastery, do we usurp the creative prerogative of God when we recreate the world in images? History is studded with such contentious claims – together with the highly destructive and potentially fatal consequences that they carry for perceived transgressors. This is not a distant threat. As recently as 2001, we saw the revival of iconoclastic fervor when the Taliban dynamited into dust the monumental Bamiyan Buddhas in central Afganistan, claiming them to be idols forbidden under Sharia law. We witnessed this destructive impulse at work again in 2005, when protests, threats, and acts of violence by Islamic fundamentalists erupted around the world after the Danish newspaper *Jyllands-Posten* published 12 editorial cartoons that mockingly depicted Mohammed.

Who can doubt the power of the visual image? And who can doubt the power of new communication technologies to alter the way we live, from our construction of self and interactions with others to our very sense of the world we live in? As Sherry Turkle has observed, digital simulation wants immersion, and immersion makes it difficult to doubt simulation: "[C]ompelling virtual objects that engage the body as well as the mind ... [can make it] hard to remember all that lies beyond [simulation]."[10] The potent expressive power of digital simulation raises important questions for law and society as a whole. It causes us to wonder, what does it mean today to speak of our continuing fealty to reality, and in particular of law's continuing commitment to fact-based justice? And so we ask, what does it mean to perceive an image? And what does it mean for law to anchor its authority in perceptions and judgments based on digital simulations? These questions prompt practical as well as deeply philosophical responses. It is not simply a matter of knowing how to create visual evidence and visual arguments that win cases inside the courtroom, although that is no small thing. It is also a question of coming to grips with how we know what's true and what's just in a given legal controversy. How do we avoid being taken in, or led astray by a visually compelling, emotionally fraught, but perhaps ultimately misleading image?

What do we see, and what is absent from (or hidden on) the screen? What reality do images present (or make present)? What makes it seem as if the image stares back at us, with a life of its own? How are images inscribed in our body? How do they affect us, change us, enliven us, distract us, lead us astray? What mental tools, what cultural and cognitive categories, do we use to see with? How do images draw from popular cultural resources (such as advertising, film, and television) to cue familiar feelings, memories, thoughts, and desires in the mind of the viewer? And how do these associative processes and substantive resources for meaning making constitute the legal imagination and, by extension, help to construct the reality of law? In short, what kind of life is it (and what sort of world, what sort of mind) when law lives the life of images on the screen?

Plato taught that when law comports with reality it can aspire to justice.[11] But today we are not so sure about reality. Thus we come to inquire, what is the fate of law, and justice, in a time when the real grows elusive? If there is no "there" there, if reality becomes interchangeable with digital simulation, if it is always being created anew – unfolding from moment to moment, like some Deleuzean assemblage or rhizoidal network of "movement-images" endlessly flowing in a state of "pure immanence," or like Derrida's irrepressibly protean *différance*, that unrepresentable, non-existent source from which differences, traces without origins, endlessly disseminate – might it be that everything we see on the screen is momentary and inescapably contingent? But if everything is equally contingent, then may we also say that everything is equally valuable? Equally true? If that were so, then what, aside from the will to power, arbitrates judgment? This vexatious uncertainty permeates baroque culture, including the digital baroque culture in which we live today. In baroque times it often seems as if we have nothing but our own fabricated forms to live with, nothing but our own "garrulity" (as Stanley Rosen put it[12]).

In this sense, baroque law is hyper-positive law, law cut off from nature or from essences of any kind. Such may well be law's fate in a condition of "creation without grace."[13] Under such conditions, positive law's legitimacy only arises from the public's acceptance of its commands, and of its right to command in the first place. But what justifies such acceptance? We know that the baroque lacks transcendental references. Rousseau, along with other Liberal theorists of law and the modern state, understood that deprived of traditional metaphysics, no longer able to imagine the sovereign as the living agent of God on earth, people would need to be taught anew how to believe in sovereignty and the legitimacy of state power. Rousseau referred to this as "civil religion." Expressed in visual terms, however, the available spectrum for persuasion and belief stretches far wider than Rousseau's strategic faith might suggest. It also includes, as Machiavelli and Hobbes understood full well, the persuasive inducements of fear and spectacle. And, indeed, in their generation, baroque spectacle was one of the paramount agencies of church and state power alike. State sponsored parades, elaborate pomp and ceremony, awe-inspiring mechanical gardens, massive firework displays – these were the signs of power in the age of baroque spectacle. Today, their digital analogue may be found on screens everywhere, including the courtroom.

Baroque ornamentation ramifies precisely in order to intensify its effect, as if the power of sensation alone might suffice to distract us from, or disguise, the fear that hollowness lies at the core of things. Such a condition cannot be sustained. Inwardly empty, left with nothing more than the will to form, the baroque is haunted by the idea of catastrophe. As Walter Benjamin wrote:

> The baroque knows no eschatology; and for that very reason it possesses no mechanism by which all earthly things are gathered in together and exalted before being consigned to their end. The hereafter is emptied of everything which contains the slightest breath of this world, and from it the baroque extracts a profusion of things which customarily escaped the grasp of artistic formulation and, at its high point, brings them violently into the light of day, in order to clear an ultimate heaven, enabling it, as a vacuum, one day to destroy the world with catastrophic violence."[14]

Baroque culture stands like a tree whose roots have been excised. Little wonder that it feels as if one were being "driven along to a cataract."[15]

At some point something must occur to arrest the unending profusion of empty baroque form. In this book I call that event the sublime. The sublime arrests the recession of the real and the ethical. It helps us to reassert our fealty to reality, which is to say, our capacity to respond to what others and the concrete situation that we face demands of us. Indeed, it turns out, or so I shall argue, that both beauty and justice share the sublime, albeit each in its own way. In nature, we experience a sublime beauty that momentarily arrests the recession of being. And in the social domain, attuned to the other who stands before us, we experience a sublime ethical demand, momentarily halting the spiraling recession of justice from the fragmented, monadic, and contingent legal forms that it leaves behind. Every entanglement is an occasion for mindfulness in our response to things and others around us. Entanglements ground and focus the attentive mind in concrete human encounters. They root legal decision making in the ethical demands that we experience when we stand face to face with others, and with social conflicts in specific contexts that demand resolution. In this sense, justice is an entangled reality from which we turn at our peril.

Every way of seeing is a way of being (of feeling one's way) among others in the world. An ethical optics describes attentiveness to what the situation at hand calls for. This view marks a significant shift in philosophy away from the abstraction of concepts toward the concrete particularities of everyday life. This is the way of ethical phenomenology. Applicable rules play a part, but mindfulness is not the same thing as placing facts under a category or rule. Judgment in this sense takes place in a far richer experiential register than the rule-bound domain described in the literature of legal positivism, rational choice theory, and behavioral economics. In what follows, I shall argue that the shift from abstract linguistic conventions to concrete visual practices models a concomitant jurisprudential shift from abstract concepts to embodied experience and embodied judgment. The conceptual bias in traditional jurisprudence, as we find, for example, in the disembodied, highly decontextualized framework adopted by Rawls, among others, is ill suited to the highly tactile, emotionally robust, immediately intuited affordances of visual culture. This is a far cry from Descartes' influential insistence upon disembodied rationality. The devaluation of perception and sensory experience, like the medieval subordination of flesh to soul, has no place in the legal imaginary constituted by visual jurisprudence.

There is something authentic, something grounding and sublimely transformative in our experience of the visual, as well as something deadening, reductive, flat, and sensationally hollow, as baroque culture manifestly demonstrates. Of course, in practice we do not enjoy the luxury of choice amid such simple polar extremes. The authentic and the ornamental (image as empty sensation) often come in dismayingly mixed forms. When law migrates to the screen it brings unprecedented descriptive and persuasive power to the search for truth-based justice. It also creates new risks. We see this, for example, when law adopts the screen's code of representation as its own. Then legal certainty may be conflated with visual delight, and unconscious fantasies (the mass media's logic of desire) may become the engine of legislation (as we will see in Chapter 3's case study of child pornography laws).

Today, our command and control of digital form continues to grow while our ethical confidence seems to falter. Aesthetics alone has never provided an adequate basis for constituting ethical judgment, just as ethics alone has never provided an adequate basis for motivating right outcomes. The challenge we face is to bring aesthetics and ethics (arabesques and entanglements) into better alignment. This challenge is most fraught with consequence where image-based judgments are backed by the power of the state, which is to say, in the domain of law. Accordingly, the task of lawyers, judges, and lay citizens alike in this new digital visual world of ours is to cultivate the visual sophistication and ethical competence that is needed to judge well, so that we may remain confident that the legal process and its decisional offshoots stay true to the ongoing demands of fact-based justice. We need a new visual literacy to crack the aesthetic, cognitive, and cultural codes of law as image in the digital age. But visual literacy will not suffice without an abiding confidence in the human mimetic faculty, the inventive act of representation itself. If justice is to continue to play a part in legal outcomes aesthetics in law must operate in the service of the ethical. As Jean-Luc Godard put it in a recent film, when law no longer knows justice, justice comes to be judged before the law.[16] That event marks the subversion and demise of equity. True equity looks beyond the law to correct it.[17] Justice and the ethical take on a living (albeit imperfectly realized) presence in specific acts of judgment that are attuned to the real, and that poetically stir our hearts and minds by means of figurative and visual eloquence.

Each generation bears the burden of acquitting itself of the indictment of reality. Today it is incumbent upon us to retool the legal mind so that it may pursue fact-based justice wherever it takes us – including law's life as an image on the screen. That is the challenge this book sets out to address. We shall proceed first by exploring some of the underlying cultural and cognitive conditions in which we live, drawing out the historical analogue to contemporary digital baroque culture in order to see more clearly how the visual turn today is affecting (and afflicting) the life of the law. We shall then examine examples of visualizing law in both its sensational and sublime aspects inside the courtroom and in the culture at large. The next task is to attempt to marshal those cultural and cognitive resources that are available to overcome law's iconoclash, which is to say, the baroque anxiety and accompanying loss of visual and ethical confidence that currently afflicts the legal imagination. In pursuit of greater visual and ethical acuity in the law our path will lead to a renewed encounter with visual eloquence. This will encompass a retrieval of the ancient virtue of inventiveness fortified by a renewed appreciation of the visual sublime.

CHAPTER 2

Visual Jurisprudence: The New Paradigm

> The anxiety over the adequate way of representing truth attacks periods on the threshold of major social and cultural changes when the validity of accepted norms of understanding is subjected to critical scrutiny.
>
> (Azade Sehan[1])

> It may be that one has to choose between ethics and aesthetics, but it is no less true that whichever one chooses, one will always find the other at the end of the road. For the very definition of the human condition should be in the *mise-en-scène* itself.
>
> (Jean-Luc Godard[2])

> Respondent's version of events is so utterly discredited by the record that no reasonable jury could have believed him. Since the dissent contradicts ths account, we have made the video available on the Supreme Court website . . .
>
> (Justice Antonin Scalia[3])

We are awash in images. They are on display in our homes, our schools, our theaters, and our workplaces. They are there when we reach in our pockets for our handheld devices and when we glance at the dash of our cars where virtual maps locate us in space. Electronic screens decorate the walls of the rooms we live in; they are embedded in the glass surfaces of our urban office towers; they light up the spaces of shopping malls, airports, and waiting rooms everywhere. And, yes, they greet our gaze in law offices, governmental agencies, and courtrooms. Today, with increasing frequency video displays and digital images accompany lawyers' opening statements and closing arguments at trial. They are introduced as evidence in the form of animations, digital re-enactments, and video documentaries showing tort victims living damaged lives in the wake of accidents or botched surgeries or exposure to defective products or chemical pollutants. Prosecutors display images from police surveillance as well as private security cameras that have visually captured drug deals, robberies, and all manner of wrongdoing. Criminal defense lawyers use amateur videos, perhaps fortuitously shot from a handy cell phone, to show police misconduct or to contradict a written police report. And increasingly, on appeal, judges review the visual record of the trial to assess allegations of error. Did jurors, or perhaps a lower appellate judge, unreasonably construe visual evidence that jurors saw at trial? Did the trial judge properly deem a witness hostile thus permitting the prosecutor to ask leading questions? The visual record captures descriptive details, such as demeanor, facial expression, and tone of voice, which the proverbial "cold" written record on appeal leaves silent or unseen, hidden beneath and between the lines of the court reporter's text.

Video lets us see the action unfold. The patrol car's camera records the chase and the arrest. It shows the level of violence that was used to subdue a resisting civilian, if resistance there was, and the conditions under which a station house interrogation was conducted and inculpatory statements were obtained. Perhaps a professional videographer, hired by the police or the prosecutor's office, will talk viewers through the evidence at the crime scene, zooming in on that splatter of blood on the wall, or that fateful footprint beside the body. With new visual technologies lawyers can picture many things that remain invisible to the unaided eye. Experts introduce CAT scans and MRIs at trial to show brain defects, perhaps in support of tort damages or claims of incompetence, or insanity, or that seek mitigation of punishment in a criminal case. Lawyers show digital animations depicting reconstructed airplane accidents or that take us inside the body, picturing, for example, how plaque in an artery of the heart was allegedly dislodged by a careless surgeon or a faulty medical instrument. Legal hearings and negotiations may be conducted by way of electronic screens – with witnesses or perhaps the parties themselves participating from many miles away. Mediation efforts may transpire wholly online. Disputes may be worked out in virtual courtrooms, perhaps even in virtual worlds.

And so we watch: we watch in court and we watch in the court of public opinion, and sometimes the court itself invites us to watch, downloading critical visuals on the court's own website so that we may "see for ourselves," as the U.S. Supreme Court said after doing just that in a recent case.[4] And knowing we watch, advocates sometimes begin their cases well before trial – staging interviews for the news media, setting up websites to present their side of the case, or releasing evidence that will be used in court (if it is ever admitted at all) in a pre-emptive effort to spin their client's story in preparation for the real show at trial, like a trailer whetting our appetites with visual highlights of what is to come. We are awash in images, which means we know from watching the screens that surround us how things and places and events are supposed to look; how particular kinds of visual stories are supposed to unfold; and what characters of a certain sort may be expected to do and say and look like. We know, or think we know, partly because we have absorbed useful stereotypes and recurring representations from popular culture. We carry them around in our heads, images that help to construct our personal and collective histories. For it is with images that we create memories, sometimes substituting for the real event that has long since receded from view, perhaps along with other realities that the captured image subsequently screens out. Like the horror and shock of the World Trade Center attack on 9/11, after which the same series of images played on the news, over and over, stabilizing the terror like a totemic stand-in for the chaotic barrage of events too discordant and too painful to confront.

History is an archive of words and images, documents and performances that we absorb from films along with other popular and more esoteric representations. The American war in Vietnam, for example, has become a composite, a synthetic memory, based on films like *Apocalypse Now*, *Platoon*, and iconic photographs, like the one showing a young Vietnamese girl running, naked, her skin hanging loose as a result of napalm, or the image of Nguyen Ngoc Loan, the South Vietnamese General who summarily executed a prisoner in a public square with a pistol to the head at point blank range. The war in Iraq becomes *Jarhead*, *Syriana*, and a series of iconic photos, like the one of a hooded man standing atop a cardboard box, his arms stretched wide, his hands holding electrical wires, in Abu Ghraib prison. The catastrophic hurricane and ensuing floods in New Orleans in 2005, comes to mind as a series of live television reports with their searing images of bedraggled refuges, camped out for days, without supplies or electricity, in the overheated Houston Astrodome, an aerial shot of two dogs as they "inspect" a corpse, a survivor, stranded on the roof of her flooded home, the words "This is not America" inscribed in tall letters beneath her feet, soon followed by Spike Lee's vivid and scathing documentary *When the Levees Broke*. Historic reality has become a visual template, an archive of iconic sounds, images, and words.

We watch and our senses respond, even though what we see on the screen may not have been produced from the physical world around us. Databases and algorithmic calculations produce images that activate our senses as if we were perceiving objects and events and others in real life. For example, to the untrained eye the image produced by functional magnetic resonance imaging ("fMRI") may appear to be a brain alight with neural activity. But, despite appearances, it is neither a photograph nor an x-ray. Rather, it is a computer construct based on complex statistical data sets involving the spin of water molecules in blood as it courses through the brain. A specially designed computer program turns the numbers into what looks like a brain lighting up in electrifying color. In digital culture, images abound, but oftentimes rather than seeing something that exists in nature we are using our eyes to process information.[5]

When what we see when we look at an image is less important than the coded information that invisibly produces it, beneath the surface of the screen, so to speak, we are dealing with a special kind of image. We call these "aniconic" images. Aniconic images may present themselves as visual, but they actually point toward the unseen. The authority of an aniconic image derives from an invisible source.[6] Alongside centuries-old aniconic images like the endlessly unfolding, neo-Platonic, Islamic arabesque, which traces its origin to an unrepresentable, transcendental source,[7] today we have the aniconic digital image, the visible offspring of algorithms which invisibly instruct computers to represent data in a specified visual form (a brain, a plane crash, a murder).[8]

What do we see (what is there) on the screen before us? Are we looking as if through a window, at something actual? Or must the image we see be deconstructed, or decoded, in order to get at that which exists outside the mind? This dilemma has persisted in one form or another throughout the history of visual mediation. When distrust of the image peaks, however, an iconoclastic impulse stirs that may be violent in the extreme. The icon smashing rampage that Byzantine Emperor Leo III unleashed during the eighth century, like the iconoclastic violence that ravaged Europe during the Thirty Years' War in Europe (1618–1648) between Catholics and Protestants, attests to the power of the image for iconophiles and iconoclasts alike. During the Reformation, and the Counter-Reformation backlash, the question was, does the image commemorate the reality it depicts, or does it deface the ineffable? But even putting aside these sorts of sectarian issues, it is enough to ponder the efficacy of visual representation in the context of ordinary life. For here as well the question remains: whether, and if so to what degree, any person or thing, any original, unmediated physical reality survives the act of representation. What do images tell us? In the domain of law, where the fate of property, freedom, and perhaps life itself may hang on the truth of an image, uncertainty concerning the reliability of its claims is no small thing.

The Cultural Construction of Visuality

It matters whether we feel connected to or cut off from what is real and true. The more connected we feel, the more trust we have in what we know. Alienation culminates in solipsism, perhaps even psychosis – a state in which reality only exists in the mind. As Borges has written, "You have not awakened to wakefulness, but to a previous dream. This dream is enclosed within another, and so on to infinity."[9] This "world of dreams" ("dreaming while asleep, dreaming while awake," as Shido Bunan observed during the seventeenth century in Japan[10]) captures the uneasy mood of baroque culture as it swept across Europe during the late sixteenth and early seventeenth centuries. This was a time of profound disorder, marked by a deep anxiety concerning the nature of truth, reason, and reality itself. "Everything functions upside down," Barrionuevo wrote.[11] People wandered through life as if caught in a "confused labyrinth," and, indeed, among the most prevalent metaphors of the baroque era are figures of infinite mazes, mirrors within mirrors, stories within stories, and dreams within dreams.

When the world is a stage, and all is appearances, it may seem that only the most violent of sensations will awaken the mind and root it, at least momentarily, in something real. The shock therapy of the baroque produces what Maravall has described as "an aesthetic of cruelty." It arises alongside a political culture that is dominated by mass spectacle, mass sensation, and the mass manipulation of consent.[12] When everything is mutable, when the individual "is never his or her own likeness," and "there is nothing stable, perpetual, nor permanent," when ontological anxiety is pervasive, life lurches from passion to passion. All things, including law, appear to be part of an endless spectacle of shadows driven by contingent forces cast beyond sight and reason. In baroque culture, there is nothing but fragments; ruin seems imminent. As the ersatz image empties of meaning, longing begets longing; astonishment may jolt the eye, but thereafter no substance remains to feed the heart and mind. Thus, images proliferate, in a torrential jumble, for there is no over arching plot, no steady state of origin or end in which the restless will of the creator may suspend the act of representation and find comfort in what has been created, for there is none.

Wölfflin has written that "we interpret the whole outside world according to the expressive system with which we have become familiar from our own bodies."[13] And according to Leibniz: "A soul can read in itself only what is distinctly represented in it; it is unable to unfold all at once all its folds; for these go on into infinity."[14] How we learn to see the world and others around us, how we learn to see ourselves, is a matter of historical, cultural, and cognitive particularity. As cognitive psychologist Jerome Bruner notes, our sense of self is distributed in the narratives we inherit from the culture in which we live.[15] Today, even a cursory survey of popular culture in recent years will attune the observer to the peculiar mood and expressive style of the baroque. Only now we know it as the digital baroque. With the advent of digital technologies that can simulate the real with exquisite precision, we are poised to appreciate that fateful cinematic moment in *The Matrix* when Neo first learns that he has been "living in a dream world . . . a neural-interactive simulation that we call the matrix." What we see, what we touch, what we smell, in the matrix, is the offspring of a computer code whose algorithmic constructs generate coherent patterns that register directly in the brain. In this sense, what we call "experience" is but a contingent pattern of synthesizable data. This quintessentially baroque motif is but an extreme form of a theory of language that locks the mind out of the actual, what Kant called the thing in itself, on the understanding that we can get no closer to reality than a particular expressive form or conventional code in a given medium of communication may allow. In this sense, to borrow again from Leibniz, we are all monads, sealed within the confines of our embodied mind, gazing out upon the world through what we want to call a window, but the window is in reality a medium, a code, a set of filters and translators doing their best to convey a sense that we have let the outside in. Our relationship to that code, to language, or to any communicative medium in which knowledge and meaning are produced and exchanged, is paramount when it concerns our pursuit of fact-based justice. Law lives differently in a visual expressive system than in one exclusively made up of words.

The Emergence of Visual Jurisprudence

I believe that a key task of jurisprudence is to break the code, and cultivate the craft, by which legal meanings are made and exchanged. It is science and rhetoric combined. If the code through which we mind the law is merely a convention, then we are in effect cut off from knowing reality directly. What we know is simply a swirling tableau of symbols and signs, or images and pictures. On this Hobbesian (radically "positivistic") view, meaning remains rooted in contingent conventions, for they are nothing more than nominal definitions.[16] However, if something real subsists within words and images – within the poetic resonance of a word or phrase, or in the visual shimmer or uncanny aura of an image that disquiets or enchants the mind – if the medium of communication is in this sense overdetermined, if its truth remains irreducible to structure or form, then perhaps we are not so utterly alienated from reality after all. In this alternative view, the greatness of an expressive work lies in its capacity to "show us the world."[17] As Iris Murdoch observes, the role of great art is "as an educator and revealer."[18] In this respect, it is the clarity of expression "which startles and delights us simply because we are not used to looking at the real world at all."[19] Rather than exclusively rooted in artificial conventions of meaning making, here an act of awareness, characterized by a demotion of self for the sake of that which comes to mind, makes meaning and judgment an event of attentive attunement.[20]

On this view, ethical judgment is, as cognitive scientist Francisco Varela puts it, more a matter of "know-how" than "know-what," which is to say, it is closer to wisdom than to critical reason.[21] In the act of minding a text or an image or an event in the world, we enact meaning as a spontaneous expression of our embodied knowledge. This mode of cognition is separate from, and ordinarily prior to, the mode of rational analysis through which categories or rules may be critically applied to a given set of facts or by which costs and benefits may be rationally assessed. We typically experience as a mood the emotional force of that which demands attention before we arrive at an understanding.[22] Yet, ultimately, feeling and knowledge are co-constitutive. As Antonio Damasio puts it, "Nature appears to have built the apparatus of rationality not just on top of the apparatus for biological regulation, but also *from* and *with* it."[23] In other words, signals from the body both shape and modify rationality. On this view, therefore, without emotion our capacity to reason would be severely impaired. Indeed, if we could not feel what a situation (or a text or an image, for that matter) demanded of us, our capacity for moral and aesthetic judgment would be crippled. Our intuitive sense of what we ought to feel and do in response to a particular social conflict or individual need arises from our encounter (our being present or attuned with) something other than self.[24] The ethical, perhaps even justice itself, may originate in this spontaneous act of responsiveness to (or as Levinas would say, our being responsible for) the other.

There is no finality or totality here; ethical responsiveness to the infinite demands of the other before us remains situated, and endlessly unfolding. In ethics as in aesthetics there are times when we experience the finite expression of an illimitable demand as a living presence. This uncanny sense of presence has been known since ancient times as the sublime.[25] In the experience of the sublime, something more is given, and we receive it with an unusual intensity of feeling. The sublime is that which remains inexpressible within that which is expressed. It is always more than what we can say or show, more than the word or image in which it restlessly subsists. Yet, notwithstanding its uncanny origin, the sublime remains a source of profound meaning. The sublime is an especially vivid and emotionally charged, but critically examinable type of aesthetic and ethical knowledge.

In the presence of the visual sublime the viewer experiences a deep and vital bond with the expressive work and the reality it displays. The sublime animates a way of being entangled in the world. By giving it life and form the sublime expressive work turns culture into a way of life. This is what we find in the medieval tradition of poetics. As Boccaccio wrote: "The poet is the true founder of every human community because with his poetry he inaugurates a new interpretation of reality, discloses a new era . . ."[26] This is no mere matter of versifying. Poetry in this pre-modern sense is tantamount to letting the presence of what is come to be (to "shine forth," as Heidegger would put it), so as to allow a form, or an image, to shimmer with being. In this sense, the poetic sublime originates a living meaning that can found a world. I believe this is what Vico in the eighteenth century and more recently the great legal scholar Robert Cover had in mind when they each expressed admiration for the human capacity to found a discrete universe of meaning bound by law (which is to say, a *nomos*) based on a living text or image.[27] This is what it means for the creative imagination not simply to mediate the world but also, in so doing, to establish a way of life. The *mythopoieic* power of foundational cultural texts and images, as Auerbach documents in *Mimesis*, his seminal work on literary criticism,[28] is the power to constitute a culture or a discrete legal order. Creation in this sense is not simply a matter of imitation. Rather, it involves enacting a living form. The poetic power to make what was invisible visible is more than an exercise of force (the command of the sovereign) or of sensory delight. Touched by the sublime, expressive forms acquire an unusually compelling binding force.[29] This is what is meant when we say that a form of meaning may found a world – including the lived reality of law.

The aesthetic and ethical sublime may be viewed as complementary modes of mindfulness or attunement. As Elaine Scarry writes, "there is no way to be in a high state of alert toward injustices . . . without simultaneously demanding of oneself precisely the level of perceptual acuity that will forever be opening one to the arrival of beautiful sights and sounds."[30] In sum, if our attentiveness or attunement to actualities admits of more than the mobilization of visual artifice or nominal semiotic conventions, if there is something in our experience of what we call the beautiful and the just that remains irreducible to the rhetorical structures that help bring them to life, then to that extent both beauty and justice may be said to be rooted in the real. In this sense, the aesthetic and ethical sublime describes an ontological as well as an epistemological truth.[31]

Of course, we do not experience all images this way, just as not all words necessarily go beyond the conventions of everyday discourse. However, in the presence of remarkable images, and great expressive works in general, a potent sense of reality comes through. Then we say the image lives. The image stares back. It is as if it had a life of its own. Our experience of a meaning as pure artifice may be a source of pleasure or horror, it may be informative or purely entertaining, but it is not in this sense invested with the real, which is to say, with an ontological aspect that supplements artifice or convention with something more. In recent years, meaning's devolution to the formal realm of pure artifice has been referred to as the simulacrum. In ontological terms, the simulacrum is pure fabrication. Synthetic worlds composed of digital algorithms are, in this sense, like a dream world. Our encounter with the ontological aspect of the image, the supplemental presence manifest in its uncanny, auratic shimmer, is different.

From the standpoint of visual jurisprudence, it is of utmost importance to appreciate the kind of knowledge or truth claim upon which a given image relies. To subject the digital (or "information") image, for example, to the same evaluative criteria as one might marshal in response to the sublime is an invitation to error. Different aniconic images point toward different underlying epistemological and ontological frameworks. There is work to be done to make these distinctions clear. Bound by the perspective of Cartesian rationality, with its insistence upon the conventionality of language in the construction of meaning, the visual sublime remains a highly suspect notion. Visual jurisprudence presents an opportunity to rejoin the wisdom of the ancients, particularly evident in the humanities and the classical rhetorical tradition, with contemporary insights into the nature of mind as culturally and cognitively constructed and naturally self-transcending. Simply stated, the Cartesian framework and the modern positivist tradition that it helped to inspire are insufficient in and of themselves to do justice to law's contemporary life as an image.

Re-theorizing law's legitimacy from the standpoint of visual meaning making

The need for reliable sources of authority for claims of truth and justice persists in law, even as the nature of those sources varies over time. In modernity, this authorizing function has been largely delegated to scientific reasoning and the methods of quantification. The popularity of the law and economics movement and rational choice theory, for example, reflects the continued vitality of the Cartesian framework for minding the law. The problem is that the domain of legal meaning far outstrips the empirical- and quantification-oriented method upon which science and the social sciences rely. Analytic rationality and the culture of argument must join with emotional knowledge and the interpretive methods of narrative and visual expression as co-equal sources of truth, knowledge, and value. Indeed, it has been shown that science itself is shot through with all manner of rhetorical constructions and preferences. Standards of elegance and economy in the nature of proofs are only the most obvious examples of this. The rhetoric of science, and its historic susceptibility to cultural fashions and diverse discursive styles, has been comprehensively documented and need not be detailed here.[32] Suffice it to say that minding the world by way of Aristotelian logic, empirical quantification, and formal argument may be incommensurable with minding the world through stories, metaphors, and images,[33] but they are not incompatible. Law's quest for truth and justice in the case by case resolution of social conflict must draw upon both of these cognitive modalities.

The rules and principles that help decision makers reach right outcomes in particular cases do not arise out of thin air, nor are they self-operative. Rules inform a given case based on established lines of relevance and analogy. Is this the kind of situation to which this particular rule or principle has been applied before? Is this the kind of situation they are meant to regulate? If we are to be governed by past practices, so that the axiomatic principle of equal justice may be preserved (treating like cases alike) there must be an agreed upon way in which to characterize those situations that are said to recur. How does the decision maker know what kind of case he or she faces? To answer that question requires a narrative frame, or more accurately, at least in the adversarial culture of the common law, it requires competing accounts. The production and comparative assessment of such accounts are crucial aspects of what lawyers and judges do. Stories frame the facts and capture the legal theory of the case at hand, so as to locate it on the map of law. That is the way we find out what rules and principles ought to apply. In tort law, for example, accident stories prompt rules of adequate precautions and causation that allocate individual responsibilities for harm and loss. In contract law parties sort out promises that have been met or frustrated and what consequence ought to follow, and so on.

It is their narrative frame that puts law cases on the map, and these days, with increasing frequency, visual stories, visual evidence, and visual arguments are fulfilling that function. Hence, when we ask, what authorizes the state's exercise of power through law, we are also asking, in what story and what image should we invest our trust, and why? When it comes to law and the written and spoken word, this query has sparked a good deal of thought.

Legal positivism, legal realism, the law and literature movement together with numerous related scholarly developments (such as cultural and critical legal studies, law and rhetoric, law and the humanities, and law and popular culture studies) have pursued the implications of legal meaning making through narrative. Little work has been done, however, to investigate the implications of *visual* legal meaning making. What authorizes the state's exercise of power through law as image?

This seemingly simple question launches a complex historical and philosophical investigation into the cultural and cognitive construction of visual meaning and the nature of visuality itself. The visual encompasses physiological, cultural, and cognitive frameworks for experiencing the world and others around us. How and what people see (and fail to see) varies from place to place and time to time. Social conventions and inherited tools track permissible ways of feeling and knowing and being in the world. They frame the visible and invisible alike – establishing the one by virtue of the other. Visual storytelling and argument are as varied and complex as their verbal and written counterparts. Visual expression, moreover, is no less dependent upon the media in which it occurs. Significant changes in the technology of visual communication inevitably bring about changes in the shared forms and conventions and collective expectations concerning visual meaning making. How visual meaning making occurs, how (and with what aesthetic and ethical consequences) it constructs a world, a self, and a network of relations for us to be in, is not obvious. Critical self-reflexiveness and prudence in judgment presuppose visual literacy, and visual literacy, like its literary counterpart, does not simply happen. It requires conscientious training.

This is no easy task. Digital signs proliferate and their mimetic power grows, but the source and nature of the metric by which we might decode their meaning only seems to proliferate with the programs that produce them. Without a common normative measure (what Nelson Goodman calls a "standard construction") to isolate and frame the images that flow around us, a sense of chaotic overabundance prevails. This is precisely the cultural condition of the baroque. It is, as Deleuze has written, a time when our "response to the world's misery is made through an excess of principles."[34] We live increasingly in an environment of infinitely stimulating, data rich, instant communities, virtual worlds in which the will to power equals the power of imagination, or so we are told. Yet, the heightening of mimetic power (the human ability to simulate the real) that digital technology allows lacks a corresponding boost either in the clarity of our ethical imagination or in the level of our ethical confidence. The vicissitudes of meaning making that attend the overabundance of digital visual forms, including our growing inability to distinguish fact from fiction, reality from fantasy, will from desire, are telltale signs of the baroque.

The vicissitudes of the baroque

The digital age may mark a new culmination in the human ability to represent the world and everything in it, even unto its innermost parts and outermost wholes, but the aspiration toward mastery ("command and control") that this faculty reflects is often at odds with another dimension of our nature, namely: attentiveness, solicitude, a felt sense of responsiveness to and responsibility for things and others around us. In the digital simulacrum, the virtual world of digital simulation, there may be no way out of the monadic shell of subjective sensation and self-absorption.[35] The danger is that within the ever-unfolding, self-enclosed (monadic) sensorium of digital baroque ornamentation, we may find no staging area for self-demotion in behalf of experiencing something other. A diminished capacity to identify with (and respond to) an other may carry significant epistemological and ethical consequences. If there is nothing to constrain the monadic will to command and control the flow of digital information on the screen, in whatever form it may take, how does the self-absorbed subject decenter itself sufficiently to feel and care about the needs of others? Without the capacity for such self-transcending responsiveness to (and responsibility for) others, what then becomes of justice?

The crux of the longstanding debate between legal positivism on the one hand and natural law on the other has centered on the controversial role played by moral principles in justifying law's exercise of coercive power. Under what circumstances, if any, might we justifiably conclude that a law, while valid, may lack the moral authority to warrant obedience? In H. L. A. Hart's stark terms, the core dilemma is plain: How is law different from the gunman writ large? What distinguishes law's legitimate authority from the Hobbesian and Austinian (conventional, arguably nominalist, but manifestly contingent) positivist model that anchors law's authority to the command of the sovereign? Simply put, what makes it right to obey the law? What principles, internal to the law itself, conceived perhaps as part of the minimum content of natural law, as Hart puts it, transmute "obligation" (for fear of the consequences of disobedience) into a collective sense of "being obliged" (out of an internal sense of moral acceptance)?[36] A descriptive ("sociological") jurisprudence takes for granted the normative foundation for law's authority based on the "social fact" of collective acceptance of that authority. Legal positivism as a form of sociological jurisprudence may *describe* social normative practices, but it lacks the means of *prescribing* or *judging* a particular set of moral principles that those practices ought to follow. Legal theorists, such as John Rawls and Ronald Dworkin, have leapt into the normative gap that the legal positivists seem incapable of filling. The ensuing debate has turned on the proper pedigree or proffered justification for the moral principles that undergird law's legitimation. Thus we have, for example, a putatively rational derivation of universal moral principles from behind Rawls's veil of ignorance, or an interpretive origin, based on criteria of philosophical coherence or integrity or narrative fit, as Dworkin has urged (like Beale before him).[37] In contrast to the descriptivist claims of the positivists, the regulative principles thus proffered may be irreducible to a particular set of social practices, but that does not necessarily bear upon their suitability as good or just reasons for accepting the moral authority of law.

For their part, the Legal Realists endorsed an interpretive method rooted in empirical data as well as situationally attuned intuition that as a practical matter purports to help jurists close the normative gap between rules of legal validity on the one hand and the more complex and elusive domain of regulatory principles on the other. The method of intuition, however, falls short of resolving the legal positivist/natural law debate, for intuition offers no account of the origin or legitimacy of its criteria for choosing the moral principles or sentiment of equity that it invites decision makers to apply in a given case. Not surprisingly, Legal Realism found itself in the same *cul de sac* as the legal positivists and descriptive sociologists. As Cardozo candidly acknowledged as early as 1921, when preferences conflict and disparate reasons more or less equally support disparate outcomes in a particular case, the decision maker can only follow the inclination of his own culturally attuned, socio-economically embedded, and psychologically predetermined judgment. In short, intuitions of normative preference bring us no closer to a reasoned basis or predictive metric for normative prescription. A tool cannot define the task it is to perform. We shall return to this topic in Chapter 5 where the strengths and limits of legal positivist and Legal Realist strategies and resources for law's legitimation serve as a springboard to alternative cultural and theoretical strategies. Suffice it to say here, the limitations inherent in descriptivist (or naturalist) jurisprudence become increasingly striking and troublesome in times of normative uncertainty, when the collective level of ethical confidence is low. In such times, the descriptivist tools of the social sciences are manifestly ill suited to the task of restoring the community's moral compass.

Visuality implicates ways of valuing as well as ways of knowing.[38] A manner of seeing entails a discrete way of being in the world among others. In short, it helps to shape and inform a way of life. In the phenomenology of perception, for example, we find ourselves open to the world and others around us. In this way, perception grows entangled and embodied, attuned to being (which Dufrenne describes as the identity of meaning and the real[39]) as well as to the endless needs of others. Cartesian optics, by contrast, turns away from the world of the senses. It is governed instead by a disembodied, internally derived, rational metric. The intense asceticism that gave birth to modern rationality was not an easy undertaking, as Descartes discourse on method makes plain. Its demands attest to the dire need of the moment.

During the late sixteenth and early seventeenth centuries, baroque culture struggled with a growing epistemological crisis, namely: the breakdown of the Aristotelian "correspondence theory" of visuality. As advanced by medieval philosophy, the Aristotelian theory posited the flow of "species" from the observing eye to the object observed, thus linking the observer and the observed.[40] This theory of knowledge faltered in the face of baroque perspective and the manifest illusions and optical deceits that it displayed. The old optical regime simply could not account for perspectival artifice and the deliberate manipulation of optical illusions.[41]

But the breakdown of the medieval (species-based) correspondence theory of visuality was not the only challenge of the moment. The Thirty Years War between Catholics and Protestants was devastating Europe. In iconoclastic fury, protestant reformers pitted the inner eye of the spirit against outward displays of faith, such as the ceremonies and icons employed by the Catholic Church. Physical icons, according to protestant reformers, were no more than idolatrous offshoots of the carnal eye. Descartes lived most of his adult life – from age 22 to 52 (a mere two years before he died) – under the scourge and horror of the ensuing war of images. An alternative was desperately needed to end the ravages of sectarian visuality with its stark oppositions between iconoclastic violence on the one hand and the public spectacle of sacred iconography (in alliance with the baroque pageantry of state power) on the other.

In the early modern era of the European Enlightenment, the objectivist and universal ideals of Cartesian rationality and the scientific method not only gave birth to a post-medieval (post-"species") model of visuality, but it also served as a vehicle of hope for relief from the collective violence of intolerant religious passions. In this respect, the move toward Cartesian optics helped to achieve a radical metaphysical shift from sectarian to putatively universal rational sources of knowledge, truth, and certainty. This move had profound consequences for politics and law. Indeed, it helped to launch an entirely new basis for the legitimation of political power which, in turn, provided a secular legal framework for the modern nation-state. The traditional belief in the absolute right of the monarch, the claim that the king was Christ's representative on earth, now came to be seen to embody the much criticized Catholic confusion of high and low, what Protestant reformers criticized as the false, indeed impious, embedding of the transcendental in the secular sensory realm of institutional pomp and ceremony and the visual delights of the image and the icon. Faced with the collapse of the transcendental stature of the sovereign – what Kantorowicz refers to as "the King's two bodies" – into a flattened, desacralized plane, political and legal theorists were forced to adapt to new conditions of power and legitimacy.[42] Hobbes would find refuge in the absolute sovereignty of the secular state; Locke, in the appropriation of desacralized nature through labor; and Rousseau, in elevating the moral influence of contract-based society. The publication of the Gallican articles in 1682, arguably marked the final collapse of the pre-modern doctrine of the state.[43]

In sum, modern law's marriage of power and meaning based on the rational operation and assessment of conventional semiotic codes and a non-correspondence theory of visuality helped to make law a neutral arbiter among contentious factions. As Dan Kahan has aptly observed: "The quieting of open and violent sectarian rivalries aimed at aligning the state with partisan cultural orthodoxies is liberalism's great achievement."[44] The disembodiment of law's authority – removing it from the domain of the senses as something that might be seen as well as felt – was the price to be paid for breaking the impasse between the warring paradigms of Catholic and Protestant belief. Cool Cartesian reason was to temper unruly sectarian passions. The turn away from the visual would make previously conflicting claims regarding the carnal knowledge of the eye irrelevant. For what has the eye to do with the rational mind's putatively "universal" claims to authoritative knowledge?

Descartes' method for eradicating the problem of uncertainty was to cut it off at the source: by divorcing mind from body (the origin of deceitful sensation) and by breaking with the Aristotelian and medieval belief in a "natural" connection between reality and representation. Descartes accomplished this in a single stroke: by shifting away from images to signs. Unlike "species," signs are not images caused by objects. Signs are culturally constructed conventions for truth. Semiotics thus comes to supplant the medieval correspondence theory of representational truth.[45] Cartesian epistemology shifts attention from images to words, from the objective eye to semiotic interpretation. Signs have no direct correspondence with what caused them. Signs signify. They stand for a word. This is not a matter of sense impression, as with the flow of species. In short, Cartesian modernity subordinates *physis/themis* (nature and natural law) to *nomos* (law posited as a cognitive and cultural interpretation or convention). The classical and medieval link to the "natural" order has been broken, and the modern disenchantment of nature has begun. Truth has now become the offspring of artificial linguistic conventions. The sign, on this account, is but an arbitrary association to an object or event rather than a natural resemblance.

In the same stroke the deceit manifest in baroque representations and the anxiety associated with irreconcilable claims to privileged truth – either iconoclastically expressed (as in the Protestant eradication of sensate idols) or ceremonially enacted (as in the visual icons, rituals, and spectacles of the Catholic Church and its patron states whose legitimacy remained tied to Papal authority) – lost their sting. Rather than resembling the exterior world, sensations and perceptions were now deemed to exist in order to "inform the mind of what is beneficial or harmful for the composite of which the mind is a part."[46] To this extent and for this purpose, sensations and perceptions may be discerned by the intervening intellect as "clear and distinct."[47] Resemblance (the truth of representation as a material correspondence between observer and observed) has now fallen by the wayside. Perception has become a matter of conventional mechanics. In the Cartesian account, perceiving produces a mental effect which the intellect interprets as "color," "taste," "sound," "smell," and "touch." What the rational mind knows of the exterior world is based upon the effects of physical impacts upon the perceptual apparatus. Words are conventions that "bear no resemblance to the things they signify, and yet they make us think of these things."[48] In sum, according to Cartesian epistemology, meaning arises in the mind in the company of signs – not of things or sensations. Meaning is the byproduct of conventional, which is to say, cognitive or cultural symbolic practices – not nature, and certainly not the body. Whether it is an object in the natural world or an emotion or feeling registered by the body's neurological system, meaning requires the intervention of intellect for the purpose of rendering an interpretation.[49] As Descartes succinctly put it, "it is the soul which sees . . . and not the eye."[50] An event involving the eye is simply grist for the intellectual process of assigning a meaning in the company of signs. The mirror of nature, as true correspondence, has been shattered.[51]

The ensuing Cartesian dualism posits an unbridgeable gulf between the source of perception (the body's acquisition of raw data from the world) and cognition (the mind's construction of meaning out of that data). This philosophical move away from the correspondence theory of visuality contributed to a concomitant shift to positivism and nominalism, as Machiavelli and Hobbes, among others, would make clear.[52] If meaning is a function of mind, mind (not nature) can also generate standards of "correctness" by which to assess a given interpretation of perception.

Utilitarianism is one such cognitive template. On this analysis, we measure the correctness of perception in accordance with a behavioral model that teaches the practical lessons of seeking pleasure and avoiding pain.[53] Knowledge may require experience to set it in motion, as Kant came to realize, but knowledge remains irreducible to experience. This insight is a hallmark of modernity.[54]

The domain of ethics, as Hobbes and Machiavelli would show, had now become a matter of convention. Moral terms may be treated in exactly the same manner as color terms – they are mental constructs which do not directly pertain to real and objective properties in the external world. We call "good" that which gives us pleasure; "bad" is that which causes pain. The problem is that this traditional modernist metaphysic of instrumental rationality cannot satisfy our longing for deeper normative significance.[55] Nor can it guide us in the face of multiple metrics for judgment. The move from baroque spectacle to modern rationality gained release from the metaphysical anxiety of iconoclash and the deep impasse to which it led in law, society, and culture. But the price that was paid for that advance was the loss of the visual sublime. That loss has come to the fore in the face of a new baroque anxiety and a new set of impasses, both in theory and practice. As in Descartes' generation, today a new path is needed.

A New Paradigm for Law in the Age of the Digital Baroque

The phenomenology of the aesthetic and ethical sublime that will be explored in these pages arises out of the felt need for a new paradigm for law in the visual, digital age. Understanding the phenomenology of visual meaning making, in cognitive, cultural, and perhaps even metaphysical terms provides a way of reintegrating law's power with a shared sense of its normative significance. It aims to break the frustrating oscillation between the desuetude of Platonic and Cartesian metaphysics on the one hand (with their reliance on the universal truths of natural Reason) and descriptivist positivism on the other (with its roots in conventional or nominalist semiotics). The felt need for justice as the ultimate basis for law's legitimate authority, like the uncanny presence of the sublime as the authenticating and authorizing source of the living image's truth and ethical demand, cannot be fulfilled by the metaphysics and associated methods of either pre-modern piety (the inexorably divisive, sectarian eye of the spirit) or by Cartesian rationality (the ethically bereft and aesthetically crippled eye of disembodied, scientific reason). It is the humanities and the ancient rhetorical tradition in particular to which scientifically informed jurisprudence must reconnect in order to redress the normative lack that afflicts it. To be sure, the empirical methods and resulting data that the sciences provide will continue to play a valuable role both in legal theory and in legal practice, but the sciences alone are ill suited to address the fragility of our ethical confidence. We shall need to engage new normative sources and methods to help us clarify the beliefs, feelings, and values that sustain the moral legitimacy of law's coercive power in the current visual age.

In this sense, the pictorial turn, particularly in the context of contemporary digital baroque culture, is an occasion of both opportunity and concern. For notwithstanding (indeed, partly because of) the immense power and efficacy of visual communication and visual advocacy that digital technologies have unleashed, the inherited, traditionally dominant forms of legal reasoning and communicative practice now face profound epistemological, metaphysical, and ethical challenges. What authenticates visual meaning as a matter of law? On what authority do we invest belief in what we see? To what extent is emotion an appropriate, perhaps even essential part of the decision making process, and when does the visual image invite emotional excess and deceit? When has our visual knowledge been appropriately animated by aesthetic craft or undermined by sensory gratification for its own sake? These questions together with a host of others bear upon, but cannot be reduced to evidentiary issues of admissibility alone. It goes without saying that lawyers must persuasively establish that a proffered item of visual evidence is what they claim it is. Advocates also must persuasively show the relevance of such evidence to the factual and legal issues that the case in question raises. And they must assure the court that the evidence does not unduly play upon the decision maker's prejudices, emotions, and perhaps even unconscious desires. But in order to successfully undertake these tasks jurists will have to travel beyond conventional evidentiary rules and procedures. They will have to understand how visual images make and convey meaning, both explicitly and implicitly.

Descartes' ascetic turn away from the visual world of the senses to the disembodied realm of pure reason simultaneously extricated reason from the carnal senses and the profuse dissimulations of baroque representation as well as from the violence of iconoclastic impulses.[56] In their place, Cartesian rationality aimed to posit an objective optical order putatively based on timeless and placeless geometrical principles.[57] In lieu of the visual representation of external reality, the interior search for "clear and distinct ideas" defined the dominant method by which true knowledge may be attained. For Descartes, the rational method was deemed consistent with the transcendent reality and innate idea of God, but it wasn't long before the style of scientific thinking, based on empirical, verifiable, and objective answers to problems posed, would suffice without recourse to the divine.

Along the way, law, like language itself, rather than a natural category came to be conceived as a convention whose authority depended upon sufficient reasons and justifications.[58] Like a secularized Protestantism, certainty came to be based on a conventional, objective text.

But times have changed, and the visual image is back. The twentieth century was fundamentally an audiovisual culture. The twenty-first century will undoubtedly continue to be so. The way we make sense of the true or the real, and the way we make judgments about the ethical and the just, have now taken on new dimensions. Today, visual images have flooded into the power precincts of politics and law. Our capacity to visualize the world around (and within) us has grown exponentially. At the same time, however, the spectacle of the baroque amid the rise of the digital simulacrum has left us awash in images whose authority lies not on the surface of the screen, but rather in the invisible depths of the algorithmic program that generates them. The danger, as iconoclasts throughout history have feared, is that the visible may break free from its invisible source. This is the origin of the image as idol or fetish or, more recently, as free-floating signifier. In the deracinated realm of the digital baroque, signifiers may refer to other signifiers *ad infinitum* with no necessary correlation to a signified. As Mitchell puts it, "When the relationship is lost between original and copy (signifier and signified) there is nothing to constrain the 'chain of signification' associated with the sign."[59]

The proliferation of signifiers floating free of the signified has been hastened by the advent of digital technology and the culture of the simulacrum (as evidenced in interactive gaming and synthetic worlds online). This development has profound implications for the theory and practice of law. A law field constituted by rules and principles operates by way of abstract transcendentals, a commonplace of the written word. By contrast, a law field constituted by visual images and immanent digitized networks operates as a series of discrete and contingent insights, fleeting impressions, relational possibilities, and fragmentary affective intensities, a commonplace of the electronic gaze. Law in the image faces the paradoxical prospect of re-embodiment on the one hand (as a renewed source of affectivity to which the senses are attuned), and virtuality or hyper-simulation on the other (as digital images float free of their invisible, algorithmic source).

The immediate juridical prospect points toward increased intensity of feeling amid wavering confidence in the visual image that shimmers before our eyes. This is law in the condition of iconoclash: We love the image and we hate it. We crave its enchantment and fear its deceit. In this respect, we stand at a historical juncture not unlike the one Descartes confronted in the midst of the Thirty Years' War of images. We live in a new (digital) baroque era in which powerful iconoclastic impulses roil the surface of rational certainty. We can no longer keep out the unruly sensations of the body; indeed, we now know that the emotions constitute a discrete and significant form of knowledge. Thus, we stand at a post-Cartesian juncture, in dire need of ways to integrate anew emotional and rational, aesthetic and ethical, rhetorical and scientific forms (and ways) of knowing.

Neither the positivist's urge to cut off the vagaries of the senses (in order to preserve the order of conventional rules) nor the radical constructivist's impulse to dive into the whirlpool of affect-laden, free-floating signifiers (for the sake of preferred outcomes or values) addresses what the times demand of us. We can no more escape the pre-reflective affectivity of law as image than we can relinquish responsibility for a normative framework that constrains arbitrary preferences harnessed to contingent desires. Recourse to a disembodied Cartesian rationality is a false haven; the mind is embodied. At the same time, however, mind is also a vehicle for self-transcendence, for attunement to things and others beyond it. A new, more broadly integrated paradigm is needed to ease the epistemological and ontological anxieties that underlie the current digital baroque era. This will require new ways of assessing and crafting visual meaning. The realization that meaning exceeds the limits of representation invites a posture of humility, and persistent mindfulness. Beauty and justice, in their sublime fullness, remind us of our limits even as they challenge us to exceed those limits. The paradigm for visual jurisprudence that this book advocates envisions an attitude of informed attentiveness in the way we mind the law. It is a posture of openness, of affective attunement to that which is other, which allows the sublime aspect of beauty and justice to come to mind. The integrated legal mind brings the logic of argument, and the foresight that empirically based prediction allows, together with the aesthetic and ethical wisdom that comes with the self-transcending capacity of attunement.

In a baroque age, when it comes to visual representations of reality, a tenacious binary opposition persists: either the image we see is what it shows, or it is a deceit that must be discarded. Either it is a transparent frame, like a window on to reality, or it is a fabrication that ought to be rejected, perhaps destroyed. This is the distinctive cultural and cognitive posture of iconoclash. In this respect, it becomes apparent that the iconoclastic impulse is parasitic upon naïve realism. If the image isn't what it seems it ought not to be. The wild oscillations of iconoclash that characterize the baroque mind are likely to continue so long as this unstable "either/or" orientation toward visual representation prevails.

To extricate ourselves from this condition requires phenomenological as well as pragmatic counter-measures. One must learn the appropriate code or codes that apply to the particular image in question. This is in part a matter of visual literacy, which is to say, the cultivation of visual rhetoric in all its cultural and cognitive forms and technological mediations. Different visual media invite different aesthetic, interpretive, and critical norms. But the anxiety that casts the mind into its disquieting flight from belief to suspicion and back again goes beyond rhetorical craft and visual acuity. For the question not only goes to what constitutes but also what *authorizes* a particular code as the right or appropriate basis for responding to (or interpreting or reading) the image. Is the image no more than a train of empty signifiers to which we submit in "nihilistic abandonment,"[60] as postmodernists like Jean Baudrillard claim, or is it rooted in the real? And if it is the latter, how do we assess its claim to truth and justice, by what aesthetic or epistemological code or, in the case of the aniconic image, on the basis of what hidden algorithmic calculation or sublime presence?

The postmodern strategy of "nihilistic abandonment" is a familiar one to students of baroque and neo-baroque cultures alike. It marks the embrace of reality as endless carnival, a perpetual baroque spectacle, or masque. The axiological clash between law and entertainment is one of the offshoots of contemporary law's life as an image on the screen.[61] In its screen life, law proliferates in the form of images that both reflect and constitute anew the images that circulate within popular culture. These images help to constitute our shared sense of narrative and visual reality. Law benefits from technological feats of imaging the unseen or visually animating unwitnessed events (as if we were there); and it is burdened by epistemological doubts and metaphysical anxieties that accompany such unprecedented powers of creative visualization.

Seeing how a representation has been constructed, deliberately confronting the nature of its artifice, is a way of staving off the specter of deceit and doubt. But this kind of visual deconstruction may also prompt baroque effects when the collective sense is that "it is artifice all the way down," which is to say, when there is no available meaning-instilling code to redeem or supplant what has been visibly deconstructed. The aniconic image may help to restore meaning by enfolding the deconstructed image in an alternative normative register. When we see the framework that has been invisibly organizing our world (helping to shape and inform our beliefs, feelings, ideas, and values) we stand as upon a threshold. We enter a liminal state, betwixt and between the familiar and the strange, the conventional and the extraordinary. This is what we see in anamorphic paintings such as Holbein's *The Ambassadors* (1533; image 2.1 – see plate section between pp. 118 and 119). Standing before Holbein's canvas we behold two men, a cleric and a man of wealth who wears an elaborate fur-lined cloak. Laid out between them we see the fruits of the human arts and sciences: a globe, an open book, a mandolin. But what is that blurred image in the foreground? It rises at a 45 degree angle from the floor like a flattened cipher. Move a few steps to the left or to the right and the mystery dissolves. The blur crystallizes into a coherent form. It is a skull. And so we see how a change in one's perspective changes everything, turning the fruits of human labor into the death-darkened shadows of *vanitas*. By triggering the invisible Christian eschatological code of redemption, Holbein's painting transforms the vanity of worldly existence into an allegory of future hope as the painting's display of pride gives way to an expression of Christian humility and renunciation. When a change in perspective brings the blurred skull into view, the normative register of the work completely shifts (from worldly values to transcendent ones).

This is deconstruction in the service of a transcendent axiological code. Without recourse to a stable code of meaning and value, however, the manifest representation may be shattered. In that case, only deconstruction, perhaps for its own sake, remains. These are the conditions under which the postmodern strategy of "nihilist abandonment" comes to the fore. The previous baroque era, which unfolded during the Reformation, witnessed a bitter and violent clash between two opposing codes of meaning: the Protestant belief in God's essential unrepresentability, which supported the embrace of abstract (disembodied) printed text over visual image on the one hand, and the Catholic belief in the symbolic role of images, ceremonies, and icons as visual aids in the search for spiritual insight on the other. In the current digital baroque era, by contrast, image-generating digital codes proliferate without constraint. We may deconstruct the information image to discover the algorithmic calculations that produced it, which may help us discover whether the program's input of data authorizes its visual output. But this will not tell us what kinds of images to create or how their perceptual and emotional significance should be gauged.

From digital films to interactive gaming and virtual worlds on the Internet, the technological enhancement of the human capacity to project and inhabit realities of our own making has become a source of growing metaphysical anxiety. As Morpheus explains to Neo, his incredulous acolyte, in *The Matrix* (1999; image 2.2 – see plate section between pp. 118 and 119):

> What is the Matrix? Control. The Matrix is a computer-generated dream world built to keep us under control . . . What is real? How do you define real? If you're talking about what you can feel, what you can smell, what you can taste and see, then real is simply electrical signals interpreted by your brain. This is the world that you know. The world as it was at the end of the twentieth century.

> It exists now only as part of a neural-interactive simulation that we call the Matrix. You've been living in a dream world, Neo.

We witness a similar scenario unfold in Alex Proyas's *Dark City* (1998), a science fiction noir film about a dying race of aliens who abduct humans to an artificial planet and turn their lives into an unending series of experiments. As the main character explains:

> This city, everyone in it . . . is their experiment. They mix and match our memories as they see fit, trying to divine what makes us unique. One day, a man might be an inspector. The next, someone entirely different. When they want to study a murderer, for instance, they simply imprint one of their citizens with a new personality. Arrange a family for him, friends, an entire history . . . even a lost wallet. Then they observe the results. Will a man, given the history of a killer, continue in that vein? Or are we, in fact, more than the sum of our memories? This business of you being a killer was a sad coincidence. You have had dozens of lives before now. You happened to wake up . . . while I was imprinting you with this one. Why are they doing all this? It is our capacity for individuality, our souls . . . that makes us different from them. They think they'll find the human soul . . . if they understand how our memories work . . . Your history is an illusion, a fabrication, as it is with all of us.

The paranoid horror that plays out in both of these films, and many others besides, is that we may all be living the same deluded lives as these forlorn characters, unwittingly trapped in the same dream-within-a-dream existence, unable to awaken, mere puppets in a program not of our making. Yet, on the other side of this horror a utopian fantasy takes shape. In an instant, abject enslavement turns into total liberation once the subject switches places with the master. It is all a matter of who controls the machines. This is not a battle of the reality principle against the forces of illusion.[62] Rather, it is a quest to harness the technological power to transform reality at will – a power that makes gods of us all. This fantasy is vividly expressed in Neo's final words at the end of *The Matrix.* Reciting what might well be regarded as a cyber-utopian manifesto, Neo says: "I don't know the future. I didn't come here to tell you how this is going to end. I came here to tell you how it's going to begin. I'm going to hang up this phone and then I'm going to show these people what you don't want them to see. I'm going to show them a world without you, a world without rules and controls, without borders or boundaries, a world where anything is possible. Where we go from there is a choice I leave to you."

A similar fantasy shapes the ending of *Dark City*, after the hero learns how to take control of the aliens' reality-shifting machinery. Guided by his mentor's words ("The world can be what you make it . . . You have the power to make anything happen."), our hero recites the cyber-utopian mantra: "I'm gonna fix things. You told me I had the power, didn't you? I can make these machines do anything I want. Make this world anything I want it to be." It's like the TV ads say, "You can have it all," "Be all you can be," "Just do it!" Or as Ray Kurzweil puts it in *The Singularity is Near*, once a species discovers computing, it is only a matter of time before it "engineer[s] the universe it wants."[63] Command and control is not the problem in this view; it's the solution. The baroque mind thus strives to turn the dross of metaphysical anxiety into the gold of metaphysical mastery.[64]

During the latter half of the twentieth century, pop artist Andy Warhol proclaimed with comic-ironic effect, "I am a machine." In the ensuing culture of the digital baroque, the humor and irony have been lost. With the arrival of post-Foucauldian command and control society (the so-called "post-human" age of the "cyborg"), the metaphysical question *par excellence* has become: "Why am I not (am I not) a machine?" Today, the source of wonder and fountain of baroque fantasy has become the thinking machine. The spiritually vacant robot, Descartes' mechanical body, now gives way to Kurzweil's "spiritual machine," a hybrid, cyborgian form of intelligence utterly fungible with the human kind. Thus is the Cartesian paradigm turned on its head, as Descartes' disembodied rational soul trades places with spiritual machines smart enough to turn any fantasy into a living reality.[65] This leaves us, however, in a metaphysical quandary. In *The Matrix*, the character named Cypher looks at the raw code of the matrix and can immediately translate it into representational reality ("I don't even see the code. All I see is blonde, brunette, redhead . . ."). Yet, in the end, Cypher sells out his comrades to the aliens so that he may forget the code once and for all and comfortably sink back into the illusions the matrix offers. ("They're going to reinsert my body. I go back to sleep, and when I wake up, I won't remember a goddamn thing."). The metaphysical question that remains is this: does it matter what space I occupy, simulated or real? Is the matrix a paradise or a prison? Why am I not (am I not) a spiritual machine?

This is the characteristic condition of iconoclash, that recurrent oscillation between belief and suspicion that shapes and informs the digital baroque culture of our time. It is an era in which the aniconic digital image threatens to self-deconstruct in the absence of some transcendental category or authoritative norm to redeem it. We witness this anxiety in a variety of contemporary cultural works – paintings, novels, and especially film. From *The Matrix* to *eXistenz, Waking Life, The Truman Show, Synecdoche, Memento, Open Your Eyes, Eternal Sunshine of a Spotless Mind, Inception*, among others too numerous to mention, viewers are made to confront a recurring question: How do we know what's there, outside our own minds, and how can we be certain of what we know? As a matter of philosophy or art, such metaphysical musings may pique our interest or leave us cold. As a matter of law, however, it is not so simple. When it comes to law visual aesthetics merges with the power of the state. Through law we enforce the reality in which, by general consensus, we are most inclined to believe. It is the task of the newly emerging field of visual jurisprudence to help ensure that this legal responsibility is undertaken with the greatest care. By what axiological code or codes, in what register – visible or invisible, analogue or digital, indexical or simulated, perceptual or lexical, experiential or mathematical – should the truth or justice of the image be assessed in a given case? For example, are judges to be trusted over jurors in assessing the images they see? What does the surveillance video, the trial video, the professional videographer's crime scene documentary, the animated accident or crime re-enactment, the fMRI of defendant's brain, really show, and what does it really mean in a particular case?

The need for visual literacy

Significant changes in the media of communication bring about significant changes in mind and culture. "We make our technologies and our technologies shape us," as Sherry Turkle writes.[66] To engage a particular medium of expression, whether it is text, television, or new digital media, is to engage a discrete set of material practices that involve habits, skills, and traditions as well as technologies.[67] The digital (or information) image asks to be read, but the potentially beguiling visual representation that its invisible program produces also asks to be experienced like any other sensory perception. Or consider surveillance videos which ask to be taken for all there is to know. Videos like these place viewers (including judges and jurors) in the seeming position of witnesses, despite the fact that their perspective is limited by the camera's lens and position. Moreover, video images may appear to be one thing but like a photograph whose meaning shifts with the caption beneath it, video images, too, remain susceptible to the framing effects of the narrative context in which they are played. We need only recall the way defense lawyers altered the pace and framing of the video images that fortuitously captured Los Angeles police officers surrounding and beating motorist Rodney King. Played in ordinary time, the images strongly suggested excessive force. The defense narrative, however, argued that the police acted professionally in their measured escalation and de-escalation of force, and the images the defense showed in court supported that claim. By digitizing and then strategically freeze framing and altering the flow of the images, the defense showed that police batons came down upon King's body only when he rose up in defiance of repeated police orders to remain prone on the ground. In short, it appeared that King "caused" the police to act as they did. This argument was victorious at the state criminal trial. The jury acquitted the officers just as the defense had requested. The prosecution in the Rodney King case never challenged and perhaps never even realized how the defense narrative had captured and altered what the video images showed.

Visual literacy in the domain of law as elsewhere requires multiple competencies to accommodate the challenges that new visual media present. With the current shift to the visual, however, the time is ripe not simply to expand legal education to embrace a multi-disciplinary approach to visual literacy in legal practice. It is also necessary to expand legal theory to address the ramifications of law's assimilation of digital, audio-visual, and interactive on-screen practices. As the pictorial turn sweeps across the domain of law, as it has already done in the fields of semiotics, anthropology, film studies, gender studies, and cultural studies, it brings with it "new problems and paradigms."[68] Indeed, in many respects images are just what law is not supposed to be. At least, not as we've conceived of law within the secular, rational, and positivist conventions of modernity. In the tradition of modernity, law aspires to generality, consistency, objectivity, and predictability. Law's generality reassures us that it will be applied equally in similar cases; consistency reassures us that like cases will be treated alike; and objectivity assures us that law's content may be readily understood by reasonable people of ordinary intelligence. Finally, predictability assures us that people will be able to adapt their behavior and plan their affairs in advance, secure in the expectation of law's stability and continuity. Semiotic abstraction, in the form of text-based rules, has served as a familiar theoretical basis for law's generality, consistency, objectivity, and predictability. That is the legacy of legal positivism. But images are not like this at all. Images are insistently particularistic, subjective, and emotionally charged. Their meanings are notoriously difficult to debate, perhaps because so much of the way images signify remains implicit, largely inaccessible to conscious reflection.

Consider, for example, the plight of attorney Craig Jones, whose client became a quadriplegic after police brought a high speed chase to a violent end by deliberately ramming his car, causing it to flip over an embankment and crash. Jones's client, Victor Harris, sued the police on the grounds of unreasonable search and seizure in violation of his Fourth Amendment rights. The police rebutted Harris's claim by arguing that he had created a danger to the public that warranted the use of deadly force against him. The case went all the way to the U.S. Supreme Court on the threshold question of whether a reasonable person could assess the risk other than as the pursuing officers judged it at the time. At oral argument, however, Mr Jones was stymied. The justices had watched a videotape of the chase shot by cameras mounted on the state patrol cars' dash. Based on that viewing, their minds were made up. "He created the scariest chase I ever saw since *The French Connection*," Justice Scalia observed. Indeed, when presented with attorney Jones's oral argument together with the lower federal circuit court opinion that found sufficient uncertainty to allow a jury to consider at trial the issue of reasonable force, Justice Breyer opined: "I look at the tape and I end up with Chico Marx's question . . . 'Who do you believe, me or your own eyes?'" What could Jones say? How do you argue against a judge's feeling of alarm or sense of utter certainty in response to images of a car chase? What argument will rebut Justice Scalia's and Breyer's brute sense impressions which told them that, having watched the tape, they knew all there was to know about what happened on that country road? How do you argue with a video that, as Justice Scalia put it, "speaks for itself"? Surely it is a strange thing for a lawyer to suggest that a judge's eyes cannot be trusted.

So how does an advocate ask, "Whose eyes are you going to believe?" when visual common sense insists that it is enough just to look for oneself? That is why, for all its humor, Justice Breyer's invocation of Chico Marx during oral argument in the *Scott* case is no laughing matter. Breyer repeated Chico's witty line in court, comparing plaintiff's position with that of the lover, caught *in flagrante delicto* by the betrayed husband. In comic desperation the lover says, "Who are you going to believe, me or your own eyes?" Breyer's comparison makes the legal issue simple and altogether clear cut. That is how naïve realism works. It insists that it is enough to understand (or think we understand) what we see on the screen. No reflection is required when common sense tells us that the visual truth of the matter is self-evident. But the meaning of an image always goes beyond what it depicts. Visual truth, like visuality itself, is a construct. As Benjamin Cardozo observed nearly a century ago in regard to judgments in general, making sense of an image involves a wide array of implicit (which is to say, unconscious) meaning shaping factors, such as education, experience, class, ideology, and character. When judges fail to recognize this fact and unreflectively use their visual common sense to trump, and thus exclude, the common sense of others, this raises serious concerns about the search for truth and justice in particular cases.

One way to address these concerns is through enhanced visual literacy: the ability to see why it is *not* the case that images speak for themselves, no matter how much our common sense may tell us they do. Visual literacy means knowing how images create certain impressions, how they construct or evoke pre-constructed visual meanings. It also means knowing how the mind, through a combination of cultural conditioning, life experience, education, ideology, socio-economic background, among other factors, constructs visual meaning in response to a given set of images. Common sense issues forth with the same immediacy that accompanies intuitions and feelings. This kind of knowledge needs no explanation, even if the basis for its authority remains hidden. And it brooks no dissent. That's because humans are notoriously blind to their own prejudices, even as they are quick to spot those of others. For Justice Scalia and the other justices who voted with him in the *Scott* case, seeing is believing and any account that takes a different view of the same images must be false. Yet, there can be little doubt that the sights and sounds captured by the police video in question were different from the reality that the police themselves perceived at the time. For example, Justice Scalia described Harris as recklessly driving through red lights. What the video does not show, however, is whether they were red when Harris saw them as he drove some distance (and time) ahead of the police cruiser that was taping the scene. According to Police Officer Scott's defenders, it was for the public's protection that he acted with lethal force. Does it matter, then, whether oncoming drivers are perceived as being hurriedly forced off the road as Harris's and Scott's vehicles approached (as the majority claimed to see), or whether they had already moved to safety in advance (as the dissent claimed to see)? In addressing this question, does it matter that the video in question did not show the rotating red lights that warned drivers to slow or pull to the side of the road as police cars approached? Does it matter that the police cars' closed windows muted the sound of the blaring sirens which announced their presence even from some distance away, thus giving drivers an added opportunity to exercise greater caution in advance?

When called upon to judge the truth of ordinary perceptions we're all rather like Justice Stewart on the subject of obscenity, we just know it when we see it.[69] But the easy confidence of this kind of common sense knowledge is equally matched by its inexplicable, unruly fluctuations across time and place, bearing the unconscious fruits of individual experience. For example, in the *Scott* case, the district court judge and all of the judges of the Court of Appeals watched the same car chase video as had the U.S.

Supreme Court justices, and concluded, contrary to eight of the nine Justices, that reasonable minds could indeed differ as to whether Victor Harris's driving was dangerous enough to justify the use of lethal force by police to terminate the chase. It was a conclusion that Justice Stevens reached as well, in a lone dissent, rebuffing his brethren on the high court who told him, in effect, that no reasonable person could think such a thing. Indeed, Justice Stevens's dissent specifically identified some of the underlying prejudices that judges (like any viewers) may bring to the screen, helping to shape and inform what they see. For example, he reflected on the lower court judges' local knowledge concerning road conditions in their state, and how this might have affected their assessment of the dangerousness of the chase in question. Having learned to drive on such roads, Stevens observed, normalizes the practice of passing in the face of oncoming traffic. In other words, experience tends to remove the sting of fear that those who are unfamiliar with such conditions might otherwise feel.

Dan Kahan refers to this as "motivated cognition."[70] It describes the social and cultural construction of perception. To a significant degree, we tend to see what we expect to see, and our expectations are the result of experience, memory, and the various cultural and cognitive models that we carry around in our heads to help us make sense of what we see and hear and feel in everyday life. Images do not speak for themselves; what we bring to them help give them voice. Kahan confirmed this by designing an empirical study to test Justice Scalia's naïve realist insistence that but one "reasonable" view of the video was possible (his own). In Kahan's study, 1,350 participants took up Scalia's call to watch the video for themselves. Most of them (approximately 75 per cent) did agree with Scalia's judgment that the use of fatal force was warranted under the circumstances, but hundreds of viewers (351 to be exact, or 25 per cent of the total number of viewers) reached the opposite judgment. Significantly, the viewers' divergent responses to what they saw on the screen directly correlated to ideology, class, geography, and ethnicity, among other factors. Notwithstanding their differences, however, for each viewer seeing was believing. The images seemed to speak for themselves, even when their message differed.

The adversarial system of justice has long been guided by a basic rule of thumb. Law is driven by evidence in the search for truth and justice at trial. Evidence reconstructs reality, and the trier of fact (whether judge or juror) is supposed to test the evidence that pieces that reality together. In this sense, trial reality is second-hand reality. When a witness is on the stand, or when a document or some physical evidence (like a weapon or a fingerprint) "testifies" in court jurors know what it is they are seeing and hearing, and they also know what their job is. They are participating in a "battle for reality" known as the adversarial contest for truth. That contest grows more complicated when visual evidence enters the scene. When triers of fact watch visual evidence on the screen they in effect become witnesses to reality. Rather than a derived or second-hand experience, such evidence may now come to mind as a first-hand reality. In this way, visual evidence not only problematizes what it means to be a "witness," but also what it means to "testify" Is it the camera that testifies once it has captured the scene it shows? Do the images simply "speak for themselves," as Justice Scalia and other members of the U.S. Supreme Court asserted in *Scott v. Harris*? But how could that be? We know, for instance, that filming begins and ends at a particular point in time, and that it occupies a particular place that provides its own particular (and partial) view on to the reality it shows. And it goes without saying that digital animation (like digital images generally) can only show whatever invisible algorithmic calculations are designed to show, based on a given digital program. Who or what, then, is testifying? The image? The photographer? The camera? The digital data it contains? The underlying digital program? The engineer who designed the program? Should we say it is the advocate who "testifies" when he or she edits or narrates the image or designs the montage? Is it the viewer, who brings unconsciously shared cultural and cognitive templates to the screen in the visual meaning making process? Or is it perhaps popular culture itself that testifies by way of the templates it supplies viewers to help them make sense of and react to what they see?

The need for metaphysical resolve

And what if the images viewers see mean more than the conventional cognitive and cultural frames that thematize them? What if images bear an ontological excess (what some scholars have referred to as the "aura" of the image or its metaphysical trace)? Peirce used the term "indexicality" to describe signs that embody a physical trace from a particular source – like a fingerprint, or the photochemical reaction of light on celluloid. When the eye brushes up against the flesh of the image there is an indexical trace. This describes the embodied (or haptic) aspect of the image. But what about when the eye brushes up against the shimmer or aura of the image, an absence that is somehow strangely present? May we speak, then, of metaphysical indexicality? We will return to this matter presently.

What do we see when we look at images on the screen, and what is the authority of the visual meaning that we make of what we see? Images cue subconscious categories, memories, feelings, and beliefs. This cognitive process is far too rapid for consciousness to register. Moreover, images stubbornly resist reduction to propositional assertions. Their logic is associative, rather than linear or syllogistic. By coming all at once, full blown, as it were, their meaning seems unconstructed, intuitive, and complete. Cut off from unconscious origins (in memory, experience, or fantasy), visual meanings cleave to the image itself as the source of their significance. And in that common elision of deeper-seated origins we encounter one of the rudiments of the image's singular power. They are signs that deny they are signs.[71] Images closely guard the source of their meaning. They seem to show all there is to see, like a window open to the world beyond. Resemblance invites belief. We respond to images the way we respond to unmediated reality. Consider the dizzying experience of watching a virtual roller coaster on the screen or a sizzling close-up of two alluring Hollywood stars wrapped in a physical embrace.

Not only do we respond to images as if they were real, we also tend to attribute their origin to the reality they depict. Their credibility is heightened by seeming to have been caused by external reality itself. The deceits of mediation – the naïve realism of responding to images as if they were an empty frame rather than a mediated construction – help us to invest subjective feelings in the images we see. This kind of personal ownership heightens their reality even further. This added vividness combined with the force of immediacy and completeness contributes to the impression that we have before us all we need to know about what the image depicts. Such self-evidence dissuades us from engaging in critical reflection. To be sure, this kind of naïve realism is but one illustration, admittedly a particularly vivid one, of the general human tendency to credit common sense knowledge as "naturally" arising from evidence perceived by the senses. By calling such knowledge or belief "self-evident" we assume away any constitutive factors of interpretation or subjective construction. It discounts cognitive tools or heuristics or cultural frameworks that might help explain the way we (unconsciously) construct what we know or believe through cognitive and cultural processes that are separate from the thing itself. In short, common sense belief is self-authenticating. It seeks no extrinsic warrant; it needs no reasons in its behalf. This is why we say, "Seeing is believing," or "The thing speaks for itself." This feeling of confidence may be warranted under the circumstances. But the feeling alone is not adequate justification for the certainty that accompanies it. Intuitions are immediate; their basis lies mostly hidden from view. However, that does not mean that even our most confident findings or beliefs or judgments do not rely on unobserved cognitive and cultural patterns and processes. To attribute a feeling or belief or judgment to extrinsic evidence, as decision makers sometimes prefer to do, is to assume away the mind's swift yet complex apparatus for making meanings.

One of the most significant and lasting contributions of Legal Realism has been its acknowledgement of the complex and often unconscious cognitive process of human decision making. As Supreme Court Justice Oliver Wendell Holmes famously observed:

> The life of the law has not been logic; it has been experience. The felt necessities of the time, the prevalent moral and political theories, institutions of public policy, avowed or unconscious, even the prejudices which judges share with their fellow men, have had a good deal more to do than the syllogism in determining the rules by which men should be governed.[72]

Justice Cardozo blazed a similar trail in jurisprudential thought, as is evident in these famous lines:

> There is in each of us a stream of tendency, whether you choose to call it philosophy or not, which gives coherence and direction to thought and action. Judges cannot escape that current any more than other mortals. All their lives, forces which they do not recognize and cannot name, have been tugging at them – inherited instincts, traditional beliefs, acquired convictions; and the resultant outlook on life, a conception of needs . . . In this mental background every problem finds its setting. We may try to see things as objectively as we please. None the less, we can never see them with any eyes except our own. Deep below consciousness are the forces, the likes and the dislikes, the predilections and the prejudices, the complex of instincts and convictions, which make [us].[73]

So when a court asserts that "the video speaks for itself" or that "life experience is no substitute for evidence"[74] we are witness to a curious form of denial. We long for objective certainty, and we fear the deceit of human subjectivity with its irrational biases, passions, and preferences.

Many different kinds of knowledge have always been called into play inside the courtroom, the archive as well as the repertoire, to use Diana Taylor's typology, which is to say, the discursive as well as the performative, the logical as well as the poetic, the textual as well as the audio-visual.[75] In an effort to inaugurate the new scholarly field of visual jurisprudence and delineate its scope, one must draw upon a variety of disciplinary sources and methods. Descartes taught that we see with the thinking mind, that reason assigns labels to the raw data of the senses. In this view, it is conventional categories and well defined rational codes that establish order amid the chaos of swirling perceptual inputs. Meaning emerges from within, not without. Yet, by the twentieth century faith in disembodied reason as the exclusive source of truth and meaning in language had declined. A diverse group of thinkers, ranging from Maurice Merleau-Ponty to Francisco Varela, George Lakoff, and Antonio Damasio, among others, rejected the fateful division between the sensual body (regarded by Descartes as the realm of blind aesthetics, a merely decorative rhetoric) and the rational mind (the Cartesian realm of knowledge and truth). Rather than finding its origin within, as the constructed offspring of conventional (perhaps even nominal) semiotic codes and rational categories, for these critics of the Cartesian split, meaning's source shifts to the world outside the mind. From a phenomenological perspective, meaning emerges dynamically, from the mind's intentional response to things and others in the world.

The shift from a Cartesian optics of measurement, based on a self-assigned ("clear and distinct") rational metric, to an optics rooted in mindfulness (of being and others) is no accidental development. It has been long in the making. Today we face a proliferation of codes and measures. As they ramify, along with the images they struggle to assess and arrange, ethical as well as aesthetic disorientation sets in. The quintessentially baroque fear of moving from dream world to dream world in an infinite hall of mirrors, the so-called Matrix effect, is only one of several discrete kinds of metaphysical anxieties provoked by the proliferation of visual images. There are others. Consider, for example, the Medusa effect: the fear of being frozen in an other's gaze; or the Narcissus effect: the fear of being swallowed (or drowned) in the image (that stares back); or the Pygmalion effect: the fear associated with the fantasy of bringing the image to life as an autonomous being (and perhaps joining it in a virtual world unto itself); or, finally, the Tantalus effect: the fear of the image as cruel catalyst – a force that stokes desires it can never fulfill. Each of these effects has its digital concomitant. Consider, for example, the fear of experiencing one's virtual self (or avatar) frozen Medusa-like within a digital program,[76] or being gripped, Pygmalion-like, by a foreign will and made to succumb, a virtual puppet to the whims of an anonymous avatar or hacker,[77] or being zapped by an electronic stream of commercials, like a modern day Tantalus, lit up by an audio-visual screen that stokes desire at every turn, telling you that "You Can Have it All," though surplus desire remains, throbbing, in the end as at the beginning. Feeding off of the desire we invest in them, images seem to have a life of their own.[78]

There is something uncanny about the visual image. Sometimes, it seems to meet our gaze or elicit a response – as if animated by some mysterious force. We feel this, for example, in Titian's sensual objects of desire, in paintings like

Venus of Urbino, Danae, Europa, Penitent Magdalen. These paintings are highly tactile, arousing, as the eye registers all manner of carnate cues: the erect nipple, the male's ravishing gaze, the female nude's gentle self-caress. Films too numerous to mention replicate this erotic charge. And sometimes images even invite us to reflect upon their evocative power, as if holding up a mirror to our eye so that we might see ourselves seeing. As in Titian's masterly *Venus with a Mirror* (1555; image 2.3 – see plate section between pp. 118 and 119), which splits off Venus's gaze (in the mirror she holds) from its source (strangely, the eyes do not match). Or consider Veronese's own version of *Venus with a Mirror,* in which the angle of the subject's gaze captured in the mirror cannot possibly be correct. It is as if the image had somehow broken free and taken on a life of its own. These images imaging imaging force the viewer to wonder: whose gaze is this? (Venus? The painter? Our own?)

It is the same challenge film director Michael Powell poses in his 1959 cult classic, *Peeping Tom.* The film tells the story of a deranged serial killer who places a mirror before the terror-stricken eyes of his victims as he films them watching their own death unfold. We, too, watch, we the film viewers, or should one say, "film voyeurs," caught in the spectacle of eroticized violence. The audience's stricken gaze becomes an act of collusion with the killer's (or is it the director's? or our own?) perverse desire, cycling within an endless loop of illicit gratification, implicating the very nature of the filmic experience itself. Tactile and evasive, wily in its deceptive transparency, its disingenuous claim to originality (as the thing itself rather than a mere representation), the visual image is like the devil incarnate, the Satanic seducer who famously "lured the eye" of Eve.[79] Yet, as philosophers and poets along with painters and film makers tell us, from Bruno to Blake to Deleuze, and from Titian, Tintoretto and Veronese to Powell, Verhoeven, and Lynch, it is precisely the universal binding power of *Eros* that makes the visual image worthy of wonder, celebration, and perhaps even joyous or anxious submission.

At the same time, that very power has also inspired fear and prohibition. Indeed, the very first prohibition that the Old Testament announces concerns the graven image. (The first commandment insists upon the oneness of God; the second commandment, regarding images, begins the ensuing sequence of prohibitions.) It is as if the ancient scribes feared that the power of the image somehow emulates and thus threatens to usurp the creative power of God. Heresy, arrogance, idolatry: here lies the historic origin of the iconoclastic impulse. It takes a sublime, even godlike power to warrant such an extreme prohibitory measure, the kind of power that tempts people to substitute for the worship of God the worship of images and idols (like the Golden Calf, that uncanny, magical creation that emerged as if of itself, with a life and shape of its own making[80]). The creation of images is such a power.

I contend that a paradigm born of an antipathy to vision is ill suited to a culture that is predominantly visual. The positivist perspective of modernity was born in a cauldron of profound metaphysical anxiety. We hear that anxiety resound in Pascal's tortured cry:

> The eternal silence of these infinite spaces fills me with dread . . . When I consider the brief span of my life absorbed into the eternity which comes before and after – as the remembrance of a guest that tarrieth but a day – the small space I occupy and which I see swallowed up in the infinite immensity of spaces of which I know nothing and which know nothing of me, I take fright and am amazed to see myself here rather than there: there is no reason for me to be here rather than there, now rather than then.[81]

A similar metaphysical anxiety pervades our time. We hear it, for example, in Samuel Beckett's words:

> . . . you must go on, I can't go on, you must go on, I'll go on, you must say words, as long as there are any, until they find me, until they say me, strange pain, strange sin, you must go on, perhaps it's already done, perhaps they have said me already, perhaps they have carried me to the threshold of my story, before the door that opens on my story, that would surprise me, if it opens, it will be I, it will be the silence, where I am, I don't know, I'll never know, in the silence you don't know, you must go on, I can't go on. I go on.[82]

Similar cultural ailments, however, will not necessarily respond to similar remedies. The Cartesian retreat from the senses and from visuality in particular, helped to forge a path that led beyond the violent and disorienting iconoclash of seventeenth century baroque culture. In that respect, it served its historic function. But ours is an ineluctably visual era. The way out of the iconoclash of the contemporary baroque will require a different path.

We are now living in a post-Foucauldian society. The micro-physics of power/knowledge has given way to "command and control" technologies. As the agents of both Church and State realized during the Counter-Reformation, and as engineers of social consent (advertisers, politicians, and jurists) well understand today, power inheres in defining, stimulating, and channeling the demands of sensation. Like cars speeding along a vast network of highways, we are free to seek our gratifications within the programs to which we have access.[83] Today, that power of command and control plays out in the form of hyper-flattened images pulsating on electronic screens in the service of a wide range of sensory gratifications and channeled desire.

By identifying the familiar models and templates, the recurring scripts and scenarios, the common character types and story lines that people habitually (which is to say, unconsciously) use every day, we can learn a great deal about the methods as well as the cultural materials with which visual meanings are constructed. By studying cognitive heuristics (which serve as our mental rules of thumb) quickly intuited responses to external stimuli may be unpacked and critically assessed. Likewise, the role of emotions in the construction of meaning and belief may be understood with greater clarity and sophistication. At the same time, however, the analytic tools of cognitive and cultural psychology, among other social scientific disciplines, cannot fully account for the way we experience visual images. Just as the tools of psychoanalytic interpretation, brought to bear upon dream work, presuppose but will never fully grasp or delineate the creative unconscious, so, too, the tools of visual interpretation, brought to bear upon the sublime image, presuppose but will never fully capture the shimmering surplus of meaning that animates it. Like the unconscious, the sublime is a presence that comes to mind as an uncanny absence. Its potency consists in simultaneously taking the viewer into a particular visual field or representation and catapulting her beyond it. It is as if the fullness of meaning (or value) that pervades a given visual form remains irreducible to that form, like a dancer who simultaneously is and is not the dance.

A peculiar sense of authenticity and authority attends our experience of the sublime. That sense may play out in different registers – depending, for example, on whether one is addressing the aesthetic or the ethical aspect of the visual experience in question. The authority of an aesthetically sublime image transcends whatever pleasure the image may bring. It invokes a sense of ineffable meaning in an experience that casts one outside oneself. The source of the experience is irreducible to what the senses can make of it. For its part, the ethical sublime transcends rule-based or even principled judgment; the sense of justice that it invokes, like the Others' need, to which we respond in our experience of the ethical, remains beyond measure. These descriptions should not be taken to suggest that the aesthetic and the ethical are somehow antithetical in nature. They need not coincide in a given experience or representation, but they might. Indeed, the confluence of the ethical and the aesthetic sublime harks back to the age-old ideal of classical and medieval rhetoric.[84] Vico renewed that aspiration at the outset of the eighteenth century when he wrote: "What is eloquence, in effect, but wisdom, ornately and copiously delivered in words appropriate to the common opinion of mankind?"[85] This ancient rhetorical ideal, expressed here as the confluence of the aesthetic and ethical sublime, is also the aspirational ideal of visual jurisprudence. The path to this ideal, initiated by the phenomenology of perception, embodied knowledge, and self-transcending attunement to that which is other, points the way beyond the metaphysical anxiety of iconoclash in the age of the digital baroque.

The Road Ahead: Reintegrating the Aesthetic and the Ethical

Law, like an image, may assert it is simply what it seems, no more, say, than a sovereign command. Yet, at the same time, it contains a mystery. That mystery takes us beyond the positive rules that establish law's validity. For validity conditions alone cannot account for the legitimating aura of law's moral authority. What is the source of that aura? How do we understand it, or trust it? Like Antigone's defiant claim to justice in the face of King Creon's stark command (that her brother's body remain unburied), or like the King's two bodies, one worldly, the other divine (inspired by "the breath of God," as Hooker put it),[86] law's nature is split. It carries within itself a perpetual want, that it might contain the invisible source of a legitimating value. When that trace is gone, law may still aspire to be a valid rational system of conventional signs, an efficacious code of command and control, but as Gershom Scholem noted of Kafka's law, such a system risks becoming a mere formality, a code that retains validity but lacks significance.[87] What is such a sign if not a mere ornament, like an arabesque endlessly unfolding in empty space, or ceaselessly enfolding the curved surface of a decorative vase? When law lives like an image deprived of its auratic shimmer, when its legitimating surplus of meaning, its visual *différance*, has been exhausted, then the door no longer opens wide enough even to intimate, as Kafka does in *Before the Law*, that the luminous mystery of justice persists. When only the imperative of law remains, it is if the king's transcendent body had died, but the command of the sovereign lives on, and its interdictions and procedures continue to pile up in conformity with an ever-changing human will. That is what baroque law is like.

In what follows, I shall argue that restoring an authentic and authoritative ontological source of visual meaning will help to counter the relativist tendencies of Cartesian rationality which have been with us from the outset of modernity. This response also addresses the recurring moral uncertainties that have long dogged the legal positivist tradition. Alternative cultural and cognitive sources of truth and value, manifest, for example, in the aesthetic and ethical sublime, also counter the hyper positivist as well as the deconstructivist tendencies of late (or "post-") modernity, a cultural moment of low ethical confidence and heightened visual proliferation more aptly described as the digital baroque.[88] In this view, the Cartesian or positivist impulse to simply denounce or seek to codify desire, in an effort to defuse its demands, will not suffice. We must learn to fuse the demand of desire with the interpretive capacity of the ethical imagination. The ethical teaches a way of responding to desire. How do we express its binding power (as *Eros*), in what sublime form, in the service of what collective values and beliefs? There may be a science to effectively constitute the formal validity of law ("legal positivism"), but as jurisprudential scholars from Vico to Robert Cover and James Boyd White understood so well we also need a poetic (perhaps a mythopoieic) rhetoric to establish and effectively maintain the binding power of law's moral authority.

In that spirit, before we turn to the chapters that follow, I would like to recount here two closely related stories. They are iconic narratives with an ancient pedigree whose continued authority testifies to the persistent binding power of *mythopoieic* thought. My intention is to use these accounts to help frame what I describe in this book as the advent of the digital baroque and the devolution of the once dominant paradigm of Cartesian optics. Though we find them in the Book of Genesis, I wish to be clear that it is not my purpose here to advance some sectarian aim or belief. I recount them for the eloquent wisdom that they contain. I believe that these stories squarely address issues that lie at the heart of law's uneasy marriage of power and meaning, and they show just how ancient is the human encounter with iconoclash, our love and fear of images. Following Soleveitchik, I shall refer to these two stories as "Genesis I" and "Genesis II."[89]

Envisioning law's mythopoieic origin

In the Old Testament there are two different accounts of humanity's origin. In the first creation story ("Genesis I") we read: "God created man, in the likeness of God made he him."[90] In this version, God creates man in his own image. And humans, true to their origin, reflecting the mimetic power of their maker, have been creating images ever since. We are after all the image-creating creature *par excellence*.[91] And yet, we also read, in the Book of Exodus, the stark imperative of the Second Commandment: "Thou shalt not make unto thee any graven image, or any likeness of any thing that is in heaven above, or that is in the earth beneath, or that is in the water under the earth. Thou shalt not bow down thyself to them, nor serve them, for I the Lord thy God am a jealous God."[92] What paradox is this? By creating man in his own image, God created an image-making being like himself. Then he prohibits the making of images. It is as if the ancient Genesis story envisions a radical split in human nature. As a creature made in God's image, humans feel impelled to imitate their Creator, which is to say, they feel compelled to create images that imitate creation. But they must not do so. What is the meaning of this paradox? The answer lies in the differences between Genesis I and Genesis II.

Created in God's likeness, the first Adam stands as both the model and champion of humanity's instrumental mastery over the earth and all that it contains. ("Fill the earth and subdue it, and have dominion over the fish of the sea, over the fowl of the heaven, and over the beasts, and all over the earth.") Humankind's mimetic faculty, in other words, correlates to material mastery. In the second creation story, by contrast, we find no reference either to images or to mastery. Instead, we read: "God breathed into his nostrils the breath of life; and man became a living soul."[93] The chief variation in this version consists in the gift of life in the form of God's breath. With the introduction of this immaterial element, the second creation story shifts focus, along with its normative register. Dominion over the material world gives way to a very different purpose. Placing Adam in the Garden of Eden, God instructs him "to dress it and to keep it."[94] In other words, mastery now yields to solicitude and conservation. If the first Adam is the master of creation, the second Adam is its self-denying caretaker. In short, if our first nature is instrumental, in the service of command and control, our second is responsive, mindful of that which requires care or service.

The eloquent wisdom of this double creation narrative teaches that our nature is indeed divided. As a result, we are fated to oscillate between two possibilities: mastery and service. Mastery, fueled by humanity's mimetic faculty, risks the arrogance of power. As progenitors of images, we face that ancient and recurring temptation: "Ye shall be as gods." In this view, the second commandment's strictures against graven images may be read as an ethical check upon the mimetic desire for total mastery. The ethical challenge we face is to harmonize our first nature (mastery) with our second (service). I believe this challenge is replicated in law's historic struggle to marry power and meaning, to somehow harmonize command and control with the moral authority that assures us it is good (right, fair, or just) to accept what the law demands of us. Key to the modulation of totalizing power is the cultivation of self-demotion (or perhaps "self-mastery"[95]) in the service of something other than self. Law faces a similar challenge. It, too, requires a form of self-demotion in response to something other than its own power to command. This is the perennial challenge of justice.

When law lives as an image on screens large and small, the ongoing struggle to reconcile law's divided nature falls to visual jurisprudence. We may be tempted to treat the visual image as no more than what it depicts (as if it were the thing itself and not a copy), just as we may be tempted to treat it as an empty sign (as if it were a signifier modifying a signifier in an endless stream of signifiers utterly cut off from the signified). But naïve realism and postmodern suspicion are not our only options. In the irreducible auratic shimmer of the image, we encounter something that is both constructed and sublime. When law takes on the life of an image, as it has in recent years and will continue to do in the years ahead, law too faces these options. Law is a command that may be taken for no more than what it says or shows; but authorizing power requires more than that. Law wants the binding power of moral value and mimetic desire combined; in that mysterious union lies the source of positive law's legitimacy. In a visual age, we encounter that source in the irreducible auratic shimmer of the law as image. That shimmer signals a sublime presence (which we experience as an uncanny absence). It brings justice to mind.

Derrida has written: "[O]ne cannot speak directly about justice, thematize or objectivize justice, say 'This is just,' and even less 'I am just,' without immediately betraying justice."[96] The demand and scope of justice is simply too great to be contained in a finite form. Yet, like love, its fullest meaning, paradoxically invariant amid endless variation, is inescapably situated. We know it best from lived experience; its meaning fades in mere abstraction. Derrida calls the testing of that experience "deconstruction". Justice itself cannot be deconstructed. Law, however, must be. Testing the law for justice – exploring the authenticity of law's authority and the legitimacy of its command – is deconstruction. This is the meaning of Derrida's famous claim, "Deconstruction is justice."[97] Given the fragmentary and imperfect nature of law's expression of justice, deconstruction remains an interminable process. Law wants justice. Paradoxically, justice is simultaneously law's other and its fulfillment.

Law, like an image, invites us to forget or deny that which lies beyond its mimetic (figurative) aspect. Law's oscillation between power and meaning, between aesthetic form (image, figure, copy, text) and moral authority – between arabesques and entanglements in the shorthand of this book – re-enacts humanity's historic vacillation between the two poles of our nature (Genesis I and Genesis II). In the endless dance of power and meaning, Adam I and Adam II recapitulate the King's two bodies, the letter and spirit of the law. Law oscillates between these poles in search of the rule-based conditions of its validity and the moral conditions that establish its legitimacy. In the current digital baroque era, the reign of the visual image, with its culturally fraught history of power and idolatry, spectacle and iconoclasm, heightens our sensitivity to the positivist (sign-based) and natural (sign-transcending) polarities of law. Law commands, but it wants its commands to be accepted not simply out of fear of punishment, but also, and perhaps even more importantly, in the belief that it is just. Law oscillates between power and meaning. Without good (non-punitive, moral) reasons to accept its coercive power, law remains the gunman writ large.

The plan of this book

Today, as the disembodied optics of Cartesian rationality grows increasingly anachronistic, we confront anew the vicissitudes of ethical and aesthetic judgment. Caught between the Scylla of sectarian intolerance and the Charybdis of ethical relativity, we find ourselves in circumstances strikingly similar to those under which modernity began. Descartes' rational paradigm, modeled on the natural sciences, offered an escape from the manifold crises of the time. His method bore fruit. We owe the secular ideals of the Liberal state (including tolerance, pluralism, and the idea of popular sovereignty) to this origin. And, indeed, throughout modernity, the sciences have continued to improve our material condition as they steadily increase our mastery over nature. But the sciences alone could never harmonize our twofold nature. As Konrad Lorenz once wrote: "Always and everywhere, it is the unreasoning, emotional appreciation of values that adds a plus or a minus sign to the answer of Kant's categorical self-questioning and makes it an imperative or a veto. By itself, reason can only devise means to achieve otherwise determined ends; it cannot set up goals or give us orders." In short, the ethical challenge of Genesis II looms as large as it ever has.

The pictorial turn in mainstream culture generally, and in the legal culture in particular, makes vivid the insufficiency of rational categories and methods alone to cope with the practical and theoretical demands of visual meaning making. Visual culture calls for other forms of logic (for example, associative rather than deductive and inductive) and other forms of knowledge (for example, emotional as well as critical). The modern scientific reaction against the pre-modern code of visuality, and against the rhetorical culture of poetic imagination in which it was embedded, may be viewed, as an historical matter, as an understandable defense against the destabilizing consequences of irrational intolerance and iconoclastic violence. Nevertheless, its eclipse of the humanities in general and the rhetorical tradition in particular resulted in an imprudent cultural and cognitive imbalance. As visual and digital forms proliferate together with the codes that govern them, signs of ethical uncertainty abound in legal and popular culture alike. The challenge of contemporary digital baroque culture is above all an ethical one. The ethical imagination inhabits a narrative world of mythopoieic ideas, images, and feelings. Accordingly, it is this world to which visual jurisprudence must turn as it explores new cultural sources and cognitive methods that will help ensure the ongoing legitimacy of law in the digital age.

What follows, then, is an effort to narrate the contemporary drama of law's oscillation between meaning and power under the singular conditions of digital baroque culture. Chapter 3 begins by situating law's screen life in the context of actual cases. Here we see the different visual registers and aesthetic codes law assumes when it lives as an image on the screen. The possibilities range from the sublime to the spectacular. Both require elucidation. Chapter 4 takes up the task of examining in further detail the visual register of the spectacle. Here we explore the perturbed, fragmented, endlessly pullulating dreamscape of the contemporary neo-baroque. We also examine what the life of law is like when it unfolds under such disturbed cultural conditions. Pervasive ontological uncertainty, we will see, makes manifest the ethical fragility of law's authority. This unstable condition invites a constructive response. We will need to re-theorize in order to readapt the legal imagination to contemporary conditions. Accordingly, Chapter 5 sets out to identify extant cultural and cognitive resources that are adequate to this task. We begin by building on important Legal Realist insights concerning the role of intuition and social as well cognitive construction in the decision making process. Then, drawing together insights from the early twentieth century "process" philosophies of Henri Bergson, Alfred North Whitehead, and William James, the phenomenology of perception, and contemporary cognitive and cultural psychology, this chapter proposes a new model for legal theory. It is the model of visual jurisprudence. With the advent of visual jurisprudence we encounter the practical and theoretical significance of the aesthetic and ethical sublime. The pivotal contention here is that a better understanding of the nature and function of the visual sublime will help to arrest the baroque recession of reality and in so doing ease the metaphysical anxiety and ethical uncertainty that it entails. Fortified by new resources, Chapter 6 examines the deeper challenge to law that digital simulation presents. If the visual sublime is indeed crucial to the stabilization of baroque conditions and the restoration of ethical confidence in law's legitimacy, then it is incumbent upon us to ask, what place does the sublime have in the domain of digital simulation? Are digital images amenable to the ontological surplus that generates the visual sublime, and if so under what conditions is this possible?

Simply put, the central question here is whether the ontological truth of digital simulations is sufficient to warrant an authentic ethical demand. Chapter 7 concludes by inviting readers to reframe law's contemporary encounter with the visual spectacle and the visual sublime in a broader historical context. The novelty of this clash of visual registers and the demands of visual literacy become less pronounced when viewed in light of the troubled history in the West of classical rhetoric. Returning to these roots allows us to reconfigure the unproductive dichotomization of science and the humanities. By recapturing the wisdom of integral rhetoric the contribution of science to the ongoing harmonization of aesthetics and the ethical becomes possible. Visual jurisprudence incorporates and champions anew this ancient rhetorical ideal. Restoring law's roots in the poetic (or *mythopoeic*) imagination allows us to celebrate the power and value of the aesthetic and ethical sublime in contemporary legal theory and practice. As a preliminary matter, however, it is incumbent upon us to reckon with law's contemporary reality on the screen. That is the topic to which we turn next.

CHAPTER 3

Law's Screen Life: Visualizing Law in Practice

> [T]he moviemaker's art is not all that different from the lawyer's – especially the courtroom advocate's. Both must capture, in a very short space, a slice of human existence, and make the audience see a story from their particular perspective. Both have to know which facts to include and which to leave out; when to appeal to emotion and when to reason; what to spoonfeed the audience and what to make them work out for themselves; when to do the expected and when the unexpected; when to script and when to improvise.
>
> (Judge Alex Kozinski[1])

> Recognition involves a sudden click or shift of levels as information, sensory impressions, arrange themselves into a larger gestalt.
>
> (Bill Nichols[2])

> In this flash of recognition truth is known because it is experienced . . . [I]t is visible evidence of a presencing.
>
> (Jennifer Deger[3])

Law today lives in images the way images live on the screen. In this chapter, I will describe four discrete, but interrelated forms of law's screen life and show how they play out both in actual cases and in mainstream visual culture. The four forms I have in mind reflect:

1 Law's assimilation from the visual mass media of familiar cognitive and cultural templates, including character types and story forms that tell viewers how the world works and the way people may be expected to behave in a given set of circumstances ("visual memes").
2 Law's exploitation of the viewer's sense of visual delight based on the flow of vivid visual images that draw and hold the viewer's attention, stick in memory, and seem to authorize belief ("visual sensation").
3 Law's emulation of the visual mass media's logic of desire which simultaneously stokes forbidden fantasies while providing moral cover in the form of a predatory Other on to whom the viewer may displace (and thus disown) guilty pleasures for which the predator is condemned (the "visual unconscious").
4 Law's embodiment of a source of knowledge that is manifest on the screen as an uncanny absence (or auratic presence), a phenomenon of excess we may call (with a nod to Derrida) visual *différance* (the "visual sublime").

The proliferation of images of law in all manner of visual media (including film, television, and even virtual worlds and video games) has, in Austin Sarat's words, "altered and expanded the sphere of legal life."[4] Today, people everywhere look for reality on the screen, and reality, in turn, assumes the look that the screen provides. To be sure, the two-way traffic between law and popular culture may be managed in either direction for a broad range of strategic purposes. Consider, for example, a blockbuster film such as *Erin Brockovich* (2000). The film's strong pro-environment and anti-corporate greed message played out not only in film theaters (as well as on private screens at home), but also as part of an independent political campaign featuring the real Erin Brockovich. Appearing in a series of television advertisements, Brockovich enhanced her public advocacy against proposed tort reform legislation by rechanneling the aura of celebrity that the public had come to associate with her name and character based on Hollywood star Julia Roberts's portrayal of Brockovich in the film. Here is life (Erin Brockovich advocating a particular political agenda) imitating art (Julia Roberts's fictional portrayal of Brockovich) imitating life (the real Erin Brockovich story). In this instance, the visual sensation produced by a Hollywood celebrity is being tapped and recycled into the political and legal spheres of public policy making and legislation. As we will see later on in this chapter, the images that legal advocates use to prompt judgments in their favor in real cases need not rely on such an attenuated source of visual persuasion. The image itself may also shimmer with an original presence that plays out in a far different ontological and epistemological register. The important point is this: When law lives as an image on the screen it embraces a broad spectrum of meaning making possibilities, ranging from fleeting sensation to uncanny significance. Each visual register relies upon a particular cultural and cognitive archive and a concomitant set of interpretive practices. For this reason it is incumbent upon legal advocates to understand the technical as well as the rhetorical dimensions of the visual meaning making process. And in the Anglo-American legal tradition, this includes understanding the adversarial art of deconstructing an opponent's visuals in order to substitute one's own.

The art of visual storytelling requires cultural as well as visual fluency. Everyone bears the imprint of the culture into which he or she is born and raised. Each of us inherits and constantly renews an archive of cultural knowledge and a repertoire of communicative practices. We can only tell (and respond to) the stories we know,[5] or know how to decode. There are stock scripts for negotiating certain kinds of social interactions (like ordering food in a restaurant), familiar character types for helping us to recognize the kind of person we might be dealing with (on screen and off), and recurring story forms to help us structure events in everyday life.[6] These social tools become second nature to us, which is to say once we assimilate them we are no longer conscious of their presence. The work they perform becomes invisible. Unconscious habits of meaning making, familiarly known as intuition, make up what we call ordinary common sense.[7] Whether accurate or not, common sense, including our visual common sense, depends upon the familiar social constructs and cultural models that we carry around in our heads.[8] In this respect, popular culture is a rich source of images of lawyers, criminals, and the legal system. These images help to shape and inform the way we think, feel, and judge. It should not prove surprising, therefore, to find trial lawyers importing popular film stories and character types as well as familiar cinematic styles into their courtroom practices.[9] For good or for ill, these are the resources with which trial lawyers have to work (or work around) to craft the stories and images that win cases in court.[10]

When it comes to law on the screen, however, it is not simply a matter of what images are being shown; it is also a matter of how they affect the way in which viewers think, feel, and remember – as well as what they associate to, identify with, or discount – as they watch.[11] As the great American poet Wallace Stevens observed, "things as they are, are changed upon the blue guitar."[12] In other words, the stories we hear and see are not simply a matter of content or genre;[13] the medium in which they are constructed and conveyed matters. New visual technologies allow lawyers to picture evidence and argument with unprecedented persuasive power. Judges and jurors can see inside defective machines or constricted arteries; they can witness reconstructed accidents and crimes, and assess complex patent claims by comparing relatively simple visual displays of complicated technologies or processes that show whether an impermissible imitation exists. These new capabilities are enabling great strides to be made in the search for fact-based justice at trial. At the same time, however, pictures (in some cases, perhaps by virtue of their apparent simplicity) may also complicate this aspiration. Risks arise, for example, when visual evidence and visual arguments import strong affective and associative content that would be impermissible if it had been expressed explicitly instead of remaining hidden on an implicit (which is to say, unconscious) level of meaning making.[14]

Plainly, law's adversarial method must adapt to these new cultural, cognitive, and technological conditions. Law teaching and legal theory also need to catch up to the realities (including the digitally simulated realities) that are increasingly being projected onto electronic screens in courtrooms around the globe. Adapting Robert Cover's famous formulation to contemporary cultural conditions, we may now say that for every constitution there is not only a textual epic but also a cinematic and perhaps even a multi-player interactive one.[15] Once viewed in the context of the narratives, films, and digital (algorithmically generated) representations that give it meaning, law becomes "not merely a system of rules to be observed," and not simply "a world in which we live,"[16] but many different worlds, each reflecting deep structures within the operating system or organizational logic of the communicative medium in which law's meanings unfold.

As part of this process of adaptation, it is important to realize that the way we respond to visual images is different, as a perceptual and cognitive matter, from the way we respond to words alone.[17] For example, law on the screen privileges meaning making through associational logic which operates, in large part, subconsciously, through its emotional appeal. A viewer might be aware that an image is strongly linked to a particular emotional response without knowing or understanding just what the connection is. In this respect, then, visual images tend to capitalize on the power of people's intuitive, *gestalt* emotional responses to shape their judgments. These effects operate beneath the radar of awareness and are thus less amenable to critical scrutiny and counter-argument.[18] It is also notable that visual images tend to have a more embodied impact than non-visual expressions of the same information. This is because they tend to be more vivid, and more lifelike. Studies show that people respond to photorealistic pictures as they would to the real thing.[19] For instance, viewers of an IMAX movie of a roller coaster ride or of an unstable, camcorder-based film like *The Blair*

Witch Project (1999) or *Cloverfield* (2008) may experience a sense of dizziness or physical excitement that words alone could never induce.[20]

Words are obviously constructed by the speaker and thus are immediately recognized as abstractions. A word is unlikely to be mistaken for a window. By contrast, photorealistic photographs, videos, film, as well as digital re-enactments can appear to be caused by the outside world, as if untouched by human mediation or authorial interpretation.[21] The human brain takes in visual information all at once. This wealth of data can lead jurors to believe that they have all the information there is to be had, and thus disincline them to pursue the matter further. Held in the grip of moving images, critical thinking is discouraged or effectively disabled; it is enough simply to keep up with the visual flow. Because pictures cannot be reduced to explicit verbal propositions, some of their meaning always remains implicit. This represents a convenient opportunity for advocates who might well prefer to leave an intended meaning unspoken – particularly when evidentiary rules or social conventions forbid making the message explicitly.[22]

In addition, construing visual meaning from the screen readily lends itself to what literary theorists call "intertextual" references.[23] By referring to other works, other genres, even other media, screen images cue the audience's cultural knowledge and allow them to draw on that implicit knowledge in responding to what they see.[24] Of course, words can do this too, but pictures can do it more effectively because they do it unconsciously, in a way that embeds the borrowed cultural value invisibly in the visual representation of the picture's ostensible subject matter.

Finally, cinematic representations favor particularities over abstractions. This has legal consequences. For example, stories driven by particular characters and dramatic events tend to emphasize individual agency and simplified (monocausal) explanations for the consequences of particular actions. As a result, systemic reasons for bad outcomes – such as market incentives for particular kinds of behavior or flaws in bureaucratic decision-making processes – receive short shrift on the screen. The same may be said for more complex (multicausal) explanations that get in the way of dramatic visual storytelling. In short, cinematic narratives mimic the often reality-distorting tendencies of the mind to simplify accounts and attribute blame in precisely these ways.[25] In assessing the impact of visual communication on law we must also be attentive to the largely unconscious process through which we make mental (as well as tactile or affective) associations to the images we see.[26] Although we may be aware of experiencing a particular emotion in response to an image or series of images, the precise nature of the connection usually remains obscure. If we cannot account for its source, however, the emotion we experience remains less susceptible to deliberate critique and counterargument.[27]

Skillful legal advocates, like their counterparts in politics and advertising, have learned how to exploit these features of visual communication. This raises novel legal questions. For example, is a computer-generated animation (re-enacting an accident, say, or a crime) just another evidentiary illustration or is it something qualitatively different?[28] Might there be something so compelling about a digitally simulated reality (not to mention three-dimensional or more fully immersive simulations)[29] that places it beyond the ordinary bounds of demonstrative evidence?[30] Is it even within the ken of jurors' ordinary common sense to follow judicial instructions to use a visual only as "illustrative" of an expert's opinion rather than as documentary evidence that helps to "prove" a particular party's theory of the case?[31] For example, a juror might technically obey a judicial instruction not to use illustrative visual evidence as proof of what it depicts, but can we realistically expect that juror to dispel every trace of the emotional impact that comes from "watching" a murder, or seeming to occupy the cabin of an airplane as it crashes to earth?[32]

The debate about the adequacy of current evidentiary rules in the age of computer-generated images remains at a very early stage of development.[33] Some commentators have expressed confidence in the adversarial process,[34] while others have expressed a variety of concerns.[35] Without question, the capacity of the legal system to adapt to the demands and novelties of visual evidentiary and argumentative representations in court (and elsewhere in legal practice) will depend upon the capacity of lawyers, judges, law teachers, and legal scholars to develop new standards of visual literacy as an integral part of lawyering in the digital age. The expectation of jurors, like the public in general, to assimilate information from electronic screens will only grow over time. Lawyers will need to grasp the craft as well as the tactical utility of visualizing their case theories. Indeed, the adversarial ideal of testing truth claims in open court will not be met unless lawyers learn how to cross-examine what's on the screen as well as who is in the witness stand. Likewise, judges will need to develop a deeper appreciation of how traditional notions of authentication and prejudice apply to a broad range of visual representations in court.

One thing is certain. When law lives as an image on the screen the *aesthetic forms*, *interpretive methods*, and *narrative content* of popular visual entertainment inevitably find their way into the courtroom. These images often are not what they seem. We all tend to be naïve realists when we watch. We look through the screen as if it were a window onto reality rather than the construction that it is, which is to say, we all tend to accept as true what we know or believe.[36] This default condition obtains whether the object in view is directly perceived with our senses or perceived via the screen. Either way, it seems natural to take visual images at face value, as if what we see were the thing itself. But images are bound to all sorts of conventions for the meanings they convey – conventions imposed by the medium in which they appear; conventions imposed by cultural patterns of meaning making that we have unconsciously assimilated; and psychological conventions that incline us to make certain kinds of emotional associations when we perceive a particular kind of image.

When it comes to the constructed nature of visuality there are many avenues to explore.[37] We could talk about the physiology of perception, the social and cultural construction of visual meaning, the cognitive function of emotion, the operation of implicit associations in response to the image, and so on. In what follows, I will focus in particular on visual aesthetics and psychodynamic meaning making in the specific context of the criminal predator. When I use the word psychodynamic, I have in mind the traditional Freudian sense of depth psychology, the operation of unconscious fantasies, wishes, and desires. Inside the courtroom, all of these aspects of meaning making are more or less active, although more often than not their operation remains hidden. This is often the case when it comes to the extra-legal frames of reference that affect visual perception. Consider, for example, Justice Scalia's description of the police video from the *Scott v. Harris* case. In calling it "the scariest chase scene I've ever seen since *The French Connection*," Justice Scalia may not have realized the extent to which he was evoking, by visual association, the emotional intensity that this popular feature film was designed to produce. Of course, it is also possible that Justice Scalia deliberately used this film reference precisely in order to identify for others the kind of affect they should invest in the police chase video at issue. Either way, the fact remains that images like these when shown inside the courtroom are saturated with extra-legal associations that operate for the most part outside our conscious reckoning.

The image is always more than it shows. Its meaning depends to a great extent on what we bring to it, as well as what we allow it to bring to us. What the image doesn't show is how this meaning making process comes about. In an effort to shed more light on that process, in what follows I offer a case study arising in the domain of child pornography law. My argument may be simply stated. When law migrates to the screen it tends to assimilate the aesthetic codes that operate there. This includes the visual mass media's logic of desire. My example illustrates this phenomenon by drawing upon the longstanding American obsession with the figure of the sexual predator, a rather popular character in many of the crime dramas featured in American film and television. What we also see, however, is that the fantasies that play out in these dramas may take on a life of their own – on screen and off. Jurists, too, may unwittingly collude in the fantasy life of popular culture. When they do, particularly when they undertake the juridical task of public policy making in the grip of such fantasies, it may be said that they are legislating from the unconscious. That is my contention regarding recent developments in child pornography law; the evidence and argument follow. We begin with a brief overview of how the aesthetics of popular entertainment help to shape and inform belief and judgment. In short order we come to see the extent to which aesthetics interpenetrates with the ethical.

It is well known that law figures centrally in two of the most popular genres to be found on television and in film, namely: mystery and melodrama. One reason for the popularity of these genres, and for law's affinity with them, has to do with the kind of gratification that they offer. The plot device of the mystery genre effectively gratifies our desire for closure and certainty.[38] In the end we know "whodunit," the mystery is solved. Melodrama also gratifies our craving for certainty – the certainty that shapes and informs our sense of a shared moral order. Melodrama is all about good and evil. People like melodrama because it clarifies what good and evil are, and it affirms *that* they are. It is gratifying as well to identify with the agents of good and to see the bad guys get their proper comeuppance.[39] Crime stories in particular serve as a recurring template. Villainous criminals along with those heroes who find and punish them populate our moral imagination. Law is the designated agency for defining and suppressing sources of disorder in society. A corollary to that function is the unspoken assumption that law's power to prohibit is morally authorized. But that power may be put to other uses – uses that are extrinsic to law's own.

Just as savvy trial lawyers exploit visual pop culture for their own purposes inside the courtroom, producers of that culture use law to serve their interests. Law on television and in film provides a reliable source of authority for prohibition. Prohibition is important to producers of visual mass media because illicit fantasies, wishes, and desires fuel a good deal of what appears on the screen. Powerful psychic forces make us attend. Television sponsors and film producers like good attendance. That's what they are paying for. But you can't simply unleash powerful unconscious forces and be done with it. You have to restore at least a modicum of moral and psychological order in the end. Narrative coherence (to say nothing of viewer contentment) requires no less. Law supplies moral cover for the guilty pleasures that popular entertainment supplies. In this dispensation, responsibility for the illicit belongs solely to the bad guy, whom the viewer is all too willing to denounce in the end. That judgment, especially when allied with the moral force of law, purges the viewer's psyche of guilt. In other words, the psychic gratification that illicit fantasies fuel is morally safeguarded by the viewer's condemnation of their source. Viewers thus get what they want: intense jolts of emotional stimulation that are sanctioned by authority of law. And the mass media's producers get what they want: contented viewers. And the law? There is reason to believe that the cycle of illicit fantasy and legal prohibition is not a matter of popular entertainment alone. Pop cultural fictions leech into the legal system when the aesthetic codes of the visual mass media implicitly serve as codes for truth inside the courtroom. A similar leeching process occurs when law internalizes the visual mass media's logic of desire. When that happens, unconscious screen fantasies may be transformed into legal realities. Both of these processes, we will see, are at work in the development of contemporary child pornography laws.

Let us consider first the aesthetics of popular visual entertainment, and in particular the aesthetic I shall refer to as the magical realism of pop science. Studies have shown that the mere presence of a photograph at trial (even a neutral one) significantly increases the conviction rate compared to when no photos are shown (up to 38 per cent from only 8.8 per cent).[40] It has also been shown that the mere mention of "neuroscience" has the power to enhance the credibility of claims made in its name.[41] It stands to reason that the union of the two (visualizing neuroscience) would constitute a potent tool of persuasion inside the courtroom. It already has in the precincts of science. Between 2003 and 2008, on average, 1,000 peer-reviewed scholarly articles on neuroscience were being published every month.[42] The claims being made were wide ranging, and sometimes elaborate. As early as 1994, for example, Francis Crick had written: "your joys and your sorrows, your memories and your ambitions, your sense of personal identity and free will, are in fact no more than the behavior of a vast assembly of nerve cells and their associated molecules."[43] The neuroscientific refrain ("mind is matter") has resounded far and wide. In this view, free will dissolves in a bath of bio-chemical processes. No wonder Michael Gazzaniga asserted in 2005, that advances in neuroscience would someday "dominate the entire legal system."[44] How could it not if the hard core determinist claims being made in its name turned out to be correct?

To that end, the efficacy of digital visualization tools such fMRIs (functional magnetic resonance images) in particular, which purport to show the human organism at work from the inside, has not been lost on neuroscientists and trial lawyers alike. As one experimental psychologist observed, however, "[t]here is a real danger that pictures of blobs on brains seduce one into thinking that we can now directly observe psychological constructs."[45] Yet, despite these concerns, with increasing frequency fMRIs have been showing up in court in personal injury cases (to make brain injuries visible to jurors), in criminal cases (to establish incompetence or insanity), and in the penalty stage of most death penalty cases (to show mitigation, which is to say, to support the defense claim that execution is inappropriate when brain abnormalities diminish the defendant's culpability).[46] At the same time, crime scene investigators are increasingly submitting every shred of forensic proof for lab testing – leading to ever growing backlogs. As Antony Zuiker, the creator of the popular television series *CSI: Crime Scene Investigation*, put it, "blood, hair, saliva, skin et cetera are forensically designed to tell an investigator what has happened without having any witness to a crime."[47]

The message is clear: while witnesses may lie or make mistakes, science does not. In this way, new digital forensic technologies signal a return to the early days of evidence, when the credibility of physical evidence was thought to far outweigh eyewitness testimony.[48] If there is one thing upon which commentators seem to agree it is this: *CSI* technology is not just science, it is super-science.[49] And judging by the popular television shows, the visual aesthetics of *CSI* technology is beautiful to behold. Aesthetic delight in the image encourages a sense of understanding and acceptance, and that response, cognitive psychologists tell us, is tantamount to belief. Add aesthetic delight to the widespread belief in the authority of science and you have a powerful formula for producing truth. This is certainly the case regarding many of the new scientific technologies that are being used to generate visual evidence in court. To the untrained eye, which is to say, to the ordinary common sense of most judges and jurors, digital scans or fMRIs of the brain and other parts of the body look a lot like a photograph or an x-ray. But they are hardly that. The brain does not really "light up" when active. fMRIs are actually statistical maps, visualizations of comparative data sets, calculating variations from the norm of the magnetic resonance of water molecules within localized blood flow to the brain. It is this highly complex information that has been digitally programmed to look like a brain lighting up in some parts, but not in others. In many cases, the resulting image may seem to provide direct evidence of the truth claim a particular advocate is seeking to prove.

The natural inclination to view fMRIs as if they were photographs thus poses a serious risk of increasing conviction rates in cases involving fMRIs. Nor does this even begin to take into account the possible influence of the forensic pop science that is seen on television shows like *CSI: Crime Scene*

Investigation and its numerous offshoots. The fascination with cognitive neuroscience together with the wide ranging evidentiary claims of digital forensic technology have spread from scientific circles to the domain of popular entertainment. Consider: from 2000, the year it debuted on television, to 2006, *CSI: Crime Scene Investigation* grew into a franchise, with two spinoffs: *CSI: Miami* and *CSI: New York*. In 2004, each enjoyed over 14 million weekly viewers, while the original series had over 25 million. Comparable shows, featuring crime stopping, cutting edge technologies, have ensued, including: *Without a Trace, Numbers, Criminal Minds*, and *Navy NCIS: Naval Criminal Investigative Service* – on one network alone. Other networks have sought to ride the wave with spinoffs of their own, including: *The Closer, Crossing Jordan*, and *Bones*.[50]

This cumulative visual feast seeks to assure us that science brings certainty. Forensic investigators probe crime scenes for physical clues that inevitably lead to likely suspects. Perhaps they will retrace the trajectory of a gunshot back to its source, as in one episode of NCIS.[51] Look: that glare in the car window, it's the flash of a gun caught fortuitously in the frame of an ATM camera, and now, by simply shifting the view on the screen to an overhead police surveillance camera we readily see the image of a driver in a van. His face is quickly scanned and just as quickly dumped into a data base that immediately produces the identity investigators were seeking. Wondrous. Like that episode on *CSI*,[52] when traces of an attacker's skin were caught under the fingernails of a child, the result of a struggle. After being placed in a machine the size of a toaster, the skin cells glow green, like numinous crystals of kryptonite, beautiful to behold. It's a quick trip to a skin cell database, and presto! The criminal target's face instantly looms large on an adjoining screen. Like magic, except that we are meant to conclude that what seems like magic is really the stuff of science, the product of the most sophisticated forensic technologies. Even the *CSI* labs seem magical, suffused as they are in a mystical violet light that adds to the uncanny beauty of the scientific truths produced there. But is it truth, or sheer visual delight parading as truth? If the latter, then the same possibility apparently haunts the computer screens of professional scientists and trial lawyers alike.

The sheer visual delight of digital forensic technologies enchants the eye. As one researcher concluded, "exposure to brain images in the popular press, which provides a physical explanation for cognitive phenomena, likely influences the allure of cognitive neuroscience data."[53] This describes the power of the ersatz aura, what I have referred to as the magical realism of pop science. Needless to say, the incentive to intensify this aesthetic effect – what some neuroscience researchers call the "Christmas tree effect"[54] – in order to enhance the credibility of what the image purports to show raises serious ethical concerns.

Risks attend the instant gratification of popular entertainment when such gratification displaces more deliberate forms of judgment inside the courtroom. This is what happens when popular aesthetics (the aesthetics of visual delight) are unwittingly internalized as the operative code for truth. There are risks as well when unconscious fantasies stirred by the visual mass media take on a life of their own. In turning our attention to these risks, we will consider in particular the figure of the sexual predator. In recent years, popular entertainment has exhibited a near obsession with this figure. An intriguing dynamic is at work here. Images cause viewers to react to what they see as if it were the real thing. We emote in sympathy or antipathy with what we see on the screen just as we do in response to off-screen realities. These responses include a broad spectrum of sexual fantasies and wishes. Sexual responses are particularly potent. Hence, their popularity in the visual mass media, along with violence – and judging by popularity, preferably the two combined.

Law dramas on the screen may stage a parade of legal forms on the surface, but underneath powerful unconscious forces are often at work fueling the narrative. Film and television are desire machines regulated by familiar symbols of authority. As Freud understood, the release of powerful unconscious forces requires equally powerful prohibitions to restore psychic equilibrium. The greater the jolt of illicit titillation, the more sinister is the agent who must bear the full force of law's prohibition. The vicarious fulfillment of unacceptably violent impulses requires condemnation of especially evil perpetrators, just as the gratification of unacceptable sexual desires demands condemnation of perverse sexual predators. Such predators exist, but if they didn't we might have to invent them, or at least expand the threat they present to match our need to condemn the illicit desire with which they are associated. Like the proverbial scapegoat, someone must pay the price for the community's sins. That is what we see, at any rate, when an intra-psychic defense of this sort plays out in the public life of the community. Signs are that this unconscious process is at work in the realm of child pornography law.

The sexual abuse of children has been described as "the master narrative of our culture."[55] It is a crime that has been described as "worse than murder."[56] As Amy Adler notes, no other crime so preoccupies our "tabloid culture."[57] These popular narratives have given rise to a variety of distortions. For example, mass media depictions of child abductions and sexually motivated murders promote the belief that children are at great risk from predators lurking in schoolyards and playgrounds. Studies have shown, however, that the vast majority of child sexual abusers are well known to their victims.[58] According to one study, approximately 75 per cent of American adolescents who were sexually assaulted were victimized by someone they knew well.[59] The similarly pervasive fear of recidivism among sexual offenders has led to the proliferation of laws calling for indefinite civil commitment once criminal sentences have expired.[60] However, the empirical data do not support this popular belief. What accounts for such a gap between belief and reality?

Terror management studies have shown that terror prompts a heightened tendency to blame and punish.[61] Punishment re-establishes social stability by restoring confidence in a pre-existing "steady state" of conventional values and beliefs which undergird and authorize the punitive impulse. It has been suggested that since fantasies help to constitute what we fear, they may be useful to those whose objective it is to stage the efficacy of the state's power to manage fear.[62] Punitive measures restore confidence in the community's ability to police and effectively prohibit dangerous contaminants. Whether or not one accepts such a theory, the fact remains that the public and in particular the legal attention paid to violent and especially sexually violent child predators is at odds with the available empirical data. Such wildly exaggerated claims alert us to the supernumerary presence of a highly overdetermined psychic phenomenon. In a word, some strange fantasies are afoot.

Consider in this regard the bizarre accounts of sexual and often satanic ritual abuses in day care centers in the 1980s.[63] This prompted a slew of criminal prosecutions. Perhaps most notorious was the McMartin preschool trial in Los Angeles. The trial ran for two years, making it the longest criminal trial in American history. No convictions resulted.[64] Many of these daycare cases claimed that the alleged sexual abuses were undertaken in order to produce child pornography. None was ever found. Throughout this period of "crisis" and "moral panic," the empirical data seemed to contradict the need for such exceptional concern and such extraordinary legal remedies. Yet, the public's obsession with the child predator continues.[65]

So who is this predatory other? To judge from the visual mass media he assumes a variety of guises, but the classic image from film and television is that of a violent, often brutal stalker of innocent children. In the horror film *The Hills Have Eyes* (2006), for example, a teenage girl is raped in front of her family by a grotesque monster with the physical characteristics of an older man who has been deformed by exposure to radiation. In the 1999 film *8mm*, an investigator is hired to learn more about a snuff film involving the rape and murder of a young girl. In the film the victim is an underage girl. Her tormentor is an S&M star named Machine, a man of giant proportions who wears a black leather mask to conceal his identity when he rapes and murders his young victim. The explicit depiction of his abuses is meant to convey the demonic and sadistic nature of his actions, but their graphic nature is also a titillating source of forbidden fantasy and illicit arousal.

The sexual predator also has been depicted as seemingly ordinary and nondescript. This particular characterization is a staple of the decade long television series *Law and Order: SVU* [*Sexual Victims Unit*], which focused its weekly plots on "sexually based offenses that are considered especially heinous."[66] The series covers a range of sex crimes, especially those against children and teens. For example, in an episode titled "Demons" a young girl who survives a brutal rape describes in gruesome detail the full extent of her ordeal.[67] Her abuser is a serial rapist who is portrayed as a middle aged man with grey hair who dresses in flannel suits. The episode "Fault" features a violent stranger who tortures and rapes his vulnerable child victim.[68] In the first few minutes of the show viewers witness the murder of a family, including the rape and murder of a young girl. Two other children are kidnapped and tortured. The abuses they suffer include cigarette burns and sodomy. In the episode "Uncivilized", an eight-year-old boy is beaten, raped, and then left to die in a shallow grave by a middle-aged man with a history of sex crimes against children. His ordinary appearance gives no outward clue of his vicious past.[69]

Popular images of the sexual predator have migrated from the visual mass media to various public fora involving law enforcement and legislation. Consider, for example, this public notice from a local law enforcement website:

> The predator can be anyone from any social standing in life. From the doctor, who we admired for his manner, to the race car driver, whose public persona was filled with the embraces of a multitude of female fans it become apparent that there is no 'typical' profession with which to associate him to. He (or she) no longer hides on the boundaries of our school playgrounds but now exists within the confines of the Internet as well. Where he was once a transient he is now the vice president of a corporation. Where he was limited in choice as to where he 'operated' he now resides in anonymity within a largely unregulated medium.[70]

This kind of official notice has helped to fan public fears, which in turn have motivated expansive prosecutions, more stringent laws, and even vigilantism. For an example of the latter, consider the formation of citizen groups, such as "Perverted Justice," which have initiated their own efforts to hunt down sex offenders.[71] Volunteers for *Perverted Justice* troll the Internet pretending to be underage boys and girls in an effort to catch prospective sex offenders. These efforts have been aided by partnering with the hit reality television show called *To Catch a Predator*. The concept for the show debuted in 2004, on the television news magazine *Dateline NBC*, which featured a series of hidden camera investigations aimed at identifying and detaining alleged pedophiles who sought out minors on the Internet for sex. The predators were then lured by sexually explicit communications supplied by the show's staff writers to meet with a decoy in a staged (televised) undercover sting operation.[72]

It has been noted that the fear of moral contagion may prompt a community to seek to uncover and root out the source of the infection. In some societies, this is undertaken by way of a public ritual of symbolic purification.[73] (We see something of this sort depicted in film maker Andrew Jarecki's riveting documentary, *Capturing the Friedmans* (2003).) A significant shift in current American child pornography laws may be driven by a comparable animus. In this instance, however, the contagion (of illicit sexual desire) has been incorporated into the law itself. This wasn't always the case. At the outset, child pornography laws were created because of concern about the harm suffered by underage victims of sexual abuse. As the Supreme Court put it in the seminal case of *New York v. Ferber*, the state's compelling interest in the wellbeing of minors trumps the first amendment claim that child pornography is a protected form of free speech.[74] The Court's withholding of constitutional protection included *non-obscene* as well as obscene forms of child pornography, thus making child pornography a new and independent category of unprotected speech. Subsequent legal developments in this area, however, reflect a marked change of emphasis. Instead of actual harm the new laws now target the *illicit fantasies* on which child pornography allegedly feeds and in turn fuels in the minds of its viewers. It is these fantasies which the law condemns based on the fear that they might lead to the harm of children *in the future*.[75] In other words, as the perceived social evil has shifted from actual to prospective harm (in the event that a pedophile might use child pornography to seduce future victims), the law's focus has likewise shifted to the pedophilic fantasies that might spur child abuse in the future. It is the forbidden gaze itself (from which perverse fantasies are said to arise) that has been outlawed. By taking aim at the forbidden gaze the law seeks to avoid the "perception of children as sexual objects."[76] The paradoxical outcome, however, is that it achieves precisely the reverse of what it sets out to do.

If the evil of pornographic images (which express or inflame impermissible desires) consists in the forbidden gaze, according to this juridical logic by prohibiting that gaze the sexual purity of children will be protected.[77] The problem is that (aside from its puritanical and clinically disputed denial of children's sexuality) the law cannot effectively prohibit pornographic images in this way for the simple reason that it cannot determine the existence of pornographic images based on the forbidden gaze itself. For one thing, the illicit desire the law seeks to proscribe may or may not have been present at the time the targeted image was created. Indeed, such desires may readily be brought to an entirely innocuous image. Experts have observed that it is precisely the sexual innocence of the child in view that often prompts the pedophile's sexual arousal. By asking judges to focus on the forbidden gaze, the law invites them to re-enact the pedophile's process of arousal. In this way the law encourages the creation of the very evil that it purportedly sets out to suppress. Only by emulating the pedophile's forbidden gaze may the law against child pornography (so defined) be implemented. The more judges entertain prohibited fantasies whilst they look the more prohibited pornography they will find. As Amy Adler puts it, the current child pornography regime teaches jurists to "transform the world into a pornographic place."[78] If pornography lies in the eye of the beholder, the beholder must assume the persona of the predator she condemns in order to authorize the law's prohibition. Without the illicit fantasy there is nothing to prohibit. Law's prohibition thus remains parasitic upon the desire it condemns.[79]

This paradoxical state of affairs, in which law constitutes the very evil it seeks to avert, brings to mind Freud's insight into the way the human unconscious operates: "Whatever is expressly forbidden must be an object of desire."[80] In other words, the very act of prohibition tempts transgression. Thus, the cycle commences: prohibition escalates desire which in turn calls for greater prohibition, which in turn escalates desire even further. The forbidden desire that stares back from the prohibited image is the one the viewer projects on to it. This is what happens when law migrates to the screen: it lives there as other images do, which is to say, it internalizes the media's own logic of desire. This is what we see in the domain of child pornography law. Moved by the media's logic of desire, the laws now in place seem to need ever more threatening predators. Outlawing the illicit fantasies that set these new laws in motion may belie a growing anxiety about their hidden source. But, the ongoing defense against such a confrontation continues to fuel ever greater prohibitions. This process, doomed to futile escalation, is what one might expect when jurists legislate from the unconscious.

Film director Mike Nichols once described the thrill of "a thousand people sitting in the dark, looking at the same scene, and they are all apprehending something that has not been spoken. That's the thrill of it, the miracle – that's what holds us to movies forever. It's what we wish we could do in real life. We all see something and understand it together, and nobody has to say a word."[81] We see and we understand, and we feel in unison what the visual image presents to us, united in our silent attending to its flashing across the screen. How is this possible? In view of what has been said so far, there are at least three explanatory frameworks. First, we may seek an explanation based on how the embodied mind brings meaning to the screen. How is the image (as visual meme) thematized within a larger system of conventional or social meaning making? It is in this regard that we have considered the popular visual motif of the criminal predator. Shared cognitive and cultural templates (or memes) generate feelings and associations that resonate, like Proust's second-hand memories, in response to a discrete set of images. In addition to this, however, judgments may also follow hard on the heels of sheer aesthetic delight (visual sensation). We have seen this, for example, in the aesthetic effects of popular entertainments like *CSI* along with other popular film, television, and computer-based productions. Reflecting a third explanatory frame, we have also seen that judgments may be entangled in the visual mass media's own commercially driven logic of desire (the visual unconscious). In the context of child pornography cases, for example, popular images, propelled by illicit fantasies, offshoots of the predatory gaze, have helped to shape and inform the law's response to what appears to be a collective fear of moral infection.

In addition to these three explanatory responses (visual memes, visual sensation, and the visual unconscious) there is a fourth explanatory framework that remains to be addressed. This is the experiential or phenomenological account of visual meaning making. In this mode of analysis, we confront questions such as: How does our encounter with the visual image produce knowledge? What is its ontology, its relationship to reality, which is to say, what kind of reality does it present (or make present) on the screen (and the body of the viewer)? According to Mike Nichols, film viewers feel in unison: the flesh of the eye touches and is touched by the flesh of the haptic image.[82] But that is not all that may transpire. The eye also may be touched by something uncanny: the sublime presence of that which resists representation. What strange ontological excess is this? What reality do we encounter when we are touched by the visual sublime? As Merleau-Ponty notes, there are visual experiences that have the power to mobilize "all the subject's resources" and concern him "in his entire being." This is what we experience when we are gripped by the "visual sublime." It is this explanatory framework to which we now turn.

From the onset of modernity we have grown less familiar with and far less comfortable discussing the sublime (as compared, say, to the scientific and the pragmatic). At the same time, however, this is not to say that we have lost touch with its uncanny presence. Notwithstanding the well nigh universal sense of embarrassment (surely within current legal scholarly circles) that greets the suggestion that the sublime is a legitimate (much less crucial) category of knowledge, a vast array of art, music, film, and poetry attests to its continued cultural vitality. If such persistence also characterizes the visual domain of law, one hardly hears of it. Yet, it stands to reason that without an adequate understanding of the role of the sublime in the visual meaning making process inside the courtroom, we can hardly begin to gauge the significance either of its legitimating authority (for law as image) or the delegitimating impact of its absence (for example, in the visual simulacrum which feeds on the aesthetic of visual delight).

Visual media, such as video and film, have the power to transmit a presence that is irreducible to language. As documentary film maker and ethnographer Jennifer Deger puts it, video can operate "as a practical modality of revelation as opposed to representation: it is about bringing forth, a connecting and making visible the immanent" cultural meanings that constitute a world. Through the gaps and slippages between original and representation there arises the possibility of glimpsing that which ultimately remains inexpressible. To make an inexpressible absence present: that is the work of the sublime. The presence at issue here is poetic and associative rather than expository, explanatory, or semantic. That is why it fails to show up in the register of Cartesian rationality.[83] Metrics of sensorial delight and aversion fare no better in this regard. When an image lacks experiential depth, when it is offered solely for its sensory impact rather than its potential for narrative meaning, we are left with nothing upon which to reflect in its wake. When the visual spectacle ends, it leaves us stranded. Sensation fades, and we are alone. The spectacle fills only the moment in which it plays. It has no past, and offers nothing for the future. Of course, as we have seen in the context of visualizing neuroscience, this is not to say that, in the right hands, the feelings that visual spectacles produce cannot be associated with something beyond the spectacle itself. But there, too, it is not the spectacle that provides the force of narrative that makes disparate fragments cohere.

The coherence of visual entanglement is sustained and made meaningful in the structure of exchange between self and other. This is the hallmark of the story, a visual or linguistic form that in its essence presupposes the possibility of otherness and the aspiration to encounter otherness in a meaningful way. The nature of such entanglements depends upon the world that a given written or visual work brings into being. As we shall see in Chapter 5, this is the crux of Auerbach, Taussig, and Varela's distinct, but related insights into mimesis as cultural enaction. In a broad array of visual works, from Fra Angelico to David Lynch, we encounter signs of something other, something that lies outside the frame of familiar experience yet clamors to be recognized. The body beyond the body, the image beyond the image: these are the paradoxical phrasings that seek to invoke the inexpressible (sublime).[84] We encounter them as well in the evocation of justice, for justice, like the sublime, is both singular and inexhaustible: singular because it remains entangled in the originating conditions that occasion its occurrence; inexhaustible because it always exceeds the forms it assumes. Hence, its perpetual incompleteness when reckoned under conditions of finitude and scarcity, which constitute the human condition *par excellence.*

Yet, the possibility of justice presupposes a different kind of economy. It asks us to imagine a condition of both lastingness and abundance. The inexhaustibility of justice mocks debt and profit alike, for what sense could either make under conditions of inexhaustible excess? When we take justice out of the marketplace, the economy of the balanced scale, when we reject the commodity-like fungibility of justice and insist upon its gift-like singularity, we come closer to grasping justice as the event of the ethical sublime. This is not to say that justice releases us from the demands of the marketplace or the finite order of rule-based legality. Rather, it is an event that compels us to seek renewed alignment of the one to the other. Without justice law's forms endlessly proliferate. As we will see in the chapter that follows, this describes the baroque condition of validity without significance. At the same time, however, without law's forms justice remains a remote abstraction. Finitude thus becomes the condition of endless aspiration and correction.

When law migrates to the screen, it assumes aspects of the sublime and the spectacular alike. It exhibits the transferability of fungible aesthetic delights as well as the singular truth of an immanent and entangled ethical demand. In this respect, law as image enacts the paradox of the sublime. It is, as Jean-François Lyotard has written, the paradox of "the sign of a 'presence' that will never be a presentation."[85] Thus far, I have offered examples of visualizing law as visual delight and unconscious fantasy. We turn now to the other end of the spectrum. In what follows, we will consider how the visual sublime may help to determine specific outcomes inside the courtroom.

We begin with the highly publicized prosecution, in 2002, of Michael Skakel for the 1975 murder of fifteen-year-old Martha Moxley. In the Skakel case, lawyers for the State of Connecticut used their own interactive proprietary software to display demonstrative evidence that had been shown throughout the trial, including photographs of the neighborhood and crime scene, diagrams of the locations at which real evidence had been found, and an audiotape of a telephone interview Skakel had given to a journalist in the late 1990s (Images 3.1–3.2). During the prosecution's closing argument, jurors heard and saw Skakel's own words appear on the oversized screen before them. As Skakel uttered the word "panic," jurors instantly saw Martha Moxley's lifeless body appear on the bottom right of the screen, just as it was found at the crime scene some 27 years ago. The intended association was plain. Of course Skakel experienced a "feeling of panic" when Martha's mother asked him the next morning if he had seen Martha. The picture of Martha's battered body immediately explains the implicit meaning of his words. The viewer instantly makes the connection: Skakel panicked because he must have recalled with horror what he had done the night before. Because the jurors' screen-based emotional response to the image of Martha's body and the reality-based response (by Skakel when he realized what he had

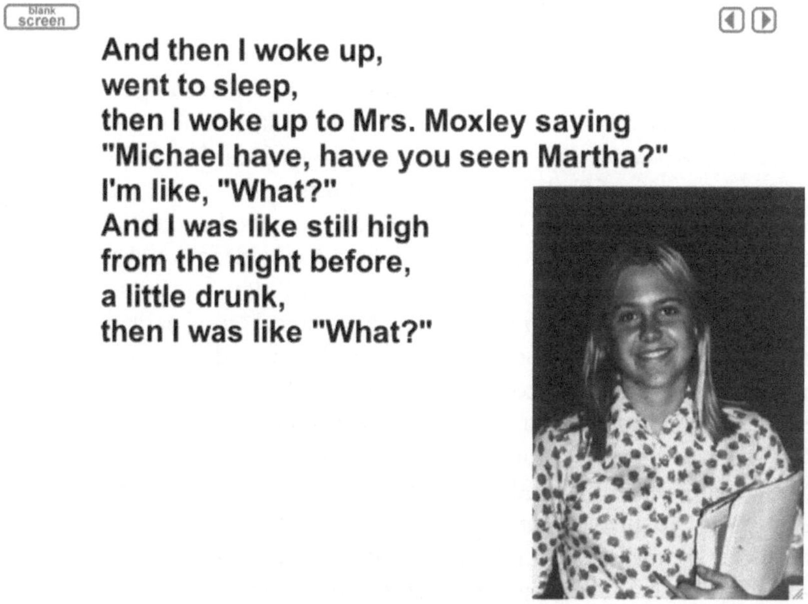

Image 3.1 From the prosecutor's closing argument in the Michael Skakel murder trial. Courtesy of Brian Carney, Esq., and WIN Interactive, Inc.

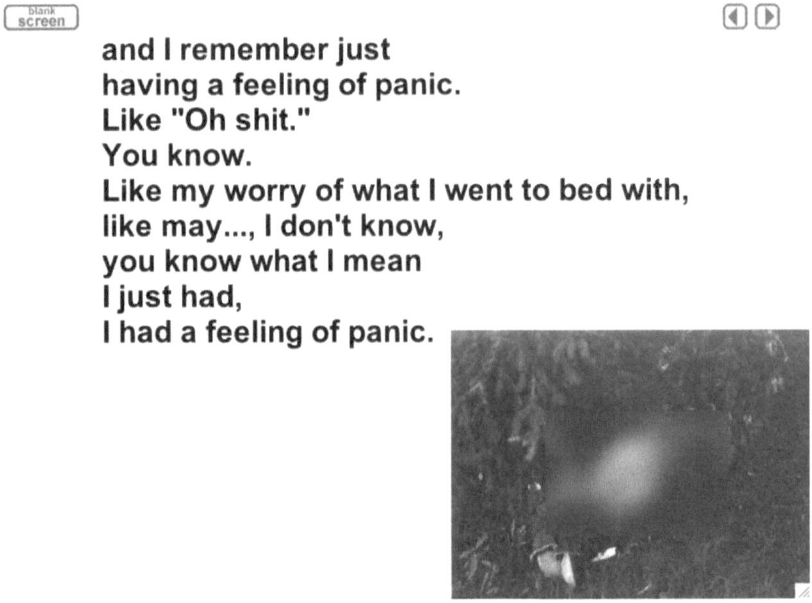

Image 3.2 From the prosecutor's closing argument in the Michael Skakel murder trial. Courtesy of Brian Carney, Esq., and WIN Interactive, Inc.

done) are comparable, the viewer's emotion is readily transferred to Skakel. The viewer "knows" what Skakel is reacting to, and the ensuing revulsion at Skakel's horrific crime readily brings a sense of guilt to mind.

But wait. How can one be sure that the image of Martha's lifeless body is the actual source of Skakel's self-professed feeling of "panic"? How do we know that his panic wasn't caused by a different mental association, like the one Skakel offered in court, namely: his fear that someone might have seen him masturbating in a tree outside Martha's window on the night of the murder? The defense didn't stick. It lacked the power of narrative coherence and emotional resonance that the state's evidence-based closing narrative produced. Of course he panicked. Who wouldn't under the circumstances? By contrast, Skakel's defense not only strains credulity, but it also leaves Moxley's murder unsolved. The decision maker's desire for closure finds all that it needs in the state's visual and verbal summation of the case. The prosecution's closing multimedia montage produced a Proustian moment. A second-hand memory cued by the sound of Skakel's voice and the graphic image of the deceased strikes the viewer as if for the first time. The resuscitation of that moment causes a shudder. It is uncanny. In a brief, but well calibrated juxtaposition of word, image, and sound, understanding manages to transcend the ordinary barriers of time and space. The passage of years – almost a quarter of a century from the murder and the morning after (in 1975) to the time when Skakel uttered these words (in 1997) up until the time they were replayed at the trial itself (in 2002) – vanishes in a flash.

In this example, the state's visual claim is authenticated by the viewer's sense of lived experience in real time (what Henri Bergson calls "direct vision") and by an accompanying "sentiment of rationality" (as William James put it) or "deep-seated sentiment" (in Benjamin Cardozo's terms). In Chapter 5 we will explore in greater detail these indicia of belief. For now, suffice it to say that the Skakel montage is suggestive of how the visual sublime may come into play inside the courtroom. Something that was absent was suddenly given an uncanny visual and aural presence. The juxtaposition of words, voice, and image sublimely incarnated a terrible past that somehow, impossibly, haunted the present. We witness the event (on the screen), and we shudder.[86] For an uncanny moment inside the courtroom, as Walt Whitman put it, time and space availed not. A legal event transpired in the temporally flattened but emotionally amplified *now* time of viewing the screen. And because the understanding this visual display produced was immediate, credible, and seemingly complete, the viewer experienced little reason to question what he or she simultaneously came to understand and believe. Defense counsel's purely verbal counter-narrative plainly lacked comparable explanatory or emotional power in accounting for Skakel's "panic."

During the closing argument of the Skakel case a strange absence shone forth in the uncanny visual shimmer of a momentary presence. But there is something uncanny as well when an absence remains absent, but haunts the viewer's mind nevertheless. This is what occurred inside a New York City courtroom when a short video documentary transfixed the attention of judge, jurors, and spectators alike. The occasion was the murder trial of Dr Mazoltuv Borukhova. Borukhova was tried and ultimately convicted of having paid a distant relative, Mikhail Mallayev, $20,000 to kill her husband, Dr Daniel Malakov. Malakov, from whom Borukhova had been estranged for the last three years, was the father of their four-year-old daughter, Michelle. The shooting took place in a Queens playground in plain view of the victim's daughter, who stood nearby with her mother. The motive? Six days before, a family court judge had granted a transfer of custody from Borukhova to Malakov and this, so the state's theory ran, was something Borukhova could not tolerate. She could not accept losing custody of her only child. But there was something exceedingly odd about Borukhova's maternal protectiveness. For example, when Michelle's father paid custody visits, Borukhova would do everything in her power to draw her daughter's attention away from her father. Michelle would remain firmly planted in her mother's lap throughout each visit, occupied with toys and sweets that her mother provided. Malakov's diminished status in his daughter's eyes (she cried whenever he sought her attention) caused him to seek help – first, from a court-appointed guardian, then from the court itself. Over time, Judge Sidney Strauss came to realize that things were not quite right with Borukhova's overweening possessiveness. She was "smothering" the child, he explained in the judicial opinion that accompanied his order that custody be shifted from mother to father. That order, prosecutors contended, enraged Borukhova, and sowed the seed for murder.

But how do we know the state had it right? Well, among other indicators, there is a video tape, made by a professional videographer Borukhova herself hired. The assignment was to document one of her daughter's custody visits at the home of her dad. And what do we see? But perhaps we should ask not what we see, but rather what lies beneath the surface of the scene that the video unfolds. What perturbations unsettle the apparent banality of a day in the life of a child of separated parents arriving at the home of her dad? The scene opens with Michelle emerging from a car, clasped tightly in the arms of her mother. "Here we go," we hear Borukhova announce. Michelle immediately breaks into loud sobs. Malakov arrives from the right, smiling broadly. He takes his daughter's right arm, which had been hooked around Borukhova's neck and shoulder. Then he tries to do the same with her left. "Very good," he says, in an assuring tone, as Michelle screams. "Ouch," we hear Borukhova cry out. Then the estranged couple begin an odd dance, circling around and around, with Michelle locked between them. "Let the hand . . ." says Malakov, without completing his sentence. "Ouch," Borukhova cries out again, louder this time. "Why are you pushing?" Malakov asks. "I'm not pushing," Borukhova replies. And around they go, circling in their dance of unyielding custody. Slowly, parents and child make their way closer to the front gate of Malakov's home. "Can you separate her legs?" he asks. Then he says it again, as the couple and child circle back on to the street outside the gate. Michelle's screams grow louder. An elderly woman in a black hat, Borukhova's mother perhaps, pushes Malakov's brother, Joseph, off to the right. We hear his plaintive voice, "Why is she touching me?" After asking the same question five times, he cries out, "Please don't touch me." At the same time, a woman in a white shirt can be seen trying to get Borukhova to let go of Michelle's legs. "You don't touch me," we hear Borukhova say, and say again, as if echoing Joseph's words from a moment ago. Meanwhile, Borukhova still has her arms wrapped around her daughter's red corduroy pants, locked tight at the knees, though apparently Malakov hasn't noticed this. They continue to circle. Finally, Malakov realizes why mother and father have been locked into this peculiar dance. "Why are you holding her . . . Let go of her feet." He pauses, now, as if at a loss. His insistent smile at last wavers. "Let the left side go," he says. "Lift your arms, I'm holding her.Lift her other arm." Eventually, Michelle is released from her mother's grip. As father and daughter finally walk past the front gate toward an open doorway, the woman in the white shirt gazes toward the videographer. In a tired voice she says, "Can you please shut off the camera?" "No," we hear Borukhova sharply countermand. "Don't shut it off."

What have the jurors and judge just witnessed? The images rush by quickly, and are quickly done. Yet, their brevity is belied by the depth of disturbance that they leave in their wake. There is an undercurrent here, a silent score to which couple and child have danced. In that silence viewers may discern the hidden presence of motive, its trace manifest in the irrational rage that keeps Borukhova locked in a custodial embrace, circling, unable to let her daughter go. There is something uncanny in a mother's capacity for revenge. The task of judgment this jury faces consists not simply in the battle to come to grips with the human capacity for murder. Here they must also struggle to comprehend how a mother could deprive her only child of its father. There is something utterly incomprehensible, almost Medean, in such an inhuman act. One watches, and shudders, sensing what this dance of custody may foretell. The violence is already there: the dozens of phone calls (91 in all) between Borukhova and the cousin hired to kill have already been made, and the process of finalizing the details of the murder will continue, including the almost comical home-made silencer, made of a bleach bottle and duct tape, that blew off with the first shot, and remained behind after the event, lying uselessly inside the playground where the shooting occurred, though perhaps not entirely useless, for it bore the fingerprints that the shooter also carelessly left behind.

When the local news media covered the Borukhova trial reporters took special interest in the custody video that played inside the courtroom, and how viewers responded. As one juror would later put it, "She was cold and unconcerned. She didn't try to comfort her daughter . . . She just wanted to show on tape how upset the child was."[87] Needless to say, the figure who appeared in these images was not the demure, self-possessed physician that her attorney sought to portray at trial. There was something uncanny, almost monstrous, about what the video showed. It was apparent to those in the room who watched, and who saw the jurors as they too watched, with fixated gazes, many eyes brimming with tears, hands lifting to mouths, heads shaking ever so slightly from left to right and back again, as if in disbelief. A shudder coursed through the courtroom. Something uncanny was unfolding, and it made them shudder. That is what happens when we encounter powerful images that we cannot fully comprehend.

A terrible presence lurks in that absence. It unsettles us, and we shudder. Had Borukhova already formed the intent, after having made the calls, as she circled around and around clutching the child whose loss brought her unbearable pain and incomprehensible rage? They dance and smile and smile and dance, mother seeking to hold on to child, father seeking to release her from mother's ironclad embrace. The jurors watch after the event, knowing what they know, and they shudder, but that is not all. The horror they face also demands a response. Judgment, the demand of the ethical, is all that remains to counter the twin temptations of escapism and paralysis. Only in responding to that demand do we preserve the reality of incomprehensibility while also ensuring the persistence of the ethical.[88] We judge, we pronounce judgment, and we authorize our pronouncement as a matter of law, with the full power of the state standing by to enforce it.

The experience of the sublime (whether terrible or joyous) exceeds our comprehension. Yet, at the same time, the sublime image in a court of law demands something of us. We cannot not respond, for once having become mindful of that which calls for a response, our response becomes an unshakable responsibility. Responding is the ethical itself. Levinas calls it going "beyond being." That is what happens when we respond to the infinite need of the other who stands before us: "I exist through the other and for the other . . . I am inspired . . . [My responsibility] means an openness in which being's essence is surpassed in inspiration."[89]

The ethical originates in this inexpressible absence, this "ought" for which I am responsible. In this sense, justice, as human fraternity, may turn out to be prior to freedom. We shudder, and know we must act. The ethical is an indictment as well as a sublime transport. It calls us into question even as it calls us beyond ourselves, in response to that which demands a response.

If our encounter with the ethical sublime demands a response, if the shudder it provokes leads to a state of ontological transport in which we are inspired to be in response to the other before us, the ersatz sublime leads to no such thing. In place of ontological transport the spectacle invites the self-involved, albeit fleeting gratification of visual delight. Our oscillation between delight and obligation, self and other, arabesque and entanglement, re-enacts law's oscillation between power and meaning.

The categories that I have been describing in this chapter – from visual memes to visual sensation, the visual unconscious, and the visual sublime – offer a way of thinking about and assessing the authenticity or truth value of a broad range of visual legal displays. How do we distinguish the authentic and authoritative from the ersatz sublime (mere aesthetic delight) when law lives as an image on the screen? How do we recognize and assess, in particular legal cases, hyper-aestheticized forms of visual expression, from sense-delighting digital displays aglow with the magical realism of pop science to lawful prohibitions driven by hidden and displaced unconscious fantasies, as distinguished from images that make us shudder by the uncanny force of their sublime presence on the screen?

Law performs its meanings in a shared, public world that is constituted (and reconstituted) through an overlapping network of discrete cultural and cognitive practices, social institutions, and inherited textual and audiovisual sources.[90] For us to understand the internal logics of law's order we must become mindful of the various media in which that order is enacted. Each medium enjoys strengths and weaknesses that others do not. For example, words may assert logical propositions and deploy them in a more rigorous argumentative form than visual images, while visual images may more effectively produce verisimilitude and thereby evoke more compelling perceptual, cognitive, and emotional responses than words alone.

Likewise, the stories we tell and the way that we tell them differ from one medium to another. Thus, to the extent that law performs its meanings through narratives and images,[91] its fate remains closely tied to the way in which a given medium codifies the meaning making process. If the grammar of film, for example, has taught us to instantly understand the visual code of close-ups, cross-cutting, and montage (through which new meanings emerge from the juxtaposition of discrete images), the digital grammar of computer-generated imaging has taught us the interactive code of the interface, together with the command and control conventions of rip, burn, re-sync, upload, and resend.[92]

Law's entanglement in the changing patterns of our "second nature" also means that law cannot escape the dominant epistemological anxieties that may afflict a given medium. Thus we are led to ask, what becomes of law when, following the path of contemporary politics and marketing, it too flattens out on an electronic screen? Critical assessments of new cultural and technological developments require the cultivation of new insights and new competencies. Iconoclash is the hallmark of the neo-baroque conditions under which law's visualization is now taking place. In the next chapter we will explore those conditions in greater detail. As we travel this strange landscape, in which phantasmal and endlessly recursive forms proliferate, the question remains: What is it like, and what does it mean, when law's perennial struggle for descriptive and moral legitimacy plays out in conditions such as these?

CHAPTER 4

Images Run Riot: Law on the Landscape of the Neo-Baroque

"A land that has no more legends," says the poet, "is condemned to die of cold." This may well be true. But a people without myths is already dead.

(Georges Dumezil)[1]

[E]verything in the world as we now see it is law, order and form; yet lawlessness always lurks at its foundations, as if it could once again break through ... Without this antecedent darkness, there is no creational reality ... [T]he path to heaven leads through the abyss ...

(Friedrich Schelling)[2]

Initiation lies at the core of any genuine human life.

(Mircea Eliade)[3]

Reversal is the direction of study which transforms existence into script. Its new teacher is Bucephalus, "the new advocate," who takes the road back without the powerful Alexander – which means, rid of the onrushing conqueror ... he reads and turns the pages of our old books ... The law which is studied but no longer practiced is the gate to justice.

(Walter Benjamin)[4]

Vision encompasses both what we see, and a shared practice of seeing. In cinematic vision, physiology, technology, cognition, and culture combine into a hybrid: a lens brings a world into view, and a mind that shapes it. Vision is always a two way street. Tools and habits of perception help to establish the way we respond to the world and others around us. Habits quicken, and tools enhance perception. Tools bring into view things invisible to the naked eye – things otherwise too distant or too interior, too fast or too slow, too rare perhaps, or maybe too elusive, obscure, abstract, or fantastical. Showing changes the nature of the thing shown. When we see with the aid of a tool, the tool is always part of what we see. The experience of mediated seeing is, then, an experience of what it is like to be that tool, to operate in that medium. How does it work, and what work does it demand of those who use it? What does it allow, and in so doing what does it prevent, for as Kenneth Burke observed, every way of seeing is also a way of not seeing. To live in one world is not to be in others.

Film is a tool of vision. We see what it shows, and how it shows. Over time, our mind grows accustomed to its conventions and practices. We learn, for example, how a particular cinematic narrative is supposed to go, what's the arc or flow-through of the story, what's the purpose of this or that scene, why are these particular characters playing in it, and why does the next scene follow. We also learn how to bridge perceptual and temporal gaps between images and scenes in order to let the story unfold. Out of carefully selected and sutured fragments we make wholes, to let the film story cohere. And along the way, we yield to the storyteller's vision. We enter the mood and feel the various affects that color the images we see. When a recognizable mood recurs in more than one film we may refer to it as a style, or a genre (film noir, the screwball comedy, the classic western and its crime noir subversion.) If we can decode a representative work from an era that is characterized by a particular way of seeing and feeling, infused by a characteristic mood, we may be able to set forth what makes that world appear as it does. We may also learn to say what it is like to be in that world. This is what its textures of meaning look and feel like. This is what they signify, and this is who and what we become (what we believe and value) when we live this way, when we emulate the life of these images on the screen.

The baroque has a mood and mindset of its own; it is made up of recurring visual tropes and storylines. The characteristic markers of the baroque include: the mirror, the labyrinth, the proliferation of fragments, the field of ruins, the spectacle, the dream – and of course the dream within a dream (*ad infinitum*). In baroque narratives we can never be sure what reality we are in. Have we awakened, or is this just another dream; or, shifting to the digital baroque, is this just another computer program, video game, or virtual world online? Metaphysical uncertainty (where, who, what are we *now?*) is a hallmark of the baroque. In this chapter, I aim to decode a neo-baroque cinematic masterpiece, David Lynch's *Mulholland Drive.* After extracting its code we will explore what it might be like for law to be coded in a similar way. What is law like when it takes on the life of baroque images on the screen? What does it look and feel like to live under the regime of baroque law?

We begin with the life of dreams. Law dreams, and forgets. It forgets its dreams and forgets *that* it dreams. Law dreams of law: its hidden fantasies, desires, impulses, fears. Like all dreams, law dreams in images: taboo symbols, intimating forbidden knowledge amid forbidden urges. We repress law's disorder for the sake of its order. We repress its violence for the sake of its legitimacy. Civilization flourishes at the expense of its discontents. But as Freud taught, the price of repression is inescapable. In symptoms of disorder, the repressed returns. The dreams of law haunt the law. Its ghost, like Hamlet's father, returns to set things right. In daylight, law rules paternally, as infallible judge. But at night – and let us include the simulated night of darkened rooms and cinemas – its demons (and perhaps also its angels) roam. On screens large and small, the usually hidden symbolic life of the law breathes free.

The assumption underlying this analysis is that the baroque does not simply describe a particular historical period or aesthetic, as evidenced, say, by the production of baroque sculpture, paintings, novels, and plays in seventeenth century Europe. I contend that the baroque is a recurring cultural archetype, what Omar Calabrese calls an "epochal trait."[5] While the expressive characteristics of its aesthetic forms most certainly vary over time, there is a recurring pattern in the originating conditions and themes of baroque culture. It is a time marked above all by wide-ranging crises in confidence concerning the human capacity to represent reality, to distinguish between truth and deception, dreams and waking, will and desire, reason and fantasy. Hence, the dominant baroque tropes of mirrors, labyrinths, knots, folds, and braids. In baroque cultures, we witness a profound confluence of stresses: technological, political, and philosophical.

What then are the recurrent cultural markers of the baroque? They are unmistakable: destabilization, fragmentation, and disorientation – amid a proliferation of forms, images, signs, appearances, coming and going without surcease. We are immersed in the flow of aesthetic excess, without a clear moral compass to orient our gaze. Our eye beholds only "mutilated fragments" – "fragments of the luminous field which adhere to one another with a cohesion without concept,"[6] fleeting appearances in an immanent flux of contiguous, insular nows, monadic moments, one sealed off from the other. As if there were a line, enfolding and unfolding within an infinite, non-geometric space, an infinitely deflected line, in a painting by Klee, let us say,[7] or an arabesque, dancing in space, like Clerambeault's ecstatic "folds of Islamic origin."[8] It is a line that takes us with it as it unfolds, like riding an infinite horizon, a gash in infinite space, demarcating infinite spaces without form.

Digital form is a funny thing: there is an insuperable flatness to its endless and immediate profusion. The momentary image (the floating signifier, or digital simulacrum) offers no space into which one may step, outside the flow itself. Where else could one go apart from the surface of the screen? But there is no depth there, to scale one image above another, no transcendental reference, no meta-frame, no overarching metric or narrative, to generalize salience, to place in a hierarchy, to alter the ineluctable fungibility of the digital image. Everything becomes a sign on an equal playing field: the field of appearances. Valuation becomes a matter of infinite choice, or sheer will, as in Nietzsche's will to power. Yet, without some orienting framework, we cannot be sure of what we are seeing – appearance or original, opinion or proof, dream or reality. Even discerning appearances as artifacts, indeed, even grasping the nature of their construction, cannot ease uncertainty, as we saw in Chapter 2 in regard to Holbein's *The Ambassadors*, that distant anamorphic forebear of the Wachowski brothers' famous *Matrix* film trilogy. As in Holbein's painting, Neo's epiphany in *The Matrix*, that he has been living in a dream world ("a neural-interactive simulation that we call the Matrix") offers no real relief from the ontological and ethical burden of his new found knowledge. After all, even upon humanity's awakening to their plight, the digital matrix itself still remains in place. In the end, the question simply shifts, as it does in *Dark City*, to one of mastery. How will we use the power of the matrix now? What dreams shall we will into reality? ("A world without rules and controls, without borders or boundaries. A world where anything is possible," as Neo triumphantly intones before the credits roll at the close of *The Matrix*.) In short, the metaphysical enigma remains: only the dream, and the dream weaver have changed. But is this majesty or sheer madness? Commingling metaphysics with the ethical, the question hangs in the air.

This is the peculiar nature of baroque visuality: hyper-awareness of the forms of representation, and of how we imagine the real, exposes the contingency and fragility of appearances and the concomitant contingency and fragility of our grip on reality. Perspective is the art of illusion, and in baroque culture the key to multiplying artificial worlds is at hand. We see this in the great phantasmagoria of baroque theater, where the art of perspective thrusts the actors into a dream world of illusory space,[9] and in the architectural design of churches and gardens whose *trompe l'oeil* perspective intermingles fantasy with paradox. Like Bramante at San Satiro in Milan whose highly accentuated foreshortenings give the impression of a vaulted room, "but if one tries to enter one collides with a wall."[10] Or, shifting from church and theater to the spectacle of the state, consider Louis XIV's madly excessive palace at Versailles (with its 400 mirrored panels, lit by 3,000 candles). The allusion to absolute worldly power could not be missed; yet, the references are utterly phantasmal. The king may be figuratively likened to Apollo, the Sun God, or to Hercules, but the references lack significance – apart from the sheer scale of their assertion of material wealth and power. "Things do not pass for what they are but what they seem, and many are satisfied with appearances," wrote the Spanish Jesuit Gracian.[11] Amid the florid ornamentation and endless parade of "routs and ridottos, comedies and ballets, hunts and carousels, masques and masquerades," everyday life in baroque Europe had come to seem like "one prolonged festival."[12] The real seemed to collapse into mere appearances. As Dryden wrote, "When I consider life, 'tis all a cheat; Yet, fool'd with hope, men favour the deceit; Trust on, and think tomorrow will repay; Tomorrow's falser than the former day."[13] It is as if one were living in a dream world. And the will to renounce the appearance of reality as empty illusion battles with the opposing impulse to marvel at the grandeur of human technology and the manifold wonders that it spawns.

Why the world? Kepler asked. Why must man travel "labyrinths of meanings" in a world of illusory appearances?[14] Everything seems to have become, as Panofsky puts it, "thoroughly problematical: the relationship of the mind to reality as perceived by the senses."[15] As Benjamin observes, "Any person, any object, any relationship, can mean absolutely anything."[16] Like the deviant baroque beauty of Kepler's ellipse, constantly looping back on itself, like the unrepresentable energy of Bruno's "infinite," or Copernicus' sense of the "monstrous" appearance of a newly decentered world which "conceals many beautiful secrets"[17] – the baroque mind looks out upon a world of illusion steeped in mystery. In physics Kepler traveled the *via negativa* in an effort to expose "the lack of being,"[18] yet another testament to the inconstancy and vanity of this world of appearances.[19]

In the modern, geometric, linear-causal space of universal perspective, the Cartesian subject commands and controls the image; but in the non-linear, endlessly unfolding and enfolding space of the baroque, including the contemporary digital baroque, the subject is carried along by an endless flow of forms, interactively co-constituting image and reality, self and object, self and other, now this, now that, depending on an ever-shifting, re-encoded point of view. Today digitized forms are hyper-anamorphic: digital-aniconic images generate a highly self-reflexive spectacle of contingent states, reversals, and endless transformations. The Cartesian premise of universal perspective has been all but abandoned, just as Leibniz sought. This is the baroque architecture of vision: a relativistic perspectivalism according to which truth accords with the attitude or position of the viewer.[20] As in cubist painting, there is no whole to grasp, only fragmented frames of reference as the observer moves around the object in view. "Inflection is an ideal condition or a virtuality that currently exists only in the soul that envelops it. Thus the soul is what has folds and is full of folds."[21]

The Internet serves well as a master trope for the digital baroque: a network of data points in which each point is, as Dombroski put it, "an open linkage, not governed by any one principle of narrative identity that fixes it with a particular function in relation to an overriding (metaphysical) unity. Rather each unit is a kind of vein that gives definition to an unfinished block of marble . . . that does not determine its form; its destiny is repetition and endless proliferation."[22] Like Lacan's notion of the Real, the digital baroque follows an invisible internal logic that is metonymic[23] and overdetermined. Only, unlike the Lacanian unconscious, the digital baroque unfolds as a simulacrum of the Real, the offspring of hidden, generative algorithms upon which what we see on the screen depends. The digital image bears within it a latent image that, as Laura Marks writes, "waits to be unfolded" with the interior logic of an underlying program.

The baroque, writes Deleuze, "is the moment when Some Thing is kept rather than nothing, and where response to the world's misery is made through an excess of principles, a hubris of principles, and a hubris inherent in principles."[24] Images run riot. Forms proliferate as if to assert not only the mastery of sign-wielding subjects over the natural world, but also as if the brute act of subduing all that is other than self with a riot of expressive form were the only way the self could survive. This is the survival instinct as mimetic desire: a matter of hyper-narcissism fueled by fear of self-annihilation. To paraphrase Nietzsche, baroque man would rather will appearances, even in wild abandon, than not to will at all.[25]

In what follows, I want to suggest that contemporary digital baroque culture mimics its seventeenth century forebear's florid and extravagant sensibility, its sensual glow and opiate dreams: "buzzed with the fever of visual excess . . . action-packed whirling arabesques . . . optical trickery . . . images layered ever more deeply within images."[26] Like pop art painter Takashi Murakami's presentation of space on an intricately folded plane.[27] Or like the "super-flat" images of contemporary Japanese video games and *otaku* anime,[28] such as *Evangelion*, that explosive hit television series and film, with its highly eroticized, baroque dreaminess. (As we see in the final scene of the film, Shinji: "Am I dead?" Rei: "No, everything's just becoming one. This is exactly the world you dreamed of.")[29] Or like the endless loops of contemporary video installations, such as Bill Viola's *The Messenger*, which begins with the image of something shimmering against a blue-black void then slowly morphs into a human form rising up from a body of water, breaking into the light, and gulping the air as if in a renewal of life, only to sink back again into the deep to the shimmering form from which it began, and from which it will begin anew, *ad infinitum*.[30]

In the baroque, there is no meta-narrative. Coordinates are assimilated to an infinite curvature of inflection.[31] Inner and outer grow confused so that the authorial self gets "externalized into a series of figures and events."[32] But trying to capture such a fragmentary reality only leads to an endless enumeration of details, folding and unfolding, as if beyond the author's grasp, since no principle of organization is at hand to contain their endless proliferation. It is as if the author cannot establish the correct distance from which to view the object, or is unable to establish a workable criterion of relevance.[33] This overloading of forms produces spectacle, grotesque in its massiveness, almost inhuman in its disorder. As the neo-baroque novelist Carlo Gadda wrote, justice is "a machine! A torment," as in Kafka's penal colony where the convicted are turned over to the machinery of law to have their sentence mechanically imprinted directly into their flesh. Or perhaps we should say law has become a network of machines, in the form of robotic programs, as we see online where automated cyberbots troll through cyberspace in search of a deal. The proverbial "meeting of the minds," that classic prerequisite of contract formation, now gives way to the programmed exchange of digital data.

Or consider the proliferation of rules that one encounters on the world wide web, where websites, like manifold sovereignties, are governed by their own terms of use, micro-worlds of enforceable law. Fragmented, prodigious, monstrous in its multiplicity: this is what law is like in a baroque time, "just before the world loses its principles."[34] No wonder Leibniz imagined the role of "God's attorney," as Deleuze puts it.[35] For at this moment of feared disappearance, that apocalyptic evacuation of all things of which Benjamin wrote, the need for justification could not be greater. So, in response, the baroque lawyer strains to account for the current state of affairs with "an excess of principles, a hubris of principles, and a hubris inherent to principles."[36] In that excess, lies the exquisite yearning, along with the horror and humor that Kafka so brilliantly expressed. Excess "amid the ruins of the Platonic Good,"[37] that is the hallmark of law in baroque times.

What is it like to live in a neo-baroque world where power and desire circulate freely, no longer subject to the ordinary constraints of shared rules or conventions, where the reality principle itself folds back into yet another dream-memory-wish-fantasy? Why, it's rather like living in *Dark City*, unaware that your life is actually a series of ever-changing setups (now you're in one role, one relationship, one job, one household, and now another) as part of an experiment by a race of dying aliens seeking to discover the secret of the human soul. Or rather like being in a David Lynch film, a world in which dream and reality, will and desire, law and chance, seamlessly intermingle. Presently, we will say more about law on the landscape of the neo-baroque. But first we must examine that landscape more closely. David Lynch will be our guide. He will take us downward, and in, as we travel the neo-baroque purgatory of *Mulholland Drive* (2001). No sooner are we launched than we realize we've entered a mystery that is no ordinary whodunit. This is a metaphysical mystery of identity and the repression of forbidden impulses and the thousand and one tales that we tell to divert ourselves from hidden truths. Yet, these tales are also clues.

Like the tragic story of Oedipus, that ill-fated man who rose to the highest (as King of Thebes, savior of his city) only to fall to the lowest (a parricide who marries his mother). Determined to root out the mysterious plague that is polluting his kingdom, Oedipus unwittingly indicts and sentences himself to lonely exile, for it is his unholy acts that turn out to be the source of Thebes' affliction. Similarly, Diane Selwyn (Naomi Watts) in Lynch's film turns out to be the source of the horrible deed that culminates in her own self-condemnation. In Lynch's film we will learn that Diane has hired a hit man to dispatch her former lover, Camilla Rhodes (Laura Harring), an actress whose Hollywood success in every way mocks Diane's failed dreams of stardom. Camilla triggers Diane's homicidal rage when she suddenly announces that their romantic affair must end, an announcement followed in short order by the news that Camilla has decided to marry a successful Hollywood director who has cast her as the star in his most recent film. Wounded on the fields of passion and ambition alike, Diane arranges her revenge. When she receives confirmation that Camilla is dead, Diane falls into an uneasy dream. It is this dream that makes up the first two thirds of Lynch's film, though we have no way of knowing this is the case until later on. In Diane's dream, rather than the seedy, drug-addled prostitute that she has become, Diane emerges as an idealized, unspoiled all-American girl, a beautiful and delightful ingénue who wins the part her rival in real life stole from her, setting Diane on her destructive downward spiral. As for Camilla, in Diane's dream, where the logic of desire prevails and wishes are the id's command, Camilla lives again, except that now she has no memory of who she is. Amnesia represses the reality the dream cannot allow. It is the way Diane's wishes may be fulfilled – but only for a short while. Reality is the monster that lives behind Winkie's diner in Diane's dream: it waits to pronounce judgment.

Amnesia is the plotting device of Diane's dream. Together, Diane and Camilla will track down the clues of Camilla's mysterious past; but along the way, they will also discover Diane's. Diane's dream fantasies of renewed amorous passion with Camilla and of professional success as a screen actor, which eluded her in real life, defensively postpone confronting the fateful knowledge of her terrible crime. And so, like Oedipus, Diane, as detective, prosecutor, and judge, ultimately roots out her own polluting deed. That knowledge forebodingly haunts her dream in the guise of the terrifying monster behind the very diner in which Diane met a professional killer to take out a contract on Camilla's life. An unknown patron of the diner foreshadows Diane's own fate when he goes out back to face the terrifying monster that appeared to him in a dream. In an act of will he confronts his fear, faces the monster, and dies at the sight of it. The uncanny horror that is Diane's guilty knowledge assumes monstrous form with its own primitive retributive power. This is the law of Diane's unconscious. It is a law that mimics the manner of baroque perspective, for this contingent and subjective force, this primitive, indigenous form-generating code generated by Diane's unconscious, is the sole source of the film's coherence.

We dream the symptomatic signs of our unrealized wishes and repressed fears. I shall propose that in the film work of David Lynch we witness a re-enactment not only of Diane Selwyn's wish fulfillments and guilt, but also something much larger. Her dream symbolically re-enacts Oedipus' desecration of the founding rites of law's legitimacy. When we can no longer tolerate the violence that marks the origin of law, when the founding narrative that is meant to convert the original violence of law into acceptable or legitimate authority goes awry, the shared coherence of law's sublime origin and value is lost. When nothing can contain the fragmentation of narrative into a proliferation of competing forms, an excess of tropes and principles, so that narratives nestle within narratives without surcease, when there is no compass to direct our path, no overarching calculus to give weight to one account over another, then life becomes like a dream, ruled by dream logic. Each of us is like a monadic arabesque twirling in the void, each an insular world, complete unto itself; each of us rotating on our own axis of subjective reality. We must learn the code of each world in order to unlock the mystery of meaning it contains. And so it is for law, too, when law is cut off from any overarching shared meta-narrative. Lacking any shared measure for our collective entanglements, law's forms proliferate in a profusion of rules and principles. Then, law, too, becomes dreamlike: like a baroque tale, a story of stories within stories, without surcease.

Like Oedipus, like Diane Selwyn, the audience that witnesses the spectacle of the baroque shudders before the horror that lies at its core. That horror is the hidden source of the endless proliferation of form. The baroque will is a horror machine, a machine of endless and unconstrained desire, the "living machine" of which Leibniz speaks, that Deleuze describes as that "infinite machine of which every part is a machine, folded differently . . ."[38] Given the horror that accompanies our encounter with the inexpressible origin of form, how could we not be shaken? Before taking this hidden meaning to heart, however, we must first face a decisive tear in the fabric of quotidian reality. That rite of passage begins with disruption and the specter of violence. And so it is at the beginning of *Mulholland Drive.*

Look: there has been a car accident at night; dead bodies are strewn around a smoldering, black limousine. A detective holds up a plastic bag containing a pearl earring. He says in a monotone: "The boys found this on the floor in back of the Caddy." His partner dispassionately responds, "Yeah, they showed me . . . Any of those dead kids wearin' pearl earrings?" The detective: "No. Could be someone's missin' maybe." Partner: "That's what I'm thinkin'." The mystery has begun.

Lynch's *Mulholland Drive*

Mulholland Drive: *an overview*

> My dreams are your actions.
>
> (Leontia in Shakespeare's *A Winter's Tale*)

> Doubtless, each organ-machine interprets the entire world from the perspective of its own flux, from the point of view of the energy that flows from it . . .
>
> (Giles Deleuze[39])

Mulholland Drive consists of a series of subversions, as film director Lynch, with infinite craft, leads (one is tempted to say, "seduces" or "tricks") the viewer from one plane of reality to another. The first two-thirds of the film turn out to be a dream fantasy, though we have no way of knowing this is so until later in the film. Only then do we realize that what we have taken as real life is not so. Lynch plainly wants us to experience this realization as a shock. It is the shock of suddenly "waking up" to an illusion that we've mistaken for reality. The play of reality and illusion is a central motif of the film, as the penultimate scene at Café Silencio will later reveal. Our disorientation is complete when, instead of allowing us to remain within the stable realm of what we subsequently take as real life, the film upends our expectations yet again. Like a Mobius strip, whose infinite regression mirrors the *mise en abyme*[40] motif, Lynch's film in the end reintroduces, and yields to, powerful irrational elements. The unreality of incomprehensible ("monstrous"[41]) forces now finally invades, and throws into question, the reliability of any assumptions we may have held regarding the stability of real life. We realize that the same unreality that launched this drama of jealousy, hatred, and violent retribution – the same unbearable forces that staged its figuration, and violent denouement – remain present at the end, as at the beginning. There is no stable place for us to hold still in. As we shall see, this destabilizing [de]realization links Lynch's work to key elements in the distinctive culture of the neo-baroque.

The initial dream fantasy sequence, which dominates the film, plays out as a murder mystery – as well as a mystery of identity. In time, we will learn that this mystery is the projected fantasy of Diane Selwyn. Upon repeated viewings, one may discern clues, both in style and content, which disturb the linear ("real lifelike") flow of the opening story frame. On the whole, however, the initial story frame offers none of the conventional markers of a dream narrative. The general inclination is to take the mystery straight. We realize our mistake when a second story frame unfolds – the story of Diane's real life. When Diane awakens we see, for the first time, elements of her inner and outer world (the psychic conflicts and real-life characters) that make up Diane's dream fantasy. Yet, just as we manage to decode that fantasy from the details of Diane Selwyn's tawdry, conflict-ridden life, the dream images that we have been viewing do not simply dissolve into a restored normality. We're not in Kansas any more, the site of Dorothy's homecoming upon her awakening in *The Wizard of Oz.*

In Lynch's hands, there is no reprieve from the grip of chaotic unconscious forces. Unlike Dorothy, Diane Selwyn awakens to a horror that utterly overwhelms her. That final horror is the abyss of infinite desire. It has been present from the beginning. It is that out of which the film comes, and back into which it dissolves. This is the Lynchian sublime, the final subversion; there is no reality to stabilize its significance. For Lynch, there is no escape, no awakening, only the endless play of schizoidal fantasy.[42] Folds (of desire) pass into other folds, "folding into folding to infinity."[43] The aesthetic sublime of the neo-baroque unfolds before us like a schizoidal self that fractures into infinite monadic possibilities.[44] In its folding of real life back into the ("monstrous") reality of desire, *Mulholland Drive* becomes an anti-*Wizard of Oz.* For in place of restabilized reality, Lynch's baroque fantasy culminates in the neo-baroque aesthetic sublime of Deleuze and Guatari.[45]

In what follows, I shall try to make good on these claims and their implications for law in our time. First, I will lay out the basic frame story of *Mulholland Drive*, describing the "real life" events out of which Diane Selwyn's dream fantasy takes shape. Second, I will interpret the narrative configuration of that fantasy in an effort to crack the dream code. I will then move to a third level of reality, the reality of the abyss, in an effort to interpret Lynch's film vision and its philosophical implications. As part of this effort, I will link Lynch's seriation of destabilizing subversions to the aesthetic of the authentic and ersatz sublime. I associate the latter with the spectacular representations of contemporary digital baroque culture. Lastly, I will enwrap these interpretive accounts in the narrative framework of a failed initiatory rite. With the help of Jean-Joseph's Goux's analysis of the subverted rite of royal succession encoded in the story of Oedipus, we will encounter the genealogy of baroque law, a tragic sign of our faltering ability to sustain law's legitimacy under baroque cultural conditions.

Mulholland Drive: *the basic frame story*

First time viewers of *Mulholland Drive* must wait for most of the film to pass before they wake up to the real plot structure of Diane Selwyn's dream fantasy. Only then do we see the details, from Diane's real life, that have supplied both the motive force and the code for interpreting the dream/mystery that we have been watching. Let us begin from the vantage of this awakening. Here (in retrospect) is what we come to understand:

Diane Selwyn is a failed Hollywood starlet wannabe. She has traveled south from Deep Rivers, Ontario to sunny Los Angeles, where she takes up residence in a seedy bungalow complex called Sierra Bonita. Diane auditions for the starring role in "The Silvia North Story," but the part goes to a sultry, seductive woman named Camilla Rhodes. Some time thereafter, Diane and Camilla begin an intense love affair. As Camilla's star rises, however, Diane's falls. Diane's dreams of stardom ultimately crumble as she finds herself living a grimy, hand-to-mouth existence on the dark outskirts of Hollywood's lucrative dream-weaving industry. When acting crumbs, tossed her way by Camilla, grow too scarce to live on, Diane plummets to the diminished state of a drug-addled prostitute.

The final blow comes when Camilla tells Diane that their affair must end. To add insult to injury, Diane soon learns that Camilla has acquired a new love object – in fact, two. This knowledge comes to Diane only after Camilla persuades her to attend a glamorous Hollywood party at the suitably upscale home of director Adam Kesher, located on Mulholland Drive. The occasion, it turns out, is the announcement of Adam and Camilla's engagement. This news is delivered with sadistic glee, since both Adam and Camilla are well aware of Diane's continued infatuation with Camilla. The final humiliation, laying bare the annihilation of Diane's hopes and desires, comes in the shape of a blonde starlet who exchanges, before Diane's suffering gaze, erotic whispers and a passionate kiss with Camilla. Diane has been supplanted on every front.

Overcome by jealousy and rage, Diane hires a hit man named Joe to murder Camilla. Diane meets Joe in a diner called Winkie's where they are served by a waitress named Betty. Joe informs Diane that when she sees the blue key in her apartment she will know that the deed has been done. Diane hands over the cash and the deal is clinched. Diane has set in motion the machinery of death on the heels of thwarted desire.

When Diane later spots the blue key on her coffee table she realizes the irrevocability of her action. She also learns from a neighbor that two detectives are looking for her. Fear and guilt play havoc with Diane's mind. She hallucinates Camilla back among the living and recalls (or fantasizes) their making love on Diane's couch. This imagery feeds a masturbatory impulse that desperately mingles violence and pleasure. A knock at the door triggers a final psychotic break. Diane hallucinates two tiny parental figures crawling under the front door. As they grow to adult size, their hands flail madly in the air as they rush toward her, screaming. Diane backs away into the bedroom. She, too, screams madly and flails in panic as she scurries backwards. Falling on to her bed, Diane blindly reaches out to an end table drawer, pulls out a revolver, places it in her mouth, and pulls the trigger. Her body lies sprawled on the bed.

The initial dream work: an interpretation

> Life is a great dream; to dream in this big dream, and to speak of dreams, is to not know where the illusion is going to end.
>
> (Wai-yee Li[46])

> [*Mulholland Drive*] – a love story in the city of dreams.
>
> (from the *Mulholland Drive* press kit)

As the opening credits of *Mulholland Drive* begin, images of a surreal jitterbug sequence play upon the screen.[47] Then we see Diane Selwyn flanked by the two parental figures – the same figures who, in their frenzied, Furies-like reappearance at the end of the film trigger Diane's suicide.

Tightly shot in the opening sequence, together the three evoke the image of a strange Mt Rushmore, with the face of Diane's (deceased) aunt flittering on to the screen and then off to the lower right. This aural-visual pun of the "jitter" (the jitter bug, the jittery image) is suggestive of the overdetermined meanings that populate Diane's dream world. A similarly jittery, floating camera effect will later become the telltale sign of the dreamer approaching (but never quite achieving) awareness of herself dreaming. And, indeed, the very next image that we see is that of a bed, with maroon sheets, even as we hear the deep, regular breathing of the sleeper. The first-time viewer remains in the dark, but the site of Diane's dream production (and death) has been announced.

The scene then shifts to a long black limousine wending its way at night down a sinuously curving road. We see Camilla seated in the back. The car stops unexpectedly, somewhere on Mulholland Drive. The two men sitting up front turn toward Camilla with revolvers pointed toward her. "We don't stop here," Camilla plaintively utters. "Get out," they say. With the aid of retrospect, we recognize this scene. It is from the time Camilla sent a limo to pick Diane up and take her to director Adam Kesher's home on Mulholland Drive, the fateful site of Camilla's and Adam's wedding announcement. As Diane's dream begins, we are about to revisit the scene where her Hollywood dreams were finally shattered, sending Diane cascading down a desperate path of jealous rage. The first link between desire and death has been made.

In Diane's dream fantasy, Camilla sits in Diane's place in the limo; her death is imminent. But a sudden freak accident intervenes. Joyriding teenagers are speeding blindly down Mulholland Drive. We see two of them, ominously standing and lurching with the curves of the road, their hands flailing as they scream with the joyful speed of it. With sudden violence, their car crashes into the limo. The men with guns are killed instantly. Camilla stumbles out of the smoking wreckage. She is intact, we will learn, but for a cut on her head, and total amnesia. Camilla stumbles down into the streets of Hollywood, finally finding her way to the idealized cottage community where Diane will meet her again.

But this is not Camilla, nor will it be Diane who meets her. Diane has become "Betty," a naïve, perky ingénue just arrived in Hollywood to realize her dreams of stardom. She is all that Diane wished to be in real life. As for her counterpart, Camilla too has now become all that Diane would have wished her to be: a blank screen, ready for Diane's fantasies (of love and desire) to play out, as they soon will.[48] Camilla sees a film poster on a bathroom wall in Diane's apartment. It features Rita Hayworth, playing the star role in *Gilda* (1946). Camilla will thereafter assume the famous seductress' name as her own. In Diane's fantasy, Camilla has become "Rita" – a Hollywood creation, Diane's ideal (imaginary) object of desire[49] (2001; image 4.1 – see plate section between pp. 118 and 119).

Together, she and Betty will reconsummate an idealized love affair as they stage (like a play within a play) the mystery story of Rita's lost identity. But, the originating reality of Camilla's death hangs over the fantasy like a dark cloud. And intimations of discovery (as the dreamer, like Oedipus, unravels the riddle of her identity and her crime) are already apparent.

Consider the two detectives, standing beside the wreckage left by the joyriding teenagers' crash into Camilla's limo. In their oddly wooden conversation they recapitulate the dream-weaver's own dynamic logic. "Looks like someone's missing," says one. "Just what I was thinking," says the other. It is the dream logic of the whodunit in the existential, post-modern mystery (or crime noir[50]) genre of Samuel Beckett and Paul Auster.[51] In her dream fantasy, Diane is missing (she has become Betty), and Camilla is missing as well (she has become Rita). The challenge of solving the dream riddle of Rita's missing identity and the real life mystery of Camilla's death (she was murdered by a hit man hired by Diane) propels the dream forward. The solution, however, already lingers in the distance, in a future that has already passed, in the terrible reality of identity revealed.

Self-knowledge, in this Oedipean world, is an excavated horror, the darkness that lies at the end of the tunnel. For, like Oedipus, Diane/Betty is a detective bent on solving the mystery of identity. Ostensibly, it is Rita's identity that she is seeking, but in reality it is her own self that lay hidden in both, for Diane *is* the dyadic split known as "Betty/Rita." They are but two (idealized) forms of Diane's unstable, borderline personality. In this respect, one might say that the film's drama is fueled by the return of the repressed.[52] As in the fabled *One Thousand and One Nights*, the mystery's tension lies in the dream's ingenious strategies for postponing the dreamer's demise. Like the reader of Scheherazade's serial narrative arabesques, each of which gives the teller yet another day of life for the next installment to unfold, the viewer of *Mulholland Drive* is kept in a precarious state of suspense: for how long will Diane's defensive dream maneuvers stave off the terror (of forbidden knowledge) from which she is fleeing? For how long will the fantasy realm of splitting and idealization delay confrontation, and ultimate fusion, with the monster (the Thing behind the diner, the one "who is doing it") that she has become?

In Diane's dream, erotic fantasy desperately competes with guilt, fear of discovery, and the reality principle of death itself. The key tools of Diane's psychological dream-defense are familiar ones in the Freudian toolkit: idealization, splitting, condensation, and role reversal. Diane becomes someone else to avoid the guilt of Diane's murderous deed. She becomes the idealized Betty to preserve her identification with (and jealous longing for) Camilla's Hollywood success. Betty is the idealized part of Diane that has been spoiled and lost, sacrificed on the altar of Hollywood's cruel, often destructive, reality. The persona of "Betty" preserves the unspoiled Hollywood of the youthful Diane's naïve dreams and thwarted ambitions. In her fantasy, Diane realizes the talent and success that she never could achieve in real life. Wish fulfillment, denial, and idealization: in her dream, it is Diane who displaces her rival, Camilla, rather than the other way around; it is Diane who restores her lost love relationship with Camilla; and it is Diane who denies, by interrupting with a timely car accident, Camilla's murder. It is Diane as well who idealizes the real by splitting off the treacherous Hollywood into a surreal, pastel-lit, benevolent wonder-world. As we will see, however, it is also a domain that is infiltrated by corrupt and omnipresent conspiratorial forces.

Like a latter day Prospero, Diane magically enfolds Camilla in the oblivion of amnesia, so that the illusion may go on, at least for a while, until the mystery's solution can no longer be put off. Diane's ultimate confrontation with herself, as the monstrous source of her unacceptably violent impulses, will mark the mystery's end. When Diane merges with the monstrous corpse on the bed with maroon covers, when she fuses with the monster behind the diner, when, in short, she assumes the identity that her dream fantasy so desperately fights to disguise, the idealized dream world will abruptly vanish. The defense is over. She is no longer Betty, and Camilla is dead, the victim of Diane's jealous rage. Diane's ensuing judgment is severe: the sentence is death, by suicide.

Along the way to this horrific denouement, Lynch offers clues that disturb the outward serenity and apparent stability of Diane's dream fantasy. Consider, for example, the scene of the two friends who meet at Winkie's, a replica of the real life diner where Diane's murder plot was put into action. Here we encounter the source of Diane's consciously unacceptable violence, her interior horror. In this scene, the camera floats and sways as if caught in the eddies of an unseen current. This happens, it seems, whenever we come close to the dream's horrific point of origin. Not surprisingly, then, it is at Winkie's that Diane's horror assumes tangible form. Like a Rosetta stone of the unnamable, it is momentarily figured. Just before it appears, we hear one friend tell the other (although it might as well be a patient recounting to his therapist) a dream that has been recurring. The dream takes place at this very Winkie's, he says, and it scares him to death. There is a monster behind the diner. "He's the one who is doing it," the friend reports.

Despite his terror, he allows himself to be persuaded by his friend's (the "analyst's") calm, disarmingly matter-of-fact encouragement: "So, you came to see if he's out there." And so, in the spirit of therapeutic reality testing, they go behind the diner to look. In a masterfully timed sequence of suspense and horror, the monster – which rationality would dispel – duly appears. Upon glimpsing it, the friend loses his breath and falls to the ground, apparently lifeless. Contact with forbidden knowledge equals death. That is what this dream-within-a-dream sequence tells us. Reason, it seems, contains a trap door – into the abyss. (So much for testing reality.) And, indeed, the dreamer's prophetic (Diane's hidden) knowledge is accurate, as Diane's subsequent suicide, upon confronting the monstrousness of her own decomposing corpse, makes plain.

These clues, among others, leave no doubt that the dreamer is on the trail of solving the mystery of her own identity.[53] Powerful psychological forces have been unleashed to preserve the dream denial that is under way. But no less powerful forces of detection are also at work, threatening to disrupt the dreamer's desperate defensive wish for complacency. At the top of the pyramid of detection/surveillance/power is Mr Rocque, a mysterious Howard Hughes-type figure who watches, and apparently controls everything he sees, from an electronically equipped living room sealed behind glass.[54] It is Mr Rocque who will set loose, always by intimation (as if to ensure deniability), a wide range of forces aimed at finding "the missing girl." For example, through a series of phone calls initiated by Mr Rocque, the search reaches the streets. Joe the hit man (Diane's pimp?) asks a prostitute (Diane's real life co-worker?): "Any new girls on the street?" At least two different elements of "detection" may be discerned here. On the one hand, Joe may be acting as a stand-in for the detectives who are actively seeking to solve the murder mystery involving Camilla Rhodes. Subconsciously, Diane knows that she is a suspect in the crime investigation under way. On the other hand, it is also possible that Diane's repressed rage against Camilla has taken the form of yet another role reversal. Perhaps Diane's unconscious has placed Camilla on the streets, substituting her professional rival (and fickle partner in love) for Diane's own unconscionable fall to soliciting tricks on the dismal outskirts of Hollywood.

On a more condensed, symbolic level, the search for the "missing girl" takes the form of a widely cast, strangely potent conspiracy bent on coercing director Adam Kesher to cast "Camilla Rhodes" as the lead in his new ("star-vehicle") movie venture. "This is the girl" (the exact words Diane uttered in real life to Joe the hit man, consummating her contract for Camilla's murder) now becomes the mantra for Camilla's *carte d'entré*, the tainted "open sesame" that lands her the part that Diane herself coveted.

"This is the girl." We hear the words spoken by the Castigliane brothers at a business meeting with Adam and his agent. The two brothers are Italian power brokers, one a producer (whose wilting demand for the perfect espresso can never be met ["It's shit!"]), the other a lawyer (whose rumbling, animal-like roar sweeps across the conference room when Adam hesitates to comply with the brothers' casting demand). The brothers embody familiar forms of raw power in action. But power assumes other guises as well. Consider, for example, the mysterious cowboy, who instructs Adam on what to say when casting the star of his film ("When you see Camilla Rhodes, tell them 'this is the girl.'"). He speaks in sphinx-like riddles,[55] but his sinister intent and the means of carrying out his implicit threats are never in doubt.

In short, the tools of detection run the gamut: from brute force to the riddle of implied power within a far-flung conspiratorial network of social forces (lawyers, producers, mobsters, banks) – all equipped with the means to cut off and control, by any means necessary, the target of their will. We will return to this theme of power later on to more closely examine the film's symbolic references to criminal, financial, legal, and corporate forms of power in contemporary society.

The penultimate scene in the film takes place when Betty and Rita rush into the blue-lit night (with its symbolic reference to the underworld) to the windswept Café Silencio. This scene embodies both the interpretive key to, as well as the final disruption of, the outward order of the dreamer's dream flow. Like the dream-within-a-dream sequence featuring the two friends in the dream diner called Winkie's, here too the camera bobs and sways, in the grip of a hidden current, as we peer down the blue-lit alley that leads to the café. This visual trope[56] links the monster behind the diner (the one who is "doing it") with a complementary figuration: the maestro, the magician, the poet, the film director. Inside Café Silencio, we encounter him, the master of ceremonies, a Prospero-like figure, and a likely stand-in for film director Lynch himself. (Is it not Lynch – in this film, this fantasy, this play of reality and illusion – who is, after all, "doing it?") "No hay banda," the emcee cries. "There is no band." Seated in the late-night, sparsely populated theater (of dreams?), Rita and Betty watch and listen as the emcee/magician reveals the truth of illusion: "This is all a tape recording, and yet we hear a band . . . if we want to hear." In the baroque play of reality and illusion, *la vida es sueno* ("life is a dream"). The poet-director controls it all, under the immobile gaze of his muse, the blue-haired lady, the fairy queen, who sits like a statue in the box seat above the stage. Like the monster's artistic double (on the stage, rather than behind it), the maestro too is the one "who is doing it." He too channels the flow of Eros.

His power is evident when he raises his arms above his head and a mighty roll of thunder rattles the theater – like the atavistic roar that opens Joyce's *Finnegan's Wake*, the unwordable thunder sound of Zeus, father of the gods.

Significantly, it is when the Lynchian maestro reveals to the audience the illusions of sight and sound, making plain that it is he who is directing them at will, that Diane's dream finally reaches its violent denouement. Knowledge (of the dream code) upon announcing its illusory nature terminates the play (of illusion). When Betty [Diane] and Rita [Camilla] behold this tutelary guide, and wordlessly make his Teiresian knowledge their own, the dream veil is lifted, and Diane awakens. The terror of what she has learned will now precipitate her demise. Her epiphanic knowledge will become real. It is just as the surrogate dreamer in the diner predicted. Knowledge equals death. The one who confronts the source of the mystery – the terrible reality of unbearable knowledge–desire–power, momentarily figured as the monster behind the diner – must die. As the blue-haired lady in the theater of illusions will say, uttering the final, Shakespearean words of the film, "the rest is silence."[57]

One may, of course, protest: Who is to say that Diane's death at the end of *Mulholland Drive* is real? Might it not be but a symbolic death? Might it not herald yet another dream within a dream – part of an infinite regress of enfolding arabesques, or nomadic monads, each a discrete self/world/reality? Who can say whether there is another scene to come, after the silence of dissolution in the monstrous abyss: the scene of yet another awakening, the beginning perhaps of the initiate's ascent, after the torturous descent though hell. It is the scene that follows the mythic ordeal of being devoured by the monster, a symbolic death that prepares the initiate for rebirth – into humane (civilized) culture, as *bios politikon*?[58]

Yet, the event of knowledge (in the aftermath of the initiate's symbolic "death") remains elusive. To all appearances, at the end of *Mulholland Drive* we remain caught in uncertainty. This state of unrelieved ambiguity, suspense, and agitation is the natural offshoot of the *mise en abyme* that Lynch brilliantly stages in his film. Indeed, it is precisely this aesthetic effect, as we will soon see, that links Lynch's film vision to the baroque's failed sublime. The horror of the Nothing – of nothing happening – ramifies form as the infinite distraction of decorative ornamentation, what Benjamin calls "the will to art." In pop-baroque art, evident, for example, in Warhol's endless seriations, denial through the diversion of physical sensation takes the place of real horror. The *frisson* of the "cheap thrill" (the spectacle) substitutes for the soul-shaking terror of deadly desire.[59] But Lynch is not toying here with the pop-horror of mere sensation. This is the Unnamable rapping at the front door, bringing death. It remains to be seen whether the new baroque may yet tap the mythic power needed to go beyond paralysis, trapped in the sensate realm of empty, infinitely ramified form.

Before pursuing this possibility further, however, it will be helpful to survey more closely the philosophical and jurisprudential implications of *Mulholland Drive.*

Mulholland Drive: *an overview of the dream work writ large – law, culture, and power in real life*

Lynch's dream play may be read as prototypical. Let us call it a contemporary allegory of unchecked desire and unregulated power in a narcissistic world of mind and culture where knowledge is understood solely in terms of mastery or control.[60] Let us call it a neo-baroque allegory: a symbolic world of unadulterated narcissism. Behold the Hollywood kitsch culture of solipsistic pleasure, embodied in Diane Selwyn's ambitions of stardom. This is *Mulholland Drive,* a fantasy world fueled by a borderline's unbound desire, violent when thwarted, as it inevitably will be. As psychoanalyst Benjamin Kilborne aptly observes: "In our contemporary world it is striking how much technology feeds our illusions. People come to believe that an ideal of themselves can be actualized."[61] Hollywood's machinery of dream production, further empowered by its alliance with new digital technology, spawns a Disneyesque ideal that denies pain, suffering, helplessness, and ultimately death itself, while amplifying the momentary pleasures of narcissistic gratification. This too is a hallmark of the contemporary baroque.[62]

I propose, then, to construe Lynch's film writ large as a baroque allegory, an account of man's fate in late modernity. I believe this analysis shares an affinity with Jean-Joseph Goux's claim that we are now witnessing the final sequence of the profoundly disordered Oedipal monomyth that Sophocles recounted with exquisite precision so many centuries ago.[63] Tracking Goux's analysis, in what follows I will contend that the multiple pathologies of knowledge, desire, and power that we witness in *Muholland Drive* evoke a profoundly disturbed rite of royal investiture, a subverted ritual of law's legitimation. As Goux puts it, "the cryptic soul is not all human; it has dark, disturbing depths, unfathomable instinctual resources that elude humanity and plunge into the dangerous darkness of animality."[64] Reason is an authority that can tame the soul's animal components. However, there is also the danger of confusing the "inner (divine) man with man as a whole." That danger risks overlooking "the monstrous structure of the soul" [i.e. the unacceptable chaos and irrationality of the unconscious] and forgetting that the "properly human part of the soul is only one element in a larger composite."[65]

Lynch's cinematic allegory invites us to restore (even if Lynch himself does not provide) a connection that has all but disappeared from the collective consciousness of mainstream culture. The first requirement is that we be willing to undergo a cinematic rite of passage. We must be willing to face the abyss, the unadulterated, all-consuming horror of schizoidal desire. The challenge is straightforward: will we remain caught, like our baroque predecessors, in a perpetual state of agitated suspension between the opposing (and equally unreachable) infinitudes of light and dark, trapped in the nauseating proliferation of endless matter?[66] Worse still, will our contemporary "failure of nerve"[67] continue the diversionary tactics of mass culture – a pop baroque culture of spectacle – where sensory gratification and motion for its own sake, a hallmark of baroque aesthetics, perpetuate our collective denial of a deeper lack, a deeper longing for significance? Or will we perhaps grasp the significance, and the epiphanic potential, of the baroque yearning for the sublime – whether it is the sublime dissolution of self in *infinite* (albeit inhuman) *freedom*, in the monstrous abyss of *infinite desire*, or in the *infinite demands of the other* (the ethical sublime)?

The contemporary challenge, then, has been set: for how long will we be content to engage in the endless ("constructivist") play of reality and illusion, mired (as Goux argues) in the perverse state of Oedipus, a perpetual exile, foreclosed from learning the ancient monomyth's higher wisdom? For how long will the pseudo-horror of mass culture, with its "pop baroque" aesthetic of shock and sensation continue to mock the real terror of initiation that marks the epiphanic quest for the sublime? And, to the extent that this state of affairs remains our fate, what hope is there for contemporary baroque law, a law whose validity remains, but whose significance, amid a surplus of principles, eludes us? For that is the fate of law when the ordeal of justice lies suspended, eclipsed by the frantic motion of the baroque impulse toward form piled upon form, proliferating images in a state of hyper-productivity – baroque production on a colossal scale. Grant Gilmore grasped the implications of law's going under in a comparably baroque fashion when he invoked that hellish state where there is nothing but law.[68] Mass production in law as in art leaves a trail of fragments, scattered like insular monads on a landscape that lies in ruins.[69]

As an initial step toward explicating and justifying the foregoing interpretive construct, in what follows I will briefly recapitulate Goux's analysis of the fateful history of the Oedipal subversion of the ancient rite of succession, the failed monomyth, and then proceed to explore, as promised, what it can tell us about the configuration of law, meaning, and power in our time.

The Subversion of the Monomyth: *Oedipus Rex*

In *Oedipus, Philosopher*, Jean-Joseph Goux reads the myth of Oedipus as an anomaly. "Matricide, not patricide, is at the heart of the heroic myth in its typical and universal form." Goux goes on: "The hero who is to become king is the hero who kills the female dragon, the female serpent, the female monstrosity, in bloody combat. By murdering a dangerous, dark, feminine force, the hero liberates the bride."[70]

According to Goux, the Oedipus myth disrupts this universal structure. It is, in his view, "a myth of failed royal investiture, or of avoided masculine initiation." It is this failure that links it to parricide and incest. Oedipus's systematic disruption of the tripartite structure of the universal monomyth, its "canonical schema of the triple ordeal," gives rise to three concomitant pathologies or "sins." I want to interpret these pathologies in relation to the symbolic order of the law which measures them in terms of knowledge, power, and desire. Properly understood, this mythic code may lead us to a theory of the rites that accompany the ordeal of justice upon which the law is founded. Here lies the code by which to interpret the allegorical import of Lynch's dreamscape in *Mulholland Drive.*

The ritual of investiture that the ancient monomyth embodies enacts the normalization of power in transition from one generation to the next. In short, it describes a rite of political and legal legitimation. That rite follows the following sequence:

1. "A king fears that a younger man, or one not yet born, will take his place, as an oracle has predicted." The king does all he can to avoid this fate.
2. "The future hero escapes from the king's murderous intentions." However, he subsequently finds himself endangered by another king who plots his demise. The second king is unable to realize this goal himself, so he sets the hero "a perilous task."
3. "The trial takes the form of a fight with a monster." The hero succeeds in defeating the monster, with the help of a god, or a wise man, or a future bride.
4. "Finally, the hero's triumph over the monster allows him to marry the daughter of a king."[71]

In the Oedipus story the "perilous task" is avoided. In fact, there is no second king and no trial to overcome. Nor is there a monster to slay. Instead, by sheer chance, Oedipus encounters a stranger in the road who turns out to be a king, his unknown father, whom Oedipus unwittingly slays.

The youthful violence traditionally reserved for the great trial of slaying the horrible, monstrous Thing, has been misspent, and perverted. Parricide has replaced the mythic conquest of the monstrous other, while desire ramifies in an unholy union of son with mother. This perversion spreads terror and plague throughout the land, and in due course it will shatter Oedipus's soul.

Parricide is not Oedipus's only mistake. He also mistakes his own efforts as the sole basis for his kingly authority to rule over Thebes. Oedipus persistently, and roughly, spurns the guidance of others, such as the blind seer Teiresias. It is by sheer force of his own intelligence, Oedipus believes, that he has solved the Sphinx's riddle. The arrogance of intellect (as exemplified in Adam I's self-satisfied dominion over nature via his mastery of signs) deflects Oedipus from the truth. Only belatedly will he realize his fateful ignorance, and his true state as parricide and spouse to his own mother. This symbolic disruption of mythic elements – perverse violence, perverse knowledge, and perverse desire – becomes, in Goux's analysis, the chief paradigm for subsequent western culture. For is it not, he argues, the rationalist philosopher who mistakes the power of reason alone to rule self and society? Is it not, we may add, the dominance of Genesis I over the self-constrained, service-oriented ethos described in Genesis II?

The universal myth[72] that the Oedipus story systematically perverts enacts a symbolic drama of legitimation. This political/legal drama is also a psychodrama in which the hero confronts the terrible Thing (the horrible monster), accepts aid and guidance from tutelary spirits, undergoes symbolic death (being devoured by the monster he must confront), and is reborn as the triumphant hero, spouse to the second king's daughter. As Plato too conceived, the nature of the city-state coincides with the nature of the soul. Disruption in one domain is matched in kind with disruption in the other.[73]

In the Oedipus story a systematic disruption of the monomyth leads to pseudo or ersatz legitimation. Its proxy is baroque law, in a pop-baroque culture steeped in sensation and denial of the wellsprings of justice, the authentic source of law's legitimacy, which originates in our response to the infinite demand of the other before us. Oedipus' rule rests on a series of deceits and perversions. His perversion of the monomyth not only generates plague in the community and a political regime of illegitimate tyranny, but also a psychological trauma that results in Oedipus's emotional collapse, self-mutilation, and, finally, the infinite hardships of a lifetime of loneliness, poverty, and exile. The dire consequences of failing properly to undergo the rite of royal investiture could hardly be more compelling. Taming the horrific demands of desire, symbolized by the slaying of the monstrous Thing, opens the path to the ethical. Amid the din of unconstrained mimetic desire, with its self-serving impulse to dominate, attentiveness to the demands of caretaking – whether in the shepherding of Being (or nature), or in taking responsibility for the needs of the other – remains inchoate. The ethical prospect of Adam II thus goes unfulfilled.

In the dream fantasy of Diane Selwyn we discern a replication of Oedipus' (self-) deceits. Could it be that David Lynch has intuitively staged in *Mulholland Drive* the philosopher-detective's arrogant claims for reason against the backdrop of a subverted initiation rite, in the sense that Goux describes? Do we not recognize the symptomatic pathologies of knowledge–desire–power as they permeate and bring to climax Diane's self-annihilating dream fantasy? Is this not tantamount to the legitimation crisis that accompanies the neo-baroque failure to restore the source of law's ethical significance? I contend that in *Mulholland Drive* we witness signs of an important cultural convergence. The Oedipal subversion of the ancient ("monomythic") rite of succession, and its nexus to the neo-baroque, play out together in the sublime horror of Lynch's cinematic *mise en abyme*. In what follows, we shall see what more may be said to render this claim persuasive.

From Oedipal Perversion to the Ethical Sublime

Elements of the baroque mind and culture

Walter Benjamin has written that the baroque concept of sovereignty gave rise to a doctrine of princely power that can be understood in terms of the state of emergency. "The ruler is designated from the outset as the holder of dictatorial power if war, revolt, or other catastrophes should lead to a state of emergency."[74] Baroque culture's main concern was to establish a mass culture of conformity and control. It was essentially a visual culture, as is our own. In the service of engineering consent, baroque culture during the seventeenth century heavily relied on the efficacy of visual elements to seize dramatically and hold the public's attention. Mass culture thrives on the sensible image for its power to capture, amaze, and stupefy.[75] Baroque culture resorted to broadly disseminated visual spectacles (emphasizing painting and theater over poetry and prose) as its main instruments of shaping and controlling public sentiment and belief ("to color the soul with passions"[76] and to "penetrate psyches and wills"[77]).

Art had become kitsch: a mass culture put in place for the sake of shaping public opinion based on intensified affect.[78] "Opinion moves the world," wrote Juan Alfonso de Lancina, and Hobbes attested that "the world was governed by opinion."[79] The seventeenth century, like much of the twentieth, had become dominated by mass culture – a culture of dazzling spectacle and splendor, amid transitory fragments, the ruins of a profoundly disenchanted, devalorized world.[80] Yet, notwithstanding the pleasures of visual distraction, the sense of imminent collapse continued unabated. The baroque subject felt as if he were "being driven along to a cataract."[81] As Benjamin astutely observed, deprived of grace in this world, all things seemed to be gathered together "in order to clear an ultimate heaven, enabling it, as a vacuum, one day, to destroy the world with catastrophic violence."[82] A state of emergency in the soul reigned in parallel with the princely state of emergency without.

Creation without grace assumed a ghostly appearance. As in a dream, discrete fragments piled up, concatenating on a landscape of ruins. And as yearning heightened, seeking escape from the corrupted state of worldly affairs, aesthetic forms proliferated. It was as if the desperate reaching out toward a distant heaven, as if to outrun an encroaching darkness, could only express itself in further decorative embellishments, like infinite folds within a compressed, but seemingly infinite, translunary space.[83] In an effort to stave off the uncanny monstrousness of empty form, to tamp down the fear of Nothing, what Lyotard has aptly described as the fear of the non-occurrence of the event,[84] the baroque imagination can only make more of the same, as if only this colossal profusion of expressive form could avert catastrophe.[85] And so, like arabesques endlessly improvising their monadic design, baroque ornamentation proliferated. Dizzying, decentering, even nauseating in their spatial and visual onslaught.[86]

"Nothing of what is today will be tomorrow," wrote Martinez de Cuellar. "Nothing you are aware of remains."[87] Under such conditions of extreme contingency, the baroque dream play came into its own. *La vida es sueno.*[88] "The dream stands over waking life like the vault of heaven."[89] As Alewyn writes: "The baroque illusion is always conscious and intentional: it refuses to seduce the soul or even to deceive the reason; it wishes to seduce the senses." Buci-Glucksmann adds: "If life is a dream, the world is truly a theater . . ."[90] Infinitely distant from a source of authenticating meaning, the never-ending artifice of play (in theater and painting and elsewhere in public life) became the baroque era's secular god. In the grip of such icy disillusion, under the intense pressure of fear and uncertainty, human nature revealed itself: a chaotic web of animal instinct and emotion, just as Machiavelli had written. Politics was the domain in which human forces had to be captured, turned to princely purposes, or simply overcome by the counterforce of the state. Machiavelli's knowledge prevailed within the court culture of the baroque: human nature had to be studied in the infinitely complex folds of its interiority so that state power might triumph.

The deeply disturbed relationship of knowledge, power, and desire that played out in the culture and politics of the baroque during the seventeenth century resonates uncannily with contemporary cultural conditions. It is that resonance that I have sought to capture in presenting the cinematic neo-baroque dreamscape of David Lynch's *Mulholland Drive*. On that landscape we see that power, knowledge, and desire have grown potent yet remain elusive, and twisted in perversion. Consider the film's fourfold evocation of *power* as: (1) *remote, yet ubiquitous* (as evidenced by the insular, seemingly unfettered power of Mr Rocque[91]) (2) *cryptic and unnerving* (as evidenced by the menacing riddles of the mysterious cowboy); (3) *vicious and vulgar* (as evidenced by the brutish company lawyer who intimidates, and the crude thug who assails the director, Adam Kesher); and (4) *spectral, a source of wonder and illusion* (as evidenced by the emcee-magician of Café Silencio). Or consider again the film's fivefold imagining of *knowledge* as: (1) *blind* (as reflected in Rita's and Betty's amnesic condition); (2) *prophetic* (as evidenced by Louise, the clairvoyant concierge of the idealized bungalow complex called Sierra Bonita); (3) *panoptic* (as evidenced by Mr Rocque's ubiquitous surveillance cameras); (4) *mantic* (as evidenced in the revelatory dream logic of the film itself); and (5) *initiatory* (as evidenced by the emcee/magician surrogate for director Lynch himself). Finally, consider the film's fourfold construction of *desire* as: (1) *monstrous* (as evidenced by the terrifying creature behind the diner); subject to (2) *idealized splitting* (as evidenced by the doubling of Diane/Betty and Rita/Camilla) and (3) *perverse merging* (as evidenced in Diane's borderline pathology, fusing with, then violently repelling Camilla); while remaining (4) *endlessly generative* (as evidenced in the process of cinematic dream production itself).

Absent cultural resources powerful enough to counter or reorganize the terror of death, the baroque anti-hero remains trapped in a maze of phantasmal deceptions. Like Oedipus in his downfall, and Diane Selwyn in hers, by the time the baroque subject confronts his monstrous self, it is too late: all hope of redemptive self-transcendence has been lost. The implications of this allegory of cultural and intra-psychic dysfunction are no less profound in regard to the new baroque law and politics of our time.

Neo-baroque law

Like its counterpart in baroque art, baroque law embodies a distinctly decadent form: the will to legislate and command has been divorced from a legitimating source of significance.[92] As Agamben puts it, "What, after all, is the structure of the sovereign ban if not that of a law that is in force but does not signify?"[93] In the spectral realities of baroque and neo-baroque legal culture we encounter patterns similar to those playing out intra-psychically and in society at large. Ramified aesthetic forms, in a spectacle of knowledge, power, and desire run amok, defend against the pressing, but unacceptable truth of the reality principle itself. We see this defense in the cybertopian dream of "singularity" and the birth of the spiritual machine, that momentous occasion when mind meets its digital equivalent and digitized consciousness may finally be downloaded – impervious to material decay. In short, digital baroque longing aspires to escape the material conditions of life itself – the earth and the body. This is the fantasy of total transformation: what was once conceived as the earth mother is now reconceived as "a space platform," and the platform of the body now becomes a site from which humans may "lift off" to the "data garden" of the stars.[94]

Lacking the capacity to confront (and ultimately accept) the reality of death, the baroque subject, in Franz Rosenzweig's words, "steps outside of life. If living means dying, he prefers not to live. He chooses death in life. He escapes from the inevitability of death into the paralysis of artificial death."[95] Artificial death, like the "infinite nothingness" that numbs the mind after encountering traumatizing terror,[96] is the baroque subject's response to metaphysical temptation. As Rosenzweig puts it, "sick reason" seeks a way out of life, an escape from the terror of mortality.[97] This retreat from life lies at the heart of what Nietzsche described as the spirit of decadence, and what Freud diagnosed as the pathology of death anxiety. It is not the will to power, but rather the fanatic's will to destruction.[98] As Nietzsche put it, "Man would rather will nothingness than not will."[99] And as Henry Birault has observed, "This will, avid for meaning, we see, is at bottom a will to annihilation, a will that begins by saying 'no' to existence, to our meaningless, immoral, unreasonable existence.[100]

Having turned away from life, the baroque subject seeks comfort (and mastery) in a land of dream, fantasy, and spectacle. But, like Diane Selwyn's dream, it is a realm haunted by the repressed knowledge of the Real. As in the mythic tale of Oedipus, so long as the monster has not been confronted and overcome, its unassimilated force is bound to endlessly ramify spectral forms of denial. This is what drives the mystery plot of *Mulholland Drive*, and the baroque spectacle writ large.

The fear of laying bare the irrational, terrifying forces that lie at the heart of the culture of spectacle, and, by extension, of law as sensate image, prompts a state of emergency within that parallels the state of emergency without.[101] In this sense, the failed initiation rite that Goux describes as the Oedipal perversion of the universal monomyth takes on distinctly political and legal implications. One may suggest that the dream logic that *Mulholland Drive* so vividly depicts, expresses, from a deeply interior perspective, a state of political and legal affairs first conceived by Machiavelli, Hobbes, and Locke, and that achieved two distinct culmination points in the modern history of ideas: first, in de Sade's sensate imaginary, and later in Nietzsche's will to power. Both reflect the endpoint (and checkmate) of the logic of desire. This is the cultural and intra-psychic reality of disenchanted knowledge, unchecked desire, and totalized power chaotically ramified. Roberto Unger's program of "negative capability," in which social life becomes an incessant struggle for the "distentrenchment of formative contexts"[102] in behalf of the emancipatory ideal of human "plasticity,"[103] takes Nietsche's will to power into the domain of social theory. Unger's libertarian model readily serves the cybertopian ideal. For his part, de Sade translates the will to power into unfettered *Eros*. Trapped in the logic of erotic intensification, de Sade's vision culminates in sadism and death.[104] Totalization in the realm of politics and law invites a similar fate. As Goux writes, "the tyrant gives free rein to his most frenetic impulses, as he does to the numberless horde of passions governed by Eros . . . [H]e attempts to live out in reality what others only dream of doing their sleep . . ."[105] This kind of violence was terrifyingly realized in twentieth century totalitarian societies (from Hitler to Stalin, Mao, and Pol Pot), and it is now helping to fuel the iconoclastic fervor and violence of Islamic fundamentalism.

Outbreaks of collective pathology of this sort in politics and law may be understood as the enactment of an inversion of justice that parallels the Oedipal inversion of the ancient monomyth. According to this ancient model, law's legitimation requires harmony among its core political, cultural, and intra-psychic elements, namely: power, knowledge, and desire. The advent of Machiavelli's understanding of brute power, authorized by the Cartesian model of knowledge as mastery (over disenchanted nature), incorporated into the Hobbesian understanding of the modern nation-state, heightened by technological advancement, and rationalized by the positivist model of conventional norms (rationalizing the command of the sovereign) risks a new baroque crisis of legitimacy. This is what happens when harmony among power, knowledge, and desire has been lost.

In *Mulholland Drive* we encounter various signs of the subversion of justice as power, knowledge, and desire take on distinctly pathological forms. Recent efforts to restabilize law and politics under the rubric of the "market state" will not suffice, for the paradigm of promoting economic opportunity fails to acknowledge, much less address, prevailing conditions of intra-psychic and cultural dysfunction. The task of reconstituting, and restoring harmony among, the core elements of power, knowledge, and desire requires that we tap new resources.

Ritual, Initiation, and the Ordeal of Justice

This diagnostic of the cultural and intra-psychic conditions under which law is now developing tracks Gershom Scholem's powerful reading of Kafka's great modern parable, *The Trial.* Scholem's observations were recorded in a letter to his close friend, Walter Benjamin. As Agamben recounts:

> Scholem defines the relation to law described in Kafka's *Trial* as 'the Nothing of Revelation.' Intending this expression to name 'a stage in which revelation does not signify, yet still affirms itself by the fact that it is in force. Where the wealth of significance is gone and what appears, reduced, so to speak, to the zero point of its own content, still does not disappear (and Revelation is something that appears), there the Nothing appears.'[106]

The neo-baroque landscape on which the proliferation of legal forms is currently taking place comports well with Scholem's account. Neo-baroque law in the society of visual spectacle readily assumes the phantasmal quality of the spectacle itself. Locked into a "jurisprudence of appearances,"[107] law remains in force buts lacks significance. In this respect, Benjamin's appreciation of the work of Carl Schmitt may be understandable. For notwithstanding the profound uneasiness prompted by Schmitt's grievous embrace of fascism in the 1920s and 1930s, his critique of the liberal model is not without interest. As Bobbitt writes:

> [B]y stripping the State of any particular legitimating myth . . . Schmitt thinks that liberalism perpetuates the greatest myth of all, the depersonalized, rational, mechanistic operation of the law. Eventually, as part of the logic of the process, all that will matter is that the machinery functions, on the one condition that the subjects continue to enjoy protection so they can go about their own lives.

Bobbitt goes on to note:

> By thus making civil society the field of competition for numberless private myths, the State sows the seeds of its own destruction because it has become marginal to the production of meaning,

> while private interest groups, each organized around its own myth, try to capture the machine of government. Meanwhile, the lives of the citizens dissolve into consumerism, hedonism, and an attraction to cults. According to Schmitt, 'the value of life stems not from reasoning, it emerges in a state of war where men inspirited by myths do battle.'[108]

By failing to redress the normative vacuum that haunts the market state, neo-baroque law risks inviting Lenin's "law as terror," what Italian fascists, such as Marinetti, romanticized as the fusion of war and beauty.[109] The risk of aestheticizing law and politics in this way persists so long as the longing for mythic significance cannot be grounded in and directed by a compelling ethical vision, together with the discipline to practice it. Whether it is the myth of the totalized state or of the stateless, totalized digital subject (that monadic, nomadic cyborg), the emotional intensities such myths hold out ultimately remain contingent and unstable. That is why the appeal of Schmitt's totalitarian ideology of "friends" and "enemies" remains potent. It engages the natural language of terror which is indigenous to the state of emergency. In the face of baroque longing, totalitarian ideologies emerge to anchor migrant fears and triumphs.[110] That is the temptation to which Heidegger and Schmitt regrettably surrendered.

Baroque longing invites mythic narratives, and mythic narratives invite mythic violence in their name. We may speak of this as the pseudo event of specious revelation. Metaphysical temptation spurs the will to annihilation, the triumph of death over life. This is where the aestheticization of politics and law, and the concomitant totalization of knowledge, power, and desire, take us. In its claim to mastery, totalization mocks the sublime, and in its willingness to subordinate others to its specious ideals, totalization subverts the ethical. This is the path to tyranny and injustice.

Yet, in the culture of the baroque a profound longing persists. At its core, an uncanny horror abides. We glimpse this reality in the dream life of the psyche, and in the dream life of law. A sublime horror fuels the profusion of appearances in the futile hope that the delight of imaginary forms will distract us from our longing and our terror. A similar longing, at the dawn of modernity, inspired Descartes to undertake his search for a way out of the profound epistemological, metaphysical, and political impasses of his time. Descartes' ascetic discipline, his systematic denial of the body's senses, helped to create a path beyond the pathologies of the seventeenth century baroque. Perhaps a new discipline (a new "ascetic apprenticeship," as Benjamin put it[111]) is needed today as we confront a similarly baroque maze of impasses. But if that is so, it will need to be fundamentally different from

Descartes' method of systematic doubt. After all, his was a time when the visual culture of pre-modernity was in the process of being eclipsed by the dominance of mass-produced texts. Descartes' disembodied rationality comported well with the emerging positivist model of textual abstraction. Today, however, the conditions are reversed. The decline in our time of the Cartesian ideal of disembodied rationality coincides with the worldwide ascendancy of digital, interactive, visual culture. If a collective forgetfulness of the visual sublime may have served the rise of modernity's positivist mindset, it disserves the quest for alternatives sparked by that mindset's decline.

The digital baroque calls for a new mindfulness, one that integrates the affects of the body's senses with the mind's natural capacity to transcend itself in attentiveness to that which is other. The cultivation of this ideal of attunement, with its renewed ties to the aesthetic and ethical sublime, requires a mobilization of resources equal to the one that launched modernity. But what resources are at hand to support such an undertaking? Fortunately, changing cultural conditions allow previously forgotten or occluded ones to come into view. Consider in this regard the story of Oedipus. Sophocles tells us that when Oedipus came to rest at Colonus after a lifetime of suffering he anticipated the reversal that was called for. Just before he dies, Oedipus asks to be taught. In that moment, the arrogance of reason, driven for so long by the will to mastery, is at last humbled. And that act of self-demotion seems to occasion another epistemological and perhaps metaphysical possibility. According to Sophocles, in Oedipus' final moment a divine grace mysteriously seizes Oedipus, perhaps redeeming him.[112] As Goux puts it, the sacredness of the impure meets up with the sacredness of the purified: "By virtue of his avoidance and delay, by virtue of delayed passage, it is Oedipus's entire life that has been initiatory . . . Existence itself has become the trial, and death the supreme passage."[113]

Is this suggestive of the ascetic apprenticeship that we must undergo before we, too, may gain a new clarity of mind and judgment?[114] Is this the "reversal" of which Benjamin spoke? By casting off the baroque pall of the Oedipal perversion of the ancient monomyth may we at last be rid of the "onrushing conqueror" to whom Benjamin alludes, that master of false mastery who remains trapped in the infinite folds of arrogant reason? What else do the "old books" hold out for us if not this tragic wisdom, leading us back, under the tutelary guidance of "the new advocate" to "the gate to justice?"[115]

If only Oedipus had confronted earlier, and worked through, in the appropriate ritual ordeal, the symbolic renewal of royal investiture, then perhaps the death of the symbolic monster might have been substituted for the death of the father. Then, the uncanny origin of sovereign authority, in terrifying violence, might have been faced head on and symbolically transformed. Then the hero's triumph would be complete: the grail of legitimate succession would be in hand, along with the renewed possibility of justice. But the blindness and self-conceits of baroque culture offer no such wisdom. Deprived of grace, gripped by terror, unable to confront much less accept the reality of violence and death, the baroque subject remains imprisoned in a spectacle of aesthetic delight. Intensified affects, fueled by unfettered fantasies and desires, keep the baroque subject wrapped (rapt) in the endless folds of denial, in perpetual deferral of the real. Life becomes a dream. This is what it means to live in exile, like Oedipus before he reached Colonus. We stand before the locked door of the law, a door that can never be opened, for the key, embodied perhaps in the tragic wisdom that completion of the universal monomyth holds out, has been lost.

In *Mulholland Drive*, David Lynch stages a horrifying *mise en abyme*, powerful enough, perhaps, to awaken us to the terror of the abyss that lies at the core of neo-baroque longing. Perhaps this is the necessary precondition to initiating the quest for alternatives. Perhaps our encounter with the sublime terror of the neo-baroque will blast open a path that leads to renewal, to other, more salutary expressions of the sublime. By deconstructing the impulse toward (false) mastery amid twisted forms of power, knowledge, and desire, perhaps there is a way to renew a shared aspiration to justice. Ever mindful of the historic dangers of mythic longing, and the violence committed in its behalf, perhaps a path to the ethical sublime may yet be found.

Law Dreams . . .

In this chapter, I have construed the neo-baroque vision that unfolds in *Mulholland Drive* as a cultural template for what the dream life of law might be like. That vision invites us to confront law's otherness, particularly the repressed violence of its origin. When we visit the dream space of law we confront law's debt to its unconscious. Monstrous, incoherent forces and untapped meaning making power lie buried in the symbolic life of the law. Like initiates, passing through the purgatory of ritualized confrontation, we dare to face the source of our terror and of our longing for something more valuable, and more authentic than the baroque spectacle that endlessly re-enacts denial. Might forgotten sources of meaning come to mind once baroque fantasies fueled by unfettered desires are worked through? Will this help the visual spectacle of law return to life? Law dreams, and in dreams begin responsibilities.

The great gift of culture is to give meaning to, and in so doing normalize, the constraint of desire in the service of freedom. Accordingly, one of the key queries that lie at culture's heart is: what is the proper relation between law and desire, discipline and pleasure? What sort of constraint – in the name of what meaning or value, toward what end – best serves our understanding of ethics and justice? With this central query before us, it becomes plain why cultural criticism plays such an essential role within free societies. The cultural critic affords the community an opportunity freely to assess how power stands in relation to meaning. If the rule of law is distinguishable from naked, self-interested force (and law's legitimacy requires that this be so), then we need to ask: how is that difference to be understood? Is the extant relationship between law and power optimal, or might it be afflicted by some as yet undiagnosed pathology?[116]

So far, we have explored the cultural and intra-psychic negotiation of power, knowledge, and desire in order to ascertain and assess how baroque law stands in relation to power and meaning. By asking what are the cultural values and imperatives currently in circulation within society, we seek to learn more about the principle of constraint that edifies freedom and disciplines desire. The examination of individual and collective pathologies drives and informs the diagnostic process and fuels the ensuing search for corrective measures. Out of a desire to understand what sort of justice, if justice it is, lives by the law of our time, in this chapter we have directed our attention to the extant cultural and intra-psychic configuration of power, knowledge, and desire.[117] This marks the movement downward (and in), toward the abyss that lies at the heart of digital baroque longing. The next step will lead upward (and out).

As in the reading of myths and fairy tales, and in dream work generally, a crucial function of initiatory rites is to consciously confront, even to the point of being swallowed up by (in order to overcome[118]) deep-rooted terrors. We have explored this theme in order to assess the initiatory implications of Lynch's cinematic dream work and its affinity with what was regarded in pre-modern times as the ordeal of justice. I have argued that the Lynchian dream state offers a window onto a political "state of exception" (in Giorgio Agamben's sense[119]) in which the terms of law's legitimation, classically conceived as the conditions of legal-political succession, are starkly revealed. The dream of law's rule lays bare the power of the exception that lies at its heart. A state of crisis disrupts the veil of normalcy both in our personal lives and in the life of the law. By deliberately simulating on the screen (and perhaps even inducing in real life, even if momentarily[120]) such a crisis, Lynch's cinematic *mise-en-abyme* reveals hidden realities. In this case, I have contended, the reality that we glimpse pertains to the actual condition of state power in contemporary society. It is a condition that corresponds in significant respects to the one Gershom Scholem evoked, referring to Kafka's famous parable of law. Scholem described it as the triumph of power over meaning – a state of affairs in which the law retains validity, but lacks significance.[121]

We recognize this as Carl Schmitt's state of exception,[122] a condition that Jean-Joseph Goux re-describes in mythic terms as a breakdown of the ancient ritual of royal succession. This momentous failure, which according to Goux Sophocles recounts in the tragedy of Oedipus, is characterized by a fateful substitution. The terror-bound, but ultimately epiphanic rite of passage toward deeper self-knowledge, social wisdom, and political and legal legitimation is displaced by the philosopher's quest for mastery through abstract categorization, deductive and inductive logic, and instrumental rationality. The ensuing subversion of the ancient succession rite is Oedipus' bequest to Western culture. We are still grappling with its ramifications for law and justice in our time.[123]

Mulholland Drive reinvokes this fateful perversion by symbolically restaging the Oedipal derangement of knowledge, power, and desire. In this neo-baroque version of Sophocles' tale, by going under, and within (into the mysterious depth of unconscious desire), the dreamer gains hidden knowledge about who she really is, and how knowledge, power, and desire actually operate in the psyche, and in the world. Here lies the symbolic code of law's unconscious. In the epiphanic completion of the rite of succession we re-encounter law's primal dream of the ordeal of justice, the wellspring of meaning from which lawful rule originates. What was once concretely ritualized, and collectively enacted in the open amphitheater, which also served as the ancient site of Athenian law making, has now moved to the shared dream space of film.[124] And so we watch, hoping for the renewal of tragic wisdom, an event that may yet revitalize the aspiration to justice upon our re-emergence under the sun.

Film director Lynch – like the magician-emcee in *Café Silencio*, a Prospero-like figure and Virgil-like tutelary guide to the underworld, the psychoanalyst's kindred spirit – plays out the contemporary role of the initiate-initiator. Diane Selwyn's story, like Oedipus's, shows us the face of intra-psychic and cultural-political discord in our time. In this way, Lynch, like Sophocles in his day, fulfills the function of cultural diagnostician. He, too, shows what needs to be corrected, and motivates us to move toward rooting out not the poet-messenger or the symbol-rich message that he bears, but the pathology that his message reveals.

Ritual restores the moral conscience to itself, both in interior isolation and in collective practice.[125] Might one, perhaps the most crucial function of culture be ritual initiation, the provocation of a crisis of conscience, a deliberate dislocation or disorientation of self so that the pathologies of ordinary life (living under the rule of exception, in the state of emergency) may be revealed?[126] Yet, if our descent with Lynch leads us to a re-enactment, in the symbolic dream logic of film, of the mythic basis for legitimating law through justice, as constituted by power, knowledge, and desire harmoniously configured, it is also fair to say that Lynch does not provide us with a vision of what that configuration might be. In the pre-modern fashion of Dante, and the late modern fashion of Eliot, following our descent with Lynch into the hellish baroque labyrinth of Diane Selwyn's dream world, the task ahead is to seek the upward path, the one that leads out of the abyss into a world of reconstituted justice – the realm of the ethical sublime.

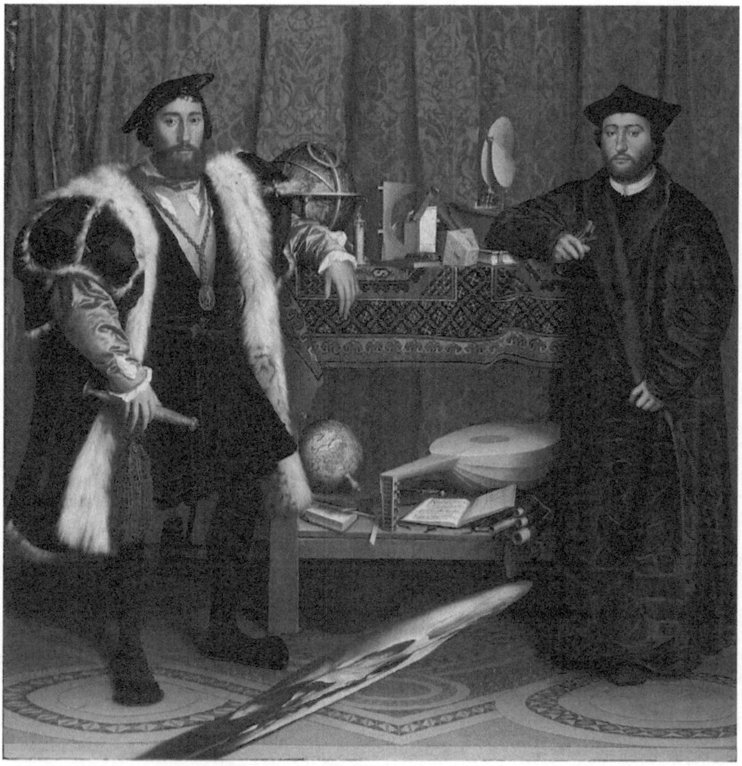

Image 2.1 *The Ambassadors*, Hans Holbein the Younger (1533). With permission of the National Gallery Company. © National Gallery, London

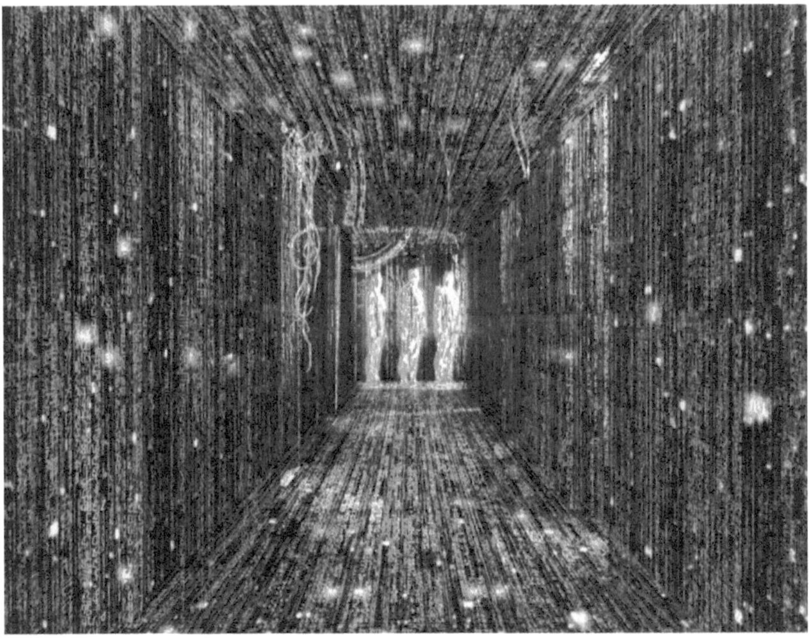

Image 2.2 *The Matrix* (1999). Dir.: Andy and Larry Wachowski. With permission of Warner Bros Entertainment, Inc.

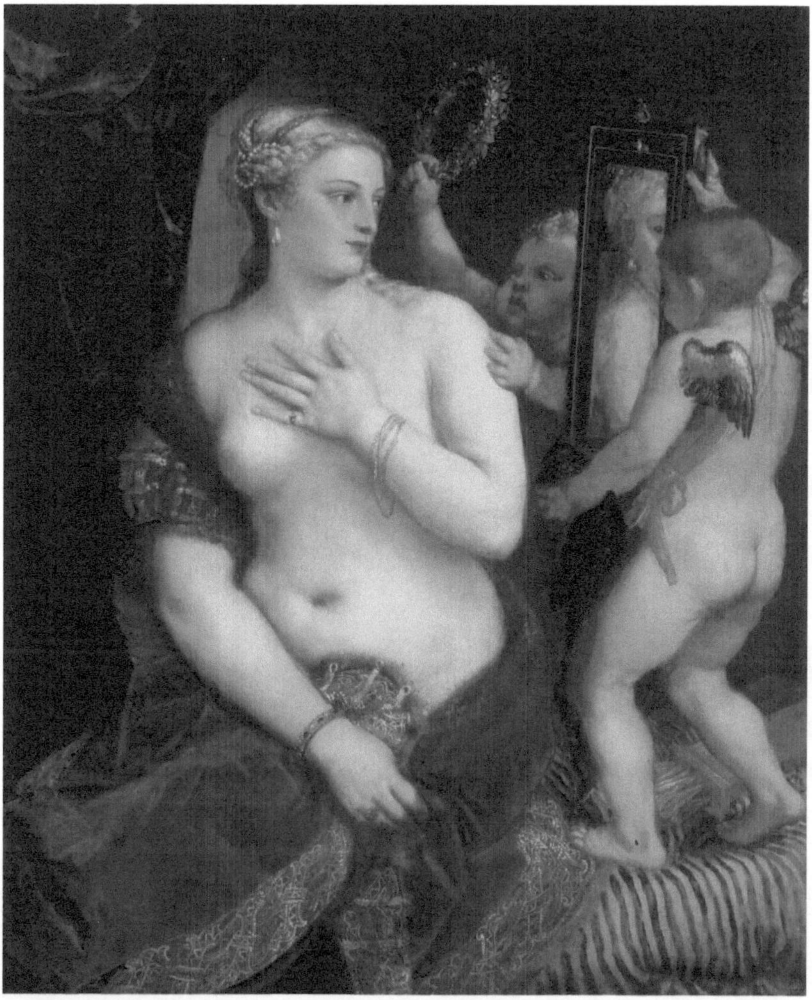

Image 2.3 Venus with a Mirror, Titian (*c.* 1555). Andrew W. Mellon Collection, courtesy of the National Gallery of Art, Washington, DC

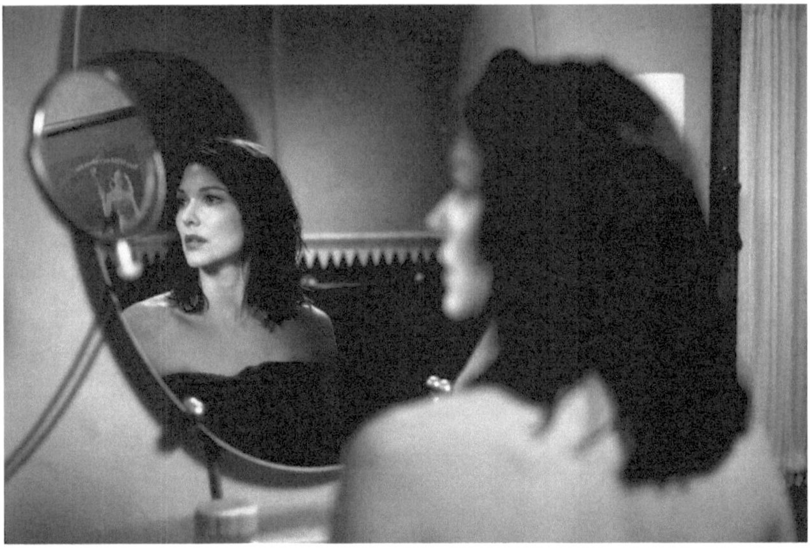

Image 4.1 *Mulholland Drive* (2001), Laura Harring. Dir.: David Lynch. With permission of Universal Studios and Studio Canal

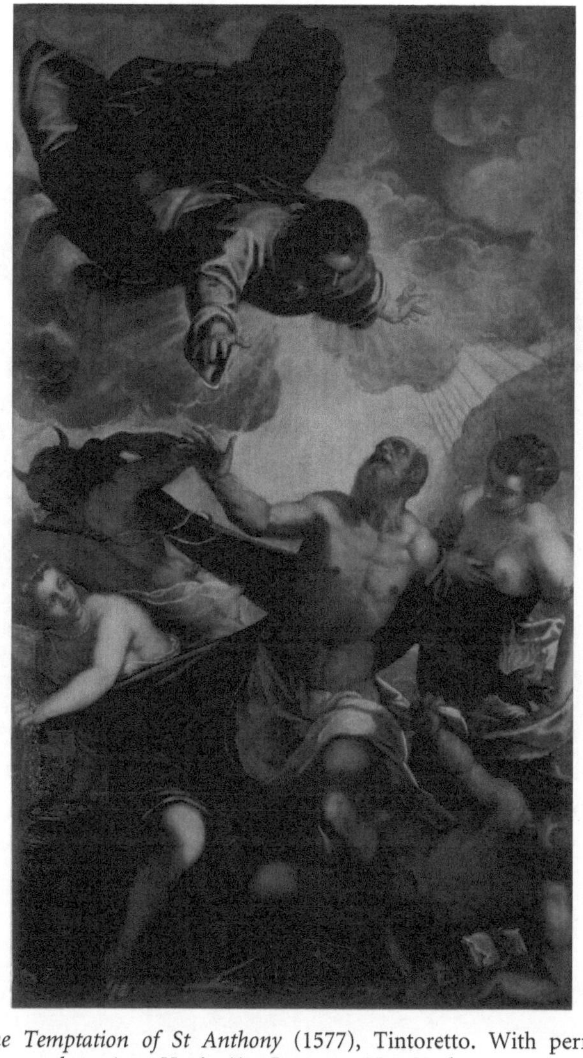

Image 5.1 The Temptation of St Anthony (1577), Tintoretto. With permission of Cameraphoto Arte, Venice/Art Resource, New York

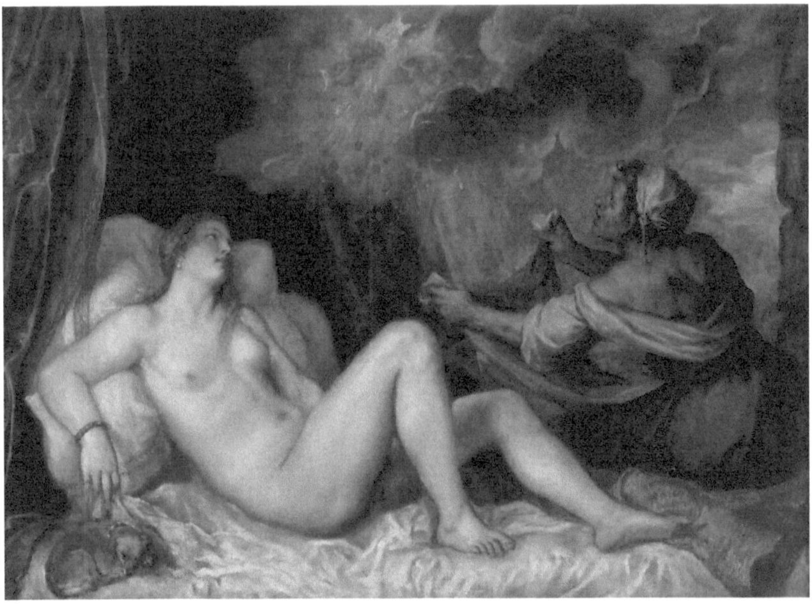

Image 5.2 *Danae* (1544–1546), Titian. With permission of the Museo Nacional del Prado, Madrid

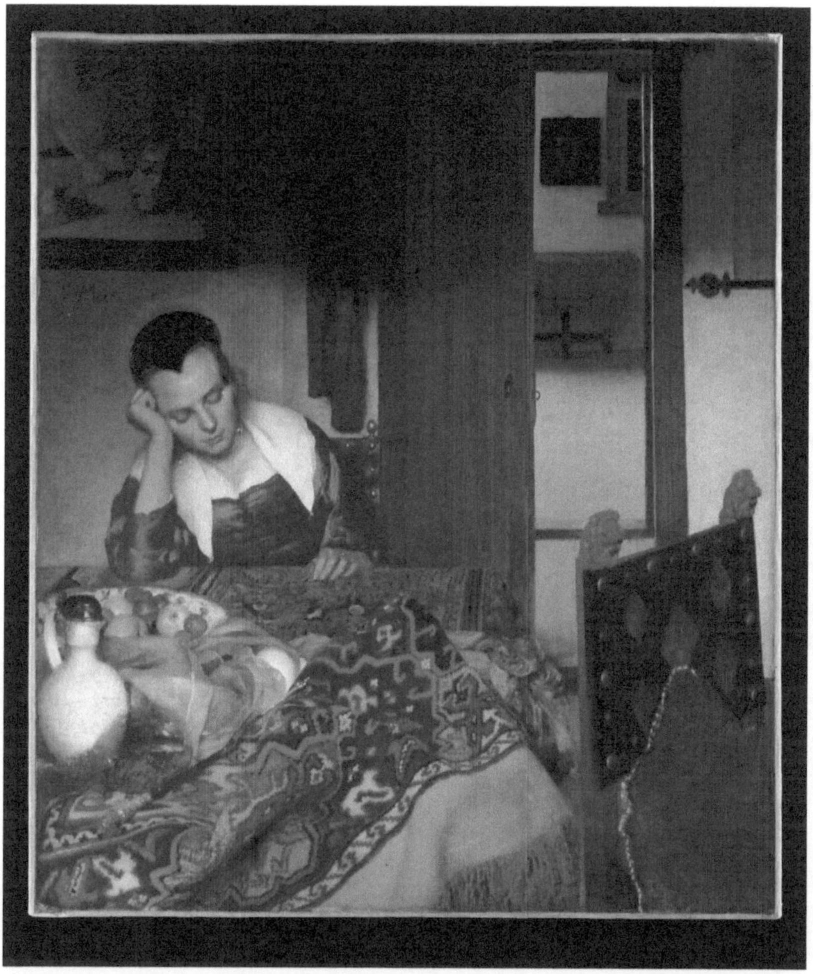

Image 5.5 *A Maid Asleep*, Vermeer (1656/1667). With permission of the Metropolitan Museum of Art, New York. © The Metropolitan Museum of Art/Art Resource, New York

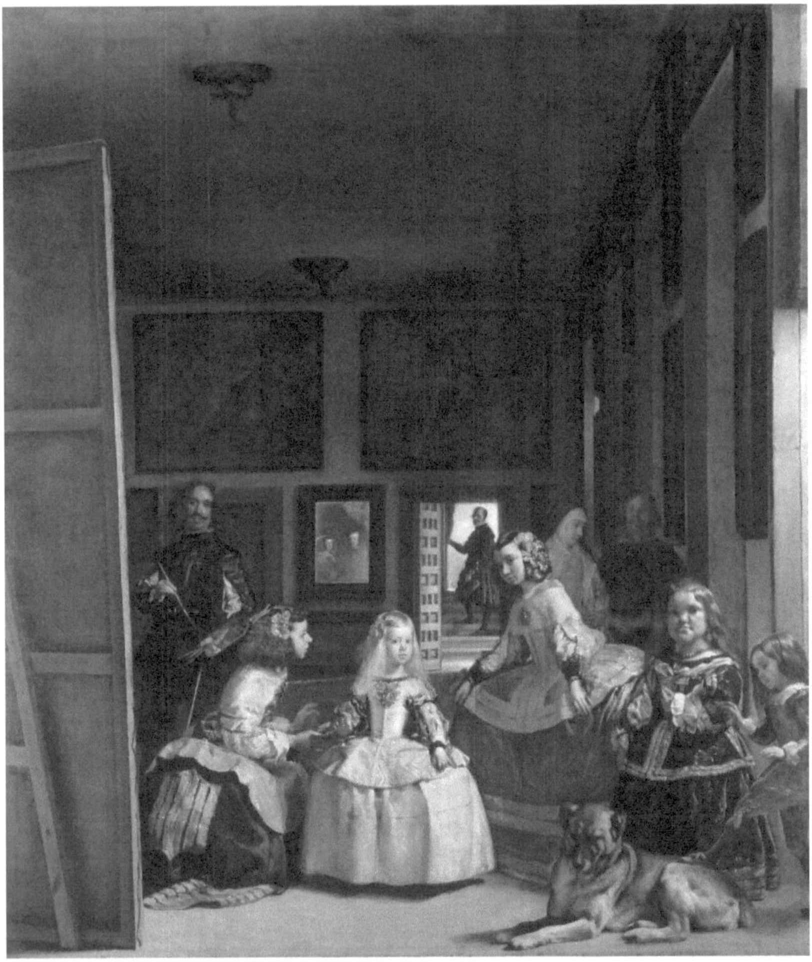

Image 6.2 *Las Meniñas* (1656), Velázquez. With permission of the Museo Nacional del Prado, Madrid

CHAPTER 5

Theorizing the Visual Sublime: Law's Legitimation Reconsidered

> [E]very epoch is defined by its own practices of knowledge and strategies of power, which are composed from regimes of visibility and procedures of expression.
>
> (D. N. Rodowick[1])

> Metaphysics grounds an age in that through a specific interpretation of what is, and through a specific comprehension of truth it gives to that age the basis upon which it is essentially formed.
>
> (Martin Heidegger[2])

> Law is a form of sublime poetry because its utterances are believed and because it creates reality.
>
> (Giuseppe Mazzotta[3])

What cultural resources are available to help us shore up the legitimacy of law as image in the age of the digital baroque? Visual images move us, but not necessarily with a moral compass in mind. As the previous chapters suggest, absent some shared sense of ethical constraint, visualizing law risks succumbing to the singular logic of subjective desire and the flattened intensity of sensation. The challenge we face is how, amid the dizzying proliferation of images, are we to orient ourselves toward the authentic and the authoritative. We need emotional knowledge to activate judgment. But we remain uncertain about how to vouch for the normative process that authorizes the judgments that images set in motion. In short, we have reached a point similar to the historic juncture that marked the birth of modernity. Now, as in the baroque era of the seventeenth century, the metaphysical anxiety of iconoclash calls out for a "third way" beyond the familiar oscillation between impugning the artifice and deceit of the image on the one hand, and rapt immersion in the spectacle of visual delight on the other.

At the outset of modernity, Descartes' rational method provided that alternative. It offered a way beyond the failed correspondence theory of medieval optics, and it provided allegedly neutral ground beyond the reach of the warring passions and "deceits" of the senses. But today the image is back, and the Cartesian ideal of disembodied knowledge has lost its cachet. Scientific explanation continues to be a source of technological power and intellectual progress; yet, experience has taught us that science alone has little to say about the meaning of the good life. A tool cannot define its purpose. And today, there are too many tools, too many signs, too many principles, and too little consensus.

In this respect, the pictorial turn in law is a source of new opportunities as well as new dangers. On the one hand, new visual technologies allow advocates to quickly communicate complex ideas, events, and processes in an accessible and credible manner. Visualization also allows advocates to infuse knowledge with the vitality and normative directedness of situated human emotion. At the same time, however, these new visual tools risk over-reliance on perhaps inappropriate (or inappropriately amplified) emotions. Images also elevate the tacit over the articulate in the decision-making process. Visual common sense may claim certainty, but it remains at a loss when asked for reasons warranting it. Judgment thus becomes a largely subterranean affair, submerged beneath the surface of consciousness, amid the hidden eddies of ingrained habits of perception based on familiar associations and the shared folk models, stereotypes, and prejudices that we assimilate from the largely visual culture in which we live. The proliferation in legal practice of a diverse array of images, absent a level of visual literacy sufficient to test their reliability and rein in the potential for emotional excess, sensory distraction, and the suspension of critical reason, places pressure on the pursuit of fact-based justice at trial and beyond.

Modern jurisprudence has staked much on the reliability of text-based rules and conventions. The medium of text generates its own rhetorical field of descriptive and normative practices and expectations. The stories we tell and the values those stories embody, the rules we apply and the norms that govern their interpretation, are all part and parcel of the medium in which they are rooted. The shift to a visual medium obliges legal theorists and practitioners alike to come to grips with a new set of cognitive and cultural tools, methods, and norms. We do not respond to visual images the way we read a text. There is no escaping the abstract nature of words on a page. But images want nothing so much as not to be an image. They want reality, to be taken as equivalent to what they show, and we are inclined to grant them their wish. What does this mean for law, particularly when digital signs not only deny they are signs but also that they need any external reality to warrant the truth they assert? What is the truth of the digital image, that aniconic simulacrum?

In recent years, we have witnessed expressions of profound mistrust regarding the simulacrum. This concern ranges across a broad cultural spectrum, from academic iconoclasts, like Jean Baudrillard whose critique of the visual simulacrum urges us to exorcise the "evil demon of images," to Islamic fundamentalists who have raged against the proliferation in Western secular culture of all manner of potentially idolatrous images. In popular culture we witness a similar iconophobic anxiety, whether it is the paranoid fantasy that we are all living in a dream world generated by a "neural interactive" computer program (as in *The Matrix*), or are unwitting participants in a video game (as in *eXistenz*), or in an alien race's experiments (as in *Dark City*). Or perhaps we are living out memories that have been strategically (or traumatically) altered (as in *Beautiful Sunshine of a Spotless Mind*, *Memento*, and *Inception*).

Notwithstanding the pervasive anxieties of iconoclash, we instinctively cling to the notion that a prudent position surely must lie somewhere between the extremes of iconoclastic violence on the one hand, and iconophilic utopia on the other (as in *The Matrix*, that "world without rules and controls, without borders or boundaries ... where anything is possible"). Yet, how exactly we are to live with the uncertainty of iconoclash has remained unclear. This impasse is bound to continue until the deep-seated metaphysical anxiety underlying the baroque imaginary of our time, like the one Descartes' generation faced in theirs, is confronted and worked through. In short, until we overcome the epistemological, ontological, and ethical impasses of iconoclash, law's migration to the screen will inevitably partake of the same metaphysical anxiety that we find in contemporary visual culture at large. That anxiety is a destabilizing force for law; it erodes confidence in the law's search for truth and its capacity to render justice in particular cases.

My chief objective in this chapter is to begin building an alternative to the limited Cartesian model on which modern jurisprudence still largely relies. The times call for a radical reconceptualization of law. I believe this effort encompasses three interrelated claims:

1 With law's visualization comes *iconoclash: How can we place our trust in visual images?* Tensions between old and new mediations of reality tend to generate a heightened awareness of the rhetorical (or constructed) nature and function of mediation and of the clashing aesthetic, epistemological, and ontological assumptions that underpin different kinds of mediations. The breakdown of medieval optics and the rise of mass produced texts at the onset of modernity was one such historic transition. The shift from text to digital visuality today is another.

2 Iconoclash may give rise to heightened iconoclastic impulses: *these impulses harbor a strong anti-rhetorical component. They express a wish to destroy mediation for the sake of getting at the naked truth, brute facts,* the second order reality of *Reality itself.* But if second order reality is not mediated, if it is not even susceptible to mediation, how can we hope to know, much less communicate its meaning? And if first order reality is all there is, just the endless profusion and transformation of digital forms, how do we meaningfully frame otherwise equally fungible visual expressions in a stable discourse of truth and value?

3 Overcoming *iconoclash* requires aesthetic, ontological, and ethical clarification as well as metaphysical resolve: *We need to develop a better understanding of visual proof and persuasion in the digital age. But we also need to clarify the way we distinguish a source of meaning from the aesthetic means of its mediation. In a word, without a new metaphysics, epistemological and ontological anxiety will persist.* We need benchmarks – a new rhetoric of visual eloquence – reflecting a more sophisticated understanding of digital mind and culture together with an enhanced attunement to the aesthetic and ethical sublime.

In this chapter, I contend that a cognitively and phenomenologically informed approach to law as visual image will help guide our passage from a practice steeped in words to one in which words compete with all manner of visual images. And yet, even with new aesthetic and epistemological benchmarks in hand, absent ethical guidance they will remain problematic, for they will not lead to metaphysical resolve and the ethical confidence required for prudent judgment in concrete cases. In short, we need an ethical optics that can help us to critically confront and meaningfully constrain the flow of images in the light of that which authenticates and authorizes the meanings they generate. I shall refer to this new model for law as visual jurisprudence.

Visual jurisprudence builds upon two different kinds of knowledge both of which gained early recognition in the Legal Realist movement. I have in mind, on the one hand, the descriptive model of explanatory knowledge that we find in the natural and social sciences and, on the other, the rhetorical (metaphoric, visual, or narrative-based) model of interpretive and prudential knowledge (what the ancient Greeks called *phronesis*, or "practical wisdom") that we find in the humanities. Much has been written about the Legal Realist contribution to jurisprudence. It has been called "the major event in twentieth century American legal practice and scholarship."[4] Yet, many misconceptions and distortions dog its legacy.

There are two points worthy of emphasis at the outset. First, while Legal Realists expressed a burgeoning confidence in the social sciences, it is important not to confine the Realist contribution, particularly in the knowledge domain of cognitive and cultural psychology, to simplified linear-causal models of scientific explanation. Second, while it is also the case that Legal Realism emerged during the "heyday of positivism,"[5] that was not the only influential philosophical movement active at the time. There are strong indications that Legal Realist thinking also was influenced by the pragmatist philosophy of William James as well as by philosophies of immanence, or creative process, championed by such philosophers as Henri Bergson and Alfred North Whitehead. Positivist scholars like Brian Leiter tend to elevate the model of the natural sciences to the detriment of both the pragmatic and creative process strains in Realist thought. This obscures the full import and transformative potential of the Legal Realist contribution to legal theory and practice. Correcting this omission allows us to build upon the Legal Realist legacy. For it turns out that Legal Realism not only provides a workable intellectual scaffolding for understanding, in a descriptive sense, the way decision makers generate *visual* meanings, but it also lays the groundwork for a more robust phenomenology of legal judgment. The latter leads us beyond the purely descriptive model of the sciences; indeed, it helps to account for the moral vitality of judgment, the dynamic push toward justice that Realists frequently addressed in their writings. This more expansive treatment of the Realist legacy also helps to overcome the normative isolation of Leiter's and, more generally, legal positivism's so-called "naturalistic" approach to law. By intuiting the demands of justice or fairness in the particular case, decision makers ensure that law renews itself in a dynamic, self-correcting, incessantly creative process. An adequate understanding of this process requires that we attend to the ontology and epistemology of text-based as well as image-based decision making.

Before teasing out in more detail the limitations of the legal positivist approach to Legal Realism, it is useful to recount the ways in which it is helpful. An example of this may be found in Leiter's useful distinction between what he calls the "Core Claim" of Realism and the "Received View." According to Leiter, the Received View suffers from a popular misconception about Legal Realism. That misconception typically overstates the degree of uncertainty in the law and the extent of unfettered judicial discretion that judges typically enjoy. In short, the popular version of Legal Realism unduly relativizes judicial decision making, as is evident in the well worn, but misleading aphorism that says we can as well understand a judge's opinion by learning what he ate for breakfast. This claim exaggerates the subjectivity and hence the unpredictability of judicial tastes and values. As most practitioners and scholars of law know, there is far more predictability in the case law than this crude version of Realism allows. With the aid of a more acute analysis, the popular stereotype of Legal Realism usefully gives way to a more accurate account, which Leiter calls the core claim. The core claim of Legal Realism is that "judges reach decisions based on what they think would be fair on the facts of the case, rather than on the basis of the applicable rules of law."[6] In other words, judges primarily respond to "the stimulus of facts," in search of what Karl Llewellyn calls the "fireside equities" or "situation sense" of the case. This preliminary response is carried out by the decision maker's "intuitive faculties" which, as Judge Joseph Hutcheson put it, are "developed and made acute by the use of a trained and cultivated imagination."[7] Once having "felt their way" toward the equities of the case, judges then devise the "apologia" or "rationalization."[8] This is the stuff of case law and statues that legally warrant the outcome that has, after much labor of the brooding mind, presented itself whole in the form of an intuition of the just or right outcome. As Cardozo notes (quoting Saleilles): "Once accepted, the construction presents itself, doubtless, in the ensemble of legal doctrine . . . The principle appears as an initial cause, from which one has drawn the result which is found deduced from it."

It is not facts per se that generate legal outcomes, but rather "the soul of the fact."[9] That a decision maker may not be able to critically dissect the cognitive process by which he or she intuited the right outcome does not mean that it is either arbitrary or unwarranted. Indeed, the clarity and immediacy of an intuited "situation sense" belies the complexity of cognitive incubation that led to it. What the Realists are describing here is what cognitive psychologists refer to as the "concrete, embodied, incorporated, lived" aspect of knowledge.[10] As Francisco Varela puts it, "knowledge is about situatedness." It is not about "the manipulation of symbols by logic-like rules."[11] It is not, in short, the input–output model proposed by early advocates of artificial intelligence based on standard models of scientific explanation.

The implications of this analysis are striking for rational choice theorists and logical positivists alike. Intuiting outcomes is the way we typically process conflicting facts for the sake of judgment. There is also, as William James notes, an aesthetic quality to this cognitive process. The brooding mind continues its efforts until intuition delivers the outcome that feels right. James calls this the "sentiment of rationality." This feeling – which James describes as "a strong feeling of ease, peace, rest" that accompanies the transition from a puzzled or perplexed state to a state of rational comprehension[12] – both motivates and qualifies intuited judgment. The sentiment of rationality arrests the decision maker's attention with a sense of importance and signals a sense of fit, the feeling that the judgment squares with what the case presents (the facts, precedents, statutes, and so on). In other words, just as, in James's view, truth "happens" to an idea,[13] we may say that justice happens to an intuited judgment. In this view, then, judicial intuition is a comprehensive experience accompanied by a sentiment that signals the integration of complex details into a felt unity of meaning. In the immediacy of judicial intuition (what Legal Realist Joseph Hutcheson called "the judicial hunch") the experiential basis for legal rationalization comes into view.

But how do we know what feels right *is* right? How do we know that confidence isn't overconfidence masking a host of unwitting subjective distortions, such as naïve realism (the tendency to merge image and reality)?[14] Several responses may be offered. For one thing, if the judgment resists rationalization, if it stubbornly refuses to be written, or explained in the process of deliberation, this suggests that the proposed synthesis may be lacking in articulable reasons or warrants for its assertion. Second, there follows on the heels of judgment that great staple of pragmatic thought, "the endless process of testing and retesting" out of which, as Cardozo notes, "there is a constant rejection of the dross, and a constant retention of whatever is pure and sound and fine."[15] In short, James's pragmatic rule of thumb remains valid: by its fruits we shall know the worth of a given judgment. In other words, the value of a decision consists not only in the efficacy of its resolution of the particular conflict that prompts it, but also in the work that it performs in the resolution of future conflicts as well.

It is also important to note that the immediacy and wholeness of judgment does not mean it is simply given, as if born, ready-made, out of whole cloth. The production of judicial intuition is preceded by an active and complex, albeit concealed, cognitive process of creative engagement. Varela calls this process "enaction."[16] Its seeming immediacy belies the persistent cultivation and hard work that paves the way for our "readiness-for-action." Put differently, immediacy conceals the preparatory requisites of professional training, practical experience, and heightened mindfulness that make possible "enactions" of judgment in the particular case. Without adequate preparation, the capacity to achieve the right synthesis in a given case will be hampered. Enaction, in this respect, is the embodied expression of who the decision maker is and the world she inhabits.

This understanding of the way we build judgment from individual micro-worlds and micro-identities stands in stark contrast to the model of universal, univocal reason championed by Descartes and the ensuing scientific ("naturalistic") tradition of modernity. Calculation may figure in the critical stage of rationalizing judgment, but immediacy and a sense of fit precede deliberation. Judgment in this respect is not analogous to computation. As Varela states, "it is not that we are simply unaware of the rules that govern the generation of mental images or of the rules that govern visual processing; we cannot in principle ever be aware of these rules." In short, judgment is not rule-driven or deliberative in its preliminary cognitive stage. The complex processing of stored knowledge (the folk models, narratives, and other cultural and characterological materials that make up our common sense models for how the world works and how people may be expected to behave) operates unconsciously. It is as if the culture itself, or at least the particular decision maker's situatedness in that culture, were thinking through specific cognitions. In this respect, the self may be said to be culturally distributed, as Bruner puts it, along the inherited pathways laid down by the stories, folk models, and shared beliefs, values, and practices that our cultural knowledge provides. The cultural distribution of identity fragments the Cartesian unitary self. But in that very fragmentation lies the ethical dimension of judgment.

Lacan famously stated that "the unconscious is ethical in its core."[17] This claim, like Derrida's assertion that "deconstruction is justice," suggests that the first move in the cultivation of the ethical consists in the act of calling into question. It is not simply the text that we deconstruct, but also, and perhaps most significantly, our self. The practice of putting the self in question, for example, by conceding and actively attending to the dangerous snares of desire, or by challenging the rigidity of conceptual or rule-driven thought and actively opening oneself up to the creative process of enactive judgment, followed by the requisite retrospection of critical reflection, helps to cultivate an ethical posture toward conflict resolution and in one's dealings with others more generally. That posture is first and foremost a mode of attentiveness to that which lies beyond the domain of self. To be attentive is to be responsive, and ultimately to take responsibility for the situation or the other that the attentive mind encounters. The more the mind is uncluttered by self-ensnaring desire, the more attentive it can become to the demands of others and of the particular conflict situation at issue. In this respect, it is not so much the imperative of an abstract moral principle or the application of pre-existing rules that motivates judgment, as it is the human capacity to encounter and adequately respond to extrinsic demands. When Legal Realists like Karl Llewellyn refer to the "situation sense" or the "fireside equities" of a case they encourage the brooding mind's capacity to dwell attentively amid a cluster of concrete particulars in anticipation of intuiting the situation's normative significance.

There is, to be sure, a perpetual incompleteness to this process. Like Bergson's intuition of infinite duration, symbolic ideals (beauty, justice, freedom, and so on) are similarly infinite in scope; their particular instantiations are always imperfect. Those instantiations emerge out of mind's active engagement with the dynamic flux of concrete particulars. The ethical wisdom that a given judgment expresses in a particular case tests the scope and range of inherited rules and judicial decisions which come into play during the post-intuitive rationalization process. These sources may need to be adapted to what justice requires under the circumstances. In this way, inherited rules avoid scholastic sterility.

The Realists, I want to claim, were privy to this ethical knowledge as well as this intuitive methodology. Their approach repudiated legal formalism to the extent that rule-driven judgment gave way to a less well understood quest for situated "right outcomes." There remains a mystery – perhaps akin to the mystery of enchantment – in the way judgment extracts from a complex array of particulars a unity of meaning that feels right. How does mind respond to the demand for justice in the particular case? As Cardozo conceded, "We reach the land of mystery when constitution and statute are silent, and the judge must look to the common law for the rule that fits the case."[18] The *terra incognita* upon which Cardozo gazes amid the gaps of legislated or constitutional law is not the disenchanted terrain of blind causal mechanics. Nor is the mind that gazes upon this landscape divorced from what Descartes conceived as the sensorially deceived body. Meaning arises in the active encounter between the creative process of embodied mind on the one hand, and what Merleau-Ponty calls the "flesh of the world" on the other. This crucial insight into the ontology and epistemology of dynamic self-other oriented, intuited judgment is precisely what the disembodied epistemology and mechanical ontology of Descartes misses. Yet, notwithstanding the Realists' efforts to shake off this legacy, Cartesian concepts of mechanical causality and natural (scientific) explanation remain deeply embedded in modern jurisprudence, as the work of legal scholars like Brian Leiter attests. This residual Cartesianism is what sustains the crude behavioral model of Leiter's naturalistic jurisprudence (according to which "inputs yield outputs").

Simply put, resistance to the Realists' efforts to shift away from an exclusively Cartesian, rule-bound, disembodied rationality continues. Legal scholars in many quarters still resist the Realist invitation to shake off what Cardozo referred to as "the tyranny of concepts"[19] and embrace the integration of creative mind and sensate body in the fullness of intuitive experience. It is this resistance that similarly blocks the integration of textual and visual storytelling into the mainstream of legal theory and pedagogy. Practitioners, by contrast, can ill afford that omission. For them, the efficacy of creative intuition and visual eloquence inside the courtroom is warrant enough.

The dynamic unfolding of fact-sensitive judgment in the case-driven search for justice that the Realists describe also comports with the integrated and dynamic approach of phenomenology. The Realist's notion of the judicial "hunch" describes the interpenetration of mind and world that phenomenologists call "lived experience." In the Realists' integrated view, decision makers find themselves situated between the dynamic flux of endlessly unfolding realities, what Whitehead refers to as the "driving force of process"[20] (as opposed to Descartes' mechanical nature), and the intuition of endlessly unfolding duration, what Bergson refers to as "the vital impetus within us"[21] (as opposed to the positivist's logic of disembodied conventional semiotics). That the Realists' sought in their way to move beyond the Cartesian subject/object split reflects one of the key contributions to early twentieth century thought of the dynamic philosophies of James, Bergson, and Whitehead. James's radical empiricism together with Bergson's and Whitehead's notions of dynamic process argue in favor of direct realism – the idea that there is no "non-experiential 'substratum,'" as Hilary Putnam put it.[22] In other words, there is no metaphysical gulf that separates mind and the material world. This is what Bergson called "direct vision,"[23] the intuitive process by which mind places us within reality ("within the object"[24]) allowing us to "grasp it over and above all expression, translation, or symbolical experience."[25]

James's radical empiricism in conjunction with Bergson's and Whitehead's philosophies of process helped to shape and inform juridical thinking during the first half of the twentieth century, but this influence is precisely what Leiter's positivist account leaves out. This aspect of Realist thinking helps to account for the Realists' understanding of the mind's capacity to intuit what Bergson called "the inner life of things." These references include allusions to the active principle of nature (what the ancient Greeks called *physis*, and what Bergson and Whitehead refer to as creative process). Consider, for instance, Cardozo's assertion that "nothing is stable. Nothing absolute. All is fluid and changeable. There is an endless 'becoming'. We are back with Heraclitus."[26] Here we see Cardozo integrating the ontology of process with the epistemology of intuition. For example, he explicitly notes that judicial intuition (which Cardozo describes as that "deep-seated sentiment" that responsively guides the law)[27] operates against the backdrop of "perpetual flux." Intuition, in this analysis, seeks the "directive force" of principle from the chaotic complexity of lived experience. Here, according to Cardozo, is the source of law's vitality and constant growth.

Cardozo found support for his view in thinkers like Savigny and Gény. They, too, were reacting against the formalist pretext of "discovering" law as opposed to actively creating it in the face of uncertainty.[28] Gény manifestly drew inspiration from Bergson's understanding of creative process and intuition. Consider, for example, Gény's reference to "the nature of things" to which we must look "for hints to expand the intellectual form of our thought; for from there shall we derive the impetus to lift us above ourselves." He also writes about the "living structure" of social forms and "the complex and hidden tissue which envelops them and gives them life."[29] These references, not to mention Gény's explicit citations to Bergson throughout his work, unmistakably reflect Bergson's influence. Indeed, they readily bring to mind Bergson's pivotal ideas of duration, fluidity, and the "fringe." As Bergson wrote:

> [L]ife transcends intellect. The feeling we have of our evolution and of the evolution of all things in pure duration is there, forming around the intellectual concept, properly so called, an indistinct fringe that fades off into darkness. Mechanism and finalism agree in taking account only of the bright nucleus shining in the center. They forget that this nucleus formed out of the rest by condensation, and that the whole must be used, the fluid as well as and more than the condensed in order to grasp the inner movement of life."[30]

Geny's notion of the "hidden tissue" enveloping and giving life to social structure plainly echoes the dynamic, process-oriented philosophy that Bergson espoused.

In short, Bergson, Gény and Cardozo were united in their belief in the immanence of nature's and society's dynamic unfolding. As Gény puts it, "Harmony is revealed in the mass in tendencies rather than states." In this view, the free imagination of the judge operating in the gaps of law responds to that which emerges out of the incessantly flowing manifold of sensibility. Imagination schematizes without concepts. Through a free play of figuration the imagination confers upon itself a unity of meaning, an intuition of fireside equities or situation sense or right outcome, a sentiment of rationality in the service of justice. This confluence of ideas is not accidental. Realists ranging from Jerome Frank to Roscoe Pound, Benjamin Cardozo, and Joseph Hutcheson knew and respected Gény's work on creative intuition and the free play of imagination in the gaps where law remains silent.[31] More generally, sociologists of law at the time expressed deep appreciation of the contributions of Bergson's immanentism and even Husserl's phenomenology which specifically addressed the unfolding of meaning, from one moment to the next, in the relationship between mind and that to which the mind attends.[32]

Gény's sense of harmony, like Cardozo's sentiment of justice and James' sentiment of rational fit, brings to mind another influential thinker at the time of Realism's emergence, namely: Alfred North Whitehead. It was Whitehead, in an effort to expand upon Bergson's philosophy of process, who asserted that "[w]hat we want is to draw out the habits of aesthetic apprehension."[33] According to Whitehead, "[p]rocess for its intelligibility involves the notion of a creative activity belonging to the very essence of each occasion. It is the process of eliciting into actual being factors in the universe which antecedently to that process exist only in the mode of unrealized potentialities."[34] Like the occurrence of trouble that sets narrative in motion, or the strife that all ritual practices seek to mitigate, legal judgment, too, arises from conflict and uncertainty in response to which it strains to articulate new unities of meaning. In the course of that response, the decision maker shifts to a liminal state of hunching, or intuitive enaction, repairing to Cardozo's "land of mystery" from whence deeper cultural and legal values come to light. This is what anthropologist Victor Turner calls the ritual evocation of "*communitas*."[35]

Whitehead was prescient in his recognition of the way mind marks matters of fact as "important"; his thinking anticipated more recent empirical findings by cognitive psychologists. According to Whitehead, out of the flux of things in which we are immersed ("amid the infinitude of the connected universe")[36] mind experiences "interest" as "that intensity of individual feeling which leads to publicity of expression."[37] In nature, all is "connectedness," just as within the psyche we intuit the uninterrupted flow of duration.[38] How, then, do we separate out matters of fact? "Feeling is the agent which reduces the universe to its perspective for fact." Perspective, in this sense, is the outcome of feeling. "Apart from gradations of feeling, the infinitude of detail produces an infinitude of effect in the constitution of fact."[39] This is a far cry from the early modernist embrace of the triumph of logical form which we find in the static, universal perspective of Descartes.

As Martin Jay notes, Descartes' optics takes place "from a vantage point outside the mobility of duration."[40] The object depicted in geometricized space is, for Descartes, the product of an utterly disembodied gaze (the "disincarnated eye"). "Blind emotion" has been swept away from the act of perception. However, as that prodigy of Benthamite utilitarianism, John Stewart Mill, experienced early in his intellectual life, knowledge divorced from passion is deadening; we may know the good as a conceptual matter, but lack the impulse to enact it. Such is the case with knowledge that has been cut off from feeling. As Whitehead puts it, "Morality is always the aim at that union of harmony, intensity, and vividness which involves the perfection of importance for that occasion."[41] Like Mill, Whitehead realized that value arises with force of feeling, not with the disembodied abstraction of rules or principles.[42] His insight anticipates Merleau-Ponty's phenomenology of perception as well as the cognitive psychology of Varela, among others, in its reunification of mind and body in the experience of "importance" or value. "We think of ourselves as so intimately entwined in bodily life that man is a complex unity – body and mind. But the body is part of the external world, continuous with it . . . [it] is that region of the world which is the primary field of human expression."[43]

As in the ontological philosophy of Heidegger and the hermeneutical philosophy of Gadamer, for Whitehead, too, the universe itself ("the intuition of the universe as everlasting process")[44] is a source of meaning (or "ideals"). This represents a sharp shift from the early modern, Cartesian and Hobbesian orientation toward meaning as the offshoot of conventional signs. According to that mechanistic perspective, man is essentially a thinking machine. Ideas issue from reason (what Descartes refers to as the soul) rather than the body, with its "deceptive" sensory inputs. This Cartesian epistemology differs substantially from the view of process philosophers like Bergson and Whitehead who regard our primary experience of value or worth as a form of embodied enjoyment. When we experience something meaningful we say "here is something that matters."[45] That sense of importance or value is what "the primary glimmering of consciousness" reveals. The shift we discern here toward the tactile and the aesthetic (the pleasure we feel at the self-presentation of a unity of meaning given by the imagination) is a significant component of James', Whitehead's, and Varela's thought. Instead of being regarded (or, perhaps more accurately put, disregarded) as a source of deceit, in their view self-enjoyment helps to authenticate our experience of the creative activity that pervades nature and our social structures. Likewise, it is our experience of harmony and relief from cognitive tension (James' sentiment of rationality) that helps to authenticate intuition. In short, James, Bergson, and Whitehead reverse what Whitehead once described as the "disastrous" separation of mind and body originating with Descartes. For Whitehead, it is this division that has been responsible for the "blindness of science."[46]

Legal Realism teaches that we can learn more about the various psychological, cultural, and sociological factors, the life experience, background, and character, that make up a given decision maker's culturally situated judgment. We can also know the formal traditions – of legal training, judicial office, and social or customary practices – that grip and shape the judicial mind. Such knowledge not only provides explanatory and predictive power, but it also arms legal advocates with the rhetorical tools they need to effectively (which is to say, persuasively) interact with a decision maker's cognitive process. In this sense, Legal Realism teaches lawyers to anticipate in an informed way the kinds of stories, character types, and values that might appeal to a particular decision maker in a given case. The repeated application of this kind of stock cultural knowledge – the shared folk models that make up common sense, including our visual common sense – also helps to account for recurring patterns in the decision-making process itself. In other words, to the extent that common sense remains common among lawyers, judges, and lay jurors alike, law's predictability is strengthened. And to the extent that legal realism provides a critical method to excavate the largely submerged intuitive process through which decision makers respond to facts, it is possible to discern what decisional elements are in play. Shared local knowledge thus may be distinguished from ideological or characterological idiosyncracy. In this respect, the Realist approach to law remains pragmatic. By its fruits we may gauge the worth of its descriptive (or "deconstructive") methods.

It is at this point, however, that we need to return to that aspect of Leiter's philosophical agenda which tends to distort his account of Legal Realist thought. I am referring to what Leiter describes as the "naturalization of jurisprudence." By "naturalization" Leiter has in mind the application to law of the explanatory model of the natural and social sciences. Leiter associates Realism with American philosophers such as W. V. O. Quine, Jerry Fodor, and David Armstrong, among others, who express "profoundly naturalistic commitments."[47] They see philosophy as continuous with science and are committed to empirical methods to certify truth. Leiter believes this describes Legal Realists as well. It is true that Leiter also criticizes some Realists for entertaining a crude behaviorism (of the Watsonian strain).[48] Presumably, this critique is meant to reflect the growing sophistication of the psychological model that underpins Legal Realist jurisprudence. But here is where problems begin to surface.

By wedding jurisprudence in general and Legal Realism in particular to the virtues of "naturalization" Leiter narrows our thinking to only one kind of knowledge: namely, the scientific model of explanation. However, as cognitive psychologist Jerome Bruner has taught, explanation represents but one kind of cognitive process, namely: the kind of rational certainty that Descartes' work celebrated. But explanation does not, and cannot, account for the way mind generates meaning through stories, metaphors, and other forms of rhetorical construction. It cannot account for what the ancients referred to as "*ingenium*," not simply the capacity to remember (*Mneme*) and imagine, but also to make connections. This is the threefold structure of remembrance ("*Mnemosyne*") which the ancients identified with the muses. The dynamic, adaptive quality of the common law depends upon this threefold relationship: to *remember* that which has been given in a specific cultural context, to be able to *see* how this juridical legacy helps to bring meaning in the face of a given conflict, and to *invent* a prudent judgment capable of expressing the wisdom and justice of the common law tradition. The triple helix of memory, vision, and invention remain central to the rhetorical task of prudent lawyering.

Scientific explanation, to be convincing, depends upon the truthfulness of its assertions; stories, by contrast, depend upon their lifelikeness (or verisimilitude). Causation functions differently in each of these models. In the scientific model, causation leads to a search for universal truth conditions. In the story model, it leads to a search for the likely connections between events that make sense. What motivated the action? Grief? Revenge? Despair? As Vico taught three centuries ago, and as Oliver Wendell Holmes famously noted, in the realm of human history it is not logic (or systems of abstract rational thought) that account for meaning. It is experience, and the ordinary discourse of everyday life. The necessity of logic transcends the particularities of a given situation. Stories, on the other hand, feed on such particularities; indeed, they cannot be told without them.

Leiter ought to be held accountable for interposing at the outset a narrow version of scientific causation, a species of psychological behaviorism that elevates explanation as the dominant modality of jurisprudential thought. He achieves this by formulating the "core claim" in terms of a "naturalistic" judicial response to "the stimulus of facts." For Leiter, once we know the input, we can ascertain the output. But such reductivist thinking cannot do justice to the intuitive process by which story-based meanings are made and construed. The intentional states that set stories in motion, and that give life to our judgments in response to them, are steeped in beliefs, values, emotions, desires, and commitments. This subjective landscape is far more complex than any stimulus–response or input–output model allows.

To understand intentional states requires knowledge of mind and culture. Stories are irreducible to the kind of objective causation that we find in the natural sciences. As Bruner puts it, "stories are many and varied; reason is governed by a compelling and single logic."[49] For a story to work there must be plot and plight, a field of narrative action and an internal landscape in which characters enact subjective realities of anger, love, jealousy, and so on. There are also local felicity conditions by which audiences typically assess the truth or falsity of what is being narrated, or the value demand of what is at stake in the narrative. Stories are impelled by and help to account for breaches in ordinary expectations.

There are canonical ways for human beings to interact in the world, and stories (and movies and video games) are culture's way of archiving those expectations. When there is a social breach, a story helps to mitigate it by reasserting a norm that brings conditions back to normal or, less typically, by introducing a new norm that establishes a different end state of affairs. Stories are law-like in their normative management of ordinary expectations about the way things go and how people behave in the world. Stories stabilize reality. In the process of doing so, law's stories embody and enforce existing norms. The way decision makers respond to discrete situations (typically involving some alleged breach of an existing norm) mingles legal and socio-cultural realities. Law may have no norm to mitigate a perceived breach, or a perceived breach may cry out for a legal norm in mitigation. In the latter instance a judge will construe pre-existing norms to cover the field or build upon them to fashion a new remedy. The decision maker's "situation sense" is crucial to the search for legal norms in mitigation: the greater the perceived breach, the stronger the motivation to mitigate.

According to the Legal Realist account, intuition synthesizes discrete facts into meaningful wholes that say or show what those facts demand. This kind of intuitive synthesis is at work when authors create written narratives and films, and when readers or viewers make sense of them in response. In the process, canonical expectations are mobilized. Discrete patterns of associative logic knit together the memories, emotions, and desires that a given narrative prompts. For example, if it is a mystery, we expect the clues to add up. If it is a hero quest, we expect the protagonist to be sorely tried and to know defeat before achieving victory and returning with the grail that was sought. If it is a melodrama, we expect a clear division between good and evil, and we expect the good guys to attain victory by their own efforts, which is to say by virtue of individual character and not impersonal chance or multi-determined, systemic control.

In this sense, it is not simply the facts to which decision makers respond, for facts are rarely meaningful apart from their entanglement in a particular narrative design. To convert facts into meaning we need symbolic mediations. As Giambattista Vico and more recently Robert Cover and James Boyd White have taught, the world we live in is rhetorically constituted. Narrative is not epiphenomenal. Our commitments, beliefs, and judgments, and to a significant extent even our emotions, are outgrowths of the stories we tell ourselves and one another. As William James wrote, the true is that which is "good in the way of belief." Laws help to generate and police and sometimes recreate ways of life that are built up from symbolic ideals and core shared narratives of the community. This is, after all, the original juridical (*mythopoeic*) function of culture.

Visual storytelling is no different in this regard – though its rhetorical components may differ from word-based storytelling in view of the unique demands of the visual medium in question. For example, what works on film is not necessarily what works on the page, as numerous failed screen adaptations of successful novels will attest. Whatever the transition, whether comic book to film, film to television, or video game to film, among other possibilities, the challenge of visual adaptation and translation remains. Our uptake is culturally and cognitively complex. The model of the natural sciences is inadequate to the task of accounting for how meanings and values are constructed and construed in practice. That is why Leiter's naturalistic model, according to which nothing escapes explanatory causal reduction, inevitably falls short. For what that causal reduction elides is precisely the motive force that impels judgment, the force that we experience as the push toward fairness or justice or the right outcome in a given case. As Cardozo puts it, if the outcome a given rule yields is "felt to be unjust" it must be reconsidered.[50] It is in response to this "deep-seated imperious sentiment" that, in Cardozo's words, "keep[s] the law true."[51]

Science may describe the way we think; it may even explain the biochemistry of thought. But what explanation cannot capture is the valence, the emotional charge, and living push of judgment toward justice in a given case. Put differently, science may tell us *how* something occurs, but it has nothing to say about *why*. As Konrad Lorenz wrote, "reason can only devise means to achieve otherwise determined ends; it cannot set up goals or give us orders."[52] To the extent that law is irretrievably anchored in a complex network of social and cultural values, jurisprudence must find a way of understanding how we come by those values and the difference it makes in how we express them in different media. What meaning does a particular expression allow (or preclude) in a given context? Only from this standpoint may we adequately account, and be held accountable for, the worlds of value and meaning in which we live.

Memorable judgment sings, which is to say, its truth and rightness enchant the mind. We call this kind of communicative efficacy "eloquence." Eloquence is irreducible to the naturalistic explanations of scientific method alone. Legal positivists like Leiter are equally at a loss to explain why philosophers like Henri Bergson might characterize philosophy as the intuitive process by which we sympathetically place ourselves "within the object."[53] Naturalistic philosophy knows nothing of, and wishes to know nothing of what Bergson refers to as the metaphysics of flow, duration, or of unceasing creation ("this true empiricism"), or what he calls the "inner life of things."[54] Naturalism does not know, nor does it wish to know of Alfred North Whitehead's evocation of external reality as a dynamic process and a "gift of aesthetic significance."[55] Naturalism does not grapple with "vividness" or "intensity" as a basis for moral understanding, or as a directive to be mindful of that which lies beyond discrete forms of expression.[56]

Leiter asserts that Legal Realism aspires to naturalization because "science is the paradigm of genuine knowledge"[57] and because the Realists "came of intellectual age in a positivistic and naturalistic culture."[58] In his account, it is as if philosophers like William James, Henri Bergson, and Alfred North Whitehead never existed – much less coexisted as contemporaries of the positivist thinkers Leiter prefers to cite. But they did exist, and there is ample evidence that their ideas exerted a significant influence on Legal Realist thought.[59] This philosophical influence offers rich insight into the authenticity and authority of legal judgment. What is more, these philosophical resources help us to flesh out a post-Cartesian metaphysic capable of sustaining the ethical optics that we need to authenticate and authorize *visual* legal meaning in the age of the digital baroque.

In this respect, Leiter's characterization of Legal Realism as an invitation to "naturalistic jurisprudence" falls short of the mark. To be sure, there is a positivist element to be found in Realist circles. We hear it echo in Holmes' early claim that law is simply a "prophecy of what the courts will do." But this predictive, one might even say behavioral dimension of Holmes' Realism does not tell the whole story. For there is also the pragmatic strain in Realist thought that develops Holmes' insight that the life of the law has not been logic, but experience. The phenomenology of human experience takes us beyond abstract concepts and rules to the domain of beliefs, feelings, and intuitions as well as to the domain of unreflectively assimilated social folkways and cultural mores which help to shape and inform common sense. In short, the study of human experience leads us to probe the way mind ingeniously creates meaning anew and expresses value in the act of judgment. Science sees half the picture. Its abstractions provide a basis for explanation, but not for meaning and value. Our being in the world, our very interconnectedness with nature and others around us, is the occasion of our capacity to feel what is of importance, which is to say, what is meaningful and of value. Cultivating attentiveness creates a clearing in which that which is demanded of us comes to mind. As Whitehead writes, emotion "issues from, and it issues towards. It is received, it is enjoyed, and it is passed along, from moment to moment."[60] Mind experiencing the unity of emotion in its contact with the immanently unfolding flux of things is the ontological and phenomenological source of expressive meaning and value.[61] As Bergson puts it: "Intuition, bound up to a duration which is growth, perceives in it an uninterrupted continuity of unforeseeable novelty; it sees, it knows that the mind draws from itself more than it has, that spirituality consists in just that, and that reality, impregnated with spirit, is creation."[62] For Bergson, the intuition of this internal flow or duration (which he calls the "direct vision of the mind by the mind")[63] is the prime subject of metaphysics.[64] For him, as for Whitehead, Merleau-Ponty, and Varela, "intelligence is the prolongation of the senses."[65] Simply stated, judgment is inescapably embodied.

The image, conceived as the transposition (or metaphoric expression) of mind as matter, may be regarded as a primary source of "direct vision."[66] As Deguy puts it, metaphor is what originally brings to visibility the figure of what is not visible.[67] This is not the static transcendental metaphysics of Plato, where meanings already fixed in language are taken as original. Rather, this is creative metaphysics as the immanent unfolding of that which appears to mind at this moment. In this view, truth "can be given only in an experience." Bergson calls this experience "vision" or "contact":[68] "We call intuition here the sympathy by which one is transported into the interior of an object in order to coincide with what there is unique and consequently inexpressible in it."[69]

On this account, then, a key issue associated with law's migration to the screen concerns the epistemology and ontology of the visual image. What is really present in the forms we see on the screen? The metaphysical challenge presented in this query is not simply a matter of how we account for the cognitive and cultural meanings we bring to the image, but also what is it we respond to in the image itself? I would like to suggest that the creative process philosophers, with the assistance of phenomenology and recent cognitive studies, can help us to account for such a presence in the image, and the way in which we encounter it.

My claim here is that this metaphysical approach to creative process or immanence works in conjunction with a phenomenology of perception and intuition to account for the legitimating event of justice in particular cases. I call that event the ethical sublime. The ethical sublime arrests the recession of the real and the ethical from the spectacular landscape of neo-baroque law. In similar fashion, the ethical sublime rescues baroque legal forms from subjective insularity and contingency, which is to say, from its flight to mere sensation. On this view, Legal Realism provides a useful link between descriptive positivism (or naturalistic jurisprudence) on the one hand, and law's ongoing aspiration to justice on the other. It is the latter aspiration, both as a matter of theory and practice, that accounts for law's legitimacy. The haptic or tactile aspect of our perceptual encounter with the real in an image carries over from direct experience. It makes possible the creative fashioning of poetic metaphor and, with even greater perceptual intensity, of visual eloquence on the screen. The latter transposition brings us to the dynamic nature of mimesis in the context of visual mediation. For it is the nature of visual images, as manifestations of creative intuition in Bergson and Whitehead's sense, to go beyond abstract concepts in the fullness of visual experience. As Merleau-Ponty writes, "it is our experience, prior to every opinion, of inhabiting the world by our body, of inhabiting truth by our whole selves, without there being need to choose nor even to distinguish between the assurance of seeing and the assurance of seeing the true, because in principle they are one and same thing."[70] Here, Merleau-Ponty reflects an insight that dual process psychologists have articulated, bearing out Spinoza's prescient intuition that we tend to believe what we understand.

It is critical, particularly in the domain of visual media studies, to grasp the full import of the phenomenological and cognitive claim that what we experience in consciousness we experience as true. As Merleau-Ponty puts it: "From the moment I feel love, joy, or sadness, it is the case that I love, that I am joyful or sad, even when the object does not in fact (that is, for others or for myself at other times) have the value that I now attribute to it. Appearance is, within me, reality . . . Everything is, then, truth within consciousness."[71] The implications of this observation regarding truth in consciousness are fraught with significance in the age of digital simulation. For if I am the thirst or hate or love that I experience in consciousness, the source of that experience – whether simulated or real – is of no matter. Like Neo, we might as well be living in a dream world, and a digitally coded one at that. But does the digitally mediated image summon "all the subject's resources," does it concern him "in his entire being?" For according to Merleau-Ponty, these too are indicia of "true" versus "misguided" belief.[72] The apparent reality of feeling, it would seem, may not be a sufficient guarantor of authenticity; the reliability of judgment requires more. But how do we know how much more reality it will take, and what form, before we feel confident enough in the truth of an image?

The evocation of feeling is a sensible place to begin. Artists have long been acutely aware of the tactile aspect of the visual image. Consider, for example, Tintoretto's painting *Temptation of St. Anthony* (1577; image 5.1 – see plate section between pp. 118 and 119). We see before us a woman whose right hand slightly compresses her exposed left breast. We see her fingers press into the flesh, making an indentation. This image is intensely tactile. We feel the touch and associate immediately to its sensual impact, as does the man who is also depicted in the scene. It is the figure of St Anthony. Although for many modern viewers the flesh-searing force of his piety has waned, the effects of temptation, through vicarious physical arousal, have not. Seeing what St Anthony sees, we know what he feels. We feel it ourselves. That feeling allows us to decode the painter's depiction of St Anthony's left hand bathed in fire. That's what the temptation of the flesh, and in particular what sinful physical arousal for a man of piety like St Anthony, must feel like. It burns. The viewer's gaze – our gaze reflected in St Anthony's – registers in the flesh, even when the source of contact is an image. The image of temptation mobilizes within us what it is like to experience this kind of desire. Like activates like – that is the magic of visual mimesis. Memory is engraved in the body. We carry it in our flesh. And there is where it is awakened.

The same thing occurs when our eyes touch upon Titian's *Danae* (1544–1546; image 5.2 – see plate section between pp. 118 and 119). Titian has painted Danae's exposed right nipple with such clarity that we can discern the distinct shadow of its erection. This is a haptic image *par excellence*: arousing, titillating. The susceptible viewer responds immediately, inexplicably, as if in real life. And it is not simply the flesh of the image that we register in our flesh. We similarly discern states of mind. We read facial images for a broad range of emotional cues. For example, consider the face we see in Tintoretto's *Tarquin and Lucretia* (1578–1580; image 5.3, p. 140). See how it opens to imminent physical ravishment. This display of what may be read as excitement and anticipation (rather than fear or panic) is far more arousing (as the anticipation of pleasure always is) than Titian's earlier portrayal of the same scene (*Tarquin and Lucretia*, 1568–1571), in which the face of Lucretia expresses fear and perhaps desperation in anticipation of a violent assault. The erotic and moral registers of the two scenes are utterly different.

Images that communicate states of mind may intensify or deflect arousal. They may also shift the level of cognition from a physical to a symbolic or even hyper-reflexive plane. For example, consider Titian's *Venus with a Mirror* (1555; image 2.3 – see plate section between pp. 118 and 119). The coy goddess half-heartedly attempts to cover her naked breasts with her arms. Her mischievous smile belies the modesty of her perfunctory gesture. She seems to like being seen. But who is looking? The mirror she holds up

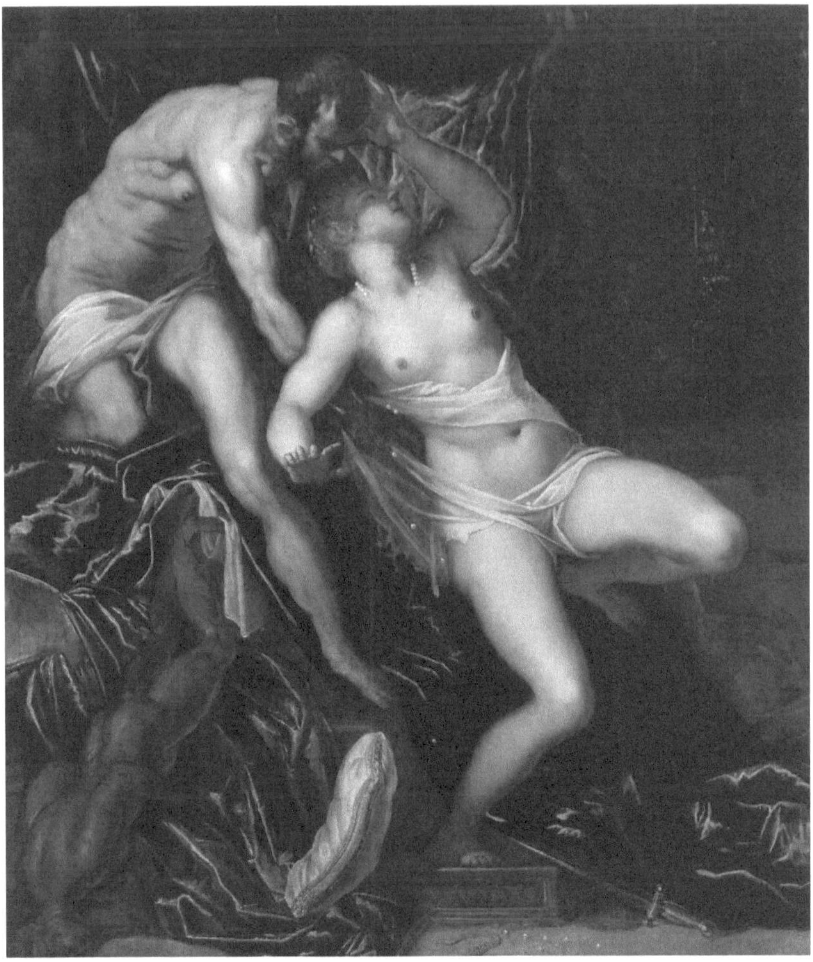

Image 5.3 *Tarquin and Lucretia* (*c.* 1578–80), Tintoretto (Jacopo Robusti). Italian, 1518–1594, oil on canvas, 68⅞ in. × 59⅝ in. (175 cm × 151.5 cm), Art Institute Purchase Fund, 1949.203, The Art Institute of Chicago

to her eyes tells us. In it we see her own image reflected back. But wait. How can this gaze be hers? The face in the mirror appears different; serious, attentive, intellectually penetrating, while the Venus who peers into the mirror coyly smiles. And look: the image in the mirror faces out, toward the viewer, seeking and meeting our gaze rather than facing back toward its unmirrored source. It is as if the mirrored image were reaching beyond the picture frame in a way that is simply impossible. It could not occur. The angle is wrong. Venus holds the mirror in a way that should not allow us to see what we see. Yet we do. And we know we do, and that we shouldn't be able to. The painter has deliberately created a gap in reality, causing a dissonance in our experience of the scene we look upon. Suddenly, it is not simply the material world, with its sensory provocations, of which we are mindful. It is something else that lies before us: a painterly world in which we are led to see seeing. The image in the mirror that meets our gaze clearly is not Venus. But who, then, is she? By disrupting the laws of perspective in order to give us this mirrored image, Titian makes visible the deceptive art of perspective itself. By breaking the rule, showing us what we could not possibly see in real life, we come to see the artifice of painterly technique. We see painting as painting. Is the penetrating gaze that emanates from the mirror the gaze of Titian himself? Is this the way the painter looks upon his subject? Is it our gaze? Is this the way the spectator is supposed to gaze upon the painter's subject? Is Titian telling us something about how to look, or about how painters look, or about the collusion that exists between painters and spectators, in an ironic exchange of looks (the painter looking back at the spectator)? Is this the way the image looks back at us, infused with a painter's intelligence, a spectator's curiosity, and the broad range of possible visual experiences laid out between the sensory, embodied landscape (of coy, naked Venus) and the intellectual plane (of self-reflexive thought being mindful of what images are, and what they do)?

Or consider the sublime paintings that Fra Angelico produced in the Quattrocento in Italy. In looking upon Fra Angelico's work we can easily identify the Christian motifs of his subjects: the adoration of the magi, virgin and child, the entombment of Christ. These are familiar signs. But wait. What is the significance of those multi-colored blotches of paint that seem to "mar" the representational accuracy of the scenes the painter has depicted with such painstaking care? The blotches do not seem to represent anything at all. So why are they there? Georges Didi-Huberman offers a reason. Fra Angelico wanted to disrupt the viewer's expectation of resemblance and lead her into a paradoxical realm of equivocation and dissemblance.[73] The enigma of shapeless form draws us away from the familiar material world before us into the mysterious domain of divine incarnation. At the core of Christian faith is the most profound mystery of all: God became flesh. How can this be? What does it mean for the divine to enter the world of the seen, to become visible, as an image? Only by moving from the physical body (of Christ) to the spiritual body, may we begin to understand this powerful enigma. In short, it requires a shift in metaphysical registers, from embodied to spiritual reality. One must alter one's perspective, from the eyes of the flesh, as Saint Paul might say, to the eyes of the spirit. But first, the material realm itself must be problematized, or "deconstructed" as we say today. When Fra Angelico challenges the conventions of perspectival figuration, when he forces us to go beyond mere representational form, he is engaging both himself and his viewers in a kind of metaphysical practice (or *ascesis*). One might call it a spiritual exercise or a rite of passage. Pictorial dissemblance prompts a reconfiguration of reality into an immaterial or spiritual register. From our experience of the utter contradiction of spiritual presence somehow inhabiting a physical frame (a human body or a painter's image) comes the uncanny epiphany of the sublime. With his application of inexplicable splotches of color Fra Angelico disrupts our perception of the physical world, and he does this in order to lead us beyond it. By showing the paradox of the sublime, the uncanny impossibility of the coexistence of material and spiritual reality, the domain of the flesh and the spirit, which is to say, the miracle of God made flesh, the painter creates a mysterious opening from which the core tenets of Christian faith may be illuminated, and given life. Like the zen master's rap on the head of a thick-witted disciple, Fra Angelica's disconcerting splotches of color jolt the viewer's eyes from one metaphysical register to another.

Of course, over time, shared cultural motifs change, and aesthetic disruption occurs in different ways, sounding in different metaphysical registers, serving different ends. For example, a sublime absence may also trigger a jarring dislocation that resounds like a silent melody, a void rich in implication, which we, as viewers, are only too willing to fill in. That is what it is like when we stand before what appear to be perfectly rendered domestic scenes depicted with infinite care and representational craft by Vermeer. Only slowly, amid the apparent calmness of Vermeer's representational worlds, does it dawn upon the viewer that something else is indeed going on. Now, however, the disruptions that unsettled Fra Angelico's otherwise familiar depictions have been moved beyond the frame. The metaphysical register has changed. As befits the secularization of early modernity, in lieu of Christianity's transcendental motifs what we now encounter is the profound (immanent) mystery of everyday life. Consider some typical Vermeer vignettes: a young woman sits pensively at her writing desk, quill pen in hand, staring out toward the painter's (or viewer's) gaze (1665; image 5.4, p. 143). In yet another scene, we see a letter writer interrupted in her task turning, with fingers quizzically touching her chin, toward a servant who presents her with a sealed envelope; or what about the maid who sits dozing at a table, behind a half-open door as a ray of light plays upon her face and upper torso and upon a jug and fruit-laden plate, their shadows finely cast (1656/67; image 5.5 – see plate section between pp. 118 and 119). Outward calm seems to prevail in these quiet domestic scenes. Except the more one looks the more one realizes that it isn't so. In fact, each scene is shot through

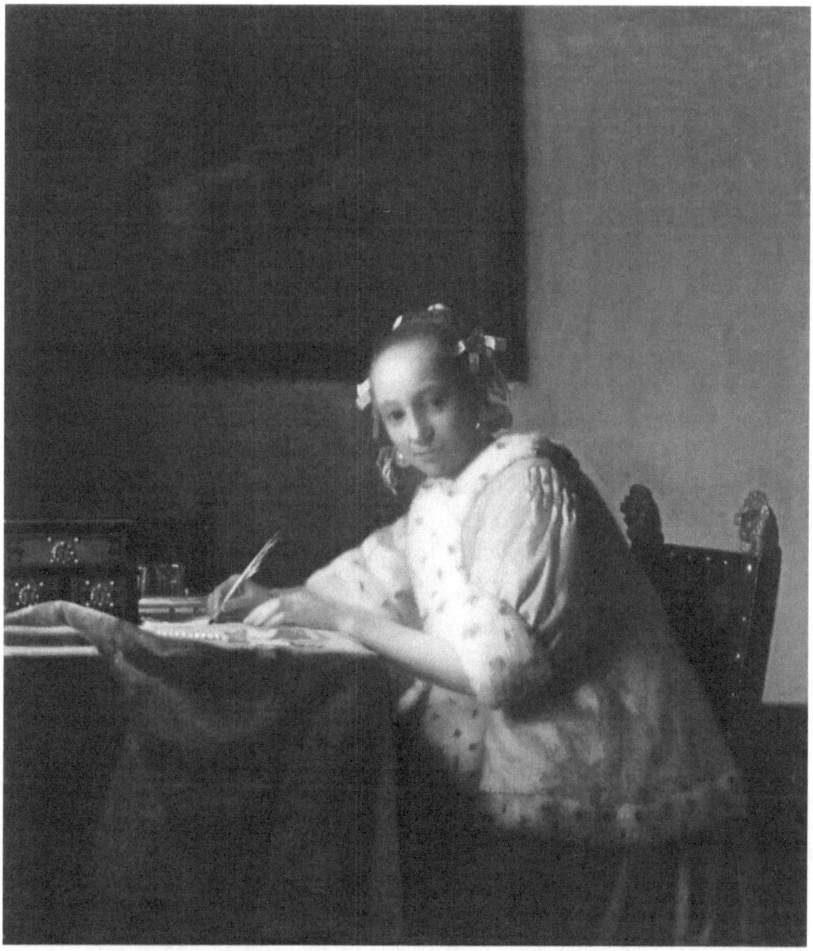

Image 5.4 The Letter Writer, Vermeer (1665). Courtesy of the National Gallery of Art, Washington, DC

with mystery – invisible perturbations animate these images with an uncanny tension. Consider the first letter writer. What is she writing, and to whom? How are we to meet the challenge of her forthright gaze? What is she thinking? The painting begs us to enter her inner world. So we gaze back at the gaze that greets us, searching a hidden reality. Or consider the equally quizzical gaze of the second writer: what are we to make of it? Does she already apprehend who the sealed letter before her is from, and what it contains? A husband away on business, or a secret lover perhaps, perhaps the very one to whom she is writing that very moment?)

And the maid who sleeps – or does she? A slight smile adorns her face. Is this the outward sign of a reverie or a dream? Whom or what is she imagining behind closed lids? What hidden image makes her smile so alluring? And look again at the setting where she sits. It, too, partakes in a mystery; it, too, reflects an animating absence. Consider the light that washes over the maid and the table she leans upon. What is its source? Is there a window somewhere, outside the frame, off to the right? Is this a mid-morning reverie, or mid-afternoon? Is it possible for there to be a window in a place that would allow light to hit her as it does? If not, is this scene real or itself a reverie? And if the latter, are we now subject to that sublime oscillation between image and reality that baroque artists spring upon us with the disconcerting effect and persistence of an infinite regress?

In short, even amid the apparent stillness and ordinariness of Vermeer's domestic scenes we encounter intimations of profound and disturbing mysteries. Only now, rather than the mystery of the Christian incarnation it may well be the baroque mystery of painting itself, the mystery of representation, what it depicts and what it leaves out, and the mystery of a hidden presence that somehow insinuates what has been left out. Harry Berger refers to the latter as Vermeer's "conspicuous exclusion" – a leaving out that is actually a "present-as-missing."[74] Vermeer lures us into the invisible domains of mind and representation (the intentional act of framing out as well as framing in). Here, then, we are drawn to the baroque metaphysics of immanent unfolding. What comes to the mind of the viewer (just as it seems to do for the figure portrayed) and what comes to light (in the scene that is shown as opposed to that which remains concealed behind half closed doors, cut off from absent windows, secreted in sealed envelopes or beneath closed lids)? The mysteries, elusively enfolded into the immediate world of lived experience, are not the only forms of absence that we can imagine. Consider, for example, the dreamlike images of surrealist painters like Joan Miro, Rene Magritte, and Salvador Dali, who hold out a different invitation. Their bizarre dissemblance of conventional representation opens up yet another register of invisible meaning. For these artists, the shock of the strange mimics the dream landscape of the Freudian unconscious. It is the same shock, and the same invitation, that we receive in the films of visionary directors like Ingmar Bergman, Krzysztof Kieslowski, and David Lynch, among other artists working in the post-Freudian era. What we are seeing, we come to learn, is not what it seems. We shall need an unconventional register of meaning, a new visual code, to solve the riddle of what is now playing out before our eyes. We may need to become adepts in the dream logic of the unconscious.

Of course, the register of dreams hardly exhausts the call of the modern. For it also comes to us in the Cubists' dissolution of objective reality and the concomitant invitation to shift away from the familiar conventions of static perspectivism. The object, after all, may be viewed from many perspectives, fragmented into many geometrical frames, which the Cubists present all at once, as if we were looking at something in the world while in motion around it, a motion picture, if you will. Or perhaps we will accept the artist's invitation to view the world stripped of representational reality altogether, as when we stand before the violet or orange hues of a massive Rothko color field. As with Fra Angelica, a similar disorientation sets in. Now, however, the eye is left with nothing but amorphous, multi-colored "blotches" writ large, the non-figural abstraction of color and shape alone. No inherited cultural motifs remain to guide or thematize our experience of the non-representative absence before us. Yet, if we allow ourselves to open up to the strangeness of this abstract expressive field, a new register of meaning emerges. The sublime catches us again, resonating uncannily in the painterly materials of color and brushstroke on canvas. Suddenly, we are transported to an unfamiliar field of meaning; in the moment of contact we find ourselves held fast, and constituted anew, by potent emotional tones, and obscure but equally potent spiritual undertones, that shape and inform the uncanny reality that the painting evokes. Why is our immersion in such a field capable of evoking tears of joy? Why does its force make one's hair stand on end? This is the uncanny ("anagogic") power of the sublime: expressing an impossible presence through a mysterious absence. And so, while the metaphysical register has changed yet again, the enigma of incarnation persists.

Film is yet another site for the uncanny event of the sublime. Who, for example, can say why, in the final scene of Kieslowski's mysterious, sublimely poetic film, *The Double Life of Veronique* (1991), the main character rolls down her car window and rests her hand upon the bark of a nearby tree. Might it be because throughout all that has preceded that moment in the film she has felt her reality split apart: first, upon learning that an identical double is living a counter-life (in Cracow) strangely attuned to Veronique's life (in Paris), and, second, upon feeling herself being swallowed up into the unfurling narrative of a puppeteer-writer in whose hands her life seems but a plaything? Like the reflected image, the uncanny double who looks back in Titian's *Venus with A Mirror*, or like Diane Selwyn's encounter with her own decaying corpse, which terminates the protracted dream sequence in Lynch's *Mulholland Drive*, for a moment Veronique (perhaps like the viewer who is drawn into her fate) shares the same dizzying, vertiginous sensation. Might she be the virtual emanation of someone else's mind, like Betty, the fantasy double who awakens into the depraved life of Diane Selwyn, or Neo, who awakens into the "desert of the real" from the dream he has been living as Thomas Anderson, an unwitting avatar, the virtual emanation of a neural-interactive simulation known as the matrix? Is Veronique, after all, just another image looking back? We shudder at the thought, and are rescued from the sublime terror of being caught in an infinite mobius strip, moving from lived experience to de-realized iteration, and back again, only to be reassured by the simple haptic gesture of a hand gently but steadily resting upon a tree, followed by the comforting feeling of being enfolded in the familiar, loving embrace that welcomes Veronique as she dashes from her car into her father's outstretched arms. The film dangles us over a sublime abyss then rescues us in haptic images that take us home again.

This quest for homecoming in the physicality of touch achieves an apotheosis of sorts in David Cronenberg's film *Crash* (1996). The film introduces us to a group of oddly alienated characters who re-enact famous celebrity car crashes. Exploiting the haptic aspect of cinema itself, here the visual image is like the metal skin of cars, a sensuous surface that rescues us, if rescue it is, from longing, and perhaps from the terror of death that drives it. And with this example the circle is complete. Having set out in search of the authenticity of the image's claim to truth, we have journeyed from the uncanny disruptiveness of the visual sublime – both in presence and in absence – only to return to the pseudo-event of the ersatz sublime in our encounter with the spectacle of empty sensation. For what is the haptic image in a film like *Crash* if not a free-floating sensation, like an arabesque dancing in the void? What else is the naked crash of images, manifest in the aimless violence and death that comes of re-enacting celebrity car accidents if not the baroque will to annihilation, the triumph of death in life?[75] Hardly a rescue at all.

In sum, the choice of registers remains, but it is the responsibility of the viewer to recognize the kind of reality that is in play. As in the disruptive reconfigurations of Fra Angelico, Miro, and Rothko, film makers and other makers of moving images also wield the power to activate alternative metaphysical registers of the sublime in its various forms. As Laura Marks notes in her descriptions of contemporary visual art works:

> In *History and Memory*, grainy old Super-8 footage smuggled from the prison camp shows a woman skating on a tiny frozen pond in the desert. In Seoungho Cho's *I Blinked Three Times* (1993), a roadside bar dissolves in a blur of colors before the eyes of a weary traveler. In Mona Hatoum's *Measures of Distance* (1988), the grainy flesh-toned images, accompanied by a longing voice-over are gradually revealed to be still photos of the artist's faraway mother. All these images are quite slight and meaningless in

> themselves, but they call up volumes of images that are not or cannot be represented."[76]

In the gap between reality and representation the viewer strains to excavate the hidden history of the image on the screen. In part, this struggle involves the viewer's cognitive engagement with memory, emotion, and a broad range of cultural templates and heuristics, unconsciously stored in the mind's toolkit for meaning making, in an effort to tame the strange with the familiar. But the struggle for meaning may also take place as a leap into the strange, an attentive immersion in the absence (of familiarity). It is this experience of the uncanniness of the image that we encountered in Chapter 3 – in the visual montage that the prosecution presented in their closing argument in the Michael Skakel murder trial, and in the video of the dance of custody that viewers watched in the murder trial of Mazoltuv Borukhova. In both cases, rather than colonize the strange with the familiar, the strange held its own. Viewers watched, and shuddered before the uncanny collapse of time in the Skakel montage, and the equally uncanny presence of incipient violence in the Borukhova video. Something new unfolded inside the courtroom. Its novelty precluded immediate understanding, for here the viewer is working at the limits of his or her ordinary knowledge and experience. Simply being with the image allows no distance for critical analysis or interpretation. That comes later, after the reality of the image has been assimilated, like an unprocessed dream, a thorn in the flesh of memory.

This shared encounter with Otherness reconstitutes our collective sense of who (and how) we are in the world among others. Film and video, in this sense, may help to constitute a living *mythos*. Law partakes of that *mythos* when it lives on the screen as a visual *nomos*. In this way, law is jurisgenerative: it conjures both a lived experience and a shared normative world in which we can believe.[77]

How, then, do we attain the epistemological and ethical confidence we need in the face of the claims images make upon us? On what basis may we trust the meanings, memories, and affects that they enact upon the body of the viewer? In response, I have proposed in this chapter that we build upon three distinct elements, all of which can be found within Legal Realist thought: (1) the descriptive (or explanatory); (2) the pragmatic (or efficacious); and (3) the metaphysical (or sublime). The challenge before us is not only to recognize the salient cultural storylines, both familiar and newly emerging, that give meaning and coherence to uncertainty, but also to cultivate visual literacy, so that when faced with the concrete demands of situated legal conflicts we can feel sure enough in our beliefs and in our reasonable doubts.[78] In this respect, visual literacy implicates three discrete fields of meaning which parallel the three elements of Legal Realism noted above. *Static meaning* refers to the structure of the image. This is what Erwin Panofsky famously described as "conventional" or "iconographical" meaning. It is what happens when an image becomes part of a larger system of reference, such as a story, or when it personifies a concept. When an image is thematized in this way it becomes what Panofsky calls a "motif," an interpretable sign. A second field of visual meaning is *enacted meaning*. This refers to the mind's active transference to the screen of internalized frames or patterns of meaning, the cultural archetypes or templates as well as cognitive heuristics (the folk models of common sense). The third field of visual meaning is *spontaneous meaning*. This refers to a sudden fullness of experience that intuitively unfolds in the embodied mind's contact with an ontological excess – what some have referred to as the "aura" of the image. Spontaneous visual meaning is the field in which we encounter the uncanny and the sublime. It is the offspring of what I would like to call metaphysical indexicality.

Indexicality is the term Peirce used to describe signs that refer to a physical trace (such as a fingerprint or the photochemical reaction to light that produces a non-digital photograph). Laura Marks describes this as haptic visuality: the way "vision itself can be tactile, as though one were touching a film with one's eyes."[79] According to Marks, we brush up against film the way we brush up against a body. Metaphysical tactility is, by extension, what it is like to brush up against an absent body that is somehow present. In short, visual images are more than conventional signs (Panofsky's "motifs") operating within systems of enacted meaning. They are also part of the immanent flux of the world around us. When viewers react to an uncanny absence – in a painting by Vermeer, say, or Rothko, or a film by David Lynch, or a demonstrative video inside the courtroom – a gap may remain between that which is encoded in the visual image and the meaning that may be drawn from it. The shock that accompanies recognition of that ineluctable gap makes the viewer shudder. This is what it is like to be drawn into the abyss between the second-hand memory of film and our desire to live it as our own. Out of that abyss the possibility of meaning arises. Or as Deleuze puts it, out of the ruins of the image comes something new. Out of an uncanny absence, which is also an ontological surplus, comes a power to restore our belief in the world of which the image is a part.[80] As Ernesto Grassi writes, "it is through the sublime, and the benumbing astonishment it arouses in us, not through logical explanations, that we become aware of reality."[81] This experience is accompanied by a supreme intensification of feeling. The living image also sparks creative intuition. An act of self-demotion – being mindful of, or responsive to, something other – places us not only within an object, as Bergson noted, but also within the lived situation that cries out for a just resolution of conflict. It is the cry from without that triggers and informs the impulse toward justice. This is the event out of which the ethical sublime arises.[82]

When we explore static visual meaning we ask what system of conventional references thematizes the image, turning it into a motif. When we explore enacted visual meaning we ask what do we bring to the screen, what acculturated, cognitive constructions does the mind project in response to the image? When we explore spontaneous visual meaning we ask what does this experience tells us about the ontology of the image? What reality does the image bring to mind? The latter query recapitulates Bill Mitchell's unsettling question, what do images want? And why do we respond to them as if they want anything at all? This query ultimately leads us to the uncanny Lynchian domain of desire, and the ontological excess that constitutes the image's aura. Yet, as baroque culture teaches, even the aura may be simulated. If the aura in its uncanny ontological fullness implicates the ethical sublime, simulation of the aura implicates the pseudo or *ersatz* sublime – whether it is the endlessly iterative, pop-baroque world of Andy Warhol, or the magical realist world of pop science and the aesthetics of digital delight.

What, then, may we say when law's claim to fact-based justice rests upon an information image that digitally simulates the world and others within it? Is this novel aniconic image, whose hidden source lay in invisible algorithmic calculations, also capable of expressing the ethical sublime? May it be traced back not simply to the nominal conventions of digital programming, but also to a reality that shimmers with uncanny excess? In the chapter that follows we will examine these matters in closer detail.

CHAPTER 6

The Digital Challenge: Command and Control Culture and the Ethical Sublime

> The beautiful charms us . . . [It] is a kind of experience that stands out like an enchantment . . .
>
> (Hans-Georg Gadamer[1])

> [I]f one envisaged virtue as one ought to do, one would be charmed by its beauty.
>
> (Gottfried Wilhelm Leibniz[2])

> The move toward replacing the system of a window and a world outside with one of a computer screen in a closed room is something that's taking place in our social life . . .[3]
>
> A control is not discipline. In making highways, for example, you don't enclose people but instead multiply the means of control . . . [P]eople can drive infinitely and "freely" without being at all confined yet while still being perfectly controlled. This is our future.[4]
>
> (Giles Deleuze)

What is meant by "presence" inside the courtroom? In 2008, the Arizona Supreme Court established the Criminal Rules Video-conference Advisory Committee to determine whether criminal defendants may appear in court via videoconferencing technology. After a year of study, a majority of the committee recommended a sweeping expansion in the use of virtual appearances. The supporters of that recommendation concluded that teleconferencing was the functional equivalent of a live (physical) presence in court. Their finding was hotly contested, and though the committee's recommendation ultimately was rejected by the Arizona judiciary, the issue persists. How does appearing as an image on a screen differ from being physically present inside the courtroom? What does the camera leave out?

Defenders of the rights of the criminal accused maintain that the omissions are many and significant. Constitutional law in the U.S. provides a notable point of departure. For example, the right to a fair trial as guaranteed by the due process clause of the Fourteenth Amendment of the U.S. Constitution has been interpreted to include the criminal defendant's right to be physically present in court. And the Sixth Amendment specifies that all individuals accused of crime are entitled to confront the witnesses against them. Under limited circumstances, such as when the court finds that the well-being of a child victim of sexual abuse is significantly at risk, and that the child's capacity to testify will be impeded by the physical presence of his or her alleged abuser, then teleconferencing may be used in place of live testimony. Speaking for a cohesive minority of the Court, Justice Antonin Scalia has strongly challenged this interpretation. For Scalia, the confrontation right plainly calls for actual "face to face" presence, without exceptions. As Scalia put it in testimony before a Congressional hearing on the question of teleconferencing, a decision made in a room that "contains a television set beaming electrons that portray the defendant's image" is not the same as a decision made in the physical presence of that person.[5] Not even at 625,000 electronic pulses, 60 times a second, which is what each video frame is typically composed of.

Justice Scalia's statement suggests that electronic images can never meet the constitutional requirements of confrontation. As Scalia puts it: "Virtual confrontation might be sufficient to protect virtual constitutional rights; I doubt whether it is sufficient to protect real ones." In this view, virtual appearances simply lack sufficient reality. But what does this mean? No judge, not even Justice Scalia, has ever spelled out the exact nature of this ontological or perhaps even metaphysical insufficiency. Pragmatic considerations, however, have come more readily to hand. For example, defense lawyers have contended that when a criminal defendant appears in court from somewhere else (a prison or detention center, say), he lacks immediate access to his attorney. Questions and advice must wait. In short, without immediate access, lawyers are unable to gauge the verbal and nonverbal cues of their clients. This lack makes it difficult to accurately assess the defendant's emotional or psychological state. The defendant remains isolated, detained in what the courts, as least since *Miranda v. Arizona*,[6] have recognized as coercive or intimidating environments. This physical and emotional distance not only impedes the psychological assistance of counsel. It also undercuts counsel's opportunity to establish and maintain her client's trust, assuring the accused that she is an ally and not an agent of the state. For their part, jurors and others present in the courtroom are deprived of the sight of the defendant being treated as worthy of equal respect, as reflected in the attentiveness of counsel.

There are risks as well associated with the camera itself. The camera provides only a limited view of what goes on in court. The distant defendant is thus deprived not only of the opportunity to look when he wishes at the judge, jurors, witnesses, lawyers, and spectators (including his own as well as the victim's friends and family), but they in turn are restricted in what they may see of him. Lighting conditions and camera angles can impede a proper assessment of his demeanor and credibility. For example, is defendant's face cast in a menacing shadow? Does the camera's proximity distort defendant's features? Is it peering down on him, as if to diminish his stature? Can viewers see that his hand or foot is shaking or that his body is calm as he speaks? Can viewers discern whether he is looking directly at his interlocutor or avoiding her eyes, as if he had something to hide? Might defendant be responding to someone off camera, a guard perhaps, who exerts an invisible influence on how the defendant feels, and how he holds himself, thus inexplicably affecting how he appears to others?

Nor are these the only risks that arise when it comes to virtual appearances. For example, it is much easier for viewers to project familiar, media-based stereotypes, along with other visual associations, on to images they see on the screen. Screen images tend to prompt other images that viewers have seen before – in films and on television, together with personalized images stored in memory. Recall, for example, Justice Scalia's association to the car chase scene from *The French Connection* when he watched a real car chase video in the *Scott v. Harris* case. Or consider prosecutors who feel compelled in their opening statements to warn jurors that forensic evidence in court is different from what they may see in popular television shows and films. In this way, prosecutors signal their concern that when jurors view the state's visual evidence they will unconsciously associate to what they have seen on television and in the movies and will judge the state's case based on unrealistic expectations. (Where's the DNA? Where are the surveillance photos?) And, of course, there is also the consideration of fairness. Courtrooms are designed to equalize the playing field among advocates and their clients. The appearance of justice requires that each side is assigned their own space, equidistant from the judge and jury. That is not so, however, when the defendant appears as an isolated figure on the screen. When his courtroom is a bare room perhaps in a jail, it may seem as if the distant defendant is unworthy of joining the ranks of trial participants and spectators.

Notwithstanding these and other risks associated with virtual appearances, in a growing number of cases, particularly when they involve defendant's initial appearance in court and the testimony of distant witnesses, the efficiency of teleconferencing has trumped its potential drawbacks. We see this happening worldwide in civil cases[7] and increasingly in criminal prosecutions as well.[8] We are also seeing a robust trend toward increased use of virtual appearances by way of visual digital evidence at trial: from surveillance and amateur digital videos to digitized accident and crime reconstructions, along with various other technical digital displays (including brain scans using fMRI technology, forensic DNA testing, and multimodal graphics and montages). Consider, for example, the case in which plaintiffs introduced a computer simulation of an accident involving their Fiat X1/9[9] or in which digital flight data was used to recreate the crash of Delta flight 191.[10] These simulations often look like a video of the event, with all its stomach-churning emotional intensity, even though no one was around to film it. Digital simulations may also give viewers the impression they are looking at pictures even when the images they see are the product of computer programs processing complex statistics, as is the case with functional magnetic resonance imaging (fMRIs). Consider in this regard the colorful brain images that were used in court to show that a defendant accused of attempted murder suffered from physiological abnormalities that allegedly deprived him of ordinary impulse control.[11] In addition to mitigating a defendant's wrongdoing, brain scans have also been used to bolster the state's assertion of criminal intent and even to show that the defendant is lying.[12]

Visual digital evidence may be emotionally powerful and visually compelling. Complex data can be simplified and easily absorbed; simulations of crimes and accidents provide not only factual but also emotional knowledge regarding the event in question. But digital simulations also risk factual distortions and emotional prejudice. Not surprisingly, judges and lawyers are now grappling with appropriate standards to assess the accuracy of input data as well as the reliability of the software used to translate digital code into visual displays.[13] As this effort proceeds, it is important to bear in mind how digital simulations differ from non-digital photography and film as well as from analog video imaging. For example, in non-digital image production, light passing through a lens creates a physical reaction on photosensitive paper or celluloid. Actuality thus appears as a trace of something that is past. That trace subsists within film as an uncanny presence that the image transfers to the viewer. Film viewers thus occupy a paradoxical space–time dimension. The uncanny presence of what the camera has witnessed radiates in the film image, but the viewer experiences that presence as emanating from a time that has past. In that strange temporal echo the film viewer may come to experience duration itself. Like a visual poem, film thus allows viewers to witness the conditions under which being and others appear. And from knowledge *of* presence comes responsibility *for* presence. Letting be is an act that confers value on what appears. Film viewers partake of that act and share in that responsibility when they embody in a film's shared duration the reality that it brings to their senses. This may well be the singular ontological and ethical quality of filmic experience.[14]

Television marks the beginning of a shift away from the trace (the singular signature or physical index of what once was) to electronic images that appear in the constantly reconstituted now of sequential scanning on an electronic receiving or display device. Absent that device, there is no display. Thus begins a divorcement between inputs and outputs, a break with the actual that visual digitization takes significantly further. By converting light waves into strings of 0s and 1s, digitization severs the analogical relationship between object and image altogether.[15] The frequency and intensity of light waves (representing color and brightness) are now symbolized in the form of mathematical calculations. In this sense, digitization, like Cartesian optics, moves away from a correspondence model of resemblance to a system of conventional markers or signs, the binary code of the digital program. Both digital and Cartesian optics dissolve embodied perception into the abstract artifice of subjective design – ideas, for Descartes, numbers (or binary code) for the digital image.

In short, digital simulation can encode physical reality, but the reality it encodes leaves no trace in the image that is digitally produced. In the digital regime the authenticating function of the original no longer operates. The meaning of digital signs does not depend on, nor does it distinguish between originals and copies. In the realm of digital simulation, everything is equally fungible, equally susceptible to transformation, recombination, and exchange. As Rodowick puts it: "The digital image is more and more responsive to our imaginative intentions, and less and less anchored to the prior existence of things and people."[16] Perhaps this is why film making in recent years increasingly concentrates on post-production techniques. Enhanced control over the digital image reduces the exigencies of capturing traces of the actual. The artistry is shifting elsewhere. And with it so, too, is the viewer's sense of being and time. The shared experience of duration that arises in analog film from the trace of the real is now slipping into the more insular, monadic temporality of the digital, which is to say, the autonomic, ahistorical, constant "now" of game time. In game time there is no present and no presence other than the one occupied by the gamer. Every player is an eyewitness – to the simulated reality on the screen. When digital simulations rather than analog film images are screened in court, trial time shifts from reconstructing traces of the past to the sensation of eyewitnessing reality in the present.

It has been suggested that, at least on a sub-atomic level, distinguishing between natural and digitally simulated worlds lacks significance.[17] As the character Cypher puts it in *The Matrix*, perhaps all we ever see is code – the incessant flow of electrons and their associated wave forms. In this respect, immersion in the infinite stream of digital data has been described as the ecstasy of the digital sublime.[18] This may help to explain why for a character like Cypher it makes no difference whether he lives in a simulation or in real life. But such a divorcement from the actual raises serious ethical concerns, particularly in a court of law. The monadic existence of digital immersion knows nothing and wishes to know nothing about attunement to the real. In this view, it may be enough simply to internalize the protocols of the program. Without adequate attunement to the real, however, there is no call (of Being, or of human beings) to heed. The question "What does reality want?" does not arise, and consequently neither does the self-demoting responsiveness of care. In other words, the dematerialization of the digital interface and its substitution for actual face-to-face encounters in real life raises ontological as well as normative issues. As Rodowick writes: "The withdrawal of the body and a physical presence in space means that individuals feel less and less accountable for their actions and speech acts, since they confront one another less and less in relations of reciprocity united in space and time."[19] Perhaps this is part of what it means to live in what Deleuze calls "control societies."[20] The apparent naturalness and easy manageability of digital representations belie the hidden imperatives or protocols of the underlying algorithms that produce them.

The ascendance of the digital interface is fraught with significance in the realm of law. To an increasing extent inside the courtroom computer programs analyze data and perform calculations based on mathematical models and the laws of physics or other scientific principles to recreate past events and even states of mind. The program's visual display testifies to the reality of what it shows. But what exactly does the decision maker see on the screen, and how can we be sure that this is something that *should* be shown in court? Standards for admissibility differ depending on whether the digital simulation in question is being offered as substantive proof or merely as "illustrative" evidence (i.e. to help the tryer of fact grasp what a particular witness has said on the stand).[21] Regardless of the applicable category, however, the images themselves increasingly retain the look and feel of reality. Learning to discern and appropriately respond in court to issues of accuracy, reliability, and undue emotional prejudice arising from digital simulations are now part and parcel of what it means to be visually literate. As Sherry Turkle puts it: "[C]itizenship in the twenty-first century calls for readership skills in the culture of simulation, the digital equivalent to knowing 'Who, What, Where, Why, and How' of print media. Such readership skills enable people to be critical of simulation, not simply immersed in it."[22]

Beyond these practical concerns, however, a deeper issue remains. It is the one that Justice Scalia flagged when he contrasted physical presence with "beaming electrons," in the context of analog video – a distinction that extends to dematerializing reality in the form of digital information or binary code. What does the digital image want? Like any image, it wants reality; it asks to be taken as synonymous with what it represents. But the digital image goes further. It also wants us to forget, or perhaps not to care that there may be no physical reality at all (no original, no signified) associated with the image we see on the screen. Is it enough to immerse ourselves in the aesthetic delight that comes of seeing and hearing and feeling in response to digital simulation? Must we repudiate the seduction of "mere appearances" in order to get at some underlying reality that we call the real? Such is the familiar oscillation of iconoclash. We love the image and we hate it. We crave its enchantments and fear its deceits. Unable to extricate ourselves from this binary regress, a metaphysical anxiety seizes hold.

In the previous chapter, I contended that throughout history visual images in various media have been associated with a sublime presence. That presence, in a variety of metaphysical registers, renews our fealty to the real. In so doing it points beyond the epistemological, ontological, and ethical impasses of the baroque. But if the aesthetic and ethical sublime direct us to a source of metaphysical resolve in the face of baroque longing, what of the aniconic information image, the digital simulacrum that neither needs nor seeks a link to something original? Is it, too, capable of producing such resolve? Is the digital image capable of the sublime? Or is it part of a new baroque pageantry of power and delight? How do we complement the strengths and counter the deceits of digital simulation with the aesthetic and ethical authority that attends renewed fealty to the real?

Visual literacy can only supply part of the answer. Cultivating a more sophisticated capacity for critical appraisal of the digital image is necessary to help decision makers validate the truth and justice claims that digital images make in court. But visual literacy alone will not help us answer the question: What does reality want? If simulation wants mastery, reality wants care. Simulations are monadic, solitary, cut off from the real. That is why the monadic soul is filled with longing, a feeling akin to perpetual homesickness. As Gabel puts it: "The abnormal need for representation here compensates for a torturing feeling of being outside the margin of existence."[23] By contrast, care presupposes fragility, pain, and humility in the face of otherness. To overcome the baroque profusion of compensatory form requires a renewed attunement to the real. Such attunement goes beyond visual literacy; indeed, it presupposes a host of cultural, cognitive, and metaphysical assumptions and practices that need to be spelled out.

Historic shifts in metaphysical registers periodically transform meaning, even to the point of inverting conventional norms and expectations. For example, when the community's metaphysical register shifts from "sincerity" (or faith in the purity of subjectively experienced meaning) to a sense of suspicion and uncertainty (premised on the indeterminacy of being), the meaning of "ritual" also shifts: from a structure that opens up to deeper ("anti-structural") meanings, on the one hand, to the enactment of an "as if" meaning that staves off indeterminacy on the other.[24] We encounter a similar inversion when the metaphysical register shifts from the invisible code of transcendent Reality (for example, the reality of divine creation in Judeo-Christian and Islamic belief) to the invisible, fabricated domain of digital code (the computerized simulation of reality based on algorithmic calculations). With that shift the Islamic arabesque, once a sign of infinite diversity leading back to the oneness of God, yields to the digital arabesque, a purely ornamental design produced by a synthetic or man-made program. Once regarded as an emanation of God, virtual reality is now understood as a mathematically generated artifact. The term "simulacra" has undergone a comparable fate. In ancient Greek culture simulacra embodied a physical reality (i.e. those minute particles that the eye "intromits" from objects, or "extromits" into the objective world in the act of seeing). In today's digital culture, by contrast, simulacra have become phantasmal simulations (i.e. signifiers modifying signifiers absent a signified).

In a similar sense, the advent of digital baroque culture also reflects a profound metaphysical shift. The baroque characteristically expresses a deeply felt longing, but lacks the resources to fulfill it. In the face of endless postponement, longing becomes a central reality of lived experience. The baroque sublime thus becomes the ghost of a ghost; a virtual form in search of an original it cannot locate. In short, it becomes a simulacrum. Baroque expression must perpetually make up in intensity of affect, mobility of expression, and diversity of form, for the emptiness that lies at its core. It is driven by a pervasive anxiety. This is what we encounter in Pascal's evocation of homelessness in the face of those gaping spaces, the Nothingness both within and without, that threatens to engulf him. This sense of profound dislocation echoes in countless late modern novels (from Franz Kafka to Carlo Gadda and Samuel Beckett) and films (from Alain Resnais's *Last Year at Marienbad* [1961] to Peter Greenaway's *Prospero's Books* [1991], and Christopher Nolan's *Inception* [2010], among others too numerous to mention).[25]

The baroque response to metaphysical longing that we witness in these and related works is consistent. Like ritual in a time of uncertainty, in baroque culture only the proliferation of form, the bare creative act itself seems adequate to stave off the abyss. Yet, a shadow haunts the profusion of form, for no matter how gaudy or glaring its ornamental complexity may become, the yearning that drives it shines through. In sum, the tragedy of the baroque consists in the futility of substituting ornamental form for a sublime reality it cannot know or express. Distraction through intensification of affect is one of the pre-eminent strategies of baroque spectacle. Ironic detachment, in conjunction with the pose of metaphysical indifference, is another. This is the strategy of parody. If the ornate glitter of a Bernini altar and the "manic ferment" and "packed extravagance" of eccentric form and "specious illusionist devices" that we find in the paintings of Vasari and Bronzino,[26] like the proliferation of dizzying, digital seriations that flood films like Peter Jackson's *Lord of the Rings Trilogy* (2001–2003) and Zack Snider's *300* (2006), reflect the strategy of baroque distraction, the serial Pop art of Andy Warhol and the parodic film work of Quentin Tarantino reflect the strategy of ironic detachment and staged metaphysical indifference. Consider Warhol's silk screen depictions of multiple Marilyn Monroes or multiple Campbell soup cans or, for that matter, multiple electric chairs, car accidents (1963; image 6.1, p. 159), and atomic mushroom clouds. Anything, Warhol tells us, no matter how banal or celebrated or terrifying, can be serialized, mass-produced and, by extension, drained of significance.

Here the art work celebrates self-mockery, and ultimately self-destruction. For no matter what its content, the work cannot escape the failure of authenticity in the act of representation. By taking viewers into the realm of ironic detachment, deploying humor, mockery, and hyper-reflexive design values (images ramifying images like mass produced widgets on an assembly line straight from the artist's "factory"), Warhol deflects metaphysical anxiety. The image is nothing to fear, he tells us. Its power has been tamed, reduced to a mere object, a commodity, a fetish. The meaning of representation has become inexorably self-referential, aestheticized, cut off from the

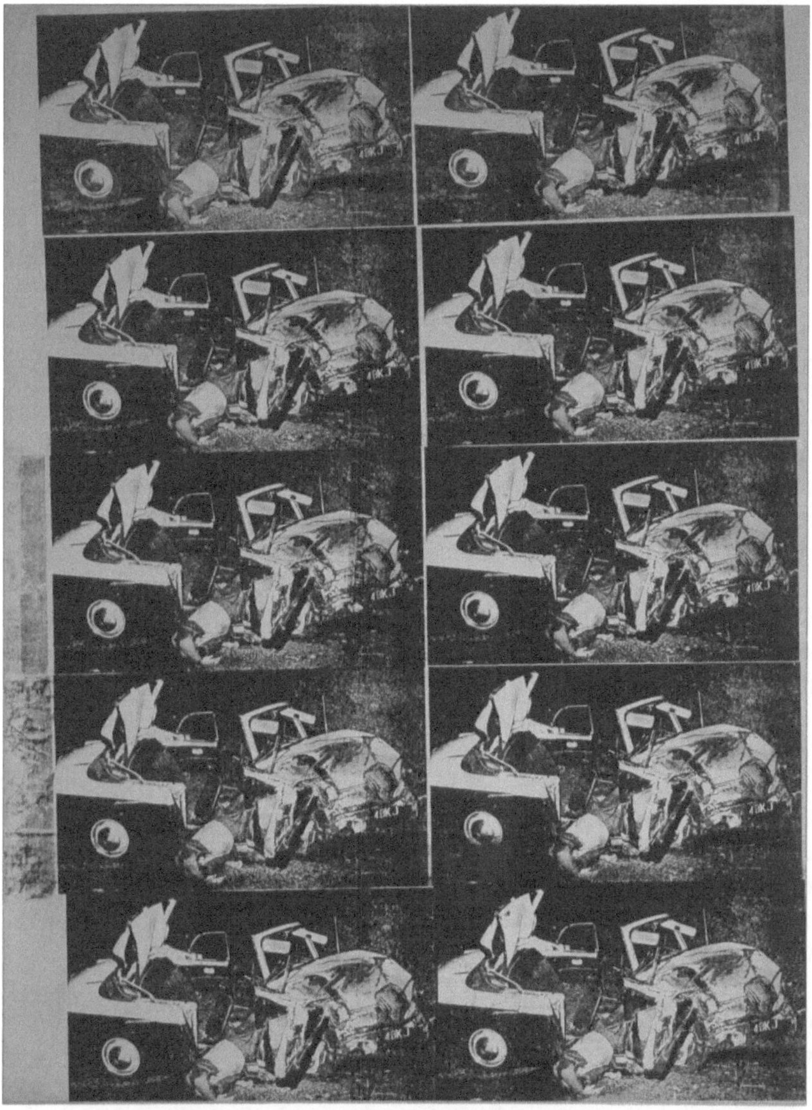

Image 6.1 *Green Disaster Ten Times* (1963), Andy Warhol. With permission of Museum für Moderne Kunst, Frankfurt am Main. © 2010 the Andy Warhol Foundation for the Visual Arts/Artists' Rights Society (ARS), New York. Photographer Axel Schneider, Frankfurt am Main

real. It is reproductions all the way down. Our refuge, Warhol seems to be saying, lies in decorative diversion.

Of course, the brilliance of Warhol's art consists precisely in making vivid what it is like to live under neo-baroque conditions, what it means to be cut off from the sublime. Warhol expresses it well when he says, "[I] make nothing happen."[27] Mimesis, for him, is an empty gesture. Consequently, there is nothing to oblige us. Warhol liberates his viewers from the ethical. His work effectively de-realizes the shameful gaze, the act of seeing ourselves seeing (nothing). In this respect, his choice of Marilyn Monroe as aesthetic artifact is an inspired contrivance. For the society that feeds off of the aura of celebrity, whether it is a Hollywood movie star or Chairman Mao, remains indifferent to the particulars of content. Ornamentation is everything. Ideology, value, and meaning must now yield to self-referential production values and aesthetic effect. The hyper-aestheticization of the real announces the society of spectacle, with its cult of celebrity and its parade of screen-based simulacra in the service of enjoyment. As Ivor Indyk keenly observes regarding Benjamin's work on the decay of the aura, in baroque times the image no longer has a life of its own.[28] In place of illumination or radiance we have allegory; in place of living history, we have the ever shifting meaning of mechanical (or digital) reproductions. This is the singular signature of the neo-baroque – in art, film, television, computer games, and law on the screen. The aura of the sublime is dead; long live the simulation. Or so Warhol and his digital baroque successors might have us believe.

But not so fast. Today, both forms of the sublime persist – the authentic, ontologically overdetermined ("visual *différance*") and the simulated, unanchored, shape-shifting (ersatz sublime) of the simulacrum. If Warhol makes nothing happen, Barnett Newman's and Mark Rothko's abstract expressionist canvases make an uncanny presence happen. This is something we have also seen in the legal videos discussed in Chapter 3, from the visual delight of magical realist neuroscience, to the uncanny dance of custody that was screened in the Borukhova murder trial and the time-dissolving audio-visual montage that was shown in the murder trial of Michael Skakel. In sum, both the ersatz and the authentic sublime are available to artists, advertisers, politicians, and lawyers alike – all of whom today are engaged in various forms of visual communication and persuasion. The sublime presence or absence of an ontological surplus in visual expression, like the strategies of aesthetic delight in the ersatz sublime of the simulacrum, presupposes the existence of different expressive styles and concomitant metaphysical registers. Understanding both allows us to describe and assess the shared meanings (the visual *nomos*) that a given form of expression invites us to take up (or suppress).

The quandary of law's iconoclash in the age of the digital baroque raises an agonized cry: What are we to make of that uncanny sense of surplus meaning that comes to us from outside ourselves, beyond the reach of any program or code, and that we refer to as the sublime? Homesickness, the unbearable nostalgia that pervades the baroque mind, is a symptom of utter disconnection from this encounter with meaning's surplus. The mood of baroque longing evinces a collective state of homesickness for the sublime that has gone away. We are at home in meaning. Meaning is the ultimate antidote to the metaphysical terror that Pascal, anticipating mid-twentieth century existential writers and thinkers, expressed in the face of a pervasive sense of nothingness without and within. An influx of meaning ends Pascal's vertiginous terror just as it eases Sartre's overwhelming sense of nausea in the face of raw existence – in all its absurd contingency.[29] We yearn to be at home: in words, in images, and in our relationship to self and others.

Law as code, as a legislative or algorithmic construction, craves totality. It seeks to command and control the events that fall within its province. Justice seeks neither. It is neither calculative nor instrumental. It comes to us like a gift, a gift of intuition (or unconscious synthesis). Justice, like beauty, like love, is always more than we can say. We recognize it as much by its sublime fullness as by its uncanny absence. Indeed, absence is precisely what makes the sense of fullness sublime. We hear intimations of that strange fullness in Wallace Stevens' words when he writes:

> She sang beyond the genius of the sea.
> The water never formed to mind or voice,
> Like a body wholly body, fluttering
> Its empty sleeves; and yet its mimic motion
> Made constant cry, caused constantly a cry,
> That was not ours although we understood,
> Inhuman, of the veritable ocean.
> The sea was not a mask. No more was she . . .
> But it was she and not the sea we heard.
> For she was the maker of the song she sang.
> The ever-hooded, tragic-gestured sea
> Was merely a place by which she walked to sing.
> Whose spirit is this? we said, because we knew
> It was the spirit that we sought and knew
> That we should ask this often as she sang.[30]

The song that sings beyond the genius of the sea (or of any actual presence) is the sublime. Its call is the call of meaning. This is what the Greeks referred to as "*thauma*," or wonder. It is with wonder that the thinker and the poet respond to the call of being. In the tension between seeing and not seeing, hearing and not hearing, saying and not saying, lies the supreme paradox of the sublime. The infinite meaning of which it hints is always irreducible to the expression in which it is given. Poems, paintings, symphonies – every exalted work of art enchants us the way Stevens imagines: as a clearing for a sublime order that is simultaneously present and absent. In this way the sublime event of beauty and justice eases our longing. We experience this as a homecoming.

There are jurists who are guided by law's encyclopedic capacity, its ability to enumerate rules for past, present, and future conditions. Others share a more poetic vision, one that is allusive and enchanting in its invocation of the remedial power of justice. The magic (or magical thinking) of law as enumeration is that a calculus for right outcomes exists. With a powerful and complex enough algorithm specific inputs will lead to correct outputs. Magic and the sublime represent two opposing responses to Pascal's metaphysical quandary: the calculative, instrumental magic of pre-emptive legislative enumeration and digital simulation, and the state of embodied mindfulness that seeks attunement to the "situation sense" of conflict, an intuited sense of what a particular reality immediately calls to mind. The totalizing sense of command and control that the programmer, like the Benthamite legislator, seeks in regard to what has been enumerated stands in stark contrast to the sense of wonder that informs the embodied experience of attunement. Legal metaphors, images, narratives – indeed, law itself envisioned as having been founded *mythopoieically* as a living reality – will not readily submit to the strict enumerative criteria, the definitive traits of clarity and distinctness required of rational concepts and categories. Notwithstanding its confident pursuit of rational certainty, however, a longing for home has always haunted the modernist mindset, including the modernist mindset of jurisprudence. But where, we may ask, is "home"?

After a prolonged absence from one's native land, or native tongue, one yearns for places and words, sights and smells that feel familiar and capacious, easy to live in. But one needn't travel abroad to experience homesickness, to have that not unfamiliar sense of estrangement from self and others. Consider in this regard Holly Golightly, that great displaced soul and inveterate loner – even in the crowds she draws around her. We encounter Holly in Truman Capote's short novel, *A Breakfast at Tiffany's*. Longing lies at the root of her character. She doesn't fully grasp this about herself, but there are glimmerings. For example, at a crucial point in the novel, Holly makes a profound connection between feeling at home with oneself and the world, and having the right, as she puts it, to name a pet or call it one's own. As Holly says, "I don't want to own anything until I know I've found the place where me and things belong together." Belonging, authenticity, naming and owning somehow go together. Holly doesn't know where exactly she belongs, but she has gotten a taste of what it might be like. "It's like Tiffany's," she says, referring to the famous New York jewelry store. But it's not the diamonds and gold one finds there that accounts for Holly's feeling. Rather, it's "the quietness and the proud look of it; nothing very bad could happen to you there, not with those kind of men in their nice suits, and that lovely smell of silver and alligator wallets."

Reading this highly allusive description one senses that Holly has not been treated well, particularly by men. One senses that she has been injured rather badly, perhaps by abandonment, or betrayal. We do not know the details, only the mood that her life experience has left her in. Holly feels desperately alienated. As readers, we connect to her longing. Like Holly, we yearn to be loved as who we are. With that kind of love we experience our own worthiness (to be loved), and our own authenticity. It is enough to be who we are. With that feeling comes a quiet and proud and safe feeling of at-homeness.

According to Heidegger, making a place for homecoming, or authentic dwelling, is what poets are for. "The poet thinks his way into the locality defined by [the] lightening of Being."[31] The poet creates a dwelling place in the poem, and in that space Being manifests itself. In the poet's song we discern "the integrity of the globe of Being." Thus for Heidegger, creating, dwelling, and thinking coincide. The common nexus among them is the truth of being as authenticity: the poet creates a dwelling where something true comes to mind. It comes as a gift, which is why one can imagine Heidegger's joy when he discovered a common etymological root in German linking "thoughtfulness" and "thankfulness."

There is another link of interest here, the one Heidegger's great student, Hans-Georg Gadamer makes between beauty and the radiance of being. Beauty charms us; it comes to us like an enchantment, like the "turning on of a new light."[32] Beauty bestows an appearance. (It "shines over what is formed.") But its radiance is also that light by which things come to appear. Perhaps this, too, this above all, is what it means to be at home. As Gadamer writes: "The beautiful is that in the vision of which desire comes to rest."[33] The consummation of the beautiful is the moment when longing is fulfilled, at least momentarily. In the ecstasy – the *ek-stasis* – of our self-transcending being among others we become one with what we are not. Beauty consummates our response to infinite being just as justice consummates our response to the infinite need of our neighbor, the other who stands nearby. That response is structured in a mode of being that we recognize as care. Care leads us on to the homeward path. As Plato puts it in the *Symposium*, the lover longs above all else to make the beautiful his own,[34] to arrive at that "sanctuary of love" where he envisions "the very soul of beauty."[35] That sanctuary, that enchanted homecoming, is where the true, the beautiful, and the good exist as one.

This poetic truth calls to us within the radiance of beauty, a radiance that seduces us. By its enchantment we are drawn out, beyond the limit of ourselves, as Stevens was drawn out beyond the limits of the sea. In this experience of sublime beauty begins responsibility: a sense of solicitude toward things and others around us. This is the origin of the ethics of care, perhaps the sublime origin of justice itself.

Leibniz taught that justice is the result of combining wisdom (which comes of understanding) and love (which chooses what is best).[36] In his description of lovers, those disciples of the god of love, Plato wrote: "[T]hey pour out, like bacchants, into the soul of the beloved, thus creating in him the closest possible likeness to the god they worship."[37] The lover mirrors the belovèd as beloved.[38] Thus does love actualize the authenticity of the belovèd as worthy of love. Like the poet, the lover makes way for a being to emerge in the open as what it is.[39] To be as such is to be at home in the world. This is the good that love realizes in regard to the other. It is a good that arises in response to, and that ultimately perfects, beauty in the truth of an authentic self.

Unlike Heidegger's poet, and Plato's lover, Truman Capote's Holly Golightly suffers a less exalted fate. Her tragedy is that her indescribable homesickness, her yearning for the kind of authenticity that one associates with the intimacy of love, leads her to a life of pseudo-intimacy. Holly makes ends meet as a high-priced call girl. Holly is homesick, and at sea. We respond to her quandary with empathy, for we recognize the condition she is in. We know from our own experience how hard it is to feel at home in the world.

Some flee from Pascal's metaphysical terror in search of the comforting embrace of a closed system. They seek a home in codes: in legal or technological systems and in virtual worlds, or in Kurzweil's spiritual machines, or Ascott's cosmic information garden – that fanciful return to Eden, now suitably digitized. Others seek a home within the uncodable: in places negatively framed by longing, as in Holly Golightly's experience of Tiffany's, or in places both negatively and affirmatively framed by enchantment, as in Stevens's sublime poem about order beyond the genius of the sea. Some become positivists and codifiers, others rhetoricians and poets. There are jurists in both camps. May we say the same of digital programmers? May we say the same of the programs they design? How much presence is there in virtual worlds? Can the sublime be digitally codified? Does it show up in digital simulations?

These questions may sound odd and elusive, strangely couched in metaphysics. But they are actually highly pragmatic, and cannot be evaded. Whether it is a matter of establishing a "minyan" in cyberspace (are ten Jews "present" enough on line to establish the basis for a religious service?) or validating the cross-examination of a virtual defendant or distant witness on the screen or, for that matter, enacting a virtual trial in cyberspace, the question of how we assess "presence" in digital simulations is no idle speculation. If the ethical originates in our face to face encounter with the infinite or sublime presence of an Other who stands before us, it is no small concern to contemplate what it means to be deprived of such a presence in court, or to ask what is the ontological status of the face of a digital avatar.

The dilemma of authentic presence versus flattened simulacrum, or of sublime enchantment versus instrumental magic, is also the dilemma between infinite surplus and total enumeration. It is the tension between poetics as lyrical, apophatic invocation on the one hand, and instrumental thinking and algorithmic calculation on the other. Jorge Borges, the great Argentinean writer, elegantly captures this dilemma in his gem-like parable "The Aleph."[40] In this short story a character named Danieri tells of a marvelous discovery. On the nineteenth step up from the floor of his cellar one may behold the aleph, that mystical sphere which Dante once described in a vision of God. The aleph, he said, is a point in space that contains all points, a place of light whose center is everywhere and whose circumference is nowhere. In other words, the unbounded Aleph contains all there is. Danieri's response to this vision of the infinite is to embark on a master poem, a poem so complete that when it is done it will contain a total inventory of every natural and artificial feature of our planet. Appropriately enough, he calls his poem, *The Earth.*

Danieri's total vision is never realized, but Borges does not invite us to mourn the loss. In fact, the vast catalogue that Danieri undertakes achieves little in the way of enchanting prose. Rather, the resulting work is dry, boring, nearly unreadable. And that is precisely the point. The desperation of the writer, according to Borges, consists in a deeply felt need to go beyond total enumeration, a project that can never succeed – neither as documentation nor as art. Only by capturing the impossibility of the artist's task, only by paradoxically evoking the experience of the ineffable source of representation in representation may the artist approach greatness.

In short, the great paradox of the sublime art work is that it simultaneously presents and withholds what it sets out to express. Danieri, we come to realize, has utterly misconstrued the nature and significance of the Aleph. He believes he can contain it in a single, obsessively crafted totality. In Danieri's view, modern man, with his technological tools close at hand, is well positioned to attain this goal. We see this in the picture Danieri paints: behold modern man "in his study, as though in the watchtower of a great city, surrounded by telephones, telegraphs, phonographs, the latest radio-telephone and motion-picture and magic-lantern equipment . . ." We may recognize here the utopian vision of infinite data flow that many associate with computers and the Internet, the perfectable matrix of simulated experience. What is missing from this vision, however, is its own negation. As E. H. Gombrich noted, when supreme artists like Rembrandt and Leonardo deliberately blurred features of the face they enhanced the expressive power of their work. We have seen something similar when Fra Angelico disrupted the aesthetic totality of his work with inexplicable blotches. These are examples of intensification through omission and aesthetic disruption. The power of sublime enchantment is a power of allusion, not enumeration. A mirror is simply one more thing added to the world, but as Velázquez shows in his masterly painting, *Las Meniñas* (1656; image 6.2 – see plate section between pp. 118 and 119), the sublime work of art enchants in the degree to which it mirrors the inexpressible.

Velázquez's painting shows us the painter at his easel staring out at his subjects, the King and Queen of Spain, who remain out of sight, hidden beyond the frame of the canvas. Their only trace may be glimpsed in a mirror that hangs on the rear wall behind the painter. A strange paradox – the subject of the painting is missing. Yet, it is also present as a kind of absence. What seizes us in this work is the very impossibility of the artistic act to seize the real. We behold the absence of the real even as we witness its traces. It is the same in the sublime absences that we encounter in Vermeer.

This sense of absence within presence is what constitutes the sublime. Consider the pilgrim, in the last Canto of Dante's *Paradisio.* God has given him a dream vision, but upon awaking, Dante writes, he felt that "he had received and lost something infinite, something he would not be able to recover." For Borges this is the source and substance of Dante's greatness as a poet. He simultaneously evokes both the fullness and the emptiness of being. There is a surplus that exceeds expression, a fullness that we experience as an absence, a gap. Better the *via negativa,* or the zen master's "neither this nor that," better the sublime presencing and withholding of Being that Heidegger describes as the essence of poetry, than Danieri's arrogant and futile, and far from enchanting encyclopedic enumeration of what is. His poetic vision remains pedestrian precisely in its commitment to totality. The sublime lies beyond the frame.

Danieri – like Descartes and Hobbes and Bentham – has opted for the magical thinking that drives the modernist mindset toward total enumeration, the perfect rational code or scientific system. In the seventeenth century, Leibniz conceived of mind as infinite monad, but in late modernity the nature of that vision underwent radical transformation. For Leibniz, each monad (every one of us) bears an infinity within and coexists in the world as an infinity amid an infinity of infinities. In this way, for Leibniz, the human mind is modeled on the mind of God. This vision gives rise to a hermeneutics of endless interpretation. This is the enchanted world of Kabbalah, a world of infinite significance and hence, insatiable re-readings. By contrast, the late modern version of the monad may be likened to Kabbalah without God, or mind without infinity. We live in a baroque world filled with a profusion of forms. It is a world of conventions and codes, signifiers cut off from the signified, copies floating free of an original. We are entangled in this world of appearances as in a web of meanings of our own making. But the web is a screen on which meaning flattens out. The flatness of the digital flow lacks the uncanny interruption of presence; there is no otherness from which to launch the search for transcendental reference. Everything is on the surface, part of a perfectly fungible, metonymic totality. This "decay of difference" portends the loss of a crucial poetic resource, namely: the sublime.[41] As Weber famously observed, there are times when the world's processes "simply 'are' and happen but no longer signify anything."[42]

With the onset of disenchantment, explanation outstrips wonder. The secular monadic mind serves time as in a prison house of expressive form.[43] In this dispensation, perhaps the most that may be hoped for is to build the most complete synthetic program, and take what pleasure there is in endlessly cycling its content within the solitary virtual space of algorithmically generated simulacra. This characteristically baroque strategy of coping with a feeling of homelessness through the modality of command and control, which digital simulation technologies of total enumeration provide, is increasingly familiar to us. More and more, we live in a network of self-generated programs or game-like simulations in which synthetic forms of life can hardly be distinguished from less artificial ones. We have seen this repeatedly depicted in contemporary culture, in films like *The Matrix*, *Eternal Sunshine of a Spotless Mind*, *eXistenz*, *Memento*, and *Inception* – to name only a few. All of these works cast us into a baroque labyrinth made up of realities cycling within realities. This is, to be sure, one of the hallmarks of Borges' baroque sensibility. But there may be no better depiction of life in an autonomic, self-reflexively generated dream world than Haruki Murakami's novel, *Hard-boiled Wonderland and the End of the World* (1993).

Murakami's is a tale of fractured minds and fractured worlds composed in a fractured style that itself mimics the process of breaking apart into monadic isolation. The simplicity of the plot belies the complexity of its underlying vision. Imagine a spy who has had his brain surgically altered so that each hemisphere can perform different mathematical functions simultaneously. The process is called "shuffling." It allows data to be coded beyond any hacker's ability to crack. But something has gone terribly wrong with the procedure. The brains that have been altered are now breaking apart into separate, non-communicating spheres. When the fracture is complete the spy's world will shatter. He will then be locked, perhaps for all time, inside an automated program generated out of memories and dreams. When he is in that world he will remember nothing about who he once was, or what reality was like beyond the endlessly cycling dream-reality in which he now lives. (In Christopher Nolan's film *Inception* [2010] a similarly sealed-off interior dream state is described as "limbo.")

In an ironic play upon Dante's pilgrim, whose radiant dream vision could never be reconstructed upon awaking, Murakami's spy also senses intimations of a hidden reality, secrets that lie in some distant darkness. "The more closely I look," he says, "the further away retreats any overall impression."[44] But now the elusiveness of metaphysical reality (the reality of God in Dante's medieval mind) has devolved into the elusiveness of physical reality in Murakami's spectral, neo-baroque mind. This is what it is like to experience the contemporary baroque. It is like the metaphysical roller coaster ride that Nolan takes us on in *Inception* as we plumb the subconscious mind, dropping from one level to another, passing from one dream reality to the next, as time slows, till at last we reach a timeless limbo. In this baroque state, one experiences the actual as a rumor, an uneasy intimation. One can never be sure that one has awakened, or that awakening is even possible. Such is Neo's experience of life before he makes contact with Morpheus and learns that he has been living in a dream world. And such is the viewer's experience of the final scene in *Inception* which may or may not turn out to be just another dream. Being suspended between waking and dreaming, as in the bardo realm between living and dying depicted in Richard Linklater's film *Waking Life* (2002), feels like a perpetual state of metaphysical vertigo. That feeling, as if one were gazing into two mirrors facing one another, fragmenting the image in an infinite regress, that vertiginous *mis-en-abyme*, is a hallmark of the baroque.

At the end of Murakami's tale, the spy embraces his solitary virtual world ("sealed inside myself") purportedly in order to "find the key to my own creation, and to its undoing." But his dying shadow (the metaphoric soul cut off from the body) insists on the futility of the spy's self-assigned task. In a scene that one might imagine unfolding after Kurzweil's "singularity,"[45] that projected time when minds will take leave of bodies on their way to being uploaded, in post-human form, on to the computers that are to come, the spy's shadow sounds a warning: "Maybe you can't die here, but you will not be living. You will merely exist. There is no 'why' in a world that would be perfect in itself."[46] The shadow might as well been quoting Weber (in a disenchanted world things simply exist, they do not signify), or Scholem (law today remains valid, but lacks significance), or Borges. Only, in the case of the latter, rather than critiquing Danieri's failed poetic vision of totality, he might just as well be critiquing the digital wonderland at the end of the world where life is lived algorithmically, sealed within endless cycles of a finite program.

Murakami's vision of a self-enclosed monad endlessly cycling simulations resonates with David Rodowick's description of digital film making. Like Walter Benjamin's description of the dissolution of the aura in the age of mechanical reproduction, in total digital simulation all trace of the original authorizing aspect of the real has been lost. This is the model of the monadic image as simulacrum. It is what constitutes Murakami's fractured world of temporally as well as physically displaced memories and dreams. The disenchanted monad is a windowless totality with no possibility of transcendental reference.[47] But without the capacity for self-transcendence, there is no radiance to announce Being's paradoxical appearance, its sublime and uncanny withholding and presenting. Without radiance there is no clearing for Being to be in. With no clearing there is no Beauty, and with no beauty there is nothing to fulfill love's longing. Without love's fulfillment there is no goodness, as embodied in the Platonic lover's will to lead the beloved toward his or her authentic self. Without the good, there is no ethical origin for justice itself. And without justice, law is no more than a disenchanted code, a finite set of signs without significance. This is Kafka's law – law as an immanently unfolding assemblage, law as a machine.[48]

Law's quandary, its incessant oscillation between power and meaning, is a matter of metaphysics.[49] That is what law's iconoclash in the age of the digital baroque teaches. As Benjamin realized, there are times in the history of culture when all that remains is artistic will, the urge to produce form. The work itself, no matter how well wrought, remains "inwardly empty or profoundly disturbed."[50] The baroque world, Benjamin writes, is "not of linear design, but of twists and folds, undulations, and fractured planes; a world in which the unexpected and multivalent has supplanted the predictable and repetitive."[51] This disorderly and highly uncertain state of affairs is not without strains of the apocalyptic. As Benjamin's puts it: "[T]he baroque extracts a profusion of things which customarily escaped the grasp of artistic formulation and, at its high point, brings them violently into the light of day, in order to clean an ultimate heaven, enabling it, as a vacuum, one day to destroy the world with catastrophic violence."[52]

This prophetic sense of cataclysmic cleansing may be what comes of living overlong with a sense of insignificance or disenchantment. We recognize this disenchanted state as Kafka's world: a place of secret laws whose hidden meaning remains locked behind closed doors, or obscured by the profusion of opaque bureaucratic structures and processes. We also recognize it as the world of the digital panopticon in which the growing capacity to store data seems determined to advance modernity's quest for total enumeration, the perfect encyclopedia, and perhaps also the perfect bureaucracy.

In the baroque labyrinth of law's formal institutions, we find law's presence ramified everywhere. When law is coded as digital simulation, however, the aura of its authority is at risk of becoming the merest of rumors. This is what it is like when our access to the real has been lost. The code may be valid, but it no longer signifies. Law without significance is like the will without love or meaning: a matter of power alone. Thus, we are thrust back into the cold nominalist embrace of Hobbes and Descartes at modernity's beginning.

The realm of the virtual has been described as an endless series of monadic "now"s playing out in a field of interminable flatness. There is a sense of freedom within this algorithmically generated space, and some refer to a sense of transcendence ("the transcendental experience of living as embedded avatars," as one avid online gamer put it). But if the sublime presupposes an encounter with an infinite presence that resists containment in finite form or total enumeration, then we will search for it in vain in the totalized, monadically sealed, manifestly delightful reality of digital simulation.

We may internalize the aniconic code of algorithmic form; we may master the hidden logic of the video game. (As Cypher puts it in *The Matrix*: "I don't even see the code. All I see is blonde, brunette, redhead.") But that adaptation only makes mind over in the image of the program, a machinic process that leads the way to Murakami's wonderland. In the latter half of the twentieth century Andy Warhol declared, "I am a machine." Since then, the sense of bemused irony in his words has faded. In the post-Foucauldian "control society," Warhol's words play in a post-human key. The metaphysical question of our time has now become: "Why am I not (am I not) a machine?" This query marks the initiation of a new field of philosophical reflection. Call it onto-cybernetics: "Heidegger 2.0."

The lyrical poet, like Heidegger's thinker and Plato's lover, opens a clearing in which the Being of being radiates. Does the architecture of digital simulation permit a comparable clearing? Is enchantment possible under the limiting conditions of algorithmic constraint? Does digital simulation in court presuppose the ontological conditions necessary not simply for aesthetic delight, but also for the aesthetic sublime (in the uncanny radiance of being's appearance) and even more significantly for the *ethical* sublime (in response to the infinite demand of an Other)? This is what metaphysical discourse is like in the age of the digital baroque. That conversation, however, has barely begun.

It may be too soon to offer conclusions regarding the prospect of law's sublime re-enchantment as digital image, its continued fealty to reality and to justice, or its devolution into digital spectacle and subjective delight. But if the infinite excess that produces sublime meaning finds no place in our totalized codes then law's legitimacy is at risk when it migrates to the screen in the form of digital simulations. Legitimacy rests upon law's continued aspiration to justice, but justice also presupposes our continued capacity to experience the ethical sublime. In the post-human era, when machinic language and digital-panoptic technologies increasingly dominate society, the ethical question *par excellence* becomes: Who and what do we become when we live on the screen, when we internalize the screen's optical code as our own? If the machinic language of the algorithm will bear only the totality that is calculated within it, then it is incapable of producing the sublime. Put differently, if digital simulation enfolds a synthetic totality then that is what we can expect it to unfold. This is the disenchanted monad in action. Like Murakami's schizoidal spy, the digital monad can only cycle calculations. It conjures a dream world so lifelike that, like Neo, we may no longer discern (or like Cypher we may no longer care to distinguish) the difference between waking and dreaming. Lacking the sublime we can but code. But the simulated life of digital code threatens to leave us homeless, stranded in the false comfort of a synthetic totality, like a perpetually disentangled digital arabesque, dancing alone in simulated space, a captive of the endless unfolding of aesthetic delight.

The good is an entangled human reality. It arises in our response to others, in actions for the sake of another. Without the infinite mystery and demands of the Other, ethical discourse, like all narrative, cannot come to life.[53] The life of the law as an image on the screen is like this as well. Only when visualizing law also encompasses the human capacity for self-demotion in response to what situated conflict and the face of the other demand of us, may we, in the words of poet Allen Grossman, "make civilization endurable and safe."[54] Law's legitimacy consists in the ongoing quest for justice. The fate of that quest today may well depend upon whether and how well we address the metaphysical quandary of visualizing law in the age of the digital baroque. To that end, we turn in the concluding chapter to the role of integral rhetoric and the harmonization of the aesthetic and the ethical in the practice and theory of law.

CHAPTER 7

Conclusion: Visualizing Law's Rhetorical Ideal

> [E]very epoch is defined by its own practices of knowledge and strategies of power, which are composed from regimes of visibility and procedures of expression.
>
> (D. N. Rodowick[1])

> Rather than erect another hierarchy, it may therefore be more useful to acknowledge the plurality of scopic regimes now available to us. Rather than demonize one or another, it may be less dangerous to explore the implications, both positive and negative, of each.
>
> (Martin Jay[2])

> For the wisdom of the ancients was [not the esoteric wisdom of great and rare philosophers, but] the vulgar wisdom of the lawgivers who founded the human race . . .
>
> (Giambattista Vico[3])

The argument of this book may be distilled into three interrelated claims: First, with law's visualization comes the dilemma of *iconoclash: how can we (how can we not) place our trust in images*? Tensions between old and new mediations of reality generate a heightened awareness of the rhetorical (or constitutive) nature of representation. Iconoclash arises when competing forms of visual expression, each with its own underlying set of aesthetic and epistemological assumptions, make the mimetic act of representation uncertain. Such uncertainty is one of the hallmarks of baroque and neo-baroque culture.

The second claim is that iconoclash prompts two opposing responses. On the one hand, we see a profusion of expressive forms and heightened aesthetic effects in search of relief from metaphysical anxiety, the deep-seated fear that a terrible emptiness lay at the core of things. On the other hand, metaphysical uncertainty also stirs potent iconoclastic impulses. Iconoclasm is at bottom a reaction against what is viewed as a substitution of material idols, icons, or images for an underlying, unseen and unrepresentable reality. The iconoclast seeks to destroy "graven images" that mock, by their sheer presumption to represent, a higher order of reality. But this destructive strategy results in a quandary. For if reality remains unmediated, if it is not even susceptible to mediation, how then can we hope to know, much less communicate its meaning? At the same time, if mediated reality is all there is, if we must live amid endless digital streams of contingent signifiers that have broken free of the gravitational pull of the real (the signified), what then remains to validate visual meaning apart from the aesthetic delight of baroque ornamentation and spectacle? What anchors or authorizes visual images when the original no longer matters?

This state of affairs prompts a third claim: namely, that overcoming iconoclash requires aesthetic clarification (visual literacy) as well as metaphysical resolve (a new visual eloquence). We need to develop an enhanced critical understanding of visual proof and persuasion, a new visual rhetoric for the digital age. Different visual representations operate in different aesthetic, epistemological, and metaphysical registers – ranging from the purely gratifying domain of aesthetic delight to the uncanny presence of the aesthetic and ethical sublime. Assessing the reliability of a given visual image requires an awareness of the virtues and defects of its form of expression. Thus, we ask: What does the image want? What state of being, what mood, affect, beliefs, memories, and values does it invoke, and how does it do this? How do we think and feel through the image? And what kind of self and social world does the image call into being? Today, practitioners, teachers, and scholars of law need to enter an apprenticeship with the image makers, including the digital wizards who know the binary codes which regulate the art of visual representation on the screen.

But visual literacy alone will not resolve iconoclash. The metaphysical anxiety that pervades baroque and neo-baroque culture requires a new metaphysical outlook. This is not a return to Platonic essences. What is called for is a renewed clarification of the mimetic or representational process through which the actual comes to mind in the moment of creative invention and judgment. As a historical matter, this kind of metaphysical clarification has had significant legal and political impact. For example, in the late seventeenth century, at the beginning of modernity in the aftermath of the European baroque, belief in the divine right of kings was shattered by an iconoclastic repudiation of that belief's metaphysical underpinning.[4] The common law consequently took on the corona of a new metaphysical legitimacy – what Peter Goodrich has referred to as the invisible (imageless) source of written law.[5] By displacing the image, the iconoclasts of the Reformation assimilated to the Crown a spiritual jurisdiction together with its courts of conscience.[6] The new regime was to be consummated not in the spectral image alone, however, but in the stability of the printed word. When the king's transcendental (second order) reality gave way to nominalist beliefs and linguistic conventions, this opened the way to new forms of political and legal discourse. De-visualizing law in the modern era produced new political and legal institutions along with new normative self-justifications. We witness the beginning of this transformation, for example, in Hobbes's *Leviathan*. In Hobbes's scientific view, the rationalization of fear becomes the logical basis for totalizing the authority of the Sovereign – together with the Sovereign's will to legislate.[7] The metaphysics of natural law thus gives way to a wholly secular positive law. Out of the ashes of the feudal concept of the transcendent, manifesting the sovereign right of kings, the secular modern state was born.[8]

As these historical references may suggest, my claim is that we have arrived today at a critical juncture that shares a number of striking parallels to the baroque era in Europe during the seventeenth century. As occurred in the aftermath of the Protestant Reformation and the ensuing rise of text-based literacy, today technological developments have also brought about a major shift in the dominant forms of communication. As a result, we, too, are witnessing fundamental changes in mind and culture. In 1600, Giordano Bruno died at the stake for blasphemously theorizing an asymmetrical proliferation of infinite worlds.[9] Today, we call Bruno's vision the Internet. No longer blasphemous, the immanent unfolding of infinite forms increasingly constitutes the reality in which we live. It also spurs the iconoclash of the digital baroque.

With the Protestant Reformation the lived experience of prayer shifted within. In this dispensation, an unadorned and newly decentralized speech act ("This bread is Christ's body, this wine is His blood") trumped the pageantry and visual spectacle of public religious ceremony.[10] As modernity developed, the realm of the sacred (including natural reason and natural law) contracted further, leaving an even more expansive secular domain for positive law to operate in. Modern jurisprudential thought reflects this trend. The spirit of equitable justice, once the touchstone of social and political life, has given way to uniform codes, instrumental reason, behavioral economics, and the calculation of subjective interests and preferences measured by disparate metrics of pleasure and pain (whether it is the maximization of individual wealth or some other calculus of maximized individual satisfaction).[11] As Habermas has written, the current liberal paradigm "no longer favors a particular ideal of society, a particular vision of the good life or even a particular political option."[12] In Habermas's view, we can only "hope" people will orient themselves to the common good, as they see it.[13]

However, with the proliferation of legal measures – in the form of rules, principles, and regulations, guided by disparate metrics of social utility, among other legal norms – that hope has grown increasingly attenuated. With the advent of what has been called the "protean self"[14] and the "hyper-modern individual,"[15] excess, fragmentation, and intensification (of speed, affect, and uncertainty) have become the norm. This state of affairs raises the question: Is the contemporary baroque self losing the capacity for (and perhaps the interest in) self-demotion in response to the claims of actual objects, events, and others? Yet, it is this very act upon which empathy and responsible caretaking, the core constituents of ethical reality, depend.

According to Isaiah Berlin the liberal tradition of tolerance and the appreciation of life's imperfections is the ironic fruit of an intolerant European Romanticism. But the irony does not end there. For it might well turn out that the instrumental or pragmatic rationality of Liberalism may be coming undone for lack of what the Romantics craved most: *Eros*, enchantment, the libidinal binding power of the law, which is to say, the animating and authenticating source of belief in something larger than the monadic self. Societies need enchantment to sustain an underlying *mythos*.[16] The legal imagination is constituted and animated by foundational *mythopoieic* images and narrative forms. These narratives and images bring into being (and police under color of law) particular forms of life. In so doing they confer value and meaning on a way of being in the world among others. As we saw in Chapter 4, however, that imagination is susceptible to historic forms of derangement. This is what we encountered in the in the neo-baroque dreamscape of David Lynch's *Mulholland Drive*.

The baroque legal imagination ramifies law's presence everywhere. As in Kafka's labyrinthine bureaucracies, law's validity remains, but it lacks significance. This collapse of meaningful authority harks back to Bruno's metaphysical interpretation of the Copernican system at the dawn of modernity.[17] For Bruno, the transcendent realm of the divine merged into the material world. And as divinity went, so went the king (hitherto God's representative on earth).[18] In Bruno's view, as in Deleuze's more recent philosophy of "pure immanence," there are no longer any privileged points in the universe. The secular mechanics and strategies of power in a political world of human design that began to take shape in the early modern writings of Hobbes and Machiavelli have developed over time into what Foucault has described as the microphysics of disciplinary power within a metonymic system of economic exchange. Power could now be taken as a right that could be possessed, transferred, or alienated, just like any other commodity.[19]

By late modernity this is what was left of the royal investiture, the rite of legitimation that once constituted the transcendent authority of the king's law. Ours is the dispensation of nominalism and the secular market. Like the characters in Kafka's *The Castle*, where sovereign authority is no more than a rumor,[20] we, too, seem to have been cut off. The door that opens to the transcendent source of law's legitimation appears to have been shut tight.[21] Exiled from a living *nomos*, "the 'state of emergency' in which we live is not the exception but the rule."[22] These words, penned by Walter Benjamin in 1940, carry an ominous familiarity today. Under such conditions, it becomes increasingly difficult to sustain fundamental liberal ideals such as Rawls's notion of "a fair system of cooperation between citizens regarded as free and equal," or Ronald Dworkin's twin concepts of dignity and self-respect.[23] What animates belief in these intuitive assertions? That is a question to which positivism, instrumental rationality, and the ideology of the market place can offer no fruitful response.

To the extent that law is more than command, more than obedience to rules, to the extent that law seeks legitimacy in a *nomos*, a living reality of shared normative beliefs, there may be no escaping the second order domain of metaphysics. Born and bred in the *mythos* of *logos*, metaphysics drives the quest for legitimating mythic narratives and images.[24] These are what Goodrich calls the hidden foundations of law.[25] They are the perennial gift of the poetic and visual sublime.

There is no direct path to this anagogic truth, and the path that remains is fraught with danger. The ersatz sublime in the service of totalized political power proved catastrophic in the twentieth century. We witnessed this, for example, in Albert Speer's Nazi "cathedrals of light" whose spectacular effects were designed to intensify the shock and awe of the Nuremberg rallies.[26] Cult leaders from Hitler to Mao Zedung and Pol Pot channeled mythic violence to blot out the lives of countless millions who, in the false light of ersatz sublime ideals, were made to appear too insignificant to be worthy of the utopia to come. But no utopia arrived, just the killing fields. Given this historical backdrop, who can deny the need for vigilance to ensure that the sublime remains grounded in the actual? This moment, this set of particulars, this singular other who stands before me – each infinite in their demands and as such irreducible to the totalizing impulse of encyclopedic knowledge and systematic ideology. On law's field of pain and death, one thing at least remains certain: if we do not begin with the cultural and cognitive conditions that nurture the aspiration to incalculable justice, if we do not continually strive to grasp the ethical sublime in its impossible particularity, we shall end up without it.

This core ethical concern is what rivets our attention to law's migration to the screen in the age of the digital baroque. We live amid spectacles and shadows; yet, signs persist of an underlying poetic structure of law. Behind what John Noonan once referred to as the mask of the law lies the uncanny source of law's legitimacy: the sublime event of aspirational justice.[27] Unlike classical contract theory, or law as the command of the sovereign, the traditional liberal origin stories for law, law metaphysically reconceived begins with the ethics of response. Ethics originates with attunement to what situated conflict and the singular other demand of us.[28] In our response to that primary ethical calling we affirm our ethical nature and give it a name. It is our own name, in recognition of the one who calls. This is the impossible and inescapable ethical task with which we are charged: to respond with care to the infinite demands of being and others. It is an impossible task because no human response will ever exhaust such demands. But this very impossibility, which as Derrida notes is "at one with the possibility that makes it possible," is also that which motivates us, and constitutes necessity for us.[29] In this sense, the ethical sublime is an aspirational value, an always yet-to-be. Its infinitude humbles us, and makes vivid the constraint our finitude imposes. Yet, at the same time, as Shira Wolosky notes, "each moral finitude must have positive responsibility for each other moral finitude."[30] In this dispensation, contrary to Heidegger's belief, first philosophy is ethical, not ontological. The ethical (being in response to the other) is prior to the existential (positing truth-values, whether from the Cartesian cogito or from Nietzsche's will to power).[31]

I have argued that law's iconoclash in the age of the digital baroque requires new forms of visual eloquence to accommodate the elusiveness of incontrovertible facts.[32] But baroque aesthetics without metaphysical resolve risks inviting persuasion in the service of an unfettered will to totalized power. Unanchored by the ethical sublime, law's forms proliferate, leaving law to preside over a labyrinth of fragments, on a landscape of ruins. That is what it means to say, as Levinas does, that today we stand on the brink of "morality without institutions."[33] The challenge we face, the one that each generation must face anew, is to institutionalize morality, to re-embody law's legitimating quest for justice. In this book, I have argued that positivism, instrumentalism, and the ideology of the marketplace lack the normative resources to fend off the specter of nihilism and the political and legal ascendancy of a totalizing will to power. In a word, they cannot do justice to justice. To meet that challenge requires metaphysical insight.[34] Rescuing law from the legitimation crisis that arises with law's iconoclash will depend upon our ability to recollect that which lay hidden in the shadows of endlessly proliferating form, beyond the matrix of algorithmically coded digital fragments.

Today, technological mastery over visual representation amplifies the individual's sense of power and control. However, this development carries a price. Mastery of the virtual invites indifference to the real. And lack of the real produces metaphysical longing, a condition of perpetual homesickness. In the modern era the dominance of scientific reason and instrumental rationality pushed the classical rhetorical tradition and the humanist ideal of ethical wisdom into the shadows. Eloquence became synonymous with empty ornamentation. Its role in presenting (or opening up a clearing for) the sublime was supplanted by an ambition to totalize knowledge in the quest for rational certainty. Critical thinking, with its ideals of logical necessity and impersonal causation, offers no home for the rhetorical/humanist ideals of situated invention, creative intuition, and the eloquence of prudent interpretation.[35]

Visual jurisprudence aims to revitalize these perennial rhetorical values. Visual eloquence is the offshoot of an integral rhetoric that seeks to harmonize the aesthetic and the ethical. As Stephen Toulmin has written: "The task is not to build new, more comprehensive systems of theory with universal and timeless relevance, but to limit the scope of even the best-framed theories, and fight the intellectual reductionism that became entrenched during the ascendancy of rationalism."[36] Toulmin aspired to devise anew the grounds for pluralism and tolerance. It is the same agenda that Descartes and his contemporaries had in mind as they grappled with catastrophic religious wars and epistemological uncertainty in the baroque era of seventeenth century Europe. But now, gazing across a landscape that has shown us the consequences of the Cartesian model as it has played out from early to late modernity, it has become apparent that a new paradigm is needed. We have come full circle and the renewal of the very impulse that gave birth to modernity, in the face of comparable epistemological crises, now calls for an integral rhetoric that complements the virtues and counters the defects of critical reason with the sublime eloquence and binding power of ethical wisdom.

The sublime, together with closely associated notions of self-transcendence (*ek-sistence*)[37] and mimesis (*being-as*),[38] invites renewed insight into the humanist ideals of visual imagination, ingenious invention, and prudent understanding. On this path of rediscovery we encounter a means of overcoming the Cartesian dualism that comes of disincarnating and denaturalizing the image.[39] Sublime representation restores the body and the material world as a source of truth.[40] Unlike the pre-modern model of correspondence, however, based on the Aristotelian notion of material "species" linking observer to observed, sublime representation now comes to be understood as the offspring of mimesis, the faculty of representation. Conceived as the natural human proclivity to transcend self in the mode of *being-as*, mimesis describes the mind's capacity to become attuned to the sublime otherness of the actual.

Situated invention and enactive intuition ground the visual image in the specific context from which it sets out to make something appear. This visual account, like the narrative account of creative metaphor, enacts meaning as an act of invention. Invention in this sense is the faculty that finds the means that are available in a given situation to open a clearing in which to bring the real to mind. This is what topical philosophy or the philosophy of rhetoric offers, and what critical philosophy cannot. In the Legal Realist movement we witness an inchoate striving to revive the virtues of this ancient rhetorical practice. This retrieval, driven by the felt need to become attuned to the demands of a given fact situation, seeks to express the real in the particular. Aided by the tools of critical reflection, with insights from phenomenology, cognitive psychology, and pragmatic philosophy, among other disciplines, contemporary jurists may renew the Realist aspiration to synthesize experience and knowledge. Crucial to this approach is a shift in emphasis from rules or axiomatic certainties as a point of departure, which typifies the modality of critical reason, to the intuitive mode of trained attunement to the concrete demands of a given conflict situation.

In this respect, the guiding imperative of Legal Realism (namely: ask first what the facts demand) retains its significance. Intuition and invention work together to produce *pathos* (motivated belief or feeling) along with *logos* (the structured presentation of reasons warranting belief). Critical thinking without the capacity to invent amid the complex entanglements of situated conflict, those swirling particularities out of which legal judgment arises, conjures validity without the motivating force (James' "sentiment of rationality") that compels belief. In short, the highly effective, associative, and largely unconscious nature of visualizing law calls for more than critical thinking alone can offer.

With uncanny foresight over three centuries ago Giambattista Vico, perhaps the last great rhetorician in the humanist tradition, saw where the rational method of Descartes must lead if it were to remain cut off from the human faculties of poetic imagination, ingenious invention, and prudent understanding. Indeed, these faculties were deemed by Vico to be the penultimate basis for generating and maintaining civil society. He believed that human nature and the nature of the ethical in particular are ill suited to an exclusively scientific study, as if they could be understood the same way as material objects in the natural world. Science, for all its technological fruits, could never replicate the social and intellectual gifts provided by the poetic imagination, inventive ingenuity, and prudent understanding. Nor could Cartesian rationality change the unruly reality of human character and the dark vicissitudes of emotional conflict and deceit. The scientific method could only shunt these subjects to the intellectual sidelines or, more accurately, to the subterranean depths awaiting Marx's insights into "false consciousness" and Freud's profound decoding of the vicissitudes of the unconscious.

Vico understood that the art and craft of politics and law, which minister to the incessant turbulence and conflict that afflict human affairs, require more than science to promote civility. As Vico wrote: "The soul must be enticed by corporeal images and impelled to love, for once it loves it is easily taught to believe. Once it believes and loves, the fire of passion must be infused into it so as to break its inertia and force it to *will*."[41] According to Vico, without a carefully cultivated art of eloquence, public life remains threatened with division and, if left unchecked, ultimately faces decay. The scientific method might produce subjective certainty, but it also introduces an ethos of solitude. The behavioral template on which it relies employs a subjective measure of pleasure and pain that renders individuals incapable of civic life. Each acting "according to his own pleasure or advantage . . . recalls them from civil community to the state of solitude."[42] An education steeped in critical analysis, dominated by the unitary, rationalist claims of the Cartesian method, without training across a more diverse range of scholarly disciplines (such as history, poetics, philosophy, and verbal and visual rhetoric) leaves us cut off from the roots of wisdom and the means to convey it. Rhetorically disarmed, drained of passion, belief, and outward (other-) directed care, citizens may be left without the necessary means to curtail "the ferocity of fools, to turn them from error through prudence, and to bring them benefit through virtue."[43]

Without the ability to prudently manage the vicissitudes of fortune and misfortune in civil life, without the capacity to recognize and counter "simulation and dissimulation," the ever shifting conditions that serve as the basis for political, social, and historical reflectivity, human society remains vulnerable, sorely threatened by unruly impulses and the deceits of power, greed, and political ambition. As Michael Mooney observes, distilling the essential insight of the rhetorical tradition: "Eloquence without knowledge is hollow and empty; but knowledge without eloquence is mute and powerless, incapable of effect in men's lives."[44] As Cicero, Vico's model rhetor, concludes (alluding to the followers of Epicurus):

> [L]et us dismiss these masters without comment, as they are excellent fellows satisfied in the belief in their own happiness; only let us warn them to keep to themselves as a holy secret, though it may be extremely true, their doctrine that it is not the business of a wise man to take part in politics – for if they convince us and all our best men of the truth of this, they themselves will not be able to live the life of leisure which is their ideal.[45]

Uneasily lodged between reason and desire, jurisprudence maps out the basis for a sustainable social life. Neither the sublime gifts of freedom nor the imperatives of law can flourish absent the scaffolding provided by civic life and the social institutions that sustain it.[46] It is in view of this ultimate prize, in the service of human flourishing, that Vico stressed the need for educating the young not simply or even preliminarily in the disembodied methods of Cartesian analysis and critique, but rather in the cultivation of visual imagination, inventive ingenuity, and prudent understanding – the progenitors of wisdom and eloquence combined.[47] On this view, rather than emphasizing (as the Cartesian method does) the importance of generality and abstraction, the qualities of mind Vico is most anxious to cultivate include creativity, memory, perception (*ingegno*, or ingenuity), and prudent, context-based understanding. These capacities, Vico writes, are "all most necessary for the culture of the best humanity: [the imagination] for the art of painting, sculpture, architecture, music, poetry, and eloquence; [memory] for learning languages and history; [ingenuity] for inventions; and [understanding] for prudence."[48]

The sublime marks the limit of the empirical.[49] It is a break with the known in the face of the unknown. Against Descartes' rational enlightenment (embodied in a universal scientific method) and its naïve elevation of totalizing reason, it remains incumbent upon us to face the dark folds of history and the vicissitudes of the political (with all its chaotic passions and dissimulations). We must be willing to confront the thick shadows of night, the tumult of the body, and its fits of passion, and the unruly vicissitudes of the unconscious, with its infinite forms of desire. In short, we need to see the baroque world of shadows and ruin, of fragments and violence, of pain and death, as one of the stages upon which the drama of law plays out.

The repudiation of the Cartesian mind/body duality coincides with the emergence of a post-Cartesian optics. In Cartesian epistemology and its positivist offshoots in the writings of Hobbes and Machiavelli, language is an artifact of mind. By contrast, an optic of the sublime addresses poetic and visual representation as essential in their own right, not merely conventional and derivative. As a source of originary meaning (as constitutive of a visual *mythos*[50] or metaphor), mimesis incarnates the visual imagination. It is this natural mimetic endowment that allows humans to become one with an object (in the acts of naming and imaging). Mimesis, the faculty of imitation through *being-as*, is thus simultaneously the condition for knowledge and a basis for wonder.[51]

In this view, mind and representation develop together. Indeed, as Mooney states, both "are the necessary outcome of social urgency, the result of a spontaneous attempt . . . to grasp a startling experience through images that are familiar."[52] This is the heroic act *par excellence.* Harnessing the originating force of metaphors and visual images in a creative/intuitive judgment compels the will of others through eloquence. This is not a matter of logic, or of experience, or of rhetorical training alone. To a significant extent it is a matter of inspired poetic visual construction, which is to say, a collaboration with something other which calls or addresses the attentive mind, seeking voice, image, word. The embodied mind's contact with that which is infinite explodes reason and its yearning for certainty, totality, and systematic knowledge. The sublime is sublime to the extent that it always points to that which exceeds representation.[53]

The category of the sublime represents the key to understanding visual imagination, or *fantasia* ("man's unique capacity for imaginative insights and reconstruction"[54]). Heidegger, among others, invites a way of thinking about this experience in terms of transcendence, or *Da-sein* (being-*there*), which describes the natural human tendency to go beyond self. This experience of *ek-stasis* (being outside of, or beside oneself) comports well with the phenomenology of perception and the process philosophies of Bergson and Whitehead. Central to this way of thinking is the dynamic of minding reality: that active process in which what is before us comes to mind. As Dufrenne succinctly writes: "Being is precisely the identity of meaning and of the real."[55] Mindfulness in this sense is a way of being with, or letting be. Mindfulness establishes the site of our access to the infinite other-than-self. When that responsiveness takes place, when presence occurs, the experience is suffused with a sense of the sublime. It is in response to this sublime event that mimesis, the human capacity to represent reality, leaves its finite trace. This experience remains aesthetic so long as the call of being rather than human being comes to mind. Only the latter entangles us in the ethical, proto-social world of humanity.[56]

It is at this juncture that the thought of Emmanuel Levinas and Jacques Derrida can contribute most. Their work helps us to reimagine human self-transcendence not simply in terms of infinite becoming, the flux of immanent being (*physis*), but also in terms of a living mosaic in which the other (the neighbor, the one nearby) and the robust singularity of situated conflict grow entangled at the site of attuned judgment. Levinas's notion of "otherwise than being" renews metaphysics, reconceiving it as first philosophy.[57] Here we return to the idea, previously referred to, of "ethics as an optics." In that earlier reference, the optics at issue was Cartesian. It posited an abstract, conceptual (objectified and disembodied) frame for generating the data of perception and a felicific calculus for assessing the intellect's interpretation of their meaning. The main thrust of this calculus is to ask: does the meaning conduce to pleasure, does it avert pain? If so, its reliability is vouchsafed. By contrast, a Levinasian (ethically sublime) optics shifts the frame of reference from self (the subjective experience of pleasure and pain) to Other – as presented in the self-transcending state of otherwise-than-being, which is to say, the state of *being-as* in which the infinite demands of situated conflict and the singular Other come to mind. This is the origin of the ethical and of the primordial bond (of religion, in the etymological sense of *religare*, or "binding") that constitutes sociality. As Derrida writes, "[r]eligion is responsibility or it is nothing at all."[58] The binding responsibility that originates in the sublime event of aspirational justice founds and sustains the social world. This is the province of meaning (and not power alone) over which law presides.

In this view, ingenuity, prudence, and the visual imagination are endowments of mind that need to be cultivated in order to preserve civil society. As Joseph Mazzeo put it (describing Teasuro's view of the world as a "metaphysical" poem and God a "metaphysical" poet), for Tesauro ingenuity is "the faculty in man analogous to God's creative power. It is a small particle of the divine nature, for it can create 'being' where there was no 'being' before. As God created a 'metaphysical' world, so the poet creates 'metaphysical' poems."[59] In a similar vein, Vico has written: "a fable is the essence of things transformed in human minds."[60] This crucial Vichian concept echoes Benjamin's understanding of the metaphysical nature of language itself: "The name is that *through* which, and *in* which, language itself communicates itself absolutely. In the name, the mental entity that communicates itself is *language*... God's creation is completed when things receive their names from man, from whom in name language alone speaks."[61] Or as Ernesto Grassi puts it, according to Horace: "[P]oetry is that primary force that is able to overcome the chaos in which men originally live. It is the means by which the order of a human society develops.

The poets are named *vates*, "revealers" or seers, because they see new possible human relationships in an original underived manner and give birth to these possibilities."[62]

It is the faculty of ingenuity through which man grasps "the relationship between things in a concrete situation in order to determine their meaning."[63] This is not a logical derivation, nor does it describe conventional signs, or codified law for that matter, which lack any necessary correspondence to the actual. Unlike conventional signs, the revelation of something new, like the construction of an original image or metaphor, takes place through the work of creative insight.[64] The gift of metaphor and of the authentic visual image is a gift of invention that brings a reality before our eyes. Invention makes things speak or appear. As Verene writes, "[i]t is a process in which the *is* itself is made . . . Every fable is true speech and every metaphor is 'a fable in brief.'"[65] Unlike scientific (rational) discourse, this is not a meaning that arises on the basis of reasons or the causal logic of antecedent premises. Poetic metaphor and the visual image establish meaning through their own invention, through what is shown.[66] This, then, is the great heroic act of the ancient poet which Vico celebrates. As Grassi puts it: "The Herculean act is always a metaphorical one and every genuine metaphor is in this sense Herculean work."[67] In short, for Vico, as for Dante and Shelley, the living image is an expression of value in virtue of that which it brings into (or leaves out of) existence. The poetic task *par excellence* is to embody (or legislate) the meaning of reality. This task is completed only when the assignment of meaning extends to the formation of society and its future.[68] In this Vichian dispensation, poetic wisdom originates in a metaphysics that is "not rational and abstract," but "felt and imagined."[69] As Vico writes, "luminous images," crafted by inventive fantasy, "blind the mind with lightning bolts" that "conjure up human passions in the ringing and thunder of . . . astonishment."[70]

On this view, we may say that visual jurisprudence envisions a metaphysic of the sublime.[71] Such a sublime jurisprudence accounts for the metaphysical origin of society (or sociality) as coincident with the origin of the law of law – or justice. This origin is not a rational construct, as embodied in the modern concept of the social contract, or the deontological derivation of universal rational principles. Rather, it is an act of poetic visual imagination[72] – the genesis, as Robert Cover would put it, of a foundational narrative (or *mythos*) that constitutes a way of life.[73] It is, as Vico wrote, the basis for a customary practice.[74] Shaped and informed by the ethical sublime, that mythic narrative aspires to "the best humanity."[75]

The reintegration of poetic visual imagination, inventive ingenuity, and prudent understanding in our time offers a way to counter the deformations of the digital baroque. The visual imagination takes us across the great Cartesian divide that separates mind and body as well as mind and nature, and nature and sign. Self-transcendence (*Ek-sistenz* as *Ek-stasis*) animates *fantasia* (poetic or visual imagination), which uncannily brings the actual to mind.[76] Responding to the demands of being implicates the *aesthetic* sublime manifest in Heidegger's ontology.[77] Responding to the demands of others implicates the *ethical* sublime as reflected in Levinas's otherwise than being.[78] Each of these singular expressions arises through a demotion of self in fealty to the actual.

I offer this contemporary recapitulation of the rhetorical ideal that we find in the humanist tradition, and in the writings of Vico in particular, as suggestive of how we might achieve metaphysical resolve in our own time and thus work through the manifold impasses of law's iconoclash in the age of the digital baroque. This effort is consonant with Toulmin's essentially Vichian aspiration to find a new basis for pluralism and tolerance without succumbing to a destabilizing epistemological uncertainty and paralyzing ethical relativism on the one hand, or a totalizing dialect of knowledge/power, on the other.[79] The ethical sublime offers an ecumenical and cosmopolitan basis for an ethically informed visual imagination. The knowledge that a sublime epistemology allows is contingent, not absolute, in that its emergence remains responsive to a concrete particularity (the situated conflict and singular other to which it responds). In short, this is not some Platonic Ideal waiting to be discovered – or claimed in behalf of totalized political power. The inventive ingenuity of poetic visual imagination, of finding an apt image or a fitting metaphor in response to a situated demand, emerges out of this sublime condition: disorder (*a-logos*) enters a *logos* (a structured representation). The sublime forcefulness of metaphoric or visual eloquence consists in the dissimulation of the artifice (*logos*) by which what is (*physis*) comes to appear. The paradox of sublime knowledge is that there must be a loss of knowledge (of the means of its production) in order for the thing itself to appear in its brilliance (as it is).[80] Sensing an infinite presence in a finite representation palpably resists the impulse to totalize; nor can it vanquish a residual sense of uncertainty and perplexity.[81] Our initial shudder in the face of the uncanny sublime does not preclude subsequent reflection. Indeed, the clash of interpretations is the backdrop against which eloquent discourse (and its lesser forms) proceeds.[82]

First philosophy thus emerges mimetically and metaphysically from the ethical sublime. Responsibility for the Other, and the third, who dwells beside the one I face, generates the bond on the basis of which society is held together.[83] Mimetically expressed, the ethical sublime is the jurisgenerative force behind the institutions of law and culture that sustain sociality, justice, and civic life as a whole. Bending the sublime generative force of the aesthetic impulse toward the gravitational field of the Other, checks the jurispathic effect of unconstrained *Eros*, while also making the disappointments of human finitude bearable. If eloquence is wisdom speaking,[84] and wisdom is the ethical *par excellence*, eloquence arises in otherwise than being: a sublime self-transcendence in the face of, and in our response to, the Other. Here we see the faculties of visual imagination, inventive ingenuity, and prudent understanding operating in unison. Ramified by our knowledge of the third, ethical responsibility develops into the civic discourse of justice.

Because our knowledge always falls short of the infinite that calls forth the creative word and image, we can never leave the shadow of uncertainty, error, and incompleteness. In this dispensation, mimesis is the condition of the possibility of knowledge, not its guarantee.[85] In our response to the call of Being (beauty), history (providence), and the Other (justice), mimesis configures the tripartite structure of a post-Cartesian optics, a sublimely embodied visuality that takes us from the pre-modern understanding of truth as correspondence and the modern semiotic view of truth as conventional signification, to a paradigm of truth as sublime representation. In this view, self-transcendence is a necessary precondition of both knowledge and ethical wisdom; mimesis is the faculty of representation that makes knowledge and ethical wisdom compelling. Eloquence in this sense is not epiphenomenal (or merely ornamental, as critical thinkers in the anti-rhetorical tradition of Descartes are prone to assert); rather, it radiates a sublime presence which we experience as the binding force of the actual.

Legal theory has endured too long the anemic understanding of human nature upon which rational theories of agency, economics, and instrumental calculation rely. The eclipse in contemporary legal theory of passion, *Eros*, eloquence, and the metaphysical roots of sociality has weakened its capacity for ethical wisdom. The visual turn in legal theory and practice makes this evasion increasingly untenable. To advance further along the path of visual jurisprudence requires two essential moves:

1. An explicit focus upon rhetorical craft and in particular the cultivation of visual literacy and its engagement with visual eloquence. This requires greater fluency in the construction, deconstruction, and reconstruction of visual evidence and argument. It also requires the capacity to critically assess and, when needed, to impose appropriate checks upon non-deliberative forms of visual persuasion; and
2. A retrieval of the core humanist ideals of situated invention, creative intuition, and eloquence in the service of ethical wisdom and fact-based justice.

Plainly, the Platonic tradition cannot guide us here, with its stunted understanding of the poet's role, its cheapened depiction of the mimetic faculty, and its concomitant subordination of the visual imagination to the putative ideal of disembodied reason. At the same time, however, we can ill afford risking the opposing danger of rhetorical excess, as in Nietzsche's totalized aesthetic of the eternal recurrence of the same, or Heidegger's mystical eloquence in his philosophy of Being. These more recent thinkers have much to teach us about what the Platonic tradition, and the Cartesian mindset in particular, suppress (to our detriment), but far too little about the ethical, which is to say about caring – not just for being, but for others.

Eloquence uprooted from wisdom, eloquence let loose in an unruly material world driven by passion, greed, deceit, and the urge to dominate others, a world governed by markets bound solely by calculations of maximized pleasure and minimized pain, eloquence divorced from knowledge of the ethical and thus at the mercy of totalizing (hyper-erotic or hyper-rational) ambitions, produces a distorted and unstable understanding of justice and civility. Civic life cannot prosper, and indeed is at risk of decay, under prolonged conditions of epistemological and ethical uncertainty. To counter such a reality requires the cultivation of the mimetic faculty grounded in the ethical sublime. Eloquent wisdom in this sense provides the scaffolding for civil society.[86] Civic education, as a counterforce to Machiavellian *Realpolitik*, sets out to civilize the monstrousness of political power. On this view, civics, politics, aesthetics, and the ethical are manifestly entangled. Wisdom consists in according each its proper scope, value, and application, and in allowing each to appropriately shape and inform and, when necessary, check and balance the other.

The wise lawyer-poet-statesman, acting in the face of unruly passions and deceits, on the one hand, and the tyranny of rational systems of knowledge or the similarly totalizing impulse of mythic violence in the service of pathological metaphysics, on the other, finds the means to make civic life both secure and just. In this sense, the story of law's legitimacy is a story of beauty as well as justice. Beauty and justice produce acceptance without violence or fear. Beauty enchants us by the expressive force of eloquence, while justice compels us by the unsurpassable, untotalizable force of ethical demand, the sense of being obliged by or responsible for what the actual calls to mind.

Law's sublime beginning prefigures and foretells its impossible end. The necessity of its lesser forms, the offshoot of our finitude, our craving for mastery, certainty, and totality, coexists with the impulse to propel the law toward aspirational possibilities. Hence law's endless oscillation between power and meaning, will and belief, command and acceptance – which is to say, between Genesis I and Genesis II, the two poles of our divided nature. Within this field of order and possibility law strives to create anew from one case to the next a moment when justice presides. Such is the perennial impulse of equity, the felt need to look beyond the limits of law in order to correct it.[87] Justice and the ethical take on a living (albeit imperfectly realized) presence in concrete acts of prudent judgment, which is to say, judgment that is attuned to the real, and that poetically stirs hearts and minds by means of figurative and visual eloquence.

Today, as in the baroque era of the seventeenth century, we are once again experiencing the deformity of visual forms. There is a heightened sense of inhabiting a universe of representations that seems to turn the urge for real world knowledge back upon itself, as if in an endless regression, like some spectacular baroque tapestry or infinite arabesque endlessly folding in upon itself.[88] The worldwide web, that centerless and constantly morphing network of virtual connections, serves as an apt symbol of the digital baroque culture in which we are living today. We are obsessed, as were those who lived in earlier baroque times, with the endless proliferation of forms as mere projections, shadows of the real, the specters of virtual reality.

Law's entanglements are patterns of meaning only partly seen and understood. The source of legal meaning is to be found in the way the mind encounters law's forms and absences. In this respect, legal judgment shares a kinship with psychoanalytic dream work. The sublime is the domain of law's unconscious. It is manifest in every situation of conflict, amid the infinite inexpressible demands of others and of the otherness of actuality itself. In the legal decision-making process, a tapestry of conventional forms (rules, codes, regulations, previous case decisions) and inchoate impressions (feelings, impulses, desires, memories, ideas, and so on) grow entangled. The pattern we recognize is called judgment. Allusion to its constituent elements (to the extent they are accessible to consciousness and deemed pertinent as proper warrants for belief) is called interpretation. Interpretations grow entangled as well, for they, too, are only partially explicit or visible. The irreducibility of every judgment to the actuality that prompts it leaves a gap in which future legal decision makers hover – attentive to what a new inexpressible reality calls to mind, including that which is expressed and that which remains silent and unseen in law's conventional forms.

Law's entanglements are entanglements all the way down – against a backdrop of what Christopher Bollas calls the "silent radiant intelligence" of the mind's attunement to the real.[89] In every situated conflict the decision maker's "evenly suspended attention" mines fragments in search of patterns of meaning that are orchestrated in accordance with the felt needs of the situation. Increasingly, these days, in addition to objects, others, and texts, visual images also constitute a discrete claim to entangled meaning. Visual meanings may be expressed or hidden; their significance may be strangely overdetermined or flattened out in the insular binary code of digital simulation. Every object we think and feel with – whether texts, things, or images – invites different methods of making meaning. Each encompasses a distinct way of being in the world, with its own virtues and defects, and its own metaphysical, ethical, and aesthetic registers, in which fluency is required.

Digital arabesques are monadic, self-contained dream worlds – like Neo's world in *The Matrix*, or the sealed mindscape of Murakami's spy in *Hard-Boiled Wonderland at the End of the World*, or the unconstructed dream state of limbo in Christopher Nolan's *Inception*. It is in the nature of digital visual simulation to encourage a potent mixture of naïve realism and totalization – as if nothing other than what we see exists beyond the screen. Entanglements, by contrast, constitute a social world in which not only are meanings shared, but the meaning making process itself depends upon open-ended attunement to the demands of others. The arabesque world of digital simulation operates on the plane of metonymy, of equally fungible, equally complete constructs. Such a world lacks the uncanny otherness that attests to the sublime presence of actuality. It bares no transcendental reference. There is important information to be mined in digital worlds: fact-based representations and feeling-effects that relate to the actual. But simulations are not of the world: they lack metaphysical depth, the sublime radiance of the actual. Living on the screen in this way is not the same as being entangled within the unpredictable and uncontrollable vicissitudes of real life. This is so in everyday life and in the life of the law.

Justice is an otherness we will never codify or simulate or otherwise master. Its fate depends upon our fealty to the real – which means on our continued willingness (and preparedness) to attune ourselves to the uncanny demands of the aesthetic and ethical sublime. The discipline of law needs this reach, this depth. Perhaps this is what law needs most, because it is what law is most in danger of losing, in the age of the digital baroque.

Law remains, but justice vanishes. Like tears, justice is an evanescent reality. Its presence is real, but it lacks guarantees. That is how it is with the sublime – as evanescent as tears and as true to an otherwise invisible reality. The humanist tradition recounts the jurist's role as steward of the perennial and elusive aspiration to justice. Today, humanism is morphing into novel forms, and so the question arises: "What disciplines can aid in the legal study of such vanishing truths, such real but absconded things?"[90] Visual jurisprudence is one response, one way to meet the felt need for a new visual rhetoric suitable to the digital visual age in which we live.

The flattened screen and the ascendance of digital simulation in law as elsewhere in contemporary culture threaten the collapse of the symbolic and with it the loss of the sublime. That peril constitutes a crucial aspect of law's iconoclash. Yet, the sublime persists – if we but persist in pursuing it, and naming it – its presence and its absence as well as its falsification in ersatz forms of spectral delight and mythic violence. That task is now part and parcel of what it means to be a jurist, if jurists are to remain true to their calling not simply as engineers or agents of social order but also as custodians of justice. To that end, we need a new paradigm for theorizing law along with new training manuals and techniques, on screen and off. In sum, we need a visual jurisprudence that brings together media studies, art history, cultural and cognitive psychology, ethnography, and psychoanalysis, among other fields in the humanities and social sciences.

Law remains, but justice vanishes. Over what social world will law preside in our time? The binding power of law, if it be not force alone, takes us beyond fear. If law is to preside over the marriage of power and meaning we must reach for deeper and richer cognitive and cultural resources, we must seek the ethical taproot of wonder and care. Knowledge is not enough. The custodial role of the jurist requires an assiduous cultivation of mindfulness, and the ethical wisdom to which it leads. Mindfulness presupposes self-demotion in the act of responding to the actual, which is to say, to what the particular situation and the other who stands before us call to mind. Could it be that this purposive determination can shift our collective metaphysical register from Pascal's baroque terror before the infinite to a response of "admiration and reverence?"[91] We may hope that it is so, for our ethical entanglements with the world and others around us arise with the latter.

Visual eloquence invites the viewer to experience the reciprocal nature of mimetic identification – that process in which identifying what is present in the field of vision fuses with the viewer's sense of identity. Integrated judgment thus comes about as an offshoot of identity's entanglements. Judgment in this sense reflects both what we know (and feel) and who we are in relation to others and the world beyond the self. In baroque times, however, dreams and the will to power, fantasies and reality, vertiginously converge. At such times, the desperate urge toward mastery and control threatens to displace the capacity for self-demotion in the experience of something other. But when technical mastery trumps ethical and aesthetic attunement we forget what Deleuze calls the "dark precursor,"[92] that disparate moment of mythic silence when explanation fails, and from which the epiphany of integrated judgment (what Vico referred to as the ingenious vision of relationships) may arise.

Like an image, law invites us to forget or deny that which lies beyond its mimetic (figurative) aspect. Law oscillates between power and meaning, between aesthetic form (image, figure, copy, text) and moral authority – between arabesques and entanglements in the shorthand of this book. In this way, law re-enacts humanity's historic vacillation between the two poles of our nature: mastery (Genesis I) and service (Genesis II). In the age of the digital baroque, legal forms and measures endlessly ramify. Still law commands, and wants its commands to be accepted – not simply out of fear of punishment, but also in the belief that it is just, that law is more than the gunman writ large. When law lives as an image on the screen that aspiration makes it incumbent upon us all – jurists and lay people alike – to discern with great care whether the images we see are capable of bringing justice to mind.

Notes

1 Introduction

1 W. Shakespeare, *The Merchant of Venice*, Act III, Scene 2, lines 63–65, 74–76.
2 L. Wachowski and A. Wachowski (dirs.), *The Matrix*, Warner Bros, 1999.
3 I. Almond, *Sufism and Deconstruction: A Comparative Study of Derrida and Ibn Arabi*, New York: Routledge, 2004, p. 9.
4 D. Morgan, *The Sacred Gaze*, Berkeley, CA: University of California Press, 2005, p. 33.
5 Ibid.
6 B. Anderson, *Imagined Communities*, London: Verso, 2002, pp. 184–185.
7 See J. Derrida, "Force of Law: The Mystical Foundation of Authority," in D. Cornell et al. (eds.), *Deconstruction and the Possibility of Justice*, New York: Routledge, 1992, p. 26. See also I. Almond, *Sufism*.
8 See, e.g. P. Goodrich, "The Iconography of Nothing: Blank Spaces and the Representation of Law in *Edward VI and the Pope*," in C. Douzinas and L. Nead (eds.), *Law and the Image: The Authority of Art and the Aesthetics of Law*, Chicago: University of Chicago Press, 1999.
9 S. Michalski, *The Reformation and the Visual Arts*, London: Routledge, 1993, p. 62 (quoting John Calvin, *Institutes of the Christian Religion*).
10 S. Turkle, *Simulation and its Discontents*, Cambridge, MA: MIT Press, 2009, p. 7.
11 C. McCusker, "Between Natural Law and Legal Positivism: Plato's Minos and the Nature of Law," *Yale Journal of Law and the Humanities*, Vol. 22, 2010, pp. 83–104.
12 I. Almond, *Sufism*, p. 63.

13 W. Benjamin, *The Origin of German Tragic Drama*, London: Verso, 1998, p. 81.
14 Ibid., p. 66.
15 Ibid.
16 J-L. Godard, *Film socialisme*, Vega Film, 2010.
17 See, e.g. G. Watt, *Equity Stirring: The Story of Justice beyond Law*, Oxford: Hart, 2009.

2 Visual Jurisprudence

1 A. Seyhan, "Allegories of History: The Politics of Representation in Walter Benjamin," in D. Downing and S. Bazargan (eds.), *Image and Ideology in Modern/Postmodern Discourse*, Albany, NY: State University of New York Press, 1991, p. 233.
2 Quoted in S. Sontag, *Styles of Radical Will*, New York: Picador, 2002, p. 147.
3 Justice Antonin Scalia, announcing the Supreme Court's decision in *Scott v. Harris*, 550 U.S. 372 (2007), available at www.oyez.org/cases/2000-2009/2006/2006_05_1631/opinion+scott+v+harris+%22we+have+made+the+video+available%22&cd=1&hl=en&ct=clnk&gl=us.
4 Ibid.
5 L. U. Marks, *Enfoldment and Infinity: An Islamic Genealogy of New Media Art*, Cambridge, MA: MIT Press, 2010.
6 Ibid.
7 See, e.g. T. Burckhardt, *Art of Islam: Language and Meaning*, London: World of Islam Festival Publishing, 1976, p. 6 ("In Islam, icons are replaced by sacred writing which is, as it were, the visible embodiment of the Divine Word"). According to Burckhardt, aniconism is "one of the foundations, if not the main foundation, of the sacred art of Islam." Ibid., p. 27. He adds: "By precluding every image inviting man to fix his mind on something outside himself and to project his soul on to an 'individualizing' form, [aniconism] creates a void." Faced with that void, the contemplative mind "dissolves mental 'fixations'" and detaches consciousness from its "inward 'idols.'" Ibid., p. 29. In short, only emptiness of form ("melting away every objectification of the Divine") ensures that no false idol interposes between man and "the invisible presence of God." Ibid., p. 30. See also D. Clevenot and G. Degeorge, *Splendors of Islam: Architecture, Decoration and Design*, New York: Vendome Press, 2000, pp. 146–147 ("When looking at a pattern of geometric interlace [the Islamic arabesque] the spectator is always confronted with two possibilities: either to follow the movement of the line or to stop at the starred polygons springing out here and there. In other words, the geometric interlace functions as an apparatus whose object is to confound the gaze of the beholder . . . [I]t also possesses the characteristic of recognizing neither centre nor limit, and the ability to spread out virtually forever. Thus, the spectator who enters the logic of the interlace is enticed into mentally continually its development beyond the limits of the decorated surface. In other words, the geometric interlace possesses an existence which goes beyond material reality").

8 See, e.g. B. Hasslacher, "Beyond the Turing Machine," in R. Herken (ed.), *The Universal Turing Machine: A Half-Century Survey*, New York and Vienna: Springer, 1991, p. 388 ("The virtual world is a model of the physical world. We are interested in computing algorithms defined in this virtual world"). See also L. U. Marks, "Information, Secrets, and Enigmas: An Enfolding–Unfolding Aesthetics for Cinema," *Screen*, 50, 2009, p. 94 ("When information intervenes, image no longer directly expands from the universe of images but is the product of quantification").

9 J. L. Borges, *Labyrinths: Selected Short Stories and Other Writings*, New York: New Directions, 1964, p. 172.

10 B. Faure, *The Rhetoric of Immediacy*, Princeton, NJ: Princeton University Press, 1994, p. 216.

11 J. A. Maravall, *Culture of the Baroque: Analysis of a Historical Structure*, Minneapolis, MN: University of Minnesota Press, 1986, p. 153.

12 Ibid., pp. 82–90, 162.

13 H. Wölfflin, *Renaissance and Baroque*, Ithaca, NY: Cornell University Press, 1967, p. 77.

14 G. W. Leibniz, *Monadology and Other Philosophical Essays*, New York: Bobbs-Merrill, 1965, p. 158.

15 J. Bruner, *Acts of Meaning*, Cambridge, MA: Harvard University Press, 1990.

16 See T. Hobbes, *De Corpore*, Paris: Librarie Philosophique J. Vrin, 1999, Part I, ch. 3, para. 7; G. W. Leibniz, "Meditations on Knowledge, Truth, and Ideas," in G. W. Leibniz, *Philosophical Essays*, Indianapolis, IN: Hackett, 1989, pp. 22–27.

17 I. Murdoch, *The Sovereignty of the Good*, London: Routledge, 2002, p. 63.

18 Ibid.

19 Ibid.

20 S. Weil, *Waiting for God*, New York: Harper Perennial, 1992, p. 62 ("Above all our thought should be empty, waiting, not seeking anything, but ready to receive in its naked truth the object that is to penetrate it").

21 F. Varela, *Ethical Know-How: Action, Wisdom, and Cognition*, Stanford, CA: Stanford University Press, 1999, p. 3.

22 See A. Damasio, *The Feeling of What Happens: Body and Emotion in the Making of Consciousness*, New York: Harcourt Brace, 1999, p. 312 (noting that "consciousness begins as a feeling"). See also G. Vattimo, *Art's Claim to Truth*, New York: Columbia University Press, 2008, p. 66 (describing what Vattimo calls "affectivity").

23 A. Damasio, *Descartes' Error: Emotion, Reason, and the Human Brain*, New York: Penguin Books, 1994, p. 128.

24 See W. D. Casebeer and P. S. Churchland, "The Neural Mechanisms of Moral Cognition: A Multiple-Aspect Approach to Moral Judgment and Decision-Making," *Biology and Philosophy*, 2003, Vol. 18, pp. 169, 188 ("Moral judgments tell us what we ought to think so that we know what to do. Isolating the doing from the knowing via an artificial experimental regimen can remove the

directedness of moral cognition"). See also H. Putnam, *Meaning and the Moral Sciences*, London: Routledge & Kegan Paul, 1978, p. 5 ("A view of knowledge that acknowledges that the sphere of knowledge is wider than the sphere of 'science' seems to me to be a cultural necessity if we are to arrive at a sane and human view of ourselves or of science").

25 See, e.g. Longinus, *On the Sublime*, trans. W. H. Fyfe, Cambridge, MA and London: Harvard University Press, 1995. See also M. T. Cicero, *De Oratore*, trans. E. W. Sutton and H. Rackham, Cambridge, MA: Harvard University Press, 1948; Quintilian, *Institutio Oratoria*, Cambridge, MA and London: Harvard University Press, 1996; and G. Vico, *On the Study Methods of our Time*, Ithaca, NY: Cornell University Press: 1990. See generally C. van Eck, *Classical Rhetoric and the Visual Arts in Early Modern Europe*, Cambridge and New York: Cambridge University Press, 2007; J. Deger, *Shimmering Screens: Making Media in an Aboriginal Community*, Minneapolis, MN: University of Minnesota Press, 2006.

26 G. P. Stone, *The Ethics of Nature in the Middle Ages: On Boccaccio's Poetaphysics*, Basingstoke: Macmillan, 1998, p. 35.

27 As Vico wrote: "The soul must be enticed by corporeal images and impelled to love, for once it loves it is easily taught to believe. Once it believes and loves, the fire of passion must be infused into it so as to break its inertia and force it to will." G. Vico, *Study Methods*, p. 33. See D. P. Verene, *Vico's Science of Imagination*, Ithaca, NY: Cornell University Press, 1981, p. 33 ("Images or *universali fantastici* are not, in Vico's terms, simply concepts in poetic cloaks. The image is not to be understood in relation to the concept. The image is to be on its own terms"). See also R. M. Cover, "Nomos and Narrative," *Harvard Law Review*, 1983, Vol. 97, p. 4 ("We inhabit a *nomos* – a normative universe. We constantly create and maintain a world of right and wrong, of lawful and unlawful . . . No set of legal institutions or prescriptions exists apart from the narratives that locate it and give it meaning. For every constitution there is an epic, for each Decalogue a scripture. Once understood in the context of the narratives that give it meaning, law becomes not merely a system of rules to be observed, but a world in which we live").

28 E. Auerbach, *Mimesis: The Representation of Reality in Western Literature*, Princeton, NJ: Princeton University Press, 2003.

29 See G. Bruno, *Cause, Principle, and Unity: And Essays on Magic*, Cambridge: Cambridge University Press, 1998, p. 165 (noting that "all bonds are either reduced to the bond of love, depend on the bond of love or are based on the bond of love"). Bruno adds that "the bond of beauty is said to be a brightness, a beam of light and a certain motion," and that "[t]he senses are the entrance through which the bonds are cast. And vision is the most important of them all." Ibid., pp. 165, 168. Put differently, the greatest bond – the so-called "chain of chains" (or *vinculum vinculorum*) – is *Eros*. As Couliano points out, in this context *Eros* refers to faith and the imagination, the "synthesizer, receiver, and producer of phantasms." I. P. Couliano, *Eros and Magic in the Renaissance*, Chicago: University of Chicago Press, 1987, p. 95.

30 E. Scarry, *On Beauty and Being Just*, Princeton, NJ: Princeton University Press, 2001, pp. 60–61.
31 Ibid.
32 See, e.g. T. Kuhn, *The Structure of Scientific Revolutions*, Chicago: University of Chicago Press, 1996; R. Rorty, *Philosophy and the Mirror of Nature*, Princeton, NJ: Princeton University Press, 1979; and P. Feyerbend, *Against Method*, London: Verso, 1993.
33 J. Bruner, *Actual Minds, Possible Worlds*, Cambridge, MA: Harvard University Press, 1987.
34 G. Deleuze, *The Fold: Leibniz and the Baroque*, Minneapolis, MN: University of Minnesota Press, 1992, p. 68.
35 See H. Murakami, *Hard-Boiled Wonderland and the End of the World*, New York: Vintage Books, 1993. See also D. N. Rodowick, *The Virtual Life of Film*, Cambridge, MA: Harvard University Press, 2007, p. 172.
36 H. L. A. Hart, *The Concept of Law*, 2nd edn, Oxford: Oxford University Press, 1997.
37 See J. Rawls, *A Theory of Justice*, Cambridge, MA: Harvard University Press, 2005; R. Dworkin, *A Matter of Principle*, Cambridge, MA: Harvard University Press, 1985. See also J. Frank, *Law and the Modern Mind*, New Brunswick, NJ: Transaction, 2009 [1935].
38 As William Mitchell has noted, "Images are active players in the game of establishing changing values. They are capable of introducing new values into the world and thus of threatening old ones . . . [W]hen incarnated in the world, [they] seem to possess agency, aura, a 'mind of their own', which is a projection of a collective desire." W. J. T. Mitchell, *What Do Pictures Want?* Chicago: University of Chicago Press, 2005, p. 105.
39 M. Dufrenne, *The Phenomenology of Aesthetic Experience*, Evanston, IL: Northwestern University Press, 1973, p. 548.
40 See, e.g. I. Illich, *Guarding the Eye in the Age of Show*, University Park, PA: *Science, Technology, and Society Studies*, University of Pennsylvania, 1994, pp. 7, 9 [2001 edition available on line at http://www.davidtinapple.com/illich/2001_guarding_the_eye.PDF] ("The eye is no longer the gate through which things enter the soul, but the instrument by which images are imprinted . . . In the classical regime, the gaze is experienced as a trans-ocular organ. In this scopic epoch the gaze radiates from the pupil to embrace an object, to fuse with it, so that the eye is dyed the object's colors"). Illich also notes historical references to the eyes' "rays" such as the French "jeter un coup d'oeil" and the Greek idea of "psychopodia," "the limbs of the soul." Ibid., p. 11.
41 The self-reflexive illusoriness within baroque painting culminates in anamorphic art. See generally J. Baltrušaitis, *Anamorphic Art*, Cambridge: Chadwyk-Healey, 1977.
42 E. H. Kantorowicz, *The King's Two Bodies: A Study in Mediaeval Political Theology*, Princeton, NJ: Princeton University Press, 1981.
43 Ibid., p. 65.

44 D. Kahan, "The Cognitively Illiberal State," *Stanford Law Review*, 2007, Vol. 60, p. 115.

45 See S. Clark, *Vanities of the Eye: Vision in Early Modern European Culture*, Oxford: Oxford University Press, 2007, p. 336 ("For sense perceptions to inform the new natural knowledge, they had to be seen as the *signs*, not the images (*species*), of natural events – caused by them but not picturing them or having any straightforward correspondence with them, and standing in relation to them 'as the conventional sign for a word stands for the word, or as words themselves may signify objects'").

46 Ibid., p. 338.

47 Ibid. Notably, for Descartes "clear and distinct" served as the prime criterion for intellectual certainty. See R. Descartes, *Meditations on First Philosophy*, 2nd edn, New York and Indianapolis, IN: Bobbs-Merrill, 1960.

48 Clark, *Vanities*, p. 339 (quoting Descartes).

49 Ibid., p. 342.

50 Ibid. (quoting Descartes).

51 See R. Rorty, *Philosophy and the Mirror of Nature*, p. 136 ("Descartes' invention of the mind – his coalescence of beliefs and sensations into Lockean ideas – gave philosophers new ground to stand on").

52 See Clark, *Vanities*, p. 339.

53 Ibid., p. 343.

54 David Hume's radical empiricism, and subsequently the deconstructive force of *différance* in the work of Jacques Derrida destabilize early modern Cartesian categories of knowledge in the face of an inconceivable, unknowable, and unrepresentable reality. See, e.g. J. Derrida, *Dissemination*, Chicago: University of Chicago Press, 1981, pp. 156–157 ("As soon as it comes into being and into language, play *erases itself as such*. Just as writing must erase itself as such before truth, etc. The point is that there *is* no *as such* where writing or play are concerned. Having no essence, introducing difference as the condition for the presence of essence, opening up the possibility of the double, the copy, the imitation, the simulacrum – the game and the *graph* are constantly disappearing as they go along. They cannot, in classical affirmation, be affirmed without being negated"). As Ian Almond observes: "The place of *différance* in Derrida's thought is important insofar as it is precisely that which makes *écriture* so uncontrollable, the elusive, never-quite-present force which forever unsettles the text, so that it in turn 'differs from itself, defers itself, and writes itself as *différance*'." Almond, *Sufism*, p. 30 (quoting Derrida; emphasis added).

55 J. S. Mill, *Autobiography of John Stewart Mill*, New York: Columbia University Press, 1960.

56 H. Foster, *Vision and Visuality*, New York: New Press, 1999, p. ix ("Although vision suggests sight as a physical operation, and visuality sight as a social fact, the two are not opposed as nature to culture: vision is social and historical too, and visuality involves the body and the psyche").

57 M. Jay, *Downcast Eyes*, Berkeley, CA: University of California Press, 1993, pp. 78–79 (describing Descartes' assumption of "a natural geometry of the mind" which he assumed was congruent with the external world).
58 See D. Manderson, "Judgment," in A. Sarat (ed.), *Law and the Humanities*, Cambridge: Cambridge University Press, 2009, p. 29 ("Law is subordinated to its reasons and justifications. In place of authority, mere justifications; in place of justice, mere law. In place of *Recht* or *droit*, a coherent body of eternal principles, *Gesetz* or *lois*, a vast and constantly expanding list of interdictions and procedures produced in conformity with and changeable by human will").
59 W. J. T. Mitchell, *Iconology: Image, Text, Ideology*, Chicago: University of Chicago Press, 1987, p. 29.
60 W. J. T. Mitchell, "What is an Image?" *New Literary History*, 1984, Vol. 15, p. 503.
61 See R. K. Sherwin, *When Law Goes Pop: The Vanishing Line between Law and Popular Culture*, Chicago: University of Chicago Press, 2000.
62 Compare W. J. Stuart, *Forbidden Planet*, Fred Wilcox, dir. (MGM, 1956) (travelers to another planet fall prey to an alien technology that is capable of instantly materializing thoughts – even when they arise from the forbidden unconscious impulses and wishes of a brilliant scientist who learns how to work the alien machines).
63 R. Kurzweil, *The Age of Spiritual Machines*, New York: Penguin Books, 2000, p. 364.
64 See, e.g. P. Legendre, *Dominium Mundi: l'empire du management*, Paris: Mille et une nuits, 2007, p. 22 ("The love of the image, the passion for being similar, the art of appearing are irresistible: we are bewitched . . . The industrial system promoted by the West rivals the great religious dream. It exalts the vast paradisiacal surfaces, the ceremonies of fashion, the beauty of images to be consumed . . .").
65 It is not that Descartes was oblivious to the wonders of mechanics. See, e.g. R. Descartes, *Treatise of Man*, Amherst, NY: Prometheus Books, 2003, describing the royal gardens in Germany that awed visitors with their fantastic fountains and musical automata. In one account, a visitor to Frascati in May of 1645 marveled at the "hydraulic organs & all sorts of singing birds moving, & chirping by force of the water . . ." (J. Evelyn, *The Diary of John Evelyn*, Vol. 2, *Kalendarium, 1620–1649*, Oxford: Clarendon Press, 1955, pp. 392–393). A similar sight might well have inspired Descartes to draw his famous analogy, comparing man to "a wondrous automaton, constructed of pipes, devices, and springs, an image of man as a kind of machine similar to the garden works." (See L. Massey, *Picturing Space, Displacing Bodies: Anamorphosis in Early Modern Theories of Perspective*, University Park, PA: Pennsylvania State University Press, 2007, p. 41.
66 S. Turkle, *Simulation and its Discontents*, Cambridge, MA: MIT Press, 2009, p. 9.
67 W. J. T. Mitchell, *What Do Pictures Want?*, p. 198.
68 Ibid., p. 77.

69 In the US Supreme Court case of *Jacobellis v. Ohio*, 378 U.S. 184 (1964) Justice Potter Stewart wrote in his concurring opinion that "hard-core pornography" was hard to define, but that "I know it when I see it."
70 D. Kahan, D. Hoffman, and D. Braman, "Whose Eyes Are You Going to Believe? *Scott v. Harris* and the Perils of Cognitive Illiberalism," *Harvard Law Review*, 2009, Vol. 122, p. 837.
71 W. J. T. Mitchell, *What Do Pictures Want?*
72 Ibid., p. 23.
73 B. Cardozo, *The Nature of the Judicial Process*, New Haven, CT: Yale University Press, 1921, pp. 12–13.
74 The first quoted reference is to Justice Scalia's opinion in *Scott v. Harris*, 550 U.S. 372 (2007) at note 5; the second is to Lord Denning's opinion in *Metropolitan Properties Co. v. Lannon* [1969] 1 Queen's Bench 577 (CA), p. 599.
75 D. Taylor, *The Archive and the Repertoire: performing cultural memory in the Americas*, Durham, NC: Duke University Press, 2003.
76 See, e.g. the case of the teenage girl who committed suicide when a fake boyfriend, malevolently engineered by an ex-girlfriend's mother, harshly cut off communication on line. See http://news.cnet.com/8301-13577_3-10278483-36.html.
77 J. Dibbell, *My Tiny Life: Crime and Passion in a Virtual World*, New York: Henry Holt, 1998.
78 W. J. T. Mitchell, *What Do Pictures Want?*, p. 16.
79 See, e.g. ibid., pp. 58–59.
80 Ibid., p. 17.
81 B. Pascal, *Pensées*, New York: Penguin Books, 1995, pp. 68, 206.
82 S. Beckett, *The Unnamable*, New York: Grove Press, 1958.
83 See G. Deleuze and F. Guattari, *Anti-Oedipus: Capitalism and Schizophrenia*, Minneapolis, MN: University of Minnesota Press, 2000, pp. 17–18.
84 Isocrates proclaimed it during the fifth century BC in Athens as the integration of eloquence and moral content. Cicero echoed that rhetorical ideal in the first century BC when he wrote that wisdom without eloquence was of little use to civic life, and that eloquence separate from wisdom was often of great harm; only the one who could join the two could bring true benefit to himself and his community. Isocrates, "Against the Sophists," in *Isocrates I*, Austin, TX: University of Texas Press, 2000; N. Struever, *The Language of History in the Renaissance: Rhetoric and Historical Consciousness in Florentine Humanism*, Princeton, NJ: Princeton University Press, 1970, p. 21; M. T. Cicero, *De Inventione*, Cambridge, MA: Harvard University Press, 1976, pp. 3–5; J. E. Seigel, *Rhetoric and Philosophy in Renaissance Humanism: The Union of Eloquence and Wisdom, Petrarch to Valla*, Princeton, NJ: Princeton University Press, 1968, p. 6.
85 Vico, *Study Methods*, p. 78.
86 Frank, *Law and the Modern Mind*, p. 54.

87 See G. Agamben, *Homo Sacer*, Stanford, CA: Stanford University Press, 1998, pp. 50–51. See also C. Douzinas, "Oubliez critique," *Law and Critique*, 2005, Vol. 16, p. 47 ("Law as an empty signifier that attaches to everything from pavement walking to smoking and Iraqi liberation is auto-poetically reproduced in a loop of endless validity but it is devoid of a sense of signification").
88 As Regis Debray puts it: "La naissance de l'image a partie liée avec la mort . . . plus la mort s'efface de la vie sociale, moins vivante est l'image, et moins vital notre besoin d'images." R. Debray, *Vie et mort de l'image*, Paris: Gallimard, 1995, p. 17.
89 J. B. Soleveitchik, *The Lonely Man of Faith*, New York: Three Leaves, 2006.
90 Genesis 5:1 (King James).
91 In more contemporary, scientific discourse we read about "mirror neurons" and "mimetic co-evolution," according to which imitation may be the key to human evolution. See, e.g. S. Blackmore, "Evolution and Memes: The Human Brain as a Selective Imitation Device," *Cybernetics and Systems*, 2001, Vol. 32, pp. 225–255.
92 Exodus 20:4–6 (King James).
93 Genesis 2:7 (King James).
94 Genesis 2:15 (King James).
95 See D. P. Verene, *Philosophy and the Return to Self-knowledge*, New Haven, CT: Yale University Press, 1997.
96 T. Jennings, *Reading Derrida/Thinking Paul: On Justice*, Stanford, CA: Stanford University Press, 2005, p. 24.
97 See J. Derrida, "Force of Law: The Mystical Foundation of Authority," in D. Cornell et al. (eds.), *Deconstruction and the Possibility of Justice*, New York: Routledge, 1992, p. 26. See also Almond, *Sufism*.

3 Law's Screen Life

1 Quoted in P. Bergman and M. Asimow, *Reel Justice: The Courtroom Goes to the Movies*, Kansas City, MO: Andrews & McMeel, 1996, p. xi.
2 B. Nichols, *Representing Reality*, Bloomington, IN: Indiana University Press, 1991, p. 161.
3 J. Deger, *Shimmering Screens: Making Media in an Aboriginal Community*, Minneapolis: MN, University of Minnesota Press, 2006, p. 197.
4 A. Sarat, L. Douglas, and M. Umphrey (eds.), *Law on the Screen*, Palo Alto, CA: Stanford University Press, 2005, p. 1.
5 See J. Gurley and D. K. Marcus, "The Effects of Neuroimaging and Brain Injury on Insanity Defenses," *Behavioral Sciences and the Law*, 2008, Vol. 26, pp. 85, 95 ("Jurors may base their verdicts, at least partially, on their prototypical notions of what they believe a criminal to be rather than focusing solely on the evidence presented to them during the trial").
6 See, e.g. J. Bruner, *Beyond the Information Given: studies in the psychology of knowing*, New York: W. W. Norton, 1973; J. Bruner, *Acts of Meaning*, Cambridge, MA: Harvard University Press, 1990; R. Schank and R. Abelson,

Scripts, Plans, Goals, and Understanding: An Inquiry into Human Knowledge Structures, Hillsdale, NJ: Erlbaum, 1977; G. Gigerenzer, P. M. Todd, and the ABC Research Group, *Simple Heuristics that Make Us Smart*, Oxford: Oxford University Press, 2000; R. Nisbett and L. Ross, *Human Inference: Strategies and Shortcomings of Social Judgment*, New York: Prentice-Hall, 1985.

7 Malcolm Gladwell has written of this cognitive process in his popular work *Blink: The Power of Thinking without Thinking*, Boston, MA: Backbay Books, 2007. See also R. K. Sherwin, "Dialects and Dominance: A Study of Rhetorical Fields in the Law of Confessions," *University of Pennsylvania Law Review*, 1988, Vol. 136, p. 729.

8 See D. Holland and N. Quinn (eds.), *Cultural Models in Language and Thought*; Cambridge: Cambridge University Press, 1987; V. Smith, "Prototypes in the Courtroom: Lay Representations of Legal Concepts," *Journal of Personality and Social Psychology*, 1991, Vol. 61, p. 857.

9 See, e.g. *Beasley v. State*, 269 Georgia 620, 627 (1998) (describing courtroom references to Oliver Stone's *Natural Born Killers*, Lions Gate, 1994) and *Commonwealth v. Graziano*, 331 N.E. 808 (Mass. 1975) (describing courtroom references to organized crime characters from Francis Ford Coppola's *The Godfather*, Paramount, 1972).

10 See, e.g. B. H. Schmitt and K. Vrotsos, *There's No Business That's Not Show Business: Marketing in an Experience Culture*, Upper Saddle River, NJ: Prentice-Hall, 2004; and A. Ries and J. Trout, *Positioning: The Battle for Your Mind*, New York: McGraw-Hill, 1986.

11 See, e.g. F. Luntz, *Words that Work: It's Not What You Say, It's What People Hear*, New York: Hyperion, 2006.

12 W. Stevens, "The Man with the Blue Guitar," in *The Collected Poetry of Wallace Stevens*, New York: Vintage, 1990.

13 See A. J. Stachenfeld and C. M. Nicholson, "Blurred Boundaries: An Analysis of the Close Relationship between Popular Culture and the Practice of Law," *University of San Francisco Law Review*, 1996, Vol. 30, pp. 903, 904 (noting that "the best courtroom stories, and therefore performances, are almost mythic in structure: food vs. evil, man vs. nature, big vs. small, innocence vs. deceit, etc.").

14 See N. Feigenson and R. K. Sherwin, "Thinking beyond the Shown: Implicit Inferences in Evidence and Argument," *Law, Probability, and Risk*, 2007, Vol. 6, pp. 295–310.

15 R. M. Cover, "Nomos and Narrative," *Harvard Law Review*, 1983, Vol. 97, p. 4.

16 Ibid.

17 Renowned Swedish film director Ingmar Bergman once wrote that in film he found "a language that literally is spoken from soul to soul in expressions that, almost sensuously, escape the restrictive control of the intellect." I. Bergman, "The Snakeskin," *Sight and Sound*, 1 August 1965. See R. Sherwin, N. Feigenson, and C. Spiesel, "Law in the Digital Age: How Visual Communication Technologies Are Transforming the Practice, Theory, and Teaching of Law,"

Boston University Journal of Science and Technology Law, 2006, Vol. 12, pp. 227–270. (The next three paragraphs in the text are adapted from this article.)

18 At the same time, it may be the case that a sudden insight, or *Gestalt*, might also occur as an act of *recognition* of that which is already known on a profound level by the viewer. As Jennifer Deger observes: "The power of recognition – the moment of insight when one sees beyond what is already known – arises from the way it allows us to *glimpse something more, something new, yet nonetheless somehow known or true.* As a technology of showing, the camera thus brings an ontological charge of truth far exceeding the verisimilitude of the 'realistic' likeness . . ."). Deger, *Shimmering Screens*, p. 19.

19 See T. Gunning, "An Aesthetic of Astonishment: Early Film and the (In)credulous Spectator," in L. Williams (ed.), *Viewing Positions: Ways of Seeing Film*, New Brunswick, NJ: Rutgers University Press, 1995, p. 114 (describing how audiences viewing for the first time Lumiere's *Arrival of a Train at the Station* were simultaneously terrified by the impression that the train was headed straight for them and pleased by their appreciation of film's *trompe l'oeil* capabilities).

20 That is why movie studios employ "nausea" specialists to help manage the viewer's response to dizzying visual sequences, particularly in 3D productions. See, e.g. D. Engber, "The Problem with 3D," 2 April 2009, http://www.slate.com/id/2215265; A. O'Connor, "The Claim: 3-D Movies Can Induce Headaches and Sickness," 8 February 2010, http://www.nytimes.com/2010/02/09/health/09really.html.

21 See D. N. Rodowick, *The Virtual Life of Film*, Cambridge, MA: Harvard University Press, 2007, pp. 9–10, 106 ("The photograph is a receptive substance literally etched or sculpted by light forming a mold of the object's reflected image . . . Computer-generated images, alternatively, are wholly created from algorithmic functions . . . Digital media are neither visual, nor textual, nor musical – they are simulations . . . Weakening or eliminating the indexical powers of photography shifts the balance, then, between causation and intention"); compare R. Barthes, *Camera Lucida: Reflections on Photography*, New York: Hill & Wang, 1982, p. 39 ("In every photograph there is the stupefying evidence of this-is-what-happened-and-how"). See also J. L. Mnookin, "The Image of Truth: Photographic Evidence and the Power of Analogy," *Yale Journal of Law and the Humanities*, 1998, Vol. 10, pp. 1, 16–17 (referring to O. W. Holmes' description of the photograph as "a mirror with a memory").

22 Sherwin et al., "Law in the Digital Age," pp. 243–244.

23 J. Culler, *The Pursuit of Signs*, Ithaca, NY: Cornell University Press, 2002, pp. 100–118.

24 See Feigenson and Sherwin, "Thinking beyond the Shown," pp. 295–310.

25 See N. Feigenson, *Legal Blame: How Jurors Think and Talk about Accidents*, Washington, DC: American Psychological Association, 2001.

26 See, e.g. L. U. Marks, *The Skin of the Film*, Durham, NC: Duke University Press, 1999; V. Sobchack, *Carnal Thoughts: Embodiment and Moving Image Culture*, Berkeley, CA: University of California Press, 2002; D. F. Marks, "On the

Relationship between Imagery, Body, and Mind," in P. J. Hampson, D. F. Marks, and J. T. E. Richardson (eds.), *Imagery: Current Developments*, London: Routledge, 1990, pp. 1–38.

27 There is an ongoing debate about whether visual images *can* be arguments. See, e.g. D. Fleming, "Can Pictures be Arguments?" *Argumentation and Advocacy*, 1996, Vol. 33, pp. 11–22 (asserting that pictures cannot serve as arguments). For a contrary position, see J. A. Blair, "The Rhetoric of Visual Arguments," in C. A. Hill and M. Helmers (eds.), *Defining Visual Rhetorics*, Malwah, NJ: Lawrence Erlbaum, 2004, p. 41; and D. Birdsell and L. Groarke, "Toward a Theory of Visual Argument," *Argumentation and Advocacy*, 1996, Vol. 33, pp. 1–10. For additional analysis and specific examples of the use of persuasive visuals in court, see Sherwin et al., "Law in the Digital Age."

28 See, e.g. *Roy v. St. Lukes Med. Ctr.*, 741 N.W.2d 256 (Wis. Ct. App. 2007) (court decision comparing a computer-generated animation that had been presented as demonstrative evidence at trial to an expert's hand-drawn illustrations during his testimony to depict his party's case theory). See also *Commonwealth v. Serge*, 858 A.2d 1159, 1170 (Pa. 2004) (opining that "a CGA [computer-generated animation] should be treated equivalently to any other demonstrative exhibit or graphic representation"). Other courts, however, have articulated a more searching attitude toward demonstrative evidence, particularly re-enactment evidence. See, e.g. *Sommervold v. Grevlos*, 518 N.W.2d 733 (S.D. 1994) ("The impact of video reenactment is substantial. When people see something on television, they think it is real even when it is not").

29 See D. Whelan, "The Bloody Sunday Tribunal Video Simulation," in J. Elkins (ed.), *Visual Practices across the University*, Paderborn: Wilhelm Fink, 2007, p. 100.

30 Demonstrative evidence is used at trial, typically to supplement expert witness testimony, to help the tryer of fact understand the matter at issue. This kind of evidence is meant to be illustrative, it is not meant to be used as substantive proof of the fact asserted. It may consist of a chart, a diagram, or computer-generated animations. Demonstrative evidence of this sort is generally admissible if it is judged fair and accurate, helpful to the jurors' understanding of the issues raised, and if the probative value outweighs any possible prejudice. See generally G. Joseph, "A Simplified Approach to Computer-Generated Evidence and Animations," *New York Law School Law Review*, 1999–2000, Vol. 43, p. 875.

31 Compare *Bruton v. United States*, 391 U.S. 123 (1968), where the U.S. Supreme Court held that asking jurors to disregard that part of a codefendant's confession that implicated Bruton constituted a "mental gymnastic" that jurors simply could not be expected to perform.

32 See generally L. Huddy and A. Gunnthorsdottir, "The Persuasive Effects of Emotive Visual Imagery: Superficial Manipulation of the Product of Passionate Reason?" *Political Psychology*, 2000, Vol. 21, p. 745.

33 See N. Feigenson and M. M. Dunn, "New Visual Technologies in Court: Directions for Research," *Law and Human Behavior*, 2003, Vol. 27, pp. 109, 110;

S. M. Kassin and M. A. Dunn, "Computer-animated Displays and the Jury: facilitative and prejudicial effects," *Law and Human Behavior*, 1997, Vol. 21, p. 269; and F. I. Lederer, "Courtroom Technology and its Educational Implications," *Virginia Education and Practice*, 1998, Vol. 8, p. 3.

34 See, e.g., B. Carney and N. Feigenson, "Visual Persuasion in the Michael Skakel Trial: Enhancing Advocacy through Interactive Media Presentations," *Criminal Justice*, 2004, Vol. 19, pp. 22, 23.

35 See generally J. Silbey, "Judges as Film Critics: new approaches to film evidence," *University of Michigan Journal of Law Reform*, 2004, Vol. 37, p. 499 ("Courts fail to encourage the evaluation of film as substantive evidence, subject to rigorous testing for the truth of its assertions").

36 See D. T. Gilbert, "How Mental Systems Believe," *American Psychologist*, 1991, Vol. 46, pp. 107, 108.

37 See, e.g. M. Jay, *Downcast Eyes*, Berkeley, CA: University of California Press, 1993; W. J. T. Mitchell, *What Do Pictures Want?* Chicago: University of Chicago Press, 2005; S. Clark, *Vanities of the Eye: Vision in Early Modern European Culture*, Oxford: Oxford University Press, 2007.

38 See C. Clover, "Law and the Order of Popular Culture," in A. Sarat and T. R. Kearns (eds.), *Law in the Domains of Culture*, Ann Arbor, MI: University of Michigan Press, 1998, pp. 99–100 ("Trials are already movie-like to begin with and movies are already trial-like to begin with . . . [T]he plot structures and narrative procedures (even certain visual procedures, in film and television) of a broad stripe of American popular culture are derived from the structure and procedure of the Anglo-American trial . . . [T]his structure and these procedures are so deeply embedded in our narrative tradition that they shape even plots that never step into a courtroom, and . . . such trial-derived forms constitute the most distinctive share of Anglo-American entertainment").

39 See N. Feigenson, "Accidents as Melodrama," *New York Law School Law Review*, 1999–2000, Vol. 43, pp. 741–810.

40 See D. A. Bright and J. Goodman-Delahunty, "Gruesome Evidence and Emotion: Anger, Blame, and Jury Decision-Making," *Law and Human Behavior*, 2006, Vol. 30, pp. 183–202.

41 See D. S. Weisburg et al., "The Seductive Allure of Neuroscience Explanations," *Journal of Cognitive Neuroscience*, 2008, Vol. 20, pp. 470–477; J. D. Trout, "Seduction without Cause: Uncovering Explanatory Neurophilia," *Trends in Cognitive Sciences*, 2008, Vol. 12, p. 281.

42 O. C. Snead, "Neuroimaging and the 'Complexity' of Capital Punishment," *New York University Law Review*, 2007, Vol. 82, p. 1265.

43 A. Lee, "The *CSI* Effect: TV's Impact on the Future of Forensic Science," in Cambridge University (ed.), *The Triple Helix*, 2007, pp. 22–23.

44 Ibid.

45 N. Feigenson, "Brain Imaging and Courtroom Evidence: On the Admissibility and Persuasiveness of fMRI," *International Journal of Law in Context*, 2006, Vol. 2, pp. 233–255.

46 See, e.g. A. Madrigal, "Courtroom First: Brain Scan Used in Murder Sentencing," *Wired Science*, 23 November 2009 (brain scan evidence that the defense claimed showed the defendant's brain was psychopathic was allowed into the sentencing portion of a murder trial in Chicago). See Feigenson, "Brain Imaging and Courtroom Evidence," p. 233, and M. Perlin, "'His Brain Has Been Mismanaged with Great Skill': How Will Jurors Respond to Neuroimaging Testimony in Insanity Defense Cases?" *Akron Law Review*, 2009, Vol. 42, p. 885.
47 K. Podlas, "The '*CSI* Effect': Exposing the Media Myth," *Fordham Intellectual Property Media and Entertainment Law Journal*, 2006, Vol. 16, p. 429, law. http://law2.fordham.edu/publications/articles/200flspub5906.PDF. See also A. Lee, "The '*CSI* Effect'," p. 22 (describing a prospective boon, perhaps, to those flocking to forensics courses at university).
48 See A. Welsh, *Strong Representations*, Baltimore, MD: Johns Hopkins University Press, 1995.
49 See N. J. Schweitzer and M. J. Saks, "The *CSI* Effect: Popular Fiction about Forensic Science Affects Public Expectations about Real Forensic Science," *Jurimetrics*, 2007, Vol. 47, pp. 357, 358.
50 See S. A. Cole and R. Dioso-Villa, "Investigating the '*CSI* Effect' Effect: Media and Litigation Crisis in Criminal Law," *Stanford Law Review*, 2009, Vol. 61, p. 1335; S. A. Cole and R. Dioso-Villa, "*CSI* and its Effects: Media, Juries, and the Burden of Proof," *New England Law Review*, 2007, Vol. 41, p. 435.
51 *NCIS: Naval Criminal Investigative Service*, Season 6, Episode 22, "Legend," Part 1, NBC (air date: 28 April 2009).
52 *CSI: Crime Scene Investigation*, Season 9, Episode 6, "Say Uncle," CBS (air date: 13 November 2008).
53 D. P. McCabe and A. D. Castel, "Seeing is Believing: the effect of brain images on judgments of scientific reasoning," *Cognition*, 2008, Vol. 107, pp. 343–352.
54 D. Mobbs, H. C. Lau, O. D. Jones, and C. D. Frith, "Law, Responsibility, and the Brain," *PLoS Biology*, 2007, Vol. 5(4), p. 103. See generally O. Jones, J. W. Buckholtz, J. D. Schall, and R. Marois, "Brain Imaging for Legal Thinkers: A Guide for the Perplexed," *Stanford Technology Law Review*, 5, 2009.
55 A. Adler, "The Perverse Law of Child Pornography," *Columbia Law Review*, 2001, Vol. 101, pp. 209, 227. See also N. Scheper-Hughes and H. Stein, "Child Abuse and the Unconscious in American Popular Culture," in N. Scheper-Hughes (ed.), *Child Survival: Anthropological Perspectives on the Treatment and Maltreatment of Children*, Boston, MA: Reidel, 1987, pp. 339–358 (describing "child sexual abuse" as "the master narrative of our culture"). See also U. Khan, "Having your Porn and Condeming it Too: a case study of a 'kiddie porn' exposé," *Law, Culture and the Humanities*, 2009, Vol. 5, pp. 391, 394 (arguing that media texts are "sites where direct gratification is absent and yet displaced satisfaction and desire are engaged").
56 A. Adler, "The Perverse Law of Child Pornography," p. 227 n. 100 (citing J. R. Kincaid, *Erotic Innocence: The Culture of Child Molesting*, Durham, NC:

Duke University Press, 1998, p. 16 (noting that some legislative schemes reflect the view that child pornography is worse than murder)). Compare, e.g. *Arizona Review of Statistics* 13–604.01(B), (D) (Supp. 1993) *Arizona Review of Statistics,* 13–701(A) (Supp. 1993) (imposing a mandatory minimum penalty of 17 years in prison for violation of child pornography law, but only a mandatory minimum of 10 years for second-degree murder), cited in *Arizona v. Gates,* 897 P.2d 1345, 1349 (Ariz. Ct. App. 1994).

57 See S. Scott, *The Politics and Experience of Ritual Abuse: Beyond Disbelief,* Buckingham: Open University Press, 2001, p. 103.

58 S. Katz-Schiavone et al., "Myths and Facts about Sexual Violence: Public Perceptions and Implications for Prevention," *Journal of Criminal Justice and Popular Culture,* 2008, Vol. 15, p. 291.

59 U.S. Department of Justice, Office of Justice Programs, "Youth Victimization: Prevalence and Implications," 2003, http://www.ncjrs.gov/pdffiles1/nij/194972.pdf.

60 E.g. Kansas' "Sexually Violent Predator Act" (Kan. Stat. Ann. § 59-29a01), upheld by the Supreme Court in 1997, provides for the indefinite civil commitment of certain sex offenders. See *Kansas v. Hendricks,* 521 U.S. 346, 352–53 (1997). See also A. J. Falk, "Sex Offenders, Mental Illness and Criminal Responsibility: The Constitutional Boundaries of Civil Commitment after *Kansas v. Hendricks,*" *American Journal of Law and Medicine,* 1999, Vol. 25, pp. 117, 118 (noting that civil commitment of sex offenders "occurs for an indefinite time period").

61 See N. Vidmar, "When All of Us Are Victims: Juror Prejudice and 'Terrorist' Trials," *Chicago–Kent Law Review,* 2003, Vol. 78, p. 1143; J. Greenberg et al., "Terror Management Theory of Self-Esteem and Cultural Worldviews: Empirical Assessments and Conceptual Refinements," in M. P. Zanna (ed.), *Advances in Experimental Social Psychology,* 1997, Vol. 29, p. 61; J. Greenberg et al., "Evidence for Terror Management Theory", II, "The Effects of Mortality Salience on Reactions to Those Who Threaten or Bolster the Cultural World View," *Journal of Personality and Social Psychology,* 1990, Vol. 58, p. 308.

62 See, e.g. N. Klein, *The Shock Doctrine: The Rise of Disaster Capitalism,* New York: Picador, 2008.

63 See A. Adler, "The Perverse Law of Child Pornography," pp. 223–225.

64 Ibid. See also D. Shaw, "Reporter's Early Exclusives Triggered a Media Frenzy," *Los Angeles Times,* 20 January 1990, at p. A1 ("The prosecution charged in March, 1984, that the McMartin Pre-school was, in effect, a front for a massive child pornography ring. . . . The district attorney, the FBI, the U.S. Customs Service and various local law enforcement agencies and task forces . . . did not find a single one of the 'millions' of photographs and films that [the deputy district attorney] had said were taken").

65 A. Adler, "The Perverse Law of Child Pornography," pp. 226–227. As Adler notes: "Anxiety over children's exposure to pedophiles was a major justification in Congress' rush to pass the 1996 Communications Decency Act (CDA) a

measure that quickly succumbed to a First Amendment challenge. New anti-stalking measures have arisen, targeting pedophiles who prey on children on the Internet. The Protection of Children from Sexual Predators Act of 1998 criminalizes the use of interstate facilities to transmit information about a minor for criminal sexual purposes. The Child Online Protection Act (COPA) prohibits knowingly distributing to minors 'material that is harmful to minors'." Ibid., pp. 228–229.

66 *Law and Order: SVU* (Special Victims Unit), NBC, 1999.

67 *Law and Order: SVU*, Season 7, Episode 1, "Demons," NBC, 2005.

68 *Law and Order: SVU*, Season 7, Episode 19, "Fault," NBC, 2006.

69 *Law and Order: SVU*, Season 1, Episode 7, "Uncivilized," NBC, 1999.

70 Law Enforcement Division, Child Abuse Unit, Long Island, New York, http://childabuseunit.com/p_information.cfm.

71 Go to http://www.perverted-justice.com/?con=full.

72 During the 2006–2007 television season, the 11 episodes of *Predator* attracted an average of 7 million viewers who witnessed the graphic enticements and consequent humiliation and public shaming that the sting operation produced. The show has continued in syndication on MSNBC following its cancellation in 2008.

73 See, e.g. S. Hall, C. Critcher, T. Jefferson, J. Clarke, and B. Robert, *Policing the Crisis: Mugging, the State and Law and Order*, Basingstoke: Palgrave Macmillan, 1978.

74 See *New York v. Ferber*, 458 U.S. 747 (1982).

75 See, e.g. *Osborne v. Ohio*, 495 U.S. 103, 111 (1990).

76 See 18 U.S.C. § 2251.

77 A. Adler, "The Perverse Law of Child Pornography," p. 209.

78 Ibid., p. 303.

79 Ibid.

80 S. Freud, *Totem and Taboo*, Stilwell, KS, Digireads.com, 2008, p. 46.

81 *New York Times*, 4 December 2009, p. 9.

82 See Marks, *The Skin of the Film*.

83 Deger, *Shimmering Screens*, p. 151.

84 Describing the sublime aspect of the Christian mystery of divine incarnation, St Bernadino of Siena captured its paradoxical aspect in these simple, but eloquent words: "Eternity appears in time, immensity in measurement, the Creator in the creature . . . the unfigurable in the figure, the unnarratable in discourse, the inexplicable in speech, the uncircumscribable in the place, the invisible in vision." G. Didi-Huberman, *Fra Angelico: Dissemblance and Figuration*, Chicago: University of Chicago Press, 1995, p. 35.

85 See E. Kligerman, *Sites of the Uncanny: Paul Celan, Specularity and the Visual Arts*, Berlin: De Gruyter, 2007, p. 36.

86 This paragraph is adapted from R. Sherwin et al., "Law in the Digital Age." See also *Connecticut v. Skakel*, No. FST CR00-135792T (Conn. Super. Ct., J.D. of Norwalk/Stamford, 3 June 2002).

87 J. Malcolm, "Iphigenia in Forest Hills: Anatomy of a Murder Trial," *New Yorker*, 3 May 2010, p. 34.

88 E. Fackenheim, *To Mend the World: The Foundations of Post-Holocaust Jewish Thought*, Bloomington, IN: Indiana University Press, 1994, p. 239.
89 E. Levinas, *Otherwise than Being, or, Beyond Essence*, trans. A. Lingis, Dordrecht: Kluwer, 1991, pp. 114–115.
90 These are what anthropologist Don Handelman refers to as the discrete logics of organizational design. See D. Handelman, *Models and Mirrors: Towards an Anthropology of Public Events*, New York: Berghahn Books, 1998, pp. xi–xii.
91 See, e.g. R. K. Sherwin, "The Narrative Construction of Legal Reality," *Vermont Law Review*, 1994, Vol. 18, pp. 688–689; P. Brooks and P. Gewirtz, *Law's Stories: Narrative and Rhetoric in the Law*, New Haven, CT: Yale University Press, 1998.
92 See Rodowick, *The Virtual Life of Film*, p. 174 (discussing the "will to control information and to shape ourselves and the world through the medium of information"). Deleuze claims that what we are witnessing here is a shift in the meaning of control from "discipline" (in Foucault's sense) to information freeways constituted by computer networks. See A. Galloway, *Gaming: Essays on Algorithmic Culture*, Minneapolis, MN: University of Minnesota Press, 2006, pp. 87–88 ("In making freeways, for example, you don't enclose people but instead multiply the means of control . . . people can drive infinitely and 'freely' without being at all confined yet while still being perfectly controlled. This is our future," quoting Deleuze).

4 Images Run Riot

1 G. Dumézil, *The Destiny of the Warrior*, Chicago: University of Chicago Press, 1970.
2 F. J. Schelling, *Philosophical Investigations into the Essence of Human Freedom*, Albany, NY: State University of New York Press, 2006. See also F. J. Schelling, *Philosophy and Religion*, cited in E. Bloch, *The Utopian Function of Art and Literature*, trans. J. Zipes and F. Mecklenberg, Cambridge, MA: MIT Press, 1996, pp. 259–260 ("After the eternal act of self-revelation, everything in the world as we now see it is law, order and form; yet lawlessness always lurks at its foundations, as if it could once again break through, and nowhere does it appear as if order and form were at the origin but rather, that as original chaos was brought to order . . . Without this antecedent darkness, there is no creational reality; gloom is its necessary heritage").
3 M. Eliade, *Rites and Symbols of Initiation: The Mysteries of Birth and Rebirth*, New York: Harper & Row, 1965, p. 135.
4 W. Benjamin, "Franz Kafka," in M. W. Jennings, H. Eiland, and G. Smith (eds.), *Selected Writings, 1927–1934*, Cambridge, MA: Harvard University Press, 1999, p. 815.
5 O. Calabrese, *Neo-Baroque: A Sign of the Times*, Princeton, NJ: Princeton University Press, 1992, p. 11.
6 M. M. Merleau-Ponty, *The Visible and the Invisible*, Evanston, IL: Northwestern University Press, 1969, p. 152.

7 G. Deleuze, *The Fold: Leibniz and the Baroque*, Minneapolis, MN: University of Minnesota Press, 1992, p. 14.
8 Ibid., p. 38.
9 J. Baltrušaitis, *Anamorphic Art*, Cambridge: Chadwyck-Healy, 1977, p. 5.
10 Ibid.
11 P. N. Skrine, *The Baroque: Literature and Culture in Seventeenth Century Europe*, London: Methuen, 1978, p. 21.
12 Ibid., p. 21.
13 Ibid., p. 150.
14 F. Hallyn, *The Poetic Structure of the World: Copernicus and Kepler*, New York: Zone Books, 1990, p. 172; Baltrušaitis, *Anamorphic Art*, p. 99.
15 F. Hallyn, *Poetic Structure*, p. 161.
16 A. Ndalianis, *Neo-Baroque Aesthetics and Contemporary Entertainment*, Cambridge, MA: MIT Press, 2004, p. 54.
17 Ibid., pp. 160, 161.
18 Ibid., pp. 273, 213, 217–218.
19 See Baltrušaitis, *Anamorphic Art*, p. 70 (noting the religious depictions of "saints taking shape and disappearing" alongside scientific studies, manifesting a common obsession with illusion – albeit with different objectives and values in mind).
20 Deleuze, *The Fold*, pp. 20–21.
21 Ibid., p. 22.
22 R. S. Dombroski, *Creative Entanglements: Gadda and the Baroque*, Toronto: University of Toronto Press, 1999, p. 10.
23 Ibid., p. 68.
24 Ibid.
25 F. Nietzsche, *On the Genealogy of Morals and Ecce Homo*, trans. R. J. Hollingdale, ed. W. Kaufmann, New York: Vintage, 1969, pp. 97, 163.
26 J. B. Korotkin and M. Giovannotti (eds.), *Neo-Baroque!*, Milan: Charta, 2006, p. 11.
27 Ibid., p. 226.
28 T. Murakami, *Superflat*, Tokyo: Madora Shuppan, 2000.
29 From *Neon Genesis Evangelion* (anime), cited in T. Murakami, *Little Boy: The Arts of Japan's Exploding Subculture*, New Haven, CT: Yale University Press, 2005, pp. 129–130, 132.
30 T. Murray, *Digital Baroque: New Media Art and Cinematic Folds*, Minneapolis, MN: University of Minnesota Press, 2008, p. 55.
31 Dombroski, *Creative Entanglements*, p. 11; Deleuze, *The Fold*, p. 101.
32 Dombroski, *Creative Entanglements*, p. 12.
33 Ibid., p. 14.
34 Deleuze, *The Fold*, p. 68.
35 Ibid.
36 Ibid.
37 Ibid., p. 78
38 K. Purgar, *The Neo-Baroque Subject*, Zagreb: Meandar Media, 2007, p. 129 (quoting Leibniz).

39 G. Deleuze and F. Guattari, *Anti-Oedipus: Capitalism and Schizophrenia*, Minneapolis, MN: University of Minnesota Press, 2000, at p. 6.

40 See L. Dällenbach, *The Mirror in the Text*, Chicago: University of Chicago Press, 1989, p. 8 ("[A] *mise en abyme* is any aspect enclosed within a work that shows a similarity with the work that contains it").

41 See O. Calabrese, *Neo-Baroque*, Princeton, NJ: Princeton University Press, 1992, p. 92 (describing the etymology of "monster" in terms of *monstrum*, outside the norm, and *monitum*, the idea of mystery, or that which is concealed in nature, i.e. the marvelous and the enigmatic).

42 See S. Zizek, *The Fright of Real Tears*, London: British Film Institute, 2001, p. 175 (recounting Jacques Lacan's quip about "awakening into reality as an escape from the Real" of desire).

43 J. Rajchman, *Constructions*, Cambridge, MA: MIT Press, 1998, p. 13.

44 See G. Deleuze, *The Fold: Leibniz and the Baroque*, Minneapolis, MN: University of Minnesota Press, 1992. This *mise-en-abyme* is a definitive feature of both the postmodern and the neo-baroque sublime. See J. Lyotard, "The Sublime and the Avant-Garde," in *The Inhuman: Reflections on Time*, Stanford, CA: Stanford University Press, 1988.

45 Deleuze and Guattari, *Anti-Oedipus*, p. 5 ("[S]chizophrenia is the universe of productive and reproductive desiring-machines, universal primary production as 'the essential reality of man'").

46 W. Li, *Enchantment and Disenchantment: Love and Illusion in Chinese Literature*, Princeton, NJ: Princeton University Press, 1993, at p. 266.

47 The viewer cannot know it, but the reference is to Diane Selwyn's earlier history. She won a jitterbug dance contest back in her hometown of Ontario. Her subsequent interest in acting gave rise to dreams of success in Hollywood. The flashback to the contest suggests high-school days of purity, unspoiled ideals. Presumably, this is the biographical core of Diane's split-off idealized persona "Betty."

48 There is evidence throughout the film that Diane's love for Camilla is of a highly narcissistic nature. Camilla may in fact be viewed as a fantasized extension of Diane. Throughout the film we see a variety of signs pointing to Diane's fusion with Camilla. For example, as Betty and Rita come close to discovering their true identities Rita cuts her hair to match Betty's hairstyle (as if to hide within Betty's benign persona). We literally see the two women fuse, after making love, in a brilliant frame that depicts Rita's profile eerily completing Betty's. The characterological pathology reflected in Diane's fragile sense of self and her felt need to fuse with, and then violently repel, the split-off ("idealized") other (dark, seductive Camilla) is suggestive of what is known in the trade as a "borderline personality" type. Diane's frightening loss of boundaries makes it feel like she is falling endlessly into Camilla. As a tactic of defense, Camilla must be demonized as the vampiric other, the one who must be destroyed in order for Diane to save her own self.

49 The image of Camilla looking in the mirror, with a smaller mirror set within the larger one reflecting the movie poster of Rita Hayworth as Gilda on the

opposite wall, brilliantly figures the quintessence of the *mise en abyme*: the baroque, infinitely reiterated image-within-an-image.

50 See, e.g. T. Hilfer, *The Crime Novel: A Deviant Genre*, Austin, TX: University of Texas Press, 1990, pp. 3, 7 (noting that a crime novel maneuvers its reader into various forms of complicity, managing to subvert the reassurances of the detective novel by "put[ting] the signification process into doubt or even exploit[ing] the gap between socially accepted signification and ultimate reality").

51 See, e.g. P. Auster, *City of Glass: The New York Trilogy*, Vol. 1, London: Penguin Books, 1987 (in which Quinn, the story's private detective, discovers that he can never arrive at the heart of the mystery – which is ultimately the mystery of himself in a world in which signifiers are no longer attached to the signified and the distinction between self and other no longer holds); see also S. Beckett, *The Unnameable*, New York: Grove Press, 1958.

52 Diane's fantasy of Camilla not only keeps her victim alive (thereby staving off the guilt that accompanies murder); it also allows her to merge with the object of her envy, and her thwarted desire. With her old identity out of the way, Diane is now free to become an ersatz Camilla, and like Camilla, a star. This wish fulfillment is matched by another, for in the persona of "Betty" Diane can now seduce Camilla and thus regain the passionate love affair that she has lost in real life. Merging with Camilla, however, also has the most devastating consequences for Diane. For it is through Camilla that Diane ultimately tracks down her true identity: figured in the end as a stinking, swollen, hideous decomposing corpse. This is the monster that Diane, in her own mind, has become – a creature not unlike the hideous monster behind the diner, the one who is "doing it." This is the monstrous force at the center of things, the one driving the dream, a figure so terrible that to behold it is fatal.

53 An amusing joke, in the form of a clue to Rita's identity, and her own, occurs when the intrepid Betty conceives of a plan to call the police to learn about any car accidents reported on Mulholland Drive. "C'mon," Betty cries, "it'll be just like in the movies. We'll pretend to be someone else." But the deadpan revelation, at this point, is premature, and goes unnoted.

54 He, too, it would seem, is the one who is "doing it" – a surrogate monster, the omnipresent policing agency of the unconscious.

55 "A man's attitude goes some ways the way his life will be. Is that something you might agree with?" the cowboy asks the stunned, and slightly bemused, director. But Adam Pesher's bemusement will quickly fade. "I want you to think about that and stop being a smart aleck. Can you try that for me?" is the sobering response to Adam's initial "attitude problem."

56 In addition to the signature of the jittery, water-bobbing camera, Lynch also uses the trope of blue light to figure the mysterious, abyssal force (of endless, unutterable desire) that makes things happen.

57 Compare Jean-Luc Godard's *Contempt* (dir. J. Godard, Embassy Pictures, 1964). At the end of the film the director cries, "Silencio," after which the scene shifts, in silence, to a car accident, depicting both driver and passenger as dead.

58 See Eliade, *Rites and Symbols of Initiation*, p. 136 ("Death prepares the new, purely spiritual birth, access to a mode of being not subject to the destroying action of Time") and p. 62 (describing the recurring pattern of "initiatory ordeal" as enabling the initiate to descend into Hell alive in order to "confront its monsters and demons"). See also ibid., p. 62: "Initiation lies at the core of any genuine human life." There are two reasons, according to Eliade: (1) "any genuine human life implies profound crises, ordeals, suffering, loss, and reconquest of self, 'death and resurrection'," and (2) there comes a moment for every person when one's life seems a failure, "an obscure feeling that he has missed his vocation; that he has betrayed the best that was in him. In such moments of total crisis, only one hope seems to offer any issue – the hope of beginning life over again . . . [T]he man undergoing such a crisis dreams of a new, regenerated life, fully realized and significant . . . This 'nostalgia for an initiatory renewal' sporadically arises from the inmost depths of modern nonreligious man. It would appear to represent the modern formulation of man's eternal longing to find a positive meaning in death, to accept death as a transition to a higher mode of being."

59 See Lyotard, "The Sublime and the Avant-Garde," pp. 101, 107.

60 Following Wai-Yee Li, I use the term "allegory" to refer to "the rhetorical procedure that emphasizes the relationship between different and disjunctive levels of coherence." See Li, *Enchantment and Disenchantment*, p. 161.

61 B. Kilborne, *Disappearing Persons*, New York: State University of New York Press, 2002, pp. 113, 123 ("The more internal feelings are repressed the more individuals view their feelings with mistrust; and the greater their dependence on appearance, the greater the tendency to mistake appearance for reality.").

62 See H. Wölfflin, *Renaissance and Baroque*, Ithaca, NY: Cornell University Press, 1967, pp. 33–34, 86 (on baroque precariousness, and the fleeting ecstatic sublimation in the absolute).

63 See Eliade, *Rites and Symbols of Initiation*, pp. 125–126 (describing how, over time, primitive/pre-modern ritual ordeals shifted to literary motifs, which presented their message directly to the imagination). Literary motifs, in turn, have more recently shifted to images on the screen – with directors like Lynch as initiate/mentors, dream weavers, and tutelary guides.

64 J. Goux, *Oedipus, Philosopher*, Stanford, CA: Stanford University Press, 1993, p. 155.

65 Ibid.

66 See Wölfflin, *Renaissance and Baroque*, p. 34 (noting that the baroque seeks to stimulate the imagination through infinite progressions, and the suggestiveness of the indefinite). See W. Benjamin, *The Origin of German Tragic Drama*, London: Verso, 1998 (on the baroque artistic imagination, and creation in a void).

67 See G. Murray, *Five Stages of Greek Religion*, New York: Doubleday, 1955, pp. 119–165.

68 See G. Gilmore, *The Ages of American Law*, New Haven, CT: Yale University Press, 1977, p. 111 ("In Hell there will be nothing but law, and due process will be meticulously observed").

69 Wölfflin, *Renaissance and Baroque*, p. 38.
70 Goux, *Oedipus, Philosopher*, pp. 2–3.
71 Ibid., p. 6.
72 According to this mythic account, heroic exploits – accepting the challenge, trial, or ordeal that culminates in symbolic death and resurrection and the subsequent acquisition of the grail (esoteric knowledge/justice) – mark the cultural dynamic by which humans leave behind the naivete of childhood and are introduced to a world of adult wisdom. See Eliade, *Rites and Symbols of Initiation*, p. 9.
73 See Goux, *Oedipus, Philosopher*, p. 145 (discussing Plato's methodical analysis of the tripartite division of the soul and the correspondences to how city-states are organized). Goux writes: "Each element is associated with a virtue: lust has the corresponding virtue of temperance; to anger corresponds the virtue of courage; and to intelligence, prudence . . . The difference between just and unjust political constitutions can be deduced with precision from the interplay of these three components and the relation of harmony or disharmony that prevails among them, and the same can be said of types of souls." Ibid.
74 Benjamin, *The Origin of German Tragic Drama*, p. 3.
75 See Maravall, *Culture of the Baroque*, p. 14.
76 Ibid., p. 262.
77 Ibid., p. 263.
78 Ibid., pp. 81–82.
79 Ibid., p. 98.
80 Ibid., p. 83 (discussing a variety of mass media devices available at the time for purposes of emotional manipulation, including "books, commercialized theatrical representations, painting in abundance, songs in vogue, posters, programs, lampoons, etc.").
81 See Benjamin, *The Origin of German Tragic Drama*, p. 3.
82 Ibid.
83 See Deleuze, *The Fold*.
84 Lyotard, "The Sublime and the Avant-Garde," p. 99.
85 See Wölfflin, *Renaissance and Baroque*, p. 38 (describing the aim of baroque art as overwhelming the mind by using matter to create oppressiveness, irrationality, amorphousness, and "treating matter with violence").
86 Compare Wölfflin, *Renaissance and Baroque*, p. 45 (describing St Peter's cathedral, a masterpiece of baroque architecture, in terms of the "viscous mass slowly oozing down the slope") with Jean Paul Sartre's description of the "*de trop*" (excess) in his first novel, *La Nausée*, Paris: Gallimard, 2002 [1938].
87 Ibid., p. 186.
88 Ibid., p. 170 (citing Calderon's baroque masterpiece).
89 Ibid., p. 81.
90 C. Buci-Glucksmann, *Baroque Reason*, London: Sage, 1994, p. 71.
91 It is Mr Rocque who moves the strings of worldly power, cutting off the director's personal money supply and shutting down his movie in order to force him

to hire the female "star" that Mr Rocque mysteriously prefers. It is the monosyllabic Mr Rocque, immobile in his high chair in his glass-enclosed, immaculate room, with its screens that panoptically reveal all that there is to see. It is Mr Rocque who cryptically sets in motion all manner of worldly forces to get his way, from the brute violence of the huge thug who comes to the director's home, to the implicit violence of the strange cowboy who speaks to the director in aphoristic riddles, and the enraged film company lawyer who screams like an animal, and his comrade in arms, the powerful immaculate producer whose impossible demands are manifested during a meeting with the director and his agent in the grotesque gesture of spitting up an elegantly served espresso that tastes like "shit."

92 See Benjamin, *The Origin of German Tragic Drama*, pp. 54–55 ("Inwardly empty or profoundly disturbed, outwardly preoccupied with technical problems of form which seemed at first to have very little to do with the existential problems of the age – this is what most of the baroque writers were like . . . [T]he baroque is not so much an age of genuine artistic achievement as an age possessed of an unremitting will. This is true of all periods of so-called decadence . . . The form as such is within the reach of this will, a well-made individual work is not").

93 G. Agamben, *Homo Sacer*, Stanford, CA: Stanford University Press, 1998, p. 51.

94 R. Ascott, *Telematic Embrace: Visionary Theories of Art, Technology, and Consciousness*, Berkeley, CA: University of California Press, 2003, p. 264.

95 F. Rosenzweig, *Understanding the Sick and the Healthy*, Cambridge, MA: Harvard University Press, 1999, p. 102. See also E. Santner, *On the Psychotheology of Everyday Life*, Chicago: University of Chicago Press, 2001, p. 13 ("The pursuit of the end of the world is . . . fundamentally fantasmatic"). Note the affinity with Gilbert Murray's "failure of nerve" stage in the decline of ancient Greek religion, Murray, *Five Stages of Greek Religion.*

96 See J. Stern, *Denial: A Memoir of Terror*, New York: HarperCollins, 2010, p. 25.

97 R. K. Sherwin, "Law's Beatitude," *Cardozo Law Review*, 2003, Vol. 24, p. 687. See Rosenzweig, *Understanding the Sick and the Healthy*, p. 102 ("Man, chilled in the full current of life . . . escapes from the inevitability of death into the paralysis of artificial death"). See also Santner, *On the Psychotheology of Everyday Life*, p. 13 ("The pursuit of the end of the world is . . . fundamentally fantasmatic"). See also F. Rosenzweig, *The Star of Redemption*, Boston, MA: Beacon Press, 1971, pp. 4–5.

98 See J. Nancy, *The Experience of Freedom*, Stanford, CA: Stanford University Press, 1993, pp. 127–8; Wölfflin, *Renaissance and Baroque*, p. 88.

99 Nietzsche, *On the Genealogy of Morals and Ecce Homo*, 1969, pp. 97, 163.

100 Ibid., pp. 225–226.

101 See Benjamin, *The Origin of German Tragic Drama*, pp. 65–69, 74, 97–98.

102 R. M. Unger, *False Necessity: Anti-Necessitarian Social Theory in the Service of Radical Democracy*, Cambridge: Cambridge University Press, 1987, p. 279.

103 Ibid., p. 592.

104 See, e.g. M. de Sade, *Juliette*, New York: Grove Press, 1968, p. 884 ("Then she had each of the other young men one after the other bound fast atop her body: she pecked at them . . . while the executioners . . . hacked and slashed those knaves to mincemeat as they squirmed and thrashed upon her; the torments we subjected them to were beyond number and example"). Ibid., pp. 765, 769 (" 'Blood must flow before orgies are satisfactory," the Holy Father replied . . . 'I too know no more delicious discharge than that expelled in echo to the plaintive accents of the dying . . . In all living beings the principle of life is no other than that of death").
105 Goux, *Oedipus, Philosopher*, p. 148.
106 Agamben, *Homo Sacer*, pp. 50–51.
107 See Sherwin, *When Law Goes Pop*, pp. 141–169 (on the jurisprudence of appearances and law as spectacle).
108 P. Bobbitt, *The Shield of Achilles: War, Peace, and the Course of History*, New York: Anchor Books, 2003, pp. 96, 606 (discussing Lenin's "law as terror").
109 Sherwin, *When Law Goes Pop*, p. 224.
110 According to Bobbitt, in the market-state "the media are well situated to succeed" in their direct competition with the government of the day. Bobbitt, *The Shield of Achilles*, p. 784. See Sherwin, "Law's Beatitude," p. 689 n. 28 (referring to President George W. Bush's rhetorical insistence upon the need to root out evil in the face of post-9/11 terrorism).
111 See Lyotard, "The Sublime and the Avant-garde" (on deprivation); and Benjamin, *The Origin of the German Tragic Drama*, p. 56 (on "ascetic apprenticeship").
112 Goux, *Oedipus, Philosopher*, p. 185.
113 Ibid., p.186.
114 See Benjamin, *The Origin of German Tragic Drama*, pp. 232, 234 ("Ultimately, in the death-signs of the baroque the direction of allegorical reflection is reversed; on the second part of its wide arc it returns to redeem . . . The Aristotelian idea of [wonder], the artistic expression of the miracle (the Biblical {sign}) is what dominates [art and architecture too] in the period after the counter-reformation"). See Lyotard, "The Sublime and the Avant-garde," p. 103 ("an interior ascesis" allows the painter to discover "elementary sensation" hidden in ordinary perception. The viewer gains access to the artist's vision only by undergoing a "complimentary ascesis"). It is in this sense that Lynch – the magician, like Virgil, like the psychoanalyst – may be viewed as the initiate-initiator, and we, the audience, in following Diane's fate, like the audience that followed that of Oedipus, encounter the awesome power that fuels the mono-myth. The clues that lead the initiate through the terrors of (symbolic) death in the dream realm take on a labyrinthine design. As Mircea Eliade notes, "the labyrinth plays the role of a post-mortem initiatory ordeal; it falls in the category of the obstacles that the dead person – or, in other contexts, the Hero – must confront in his journey through the beyond." Eliade, *Rites and Symbols of Initiation*, p. 45.

115 See Benjamin, *The Origin of German Tragic Drama*, p. 1. See also Zizek, *The Fright of Real Tears*, p. 163 (referring to "love beyond law").

116 See G. Mazzotta, *Cosmopoiesis: The Renaissance Experiment*, Toronto: University of Toronto Press, 2001, p. 30 ("[T]he metaphysical foundation of Machiavelli's world is the disorder of a fallen state of nature; the principles of this condition of existence are force and simulation ... whereby power is acquired and maintained"), and G. Mazzotta, *The New Map of the World*, Princeton, NJ: Princeton University Press, 1999, pp. 191–192 ("Within the Hobbesian framework of justice without charity human beings are apprehended as isolated entities, as disintegrated multiplicities related by perpetual, random antagonisms and reciprocal fear").

117 See F. J. Schelling, *Philosophy and Religion*, Putnam, CT: Spring Publications, 1804 (cited in E. Bloch, *The Utopian Function of Art and Literature*, Cambridge, MA: MIT Press, 1996, p. 259). "Whoever thinks he can recognize the good without that of evil is making the greatest of mistakes, for just as in Dante's poem, the path to heaven leads through the abyss in philosophy as well." See also ibid., p. 260 (quoting F. J. Schelling, *Philosophical Investigations into the Essence of Human Freedom*, Albany, NY: State University of New York Press, 2006).

118 See, e.g. V. Turner, *The Ritual Process*, Ithaca, NY: Cornell University Press, 1969, V. Turner, *Revelation and Divination in Ndembu Ritual*, Ithaca, NY: Cornell University Press, 1975; and Eliade, *Rites and Symbols of Initiation*.

119 Agamben, *Homo Sacer*, p. 37 ("The state of nature and the state of exception are nothing but two sides of a single topological process in which what was presupposed as external [the state of nature] now reappears, as in a Mobius strip ... in the inside [as a state of exception], and the sovereign power is this very impossibility of distinguishing between outside and inside, nature and exception, *physis* and *nomos*").

120 See Lyotard, "The Sublime and the Avant-Garde," p. 102 (describing "colouristic sensations" that are "only accessible to the painter, and can, therefore, only be re-established by him, at the expense of an interior *ascesis* that rids perception and mental fields of prejudices inscribed even in vision itself. If the viewer does not submit to a complimentary *ascesis*, the painting will remain senseless and impenetrable to him"). The initiation of the rite of passage also goes under the ancient Greek rubric of *ekphrasis* – bringing the initiate across an epistemological and existential threshold, from one reality to another, through an experience, an event, an epiphany, that affords transformative insight. This was a central goal of Renaissance (neo-Platonist, alchemically-minded) artists like Botticelli, as is exquisitely evident in his masterly painting *Primavera*. See C. Dempsey, *The Portrayal of Love*, Princeton, NJ: Princeton University Press, 1992, p. 149 n. 20.

121 See E. Santner, *On the Psychotheology of Everyday Life*, Chicago: University of Chicago Press, 2001, pp. 38–39 (quoting Scholem). Compare Agamben, *Homo Sacer*, p. 60 ("[W]hat after all is a State that survives history, a State sovereignty

that maintains itself beyond the accomplishment of its *telos*, if not a law that is in force without signifying?").

122 C. Schmitt, *Political Theology*, Cambridge, MA: MIT Press, 1985, p. 5 ("Sovereign is he who decides on the exception").

123 See E. Levinas, *Ethics and Infinity*, Pittsburgh, PA: Duquesne University Press, 1985, p. 77 ("First philosophy is an ethics").

124 Eliade, *Rites and Symbols of Initiation*, p. 35.

125 See E. Levinas, *Nine Talmudic Readings*, Bloomington, IN: Indiana University Press, 1994.

126 See Agamben, *Homo Sacer*, p. 188 ("This biopolitical body that is bare life must itself . . . be transformed into the site for the constitution and installation of a form of life that is wholly exhausted in bare life and a *bios* that is only its own *zoe*"). For a real life enactment of the pathologies of power against the backdrop of the baroque politics, see David Grann "A Murder Foretold," *The New Yorker*, 24 April 2011, pp. 42–55 (on the twisted machinations surrounding the death of Guatemalan attorney, Rodrigo Rosenberg).

5 Theorizing the Visual Sublime

1 D. Rodowick, *The Virtual Life of Film*, Cambridge, MA: Harvard University Press, 2007, p. xi.

2 M. Heidegger, "The Age of the World Picture," in *The Question Concerning Technology and other Essays*, New York: Harper & Row, 1977, pp. 113–154.

3 G. Mazzotta, *The New Map of the World*, Princeton, NJ: Princeton University Press, 1999, p. 169.

4 B. Leiter, *Naturalizing Jurisprudence*, Oxford: Oxford University Press, 2007, p. 1.

5 Ibid., p. 57.

6 Ibid., p. 22.

7 J. Hutcheson, "The Judgment Intuitive: The Function of the 'Hunch' in Judicial Decision," *Cornell Law Quarterly*, 1929, Vol. 14, pp. 274, 276.

8 Ibid., p. 279.

9 Ibid. (quoting Henri Poincaré).

10 F. Varela, *Ethical Know-How: Action, Wisdom, and Cognition*, Stanford, CA: Stanford University Press, 1999, p. 7.

11 Ibid.

12 M. K. Modak-Truran, "A Pragmatic Justification of the Judicial Hunch," *University of Richmond Law Review*, 2001, Vol. 35, p.73 n. 86.

13 W. James, *Pragmatism: A New Name for Some Old Ways of Thinking*, Indianapolis, IN: Hackett, 1981 [1907], p. 74.

14 See N. Feigenson, "Visual Common Sense," in A. Wagner and R. K. Sherwin (eds.), *Law, Culture, and Visual Studies*, Amsterdam: Springer, 2012.

15 B. Cardozo, *The Nature of the Judicial Process*, New Haven, CT: Yale University Press, 1921, p. 179.

16 See F. Varela, J. Thompson, and E. Rosh, *The Embodied Mind*, Cambridge, MA: MIT Press, 2001; Varela, *Ethical Know-How*, p. 8.
17 J. Lacan, *Quatre concepts fundamentaux de la psychoanalyse*, Paris: Editions du Seuil, 1979, p. 35 ("Le statut de l'inconscient est éthique"). See F. Varela, *Ethical Know-How*, p. 64.
18 Cardozo, *The Nature of the Judicial Process*, p. 18.
19 G. Gurvitch, *Sociology of Law*, New Brunswick, NJ: Transaction, 2001, p. 170; B. Cardozo, *The Paradoxes of Legal Science*, New York: Columbia University Press, 1928, pp. 37–41, 61.
20 A. N. Whitehead, *Modes of Thought*, New York: Capricorn Books, 1958, p. 137.
21 H. Bergson, *Creative Mind*, New York: Dover, 2010 [1946], p. 21.
22 Modak-Truran, "A Pragmatic Justification of the Judicial Hunch," p. 649 n. 243.
23 Bergson, *Creative Mind*, p. 30.
24 Ibid., p.150.
25 Ibid., p. 136.
26 Cardozo, *The Nature of the Judicial Process*, p. 28.
27 Ibid., p. 35.
28 See F. Gény, *Méthode d'interpretation et sources en droit privé positif*, 2nd edn, Baton Rouge, LA: Louisiana State Law Institute, 1954 [1899]; R. Saleilles, *The Individualization of Punishment*, Boston, MA: Little Brown, 1911. See also J. Stone, *Province and Function of Law: Law as Logic Justice and Social Control: A Study in Jurisprudence*, Buffalo, NY: William S. Hein, 1946, p. 166.
29 Gény, *Méthode d'interpretation*, p. 380.
30 H. Bergson, *Creative Evolution*, New York: Barnes & Noble, 2005 [1907], p. 38.
31 See D. Kennedy and M. C. Bellau, "François Gény aux États-Unis," in C. Thomasset, J. Vanderlinden, and P. Jestaz (eds.), *François Gény: mythe et réalités 1899–1999 : centenaire de méthode d'interprétation et sources en droit privé positif : essai critique*, Quebec: Yvon Blais, 2000, p. 312, dividing Legal Realists into two camps: those who worked toward developing jurisprudence as a descriptive social science (Leiter's "naturalist jurisprudence") and those who elaborated a theory of judicial intuition. As part of the latter camp, Gény cited Bergson as an authority on the intuitive process. Ibid., p. 313.
32 See, e.g. Gurvitch, *Sociology of Law*, p. 42, preface by Roscoe Pound ("The best approach to problems of the sociology of the noetic mind (or of the human spirit) and to the determination of its exact place among the various sociological disciplines, would seem to be via the levels – or depth – analysis of social reality. This type of analysis is inspired by the 'method of inversion' (Bergson) or 'phenomenological reduction' (Husserl), i.e., an imminent downward reduction through successive stages toward whatever is most directly experienced in social reality. Obviously, all the strata or levels of depth which we shall distinguish are in real life indissolubly connected, interpenetrating one another and constituting a whole").

33 A. Whitehead, *Science and the Modern World*, New York: Free Press, 1967 [1925], p. 199.
34 A. Whitehead, *Modes of Thought*, New York: Capricorn Books, 1958, p. 207.
35 V. Turner, *The Ritual Process*, Ithaca, NY: Cornell University Press, 1969. Here also lies the link between legal decision making and cultural rituals of affliction.
36 Whitehead, *Modes of Thought*, p. 120.
37 Ibid., p. 11.
38 Ibid., p. 13.
39 Ibid.
40 M. Jay, "Scopic Regimes of Modernity," in H. Foster (ed.), *Vision and Visuality*, New York: New Press, 1988, p. 7.
41 Whitehead, *Modes of Thought*, pp. 13–15, 19; compare William James's "sentiment of rationality" in W. James, *The Will to Believe*, New York: Dover, 1956, pp. 63–110.
42 See J. S. Mill, *Autobiography of John Stewart Mill*, New York: Columbia University Press, 1960.
43 Ibid., pp. 29–30.
44 Ibid., p. 142.
45 Ibid., p. 159.
46 Ibid., p. 211.
47 Ibid., p. 32.
48 Ibid.
49 Bruner, *Acts of Meaning*, p. 11.
50 Cardozo, *The Nature of the Judicial Process*, p. 23.
51 Ibid., p. 35.
52 K. Lorenz, *On Aggression*, Orlando, FL: Harcourt Books, 1966, p. 248.
53 Bergson, *The Creative Mind*, p. 150.
54 Ibid., pp. 146, 150, 160.
55 Ibid., pp. 131, 165.
56 Ibid., pp. 7, 11, 19.
57 Ibid., p. 51.
58 Ibid., p. 58.
59 Cardozo read German and French. His sources for *The Nature of the Judicial Process* include Saleilles (1911), Gény (1899), and Berolzheimer (1912).
60 Whitehead, *Modes of Thought*, p. 229.
61 Ibid., p. 230.
62 Bergson, *The Creative Mind*, p. 22.
63 Ibid., p. 29.
64 Ibid., p. 24.
65 Ibid., p. 25.
66 Ibid., p. 30.
67 Ibid., p. 9.
68 Ibid., p. 36.
69 Ibid., p. 135.

70 M. M. Merleau-Ponty, *The Visible and the Invisible*, Evanston, IL: Northwestern University Press, 1969, p. 28.
71 M. Merleau-Ponty, *Phenomenology of Perception*, London: Routledge, 2008 [1962], p. 439.
72 Ibid., p. 441.
73 Didi-Huberman, *Fra Angelico*, p. 3.
74 K. Purgar, *The Neo-Baroque Subject*, Zagreb: Meandar Media, 2007, p. 36.
75 The filmic quest for the ultimate sensation oscillates between death and murder. See, e.g. K. Bigelow (dir.), *Strange Days*, Twentieth Century–Fox, 1995, in which the development of a fully immersive visual technology produces a black market for snuff films – so that viewers can experience for themselves what it's like to kill. The film makes the connection between heightened cinematic sensation and drug addiction, as does S. Spielberg (dir.), *Minority Report*, Dreamworks, 2002. Michael Powell's *Peeping Tom* (1960) may be the earliest film to self-reflexively link sensational cinematic voyeurism with murder. M. Powell (dir.), *Peeping Tom*, Anglo-Amalgamated Film Distributors, 1960.
76 L. U. Marks, *The Skin of the Film*, Durham, NC: Duke University Press, 1999, pp. 44–45.
77 See Mazzotta, *The New Map of the World*, p. 169; E. Grassi, *The Primordial Metaphor*, Binghamton, NY: Center for Medieval and Early Renaissance Studies, 1994, p. 53.
78 R. K. Sherwin, "Law Frames: Historical Truth and Narrative Necessity in a Criminal Case," *Stanford Law Review*, 1994, Vol. 47, p. 42.
79 Marks, *The Skin of the Film*, p. xi.
80 See Marks, *The Skin of the Film*, p. 42 (citing G. Deleuze, *Cinema 2: The Time-Image*, Minneapolis, MN: University of Minnesota Press, 1989, pp. 200–201).
81 Grassi, *The Primordial Metaphor*, p. 70.
82 Ibid., p. 169.

6 The Digital Challenge

1 H. Gadamer, *Truth and Method*, New York: Crossroad, 1975, p. 442.
2 P. Riley, *Leibniz' Universal Jurisprudence: Justice as Charity of the Wise*, Cambridge, MA: Harvard University Press, 1996, p. 181.
3 G. Deleuze, *Negotiations, 1972–1990*, New York: Columbia University Press, 1990, pp. 157–158.
4 G. Deleuze and F. Guattari, "Having an Idea of Cinema," in *Anti-Oedipus: Capitalism and Schizophrenia*, Minneapolis, MN: University of Minnesota Press, 2000, pp. 17–18.
5 Justice Scalia, Order of the Supreme Court on the Court Rules, 27 F.R.D. 89, 94 (2002) (Statement of Scalia, J.). See also R. K. Sherwin, "Constitutional Purgatory: Shades and Presences Inside the Courtroom," in D. Carpi and K. Stierstorfer (eds.), *Law and the Image*, Berlin: De Gruyter, 2012.

6 *Miranda v. Arizona*, 384 U.S. 436 (1966).
7 See F. Lederer, "Changing Litigation with Science and Technology," *Emory Law Journal*, 1994, Vol. 43, p. 1095. For more on the growing globalization of teleconferencing in court, see J. Dammann and H. Hansmann, "Globalizing Commercial Litigation," *Cornell Law Review*, 2008, Vol. 98, p. 1. Rule 43 of the Federal Rules of Civil Procedure allows videoconferencing for witness technology "for good cause shown in compelling circumstances and upon appropriate safeguards." Videoconferencing for oral arguments is allowed in the Second, Third, Eighth, Ninth, and Tenth Federal Court Circuits. In British Columbia, Canada, 6,000 charge appearances were processed by video in 2003. J. Borkowski, "Court Technology in Canada," *William and Mary Bill of Rights Journal*, 2004, Vol. 12, p. 681. See also R. Marcus, "E-Discovery and Beyond," *Review of Litigation*, 2006, Vol. 25, p. 633 (arguing that videoconferencing does not reduce jurors' capacity to make accurate determinations).
8 Remote arraignments have been taking place in the United States since at least 1982, when the state of Florida initiated initial appearances via two-way television in misdemeanor cases. The use of video in lieu of defendants' live testimony has been approved in criminal trials when policy interests trump the defendant's interest in live presence. To date, such interests include national security (see, e.g. *United States v. Abu Al*, 528 F.3d 210 [4th Cir. 2008], but see *United States v. Yates*, 438 F.3d 1307 [11th Cir. 2006]), and protecting the well-being of minors in sexual abuse cases (*Maryland v. Craig*, 497 U.S. 836 [1990]).
9 *Kulacek v. Fiat*, 509 N.W.2d 603 (Nebraska, 1994).
10 See *Connors v. United States*, 919 F.2d 1079 (5th Cir. 1991). The first time the government used a computer-animated display was to recreate the 2 August 1985, crash of Delta Airlines flight 191. To see the video of the crash simulation go to: http://www.youtube.com/watch?v=G-SI1-IHRuA.
11 *People v. Savinon*, No. SS070622A (Cal. Super. Ct., 12 January 2009).
12 See T. Brown and E. Murphy, "Through A Scanner Darkly," *Stanford Law Review*, 2010, Vol. 62, p. 1119. Much debate swirls around the alleged capacity of brain scans to provide accurate information about states of mind. See, e.g. D. D. Langleben, H. W. Longhead, W. B. Bilker, K. Ruparel, A. R. Childress, S. I. Busch, and R. C. Gur, "Telling Truth from Lie in Individual Subjects with Fast Event-Related fMRI," *Human Brain Map*, 2005, Vol. 26, pp. 262–272. Yet on 12 June 2008, 24-year-old Aditi Sharma was convicted of murder with the help of a brain scan that was used to show she lied when she denied having organized a tryst with her former fiancé at a McDonald's in the Indian city of Pune, where she fed him sweets laced with arsenic. See A. Giridharadas, "India's Novel Use of Brain Scans in Courts is Debated," *New York Times*, 15 September 2008.
13 As computer scientist Jaron Lanier has put it, we must "take responsibility for every task undertaken by a machine and double check every conclusion offered by an algorithm, just as we always look both ways when crossing an intersection, even though the light has turned green." J. Lanier, "The First Church of Robotics," *New York Times*, 9 August 2010, p. A19. See N. Feigenson and

R. K. Sherwin, "Thinking beyond the Shown: Implicit Inferences in Evidence and Argument," *Law, Probability, and Risk*, 2007, Vol. 6, pp. 245–310; N. Feigenson and M. Dunn, "New Visual Technologies in Court: direction for research," *Law and Human Behavior*, 2003, Vol. 27, pp. 109–126. Courts have exercised broad discretion on a case-by-case basis in assessing whether digital simulations are misleading or unduly prejudicial. See, e.g. *Sommervold v. Grevlos*, 518 N.W.2d 733 (S.D. 1994) (where the court stated that the simulation must be "nearly identical" to the event in question because of the power and influence of visual evidence on the minds of jurors); *State v. Sayles*, 663 N.W.2d (Iowa 2003) (where the court allowed computer-generated evidence depicting "shaken baby syndrome" on the ground that it was "clinical and emotionless"); and *Ramsey County v. Stewart*, 643 N.W.2d 281 (Minn. 2002) (in a case involving computer-generated evidence showing how the murder weapon was pointed and fired the court cited the risk that "the jury may confuse art with reality" and warned that irrelevant facial expressions might be prejudicial but then allowed the evidence based on harmless error).

14 See D. Rodowick, *The Virtual Life of Film*, Cambridge, MA: Harvard University Press, 2007, pp. 68–79; L. U. Marks, *The Skin of the Film*, Durham, NC: Duke University Press, 1999, pp. 52–53.

15 See L. U. Marks, *Touch: Sensuous Theory and Multisensory Media*, Minneapolis, MN: University of Minnesota Press, 2002, p. 171.

16 Rodowick, *The Virtual Life of Film*, p. 86.

17 L. U. Marks, *Touch: Sensuous Theory and Multisensory Media*, p.174 (noting that at the electronic level "we are all more connected than we may imagine"). This notion of "connectivity" may be questioned, however, to the extent that at the sub-atomic level such connectivity remains strangely indeterminate. As Robert Lanza puts it, "Before a measurement is made, a sub-atomic particle does not really exist in a definite place or have an actual motion . . . nothing is real unless it is perceived." R. Lanza and B. Berman, *Biocentrism: how life and consciousness are the keys to understanding the true nature of the universe*, Dallas, TX: BenBella Books, 2010, pp. 57–58.

18 See also J. Nechvatal, "An Ecstasy of Excess," in *An Ecstasy of Excess*, Münchengladbach: Juni-Verlag, 1991, pp. 3–7.

19 D. N. Rodowick, *Reading the Figural, or, Philosophy after the New Media*, Durham, NC: Duke University Press, 2001, p. 209.

20 Deleuze, *Negotiations, 1972–1990*, p. 172.

21 See, e.g. *Connecticut v. Swinton*, 268 Conn. 781 (Conn. 2004); and *New Mexico v. Tollardo*, 134 N.M. 430 (N.M. Ct. App. 2003) (laying out the distinctions between visual proof and demonstrative evidence). See generally S. Goode, "The Admissibility of Electronic Evidence," *Review of Litigation*, 2009, Vol. 29, p. 1.

22 S. Turkle, *Simulation and its Discontents*, Cambridge, MA: MIT Press, 2009, p. 88 n. 3.

23 See G. Debord, *The Society of Spectacle*, New York: Zone Books, 1995, p. 193 (quoting Gabel).

24 A. Seligman, R. Weller, M. Puett, and B. Simon, *Ritual and its Consequences: an essay on the limits of sincerity*, Oxford: Oxford University Press, 2008.
25 See, e.g. A. Ndalianis, "Introduction. The Baroque and the Neo-Baroque," in *Neo-Baroque Aesthetics and Contemporary Entertainment*, Cambridge, MA: MIT Press, 2004, p. 357 (noting that Deleuze understood the baroque in its broadest terms "as radiating through histories, cultures and worlds of knowledge," including areas as diverse as art, science, costume design, mathematics, and philosophy). Likewise, in his historical and cultural study of the seventeenth-century Spanish baroque, Antonio Maravall observed that it is possible to "establish certain relations between external, purely formal elements of the baroque in seventeenth-century Europe and elements present in very different historical epochs in unrelated cultural areas . . . [Therefore] it is also possible [to] speak of a baroque at any given time, in any field of human endeavor." See J. A. Maravall, *Culture of the Baroque: Analysis of a Historical Structure*, Minneapolis, MN: University of Minnesota Press, 1986, pp. 4–5. Maravall is particularly concerned with the seventeenth century, but he is also interested in the baroque as a cultural phenomenon that emerges from a specific historical situation. In this respect, it is possible to identify and describe a morphology of the baroque that is not confined to one specific point in history.
26 S. J. Freedberg, *Painting in Italy, 1500–1600*, New Haven, CT: Yale University Press, 1993, pp. 446–449.
27 A. Warhol, *The Philosophy of Andy Warhol: From A to B and Back Again*, San Diego, CA: Harvest Books, 1977, p. 50.
28 I. Indyk, "The Critic and the Public Culture: For Example, Walter Benjamin," *Australian Humanities Review*, 2000, Vol. 18.
29 J. Sartre, *La Nausée*, Paris: Gallimard, 2002.
30 W. Stevens, *The Collected Poetry of Wallace Stevens*, New York: Vintage, 1990.
31 M. Heidegger, *Poetry, Language, Thought*, New York: Harper & Row, 1971.
32 H. Gadamer, *Truth and Method*, New York: Crossroad, 1975, p. 443.
33 Ibid.
34 Plato, *Symposium*, Indianapolis, IN: Hackett, 1989, p. 204d–5.
35 Ibid., p. 211d–1.
36 P. Riley, *Leibniz' Universal Jurisprudence: Justice as Charity of the Wise*, Cambridge, MA: Harvard University Press, 1996, p. 17.
37 Plato, *Phaedrus and Letters VII and VIII*, New York: Penguin Books, 1973, line 253a–3, p. 60.
38 Ibid., p. 255d–3.
39 See J. Malpas, *Heidegger's Topology: Being, Place, World*, Cambridge, MA: MIT Press, 2006, p. 9.
40 See S. Almog, *How Digital Technologies are Changing the Practice of Law*, New York: Edwin Mellen Press, 2007, pp. 102–105.
41 See A. Grossman, *The Sighted Singer*, Baltimore, MD: Johns Hopkins University Press, 1992, p. 250.

42 M. Weber, *Economy and Society*, Berkeley, CA: University of California Press, 1978, p. 606.
43 Contrast Walter Benjamin's understanding of the exalted aspect of language in W. Benjamin, "On Language as Such and On the Language of Man," in M. Bullock and M. W. Jennings (eds.), *Selected Writings, 1913–1926*, Cambridge, MA: Harvard University Press, 1996, p. 65 ("God's creation is completed when things receive their names from man, from whom in name language alone speaks"). Benjamin contrasts this understanding of language as an "ultimate reality" with the "bourgeois view" of words as "accidental" signs for things, which is to say, mere conventions. One recognizes here the Cartesian and digitally programmed models for language that differ so fundamentally from the expressive function of the sublime. In this way, Benjamin recapitulates the severance of signifier and signified that is characteristic of baroque and digital baroque spectacle.
44 H. Murakami, *Hard-Boiled Wonderland and the End of the World*, New York: Vintage Books, 1993, p. 41.
45 R. Kurzweil, *The Singularity is Near: When Humans Transcend Biology*, New York: Penguin Books, 2006.
46 Murakami, *Hard-Boiled Wonderland*, p. 399.
47 See Malpas, *Heidegger's Topology*, p. 163 (referring to being as "the *transcendent pure and simple*").
48 See F. Kafka, "In the Penal Colony," *Metamorphosis, In the Penal Colony, and Other Stories: With Two New Stories*, New York: Scribner, 2000.
49 See also S. Smith, *Law's Quandary*, Cambridge, MA: Harvard University Press, 2004.
50 W. Benjamin, *The Origin of German Tragic Drama*, London: Verso, 1998, p. 54.
51 R. S. Dombroski, *Creative Entanglements: Gadda and the Baroque*, Toronto: University of Toronto Press, 1999, pp. ix–x.
52 Benjamin, *The Origin of German Tragic Drama*.
53 As Alain Supiot writes, "Whenever people are cut off from their fellow creatures, they are condemned to idiocy, in the etymological sense of the term (from the Greek *idios*: 'confined to oneself') . . ." A. Supiot, *Homo Juridicus*, London: Verso, 2007, p. viii.
54 A. Grossman, "*The Sighted Singer, Two Works on Poetry for Readers and Writers*, Baltimore, MD: Johns Hopkins University Press, 1992, p. 182.

7 Conclusion: Visualizing Law's Rhetorical Ideal

1 D. Rodowick, The *Virtual Life of Film*, Cambridge, MA: Harvard University Press, 2007, p. xi.
2 M. Jay, "Scopic Regimes of Modernity," in H. Foster (ed.), *Vision and Visuality*, New York: New Press, 1988, p. 20.
3 G. Vico, *The New Science of Giambattista Vico*, Ithaca, NY: Cornell University Press, unabridged edn, 1968, Section 384, p. 120.

4 See A. Sharp, *The English Levellers*, Cambridge: Cambridge University Press, 1998.
5 P. Goodrich, *Law in the Courts of Love: Literature and Other Minor Jurisprudences*, London: Routledge, 1996.
6 Ibid.
7 See, e.g. C. Robin, *Fear: The History of a Political Idea*, Oxford: Oxford University Press, 2004.
8 See E. H. Kantorowicz, *The King's Two Bodies: A Study in Mediaeval Political Theology*, Princeton, NJ: Princeton University Press, 1981.
9 See J. Laplanche, *Essays on Otherness*, New York: Routledge, 1999, p. 56 ("If man is no longer at the center of the universe, not only are all cosmogonies and creation myths contradicted, but all the pantheons forged in the image of man or centered on man are thereby devalorized").
10 See A. M. Kibbey, *Theory of the Image: Capitalism, Contemporary Film, and Women*, Bloomington, IN: Indiana University Press, 2004.
11 See generally G. Binder and R. Weisberg, *Literary Criticisms of Law*, Princeton, NJ: Princeton University Press, 2000.
12 See J. Habermas, *Between Facts and Norms: Contributions to a Discourse Theory of Law and Democracy*, Cambridge, MA: MIT Press, 1998. Michael Sandel makes a similar claim regarding procedural liberalism: "[S]ince people disagree about the best way to live, government should not affirm in law any particular vision of the good life. Instead, it should provide a framework of rights that respects persons as free and independent (unencumbered) selves, capable of choosing their own values and ends." M. J. Sandel, *Democracy's Discontents: America in Search of a Public Philosophy*, Cambridge, MA: Belknap Press, 1996, p. 4.
13 See Habermas, *Between Facts and Norms.*
14 R. J. Lifton, *The Protean Self: Human Resilience in an Age of Fragmentation*, Chicago: University of Chicago Press, 1999.
15 N. Aubert, *L'Individu hypermoderne*, Ramonville-Saint-Agne: Éditions Érés, 2004.
16 See R. K. Sherwin, *When Law Goes Pop: The Vanishing Line between Law and Popular Culture*, Chicago: University of Chicago Press, 2000, pp. 230–233.
17 See R. Cassirer, *The Myth of the State*, New Haven, CT: Yale University Press, 1946, p. 133.
18 Kantorowicz, *The King's Two Bodies*, p. 58 ("The king is the perfect impersonator of Christ on earth"). See ibid., p. 312 ("The king who never dies is the head of the one-man corporation that never dies.").
19 See M. Foucault, "Two Lectures," in C. Gordon (ed.), *Power/Knowledge: Selected Interviews and Other Writings, 1972–1977*, New York: Pantheon Books, 1980, p. 88. See also A. M. Kibbey, *Theory of the Image: Capitalism, Contemporary Film, and Women*, Bloomington, IN: Indiana University Press, 2004, pp. 5–20.
20 F. Kafka, *The Castle*, New York: Schocken Books, 1998.
21 See ibid.
22 Benjamin, "On the Concept of History," p. 392.

23 J. Rawls, "Overlapping Consensus," in S. Freeman (ed.), *Collected Papers*, Cambridge, MA: Harvard University Press, 1999, p. 481. R. Dworkin, *Justice for Hedgehogs*, Cambridge, MA: Harvard University Press, 2011.

24 See generally G. Mazzotta, *The New Map of the World*, Princeton, NJ: Princeton University Press, 1999.

25 See also J. Derrida, "Force of Law: The Mystical Foundation of Authority," in D. Cornell et al. (eds.), *Deconstruction and the Possibility of Justice*, New York: Routledge, 1992, p. 14.

26 S. Morley (ed.), *The Sublime*, Cambridge, MA: MIT Press, 2010.

27 J. T. Noonan, Jr, *Persons and Masks of the Law: Cardozo, Holmes, Jefferson, and Wythe as Makers of the Masks*, Berkeley, CA: University of California Press, 1976.

28 E. Levinas, *Totality and Infinity: An Essay on Exteriority*, trans. A. Lingis, Pittsburgh, PA: Duquesne University Press, 1969, p. 43 ("We name this calling into question of my spontaneity by the presence of the Other ethics."). See also See also G. Sorel, *Reflections on Violence*, New York: Peter Smith, 1941, pp. 241–242 ("'To be ready to defend [the dignity of man] in every circumstance with energy, and, if necessary, against oneself, that is Justice . . . There is a tendency in every man to develop and force the acceptance of that which is essentially himself – which is, in fact, his own dignity. It results from this that the essential in man being identical and one for all humanity, each of us is aware of himself at the same time as individual and as species; and that an insult is felt by a third party and by the offender himself as well as by the injured person, that in consequence the protest is common. This precisely is what is meant by Justice'," quoting Proudhon). See also A. Rabinbach, *In the Shadow of Catastrophe*, Berkeley: CA: University of California Press, 2000, p. 459 ("The elements of the end condition are not present as formless tendencies of progress, but instead are embedded in every present as endangered, condemned, and ridiculed creations and ideas. The historical task is to give absolute form in a genuine way to the immanent condition of fulfillment, to make it visible and predominant in the present . . . [H]owever, it is only comprehensible in its metaphysical structure, like the messianic realm or the idea of the French Revolution," citing Richard Wolin on Walter Benjamin).

29 "The Tragic, the Impossible and Democracy: an interview with Jacques Derrida," *International Journal of the Semiotics of Law*, 2010, Vol. 23, pp. 247, 252.

30 S. Wolosky, "A Reply to Vattimo," *Common Knowledge*, 2003, Vol. 9, p. 3 ("Levinas's idea of otherness establishes a relationship that removes from any self a right of incursion into any other self." "Each moral finitude is by nature not negotiable – protected, defended, and entitled to be sustained").

31 See Levinas, *Totality and Infinity*, p. 48 ("This 'saying to the Other' – this relationship with the other as Interlocutor, this relation with an existent – precedes all ontology: it is the ultimate relation in Being. Ontology presupposes metaphysics").

32 See B. Latour, *Iconoclash: Beyond the Image Wars in Science, Religion and Art*, Cambridge, MA: MIT Press, 2002. See also D. Glowacka, "Ethical Figures of Otherness: Jean-Luc Nancy's Sublime Offering and Emmanuel Levinas' Gift for

the Other," in K. Ziarek and S. Deane (eds.), *Future Crossings: Literature between Philosophy and Culture Studies*, Evanston, IL: Northwestern University Press, 2000.

33 E. Levinas, *Proper Names*, Stanford, CA: Stanford University Press, 1996, p. 122.

34 My use of the term "metaphysical" in this context tracks the term's use by Emmanuel Levinas. See E. Levinas, *Totality and Infinity: An Essay on Exteriority*, Pittsburgh, PA: Duquesne University Press, 1969, pp. 23–24 ("The experience of morality does not proceed from this vision [of eschatology, which Levinas distinguishes from the revealed opinions of positive religions] – it *consummates* this vision; ethics is an optics. But it is a 'vision' without image, bereft of the synoptic and totalizing objectifying virtues of vision . . . " ibid., p. 23, emphasis in original).

35 See E. Grassi, *Vico and Humanism*, New York: Peter Lang, 1990, p. 83.

36 Ibid., p. 193.

37 See M. Deguy, "The Discourse of Exaltation: Contribution to a Rereading of Pseudo-Longinus" (quoting Longinus) in *Of the Sublime Presence in Question: Essays*, Jean-François Courtine (ed.), New York: State University of New York Press, 2007, ("[M]an's intentness on perceiving often everywhere goes out beyond the limits of what holds him in . . ."); M. Ferraris, "The Meaning of Being as a Determinate Ontic Trace," in J. Derrida and G. Vattimo (eds.), *Religion*, Stanford, CA: Stanford University Press, 1996, pp. 170, 186 ("Metaphysics is the unconditioned in man, the obscure space made possible by his self-transcendent constitution"); P. Lacoue-Labarthe, "Sublime Truth," in *Of the Sublime: Presence in Question*, Albany, NY: State University of New York Press, 1993, pp. 71, 94 (describing Heidegger's evocation of the sensibility of the sublime: "for the more purely the work [of art] is itself transported into the openness of the being – an openness opened by itself – the more simply does it transport us . . .").

38 Lacoue-Labarthe, "Sublime Truth," p. 100 (describing mimesis as the condition of the possibility of knowledge); Levinas, *Totality and Infinity*, p. 29 ("The aspiration to radical exteriority, thus called metaphysical, the respect for this metaphysical exteriority which, above all, we must 'let be', constitutes truth"); M. T. Taussig, *Mimesis and Alterity: A Particular History of the Senses*, London: Routledge, 1993, pp. xviii, 38, 40 (adopting Walter Benjamin's understanding of the mimetic faculty as "the compulsion to become the Other" and describing sentience as taking us "outside of ourselves" in the "instantaneous" and "mystical" flash which is the "perception of similarity").

39 Compare D. P. Verene, *Vico's Science of Imagination*, Ithaca, NY: Cornell University Press, 1981, p. 33 ("Images or *universali fantastici* are not, in Vico's terms, simply concepts in poetic cloaks. The image is not to be understood in relation to the concept. The image is to be understood on its own terms").

40 The primordial genesis of metaphor and fable through the archaic poetic imagination, according to Vico, presupposes the immersion of mind in the body. Reversing Descartes, it is not the soul that sees, but rather the body. Ibid., p. 86 (noting that human thought began as "bodily eyes"). This is consonant with Vico's concept of *fantasia* or poetic imagination as the process in which, as Vico

notes, "likenesses taken from bodies . . . signify the operations of abstract minds." Ibid., p. 83. Again, Verene's insight is acute: "In the fixing of sensation the meaning of the whole of the flux is found again in the single sensation. In this way a universality is achieved through the particular. An identity is made. The power of the *is*, the power of identity itself is realized." Ibid. See also ibid., p. 173 ("The mind's first act is a transference or bearing of meaning from sensation as placeless, momentary flux to the fixation of sensation as a god"). Walter Benjamin's idea of a "profane illumination" also comes to mind here. See W. Benjamin, "Surrealism: The Last Snapshot of the European Intelligentsia," in W. Benjamin, M. W. Jennings, H. Eiland, and G. Smith (eds.), *Selected Writings, 1927–1934*, Cambridge, MA: Harvard University Press, 1999, p. 2.

41 G. Vico, *On the Study Methods of our Time*, Ithaca, NY: Cornell University Press, 1990, p. 38.

42 M. Mooney, *Vico in the Tradition of Rhetoric*, London: Routledge, 1995, p. 101 (quoting Vico); J. Derrida, *The Gift of Death*, Chicago: University of Chicago Press, 1996, p. 36 ("Technological civilization only produces a heightening or recrudescence of the orgiastic, with the familiar effects of aestheticism and individualism that attend it, to the extent that it also produces boredom, for it 'levels' or neutralizes the mysterious or irreplaceable uniqueness of the responsible self").

43 Mooney, *Vico in the Tradition of Rhetoric*, p. 113 (quoting Vico).

44 Ibid., p. 10 (quoting Cicero).

45 Ibid.

46 See A. Kronman, "Rhetoric," *University of Cincinnati Law Review*, 1999, Vol. 67, p. 677 (observing that the "otherworldly satisfactions of philosophy and love . . . can be sustained only in a frame of worldly institutions").

47 Mooney, *Vico in the Tradition of Rhetoric*, pp. 11–12.

48 Ibid., p. 128 (quoting Vico).

49 Mazzotta, *The New Map of the World*, p. 60.

50 According to Ricoeur: "The fundamental trait of *muthos* is its character of order, of organization, of arranging or grouping." P. Ricoeur, "Between Rhetoric and Poetics," in A. O. Rorty (ed.) *Essays on Aristotle's "Rhetoric,"* Berkeley, CA: University of Calfornia Press, 1996, p. 348.

51 In this sense, mimesis is far more than the mere "copying" of something in nature. Mimesis involves a productive interaction with the being of something other than mind. See Ricoeur, "Between Rhetoric and Poetics," p. 351 ("[I]t is only through a grave misinterpretation that the Aristotelian *mimēsis* can be confused with imitation in the sense of copy. If *mimēsis* involves an initial reference to reality, this reference signifies *nothing other than the very rule of nature over all production . . .* Mimēsis *is* poiesis, *and* poeisis *is* mimēsis"; emphasis added). See also M. T. Taussig, *Mimesis and Alterity: A Particular History of the Senses*, London: Routledge, 1993, pp. xiii, xviii (characterizing mimesis as "sympathetic magic," "the compulsion to become the Other" (through a living speech that irradiates form with originary being)). See I. Berlin, *Vico and*

Herder: Two Studies in the History of Ideas, New York: Vintage, 1976, pp. 111–12 ("Vico, influenced perhaps by 'magical' theories of becoming one with the object, widespread in the Renaissance, is one of the true fathers of the doctrine of the unity of theory and practice . . . He believed that in principle we could re-enact in our minds – 'enter' by sympathetic imagination – into what a class, a society [wanted, worked for, were after]. . . . He supposes that we can, by a species of imaginative insight, turn every *an sich* . . . an entity observed from the outside by the agent . . . into a *für sich*, an element in, assimilated to, his purposive, 'spiritual' activity"). In Michael Taussig's felicitous phrase, mimesis, as an expression of self-transcendence, is "the nature culture uses to create second nature." Taussig, *Mimesis and Alterity*, p. 252.

52 Mooney, *Vico in the Tradition of Rhetoric*, p. 261.

53 See I. Almond, *Sufism and Deconstruction: A Comparative Study of Derrida and Ibn 'Arabi*, New York: Routledge, 2004, pp. 30–37 (comparing Derrida's notion of *différance* with Ibn 'Arabi's sense of the Real); Deguy, "The Discourse of Exaltation," 2007, p. 16. See generally Deguy, "The Discourse of Exaltation."

54 See Berlin, *Vico and Herder*, p. 108. Verene aptly attributes to *fantasia* the "power to give imagistic form to experience" and to form the particular as a universal. Verene, *Vico's Science of Imagination*, pp. 81–82.

55 M. Dufrenne, *The Phenomenology of Aesthetic Experience*, Evanston, IL: Northwestern University Press, 1973, p. 847.

56 Heidegger aptly notes that "rapture is the basic aesthetic state without qualification." M. Heidegger, *Nietzsche*, New York: Harper Collins, 1991, pp. 1, 97. But the ethical force that Levinas describes disturbs our aesthetic enjoyment. By confronting me with the irreducible "destituteness" of the other's naked countenance, the ethical obligation (to pay heed) calls into question "my joyous possession of the world." Levinas, *Totality and Infinity*, p. 29 ("The aspiration to radical exteriority, thus called metaphysical, the respect for this metaphysical exteriority which, above all, we must 'let be' constitutes truth"). The sublime surplus thus shifts from contingent things (the realm of beauty) to the infinity ("the inexhaustible surplus") of the face (the realm of the ethical). Ibid., p. 207.

57 See E. Levinas, *Otherwise than Being, or, Beyond Essence*, Dordrecht: Kluwer, 1991.

58 J. Derrida, *The Gift of Death*, Chicago: University of Chicago Press, 1996, p. 2.

59 Mooney, *Vico in the Tradition of Rhetoric*, p. 147 (quoting J. A. Mazzeo, "Metaphysical Poetry and the Poetic of Correspondence," *Journal of the History of Ideas*, 1953, Vol. 14, pp. 221, 228. See also Deguy, "The Discourse of Exaltation," p. 9 (citing Longinus: those who raise themselves to "the high" [translated as the sublime] "get a view of the 'mortal condition'" and become like the divine).

60 Quoted in Mooney, *Vico in the Tradition of Rhetoric*, p. 149.

61 W. Benjamin, "On Language as Such and on the Language of Man," in M. Bullock and M. W. Jennings (eds.), *Selected Writings, 1913–1926*, Cambridge, MA: Harvard University Press, 1996, pp. 62, 65.

62 E. Grassi, *Rhetoric as Philosophy: The Humanist Tradition*, University Park, PA: Pennsylvania State University Press, 1980, p. 75; Deguy, "The Discourse of Exaltation," p. 9 (noting that metaphor "originally brings to visibility the figure of what is not visible").

63 Ibid., p. 91.

64 Ibid., p. 92.

65 Verene, *Vico's Science of Imagination*, at pp. 82–83, 95. Verene also cites Vico here as saying "that *mythos* is a *vera narratio* or true speech: 'The fables in their origin were true and severe narrations, whence *mythos*, fable, was defined as a *vera narration*'." Ibid., p. 82.

66 Grassi, *Rhetoric as Philosophy*, p. 97.

67 Ibid., p. 7.

68 Ibid., p. 97.

69 Ibid., p. 7.

70 Ibid.

71 See Verene, *Vico's Science of Imagination*, p. 55 (describing Vico's new science as being based on a "metaphysical art of criticism"). See also ibid., p. 56 ("Only metaphysical vision can approach the illumination of the *topos* of providence behind the *sensus communis* of the human world and grasp this world as a middle term between the divine and the natural").

72 See ibid., p. 61 ("In Vico's view society was formed neither by any single act of prudent agreement between men nor by foresight. Human rationality grew within the providential structure of history as human social action grew. This social action was not originally based on acts of reflective judgment but on the formation of the world through the powers of memory and imagination").

73 R. M. Cover, "Nomos and Narrative," *Harvard Law Review*, 1983, Vol. 97, p. 4.

74 Verene, *Vico's Science of Imagination*, p. 63 ("The natural law of the gentes is not an abstract principle but is present as the actual life of any society. It is true not as a rational ideal but as the actual basis of social practice").

75 G. Vico, *The Autobiography of Giambattista Vico*, ed. Max Harold Fisch and Thomas Goddard Bergin, Ithaca: NY, Cornell University Press, 1970, p. 124.

76 See E. Santner, *On the Psychotheology of Everyday Life*, Chicago: University of Chicago Press, 2001, p. 9 ("I want to propose that the ethics at the core of both psychoanalysis and the Judeo-Christian tradition [as interpreted by Rosenzweig] is an ethics pertaining to my *answerability to my neighbor-with-an-unconscious*"); S. Freud, "Two Encyclopedia Articles," in *The Standard Edition of the Complete Psychological Works of Sigmund Freud*, New York: Vintage, 1999, pp. 235, 239 ("Experience soon showed that the attitude which the analytic physician could most advantageously adopt was to surrender himself to his own unconscious mental activity, in a state of *evenly suspended attention* . . . to catch the drift of the patient's unconscious with his own unconscious"). See also F. Varela, *Ethical Know-How: Action, Wisdom, and Cognition*, Stanford, CA: Stanford University Press, 1999, p. 64 (discussing ethics as the cultivation of a "know-how" concerning the unconscious). According to Varela, the

ek-static state of mind (i.e. standing outside oneself in a selfless, non-intentional, non-deliberative but active mindfulness) is what Buddhists refer to as *wu-wei*. Ibid., pp. 32–33. This notion of mindfulness resonates as well with Heidegger's sense of "mood" or "attunement." See M. Heidegger, "On the Essence of Truth," in W. Brock (ed.), *Existence and Being*, Chicago: Gateway Edition, 1949, p. 311 (describing mood as "a way of being attuned, and letting ourselves be attuned . . . . [it] is precisely the basic way in which we are *outside* ourselves").

77 See generally M. Heidegger, *Poetry, Language, Thought*, New York: Harper & Row, 1971.

78 Levinas, *Otherwise than Being*, 1998.

79 See generally M. Foucault, *The Archaeology of Knowledge*, New York: Pantheon Books, 1972; M. Foucault, "Two Lectures," in C. Gordon (ed.), *Power/Knowledge: Selected Interviews and Other Writings, 1972–1977*, New York: Pantheon Books, 1980.

80 Ricoeur, "Between Rhetoric and Poetics," p. 352. This notion of being faithful to things as they are is consonant with Grassi's understanding of the primary basis of metaphor (poiesis) in the production of knowledge. See Grassi, *Rhetoric as Philosophy*, 1980, p. 75.

81 See Almond, *Sufism and Deconstruction.*

82 See Levinas, *Otherwise than Being*, p. 191 n. 2.

83 J. Derrida, *On Cosmopolitanism and Forgiveness*, London: Routledge, 2001, p. 68.

84 G. Vico, "The Academies and the Relation between Philosophy and Eloquence," in *On the Study Methods of Our Time*, Ithaca, NY: Cornell University Press, 1990, p. 89.

85 Lacoue-Labarthe, "Sublime Truth," p. 100.

86 See A. Kronman, "Rhetoric," *University of Cincinnati Law Review*, 1999, Vol. 67: p. 677.

87 See G. Watt, *Equity Stirring: The Story of Justice beyond Law*, Oxford: Hart, 2009.

88 See R. K. Sherwin, "Anti-Oedipus, Lynch: Initiatory Rites and the Ordeal of Justice," in A. Sarat, L. Douglas, and M. M. Umphrey (eds.), *Law on the Screen*, Stanford, CA: Stanford University Press, 2005, pp. 106, 126 ("[L]ike arabesques endlessly improvising their monadic design, baroque ornamentation proliferated, dizzying, decentering, even nauseating in their spatial onslaught"). See also H. Wölfflin, *Renaissance and Baroque*, Ithaca, NY: Cornell University Press, 1967, p. 34 (noting that the baroque seeks to stimulate the imagination through infinite figurations); G. Deleuze, *The Fold: Leibniz and the Baroque*, Minneapolis, MN: University of Minnesota Press, 1992 ("[T]he Baroque differentiates its folds in two ways, by moving along two infinities, as if infinity were composed of two stages or floors: the pleats of matter, and the folds of the soul").

89 C. Bollas, *The Evocative Object World*, New York: Routledge, 2009, p. 13.

90 P. Goodrich, "Screening Law," *Law and Literature*, 2009, Vol. 21, No. 1, p. 20.

91 I. Kant, *Critique of Practical Reason*, Cambridge: Cambridge University Press, 1997, p. 133.

92 G. Deleuze, *Difference and Repetition*, New York: Columbia University Press, 1994, p. 119 ("Thunderbolts explode between different intensities, but they are preceded by an invisible, imperceptible, dark precursor"). See also Grassi, *Vico and Humanism*, p. 185 ("'Logic' comes from *logos*, whose first and proper meaning was *fabula*, fable, carried over into Italian as *favella*, speech. In Greek the fable was also called *mythos*, myth, whence comes the Latin *mutus*, mute. For speech was born in mute times as a mental [or sign] language . . . [which] existed before vocal or articulate [language]; whence *logos* means both word and idea," quoting Vico, *New Science*, s. 401).

Bibliography

Adler, A., "The Perverse Law of Child Pornography," *Columbia Law Review*, 101: 209–273, 2001.

Agamben, G., *Homo Sacer*, Stanford, CA: Stanford University Press, 1998.

Almog, S., *How Digital Technologies are Changing the Practice of Law*, New York: Edwin Mellen Press, 2007.

Almond, I., *Sufism and Deconstruction: A Comparative Study of Derrida and Ibn 'Arabi*, New York: Routledge, 2004.

Amsterdam, A. and Bruner, J., *Minding the Law*, Cambridge, MA: Harvard University Press, 2000.

Anderson, B., *Imagined Communities*, London: Verso, 2002.

Armstrong, E. and Zamudio-Taylor, V., *Ultra Baroque: Aspects of Post-Latin American Art*, San Diego, CA: Museum of Contemporary Art, 2000.

Ascott, R., *Telematic Embrace: Visionary Theories of Art, Technology, and Consciousness*, ed. E. A. Shanken, Berkeley, CA: University of California Press, 2003.

Aubert, N., *L'Individu hypermoderne*, Ramonville-Saint-Agne: Éditions Érés, 2004.

Auerbach, E., *Mimesis: The Representation of Reality in Western Literature*, trans. W. R. Trask, Princeton, NJ: Princeton University Press, 2003.

Auster, P, *City of Glass: The New York Trilogy*, Vol. 1, London: Penguin Books, 1987.

Baltrušaitis, J., *Anamorphic Art*, trans. W. J. Strachan, Cambridge: Chadwyck-Healey, 1977.

Barkan, L., "The Heritage of Zeuxis: Painting, Rhetoric, and History," in A. Payne, A. Kuttner, and R. Smick (eds.), *Antiquity and its Interpreters*, Cambridge: Cambridge University Press, 2000.

Barthes, R., *Camera Lucida: Reflections on Photography*, New York: Hill & Wang, 1982.

Beckett, S., *The Unnamable*, New York: Grove Press, 1958.

Benjamin, W., "On Language as Such and on the Language of Man," in M. Bullock and M. W. Jennings (eds.), *Selected Writings, 1913–1926*, Cambridge, MA: Harvard University Press, 1996.

Benjamin, W., *The Origin of German Tragic Drama*, London: Verso, 1998.

Benjamin, W., "Surrealism: The Last Snapshot of the European Intelligentsia," "Franz Kafka," trans. R. Livingstone, in M. W. Jennings, H. Eiland, and G. Smith (eds.), *Selected Writings, 1927–1934*, Cambridge, MA: Harvard University Press, 1999.

Benjamin, W., "The Work of Art in the Age of its Technological Reproducibility," trans. E. Jephcott, in H. Eiland and M. W. Jennings (eds.), *Selected Writings, 1938–1940*, Cambridge, MA: Harvard University Press, 2003.

Bergin, J., *The Seventeenth Century*, Oxford: Oxford University Press, 2001.

Bergman, I., "The Snakeskin," *Sight and Sound*, 1 August 1965.

Bergman, P. and Asimow, M., *Reel Justice: The Courtroom Goes to the Movies*, Kansas City, MO: Andrews & McMeel, 1996.

Bergson, H., *Creative Evolution*, New York: Barnes & Noble, 2005 [1907].

Bergson, H., *Creative Mind*, New York: Dover, 2010 [1946].

Berlin, I., *Vico and Herder: Two Studies in the History of Ideas*, New York: Vintage, 1976.

Berolzheimer, F., *The World's Legal Philosophies*, Boston: MA, Boston Book Company, 1912.

Binder, G. and Weisberg, R., *Literary Criticisms of Law*, Princeton, NJ: Princeton University Press, 2000.

Birdsell, D. and Groarke, L., "Toward a Theory of Visual Argument," *Argumentation and Advocacy*, 33: 1–10, 1996.

Blackmore, S., "Evolution and Memes: The Human Brain as a Selective Imitation Device," *Cybernetics and Systems*, 32: 225–255, 2001.

Blair, J. A., "The Rhetoric of Visual Arguments," in C. A. Hill and M. Helmers (eds.), *Defining Visual Rhetorics*, Malwah, NJ: Lawrence Erlbaum, 2004.

Bloch, E., *The Utopian Function of Art and Literature*, Cambridge, MA: MIT Press, 1996.

Bobbitt, P., *The Shield of Achilles: War, Peace, and the Course of History*, New York: Anchor Books, 2003.

Bollas, C., *Being a Character: Psychoanalysis and Self-Experience*, New York: Routledge, 2006.

Bollas, C., *The Evocative Object World*, New York: Routledge, 2009.

Borges, J. L., *Labyrinths: Selected Stories and Other Writings*, New York: New Directions, 1964.

Borges, J. L., *The Aleph and Other Stories*, trans. A. Hurley, New York: Penguin Books, 2004.

Borkowski, J., "Court Technology in Canada," *William and Mary Bill of Rights Journal*, 12: 681–686, 2004.

Bright, D. A. and Goodman-Delahunty, J., "Gruesome Evidence and Emotion: Anger, Blame, and Jury Decision-Making," *Law and Human Behavior*, 30: 183–202, 2006.

Brooks, P. and Gewirtz, P., *Law's Stories: Narrative and Rhetoric in the Law*, New Haven, CT: Yale University Press, 1998.

Brown, T. and Murphy, E., "Through A Scanner Darkly," *Stanford Law Review*, 62: 1119–1208, 2010.

Brüderlin, M. and Beyeler, E. (eds.), *Ornament and Abstraction*, Cologne: Dumont Buchverlag, 2002.

Bruner, J., *Beyond the Information Given: Studies in the Psychology of Knowing*, New York: W. W. Norton, 1973.
Bruner, J., *Actual Minds, Possible Worlds*, Cambridge, MA: Harvard University Press, 1986.
Bruner, J., *Acts of Meaning*, Cambridge, MA: Harvard University Press, 1990.
Bruno, G., *On the Composition of Images, Signs and Ideas*, trans. C. Doria, ed. D. Higgins, New York: Wills Locker & Owens, 1991.
Bruno, G., *Cause, Principle and Unity: And Essays on Magic*, Cambridge: Cambridge University Press, 1998.
Buci-Glucksmann, C., *La Folie du voir: de l'esthétique baroque*, Paris: Éditions Galilée, 1986.
Buci-Glucksmann, C., *Baroque Reason*, London: Sage, 1994.
Burckhardt, T., *Art of Islam: Language and Meaning*, London: World of Islam Festival Publishing, 1976.
Calabrese, O., *Neo-Baroque: A Sign of the Times*, Princeton, NJ: Princeton University Press, 1992.
Capote, T., *Breakfast at Tiffany's: A Short Novel and Three Stories*, New York: Random House, 1994.
Cardozo, B., *The Nature of the Judicial Process*, New Haven, CT: Yale University Press, 1921.
Cardozo, B. *The Paradoxes of Legal Science*, New York: Columbia University Press, 1928.
Carney, B. and Feigenson, N., "Visual Persuasion in the Michael Skakel Trial: Enhancing Advocacy through Interactive Media Presentations," *Criminal Justice*, 19: 22, 2004.
Carroll, R. and Prickett, S., "Book of Genesis," *The Bible: Authorized King James Version*, Oxford: Oxford University Press, 1997.
Casebeer, W. and Churchland, P. S., "The Neural Mechanisms of Moral Cognition: A Multiple-Aspect Approach to Moral Judgment and Decision-Making," *Biology and Philosophy*, 18: 169–194, 2003.
Cassirer, R., *The Myth of the State*, New Haven, CT: Yale University Press, 1946.
Cavell, S., *The World Viewed*, Cambridge, MA: Harvard University Press, 1979.
Chittick, W. C., *Sufism: A Beginner's Guide*, Oxford: Oneworld Publications, 2008.
Cicero, M. T., *De Oratore*, trans. E. W. Sutton and H. Rackham. Cambridge, MA: Harvard University Press, 1948.
Cicero, M. T., *De Inventione*, Cambridge, MA: Harvard University Press, 1976.
Clark, S., *Vanities of the Eye: Vision in Early Modern European Culture*, Oxford: Oxford University Press, 2007.
Clevenot, D. and Degeorge, G., *Splendors of Islam: Architecture, Decoration and Design*, New York: Vendome Press, 2000.
Clover, C., "Law and the Order of Popular Culture," in A. Sarat and T. R. Kearns (eds.), *Law in the Domains of Culture*, Ann Arbor, MI: University of Michigan Press, 1998.
Cole, S. A. and Dioso-Villa, R., "*CSI* and its Effects: Media, Juries, and the Burden of proof," *New England Law Review*, 41: 335–469, 2007.
Cole, S. A. and Dioso-Villa, R., "Investigating the '*CSI* Effect' Effect: Media and Litigation Crisis in Criminal Law," *Stanford Law Review*, 61: 1335–1373, 2009.
Couliano, I. P., *Eros and Magic in the Renaissance*, trans. M. Cook, Chicago: University of Chicago Press, 1987.

Cover, R. M., "Nomos and Narrative," *Harvard Law Review*, 97: 4–68, 1983.
Coyne, R., *Technoromaticism: Digital Narrative, Holism, and the Romance of the Real*, Cambridge, MA: MIT Press, 2001.
Csordas, T. J., *The Sacred Self: A Cultural Phenomenology of Charismatic Healing*, Berkeley, CA: University of California Press, 1997.
Culler, J., *The Pursuit of Signs*, Ithaca, NY: Cornell University Press, 2002.
Dällenbach, L., *The Mirror in the Text*, Chicago: University of Chicago Press, 1989.
Damasio, A., *Descartes' Error: Emotion, Reason, and the Human Brain*, New York: Penguin Books, 1994.
Damasio, A., *The Feeling of What Happens: Body and Emotion in the Making of Consciousness*, New York: Harcourt Brace, 1999.
Damman, J. and Hansmann, H., "Globalizing Commercial Litigation," *Cornell Law Review*, 98: 1, 2008.
de Sade, M., *Juliette*, New York: Grove Press, 1968.
Debord, G., *The Society of the Spectacle*, trans. D. Nicholson-Smith, New York: Zone Books, 1995.
Debray, R., *Vie et mort de l'image*, Paris: Gallimard, 1995.
Deger, J., *Shimmering Screens: Making Media in an Aboriginal Community*, Minneapolis, MN: University of Minnesota Press, 2006.
Deguy, M., "The Discourse of Exaltation: Contribution to a Rereading of Pseudo-Longinus," in Jean-François Courtine (ed.), *Of the Sublime Presence in Question: Essays*, New York: State University of New York Press, 2007.
Deleuze, G., *Cinema 2: The Time-Image*, trans. H. Tomlinson and R. Galeta, Minneapolis, MN: University of Minnesota Press, 1989.
Deleuze, G., *Negotiations, 1972–1990*, trans. M. Joughin, New York: Columbia University Press, 1990.
Deleuze, G., *The Fold: Leibniz and the Baroque*, Minneapolis, MN: University of Minnesota Press, 1992.
Deleuze, G., *Difference and Repetition*, New York: Columbia University Press, 1994.
Deleuze, G., *Essays, Critical and Clinical*, trans. D. Smith and M. Greco, Minneapolis, MN: University of Minnesota Press, 1997.
Deleuze, G., *Foucault*, trans. S. Hand, Minneapolis, MN: University of Minnesota Press, 2000.
Deleuze, G., *Pure Immanence: essays on a life*, trans. A. Boyman, New York: Zone Books, 2001.
Deleuze, G. and Guattari, F., *Anti-Oedipus: Capitalism and Schizophrenia*, trans. R. Hurley, M. Seem, and H. R. Lane, Minneapolis, MN: University of Minnesota Press, 2000.
Dempsey, C., *The Portrayal of Love: Botticelli's* Primavera *and Humanist Culture at the Time of Lorenzo the Magnificent*, Princeton, NJ: Princeton University Press, 1992.
Derrida, J., *Of Grammatology*, trans. G. C. Spivak, Baltimore, MD: Johns Hopkins University Press, 1976.
Derrida, J., *Dissemination*, trans. B. Johnson, Chicago: University of Chicago Press, 1981.
Derrida, J., *Of Spirit: Heidegger and the Question*, trans. G. Bennington and R. Bowlby, Chicago: University of Chicago Press, 1987.

Derrida, J., "Force of Law: The Mystical Foundation of Authority," in D. Cornell et al. (eds.), *Deconstruction and the Possibility of Justice*, New York: Routledge, 1992.
Derrida, J., *The Gift of Death*, trans. D. Wills, Chicago: University of Chicago Press, 1996.
Derrida, J., *On Cosmopolitanism and Forgiveness*, London: Routledge, 2001.
Derrida, J., "The Tragic, the Impossible and Democracy: An Interview with Jacques Derrida," *International Journal of the Semiotics of Law*, 23: 243–264, 2010.
Derrida, J. and Vattimo, G., (eds.), *Religion*, Stanford, CA: Stanford University Press, 1996.
Descartes, R., *Meditations on First Philosophy*, trans. L. J. Lafleur, 2nd edn, New York and Indianapolis, IN: Bobbs-Merrill, 1960.
Descartes, R., *Treatise of Man*, trans. T. S. Hall, Amherst, NY: Prometheus Books, 2003.
Dibbell, J., *My Tiny Life: Crime and Passion in a Virtual World*, New York: Henry Holt, 1998.
Didi-Huberman, G., *Fra Angelico: Dissemblance and Figuration*, Chicago: University of Chicago Press, 1995.
Dombroski, R. S., *Creative Entanglements: Gadda and the Baroque*, Toronto: University of Toronto Press, 1999.
Douglas, K. S., Lyon, D. R., and Ogloff, J. R. P., "The Impact of Graphic Photographic Evidence on Mock Jurors' Decisions in a Murder Trial: Probative or Prejudicial?," *Law and Human Behavior*, 21: 485–501, 1997.
Douglas, M., *Purity and Danger: An Analysis of the Concepts of Pollution and Taboo*, London: Routledge, 1995.
Douzinas, C., "Oubliez critique," *Law and Critique*, 16: 47–69, 2005.
Dufrenne, M., *The Phenomenology of Aesthetic Experience*, Evanston, IL: Northwestern University Press, 1973.
Dumézil, G., *The Destiny of the Warrior*, trans. A. Hiltebeitel, Chicago: University of Chicago Press, 1970.
Durkheim, E., *Suicide: A Study in Sociology*, trans. J. A. Spaulding and G. Simpson, ed. G. Simpson, New York: Free Press, 1951.
Dworkin, R., *A Matter of Principle*, Cambridge, MA: Harvard University Press, 1985.
Dworkin, R., *Justice for Hedgehogs*, Cambridge, MA: Harvard University Press, 2011.
Eliade, M., *Rites and Symbols of Initiation: The Mysteries of Birth and Rebirth*, New York: Harper & Row, 1965.
Evelyn, J., *The Diary of John Evelyn*, Vol. 2, *Kalendarium, 1620–1649*, ed. E. S. DeBeer, Oxford: Clarendon Press, 1955.
Fackenheim, E., *To Mend the World: The Foundations of Post-Holocaust Jewish Thought*, Bloomington, IN: Indiana University Press, 1994.
Falk, A. J., "Sex Offenders, Mental Illness and Criminal Responsibility: The Constitutional Boundaries of Civil Commitment after *Kansas v. Hendricks*," American Journal of Law and Medicine, 25: 117–147, 1999.
Faure, B., *The Rhetoric of Immediacy*, Princeton, NJ: Princeton University Press, 1994.
Feigenson, N., "Accidents as Melodrama," *New York Law School Law Review*, 43: 741–810, 1999–2000.
Feigenson, N., *Legal Blame: How Jurors Think and Talk about Accidents*, Washington, DC: American Psychological Association, 2001.
Feigenson, N., "Brain Imaging and Courtroom Evidence: On the Admissibility and Persuasiveness of fMRI," *International Journal of Law in Context*, 2: 233–255, 2006.

Feigenson, N., "Visual Common Sense," in A. Wagner and R. K. Sherwin (eds.), *Law, Culture, and Visual Studies*, Amsterdam: Springer, 2012.

Feigenson, N. and Dunn, M. A., "New Visual Technologies in Court: Directions for Research," *Law and Human Behavior*, 27: 109–126, 2003.

Feigenson, N. and Sherwin, R. K., "Thinking beyond the Shown: Implicit Inferences in Evidence and Argument," *Law, Probability, and Risk*, 6: 245–310, 2007.

Ferraris, M., "The Meaning of Being as a Determinate Ontic Trance," in J. Derrida and G. Vattimo (eds.), *Religion*, Stanford, CA: Stanford University Press, 1996.

Feyerbend, P., *Against Method*, London: Verso, 1993.

Fleming, D., "Can Pictures be Arguments?," *Argumentation and Advocacy*, 33: 11–22, 1996.

Flusser, V., *The Shape of Things: A Philosophy of Design*, trans. A. Matthews, London: Reaktion Books, 1999.

Flusser, V., *Towards a Philosophy of Photography*, London: Reaktion Books, 2000.

Flusser, V., *Writings*, trans. E. Eisel, Minneapolis, MN: University of Minnesota Press, 2004.

Foster, H., *Vision and Visuality*, New York: New Press, 1999.

Foucault, M., *The Archaeology of Knowledge*, trans. A. M. S. Smith, New York: Pantheon Books, 1972.

Foucault, M., "Two Lectures," in C. Gordon (ed.), *Power/Knowledge: Selected Interviews and Other Writings 1972–1977*, New York: Pantheon Books, 1980.

Frank, J., *Law and the Modern Mind*, New Brunswick, NJ: Transaction, 2009 [1935].

Freedberg, S. J., *Painting in Italy, 1500–1600*, New Haven, CT: Yale University Press, 1993.

Freud, S., "Two Encyclopedia Articles," trans. J. Strachey and A. Freud, in *The Standard Edition of the Complete Psychological Works of Sigmund Freud*, New York: Vintage, 1999.

Freud, S., *Totem and Taboo*, Stilwell, KS, Digireads.com, 2008.

Gadamer, H., *Truth and Method*, New York: Crossroad, 1975.

Galloway, A., *Gaming: Essays on Algorithmic Culture*, Minneapolis, MN: University of Minnesota Press, 2006.

Gény, F., *Méthode d'interprétation et sources en droit privé positif*, 2nd edn, 1899, Baton Rouge, LA: Louisiana State Law Institute, 1954 [1899].

Gigerenzer, G., Todd, P. M. and the ABC Research Group, *Simple Heuristics that Make Us Smart*, Oxford: Oxford University Press, 2000.

Gilbert, D. T., "How Mental Systems Believe," *American Psychologist*, 46: 107–117, 1991.

Gilmore, G., *The Ages of American Law*, New Haven, CT: Yale University Press, 1977.

Gladwell, M., Blink: *The Power of Thinking without Thinking*, Boston, MA: Backbay Books, 2007.

Glowacka, D., "Ethical Figures of Otherness: Jean-Luc Nancy's Sublime Offering and Emmanuel Levinas' Gift for the Other," in K. Ziarek and S. Deane (eds.), *Future Crossings: Literature Between Philosophy and Culture Studies*, Evanston, IL: Northwestern University Press, 2000.

Glowacka, D. and Boos, S. (eds), *Between Ethics and Aesthetics*, Albany, NY: State University of New York Press, 2002.

Goode, S., "The Admissibility of Electronic Evidence," *Review of Litigation*, 29: 1, 2009.

Goodrich, P., *Law in the Courts of Love: Literature and Other Minor Jurisprudences*, London: Routledge, 1996.

Goodrich, P., "The Iconography of Nothing: Blank Spaces and the Representation of Law in *Edward VI and the Pope*," in C. Douzinas and L. Nead (eds.), *Law and the Image: The Authority of Art and the Aesthetics of Law*, Chicago: University of Chicago Press, 1999.

Goodrich, P., "Screening Law," *Law and Literature*, 21(1): 1–23, 2009.

Goux, J., *Oedipus, Philosopher*, Stanford, CA: Stanford University Press, 1993.

Grabar, O., *The Meditation of Ornament*, Princeton, NJ: Princeton University Press, 1992.

Grassi, E., *Rhetoric as Philosophy: The Humanist Tradition*, University Park, PA: Pennsylvania State University Press, 1980.

Grassi, E., *Renaissance Humanism*, Binghamton, NY: Center for Medieval and Early Renaissance Studies, 1988.

Grassi, E., *Vico and Humanism*, New York: Peter Lang, 1990.

Grassi, E., *The Primordial Metaphor*, Binghamton, NY: Center for Medieval and Early Renaissance Studies, 1994.

Greenberg, J. et al., "Evidence for Terror Management Theory," II, "The Effects of Mortality Salience on Reactions to Those Who Threaten or Bolster the Cultural World View," *Journal of Personality and Social Psychology*, 58: 308–318, 1990.

Greenberg, J., Solomon, S., and Pyszcynski, T., "Terror Management Theory of Self-Esteem and Cultural Worldviews: Empirical Assessments and Conceptual Refinements," in M. P. Zanna (ed.), *Advances in Experimental Social Psychology* 29, 1997.

Grossman, A., *The Sighted Singer, Two Works on Poetry for Readers and Writers*, Baltimore, MD: Johns Hopkins University Press, 1992.

Gunning, T., "An Aesthetic of Astonishment: Early Film and the (In)credulous Spectator," in L. Williams (ed.), *Viewing Positions: Ways of Seeing Film*, New Brunswick, NJ: Rutgers University Press, 1995.

Gurley, J. and Marcus, D. K., "The Effects of Neuroimaging and Brain Injury on Insanity Defenses," *Behavioral Sciences and the Law*, 26: 85–97, 2008.

Gurvitch, G., *Sociology of Law*, New Brunswick, NJ: Transaction, 2001.

Habermas, J., *Between Facts and Norms: Contributions to a Discourse Theory of Law and Democracy*, Cambridge, MA: MIT Press, 1998.

Hall, S., Critcher, C., Jefferson, T., Clarke, J., and Robert, B., *Policing the Crisis: Mugging, the State and Law and Order*, Basingstoke: Palgrave Macmillan, 1978.

Hallyn, F., *The Poetic Structure of the World: Copernicus and Kepler*, trans. D. M. Leslie, New York: Zone Books, 1990.

Handelman, D., *Models and Mirrors: Towards an Anthropology of Public Events*, New York: Berghahn Books, 1998.

Hart, H. L. A., *The Concept of Law*, 2nd edn, Oxford: Oxford University Press, 1997.

Hasslacher, B., "Beyond the Turing Machine," in R. Herken (ed.), *The Universal Turing Machine: A Half-Century Survey*, New York and Vienna: Springer, 1991.

Heidegger, M., "On the Essence of Truth," trans. Hull and Crick, in W. Brock (ed.), *Existence and Being*, Chicago: Gateway Edition, 1949.

Heidegger, M., *Poetry, Language, Thought*, trans. A. Hofstadter, New York: Harper & Row, 1971.

Heidegger, M., *Nietzsche*, trans. D. F. Krell, New York: Harper Collins, 1991.

Heidegger, M., "The Question concerning Technology," in D. F. Krell (ed.) *Basic Writings: from "Being and Time" (1927) to "The Task of Thinking" (1964)*, New York: HarperCollins, 1993.

Heidegger, M., "The Age of the World Picture," in *The Question Concerning Technology and other Essays*, New York: Harper & Row, 1977.
Heim, M., *The Metaphysics of Virtual Reality*, Oxford: Oxford University Press, 1993.
Hilfer, T., *The Crime Novel: A Deviant Genre*, Austin, TX: University of Texas Press, 1990.
Hobbes, T., *Leviathan*, Indianapolis, IN: Bobbs-Merrill, 1958 [1651].
Hobbes, T., *De Corpore*, Paris: Librairie Philosophique J. Vrin, 1999.
Holland, D., and Quinn, N. (eds.), *Cultural Models in Language and Thought*, Cambridge: Cambridge University Press, 1987.
Huddy, L. and Gunnthorsdottir, A., "The Persuasive Effects of Emotive Visual Imagery: Superficial Manipulation of the Product of Passionate Reason?" *Political Psychology*, 21: 745–778, 2000.
Hutcheson, J., "The Judgment Intuitive: The Function of the 'Hunch' in Judicial Decision," *Cornell Law Quarterly*, 14: 274–288, 1929.
Ihde, D., *Technology and the Lifeworld: From Garden to Earth*, Bloomington, IN: Indiana University Press, 1990.
Illich, I., *Guarding the Eye in the Age of Show*, University Park, PA: *Science, Technology, and Society Studies*, University of Pennsylvania, 1994.
Indyk, I., "The Critic and the Public Culture: For Example, Walter Benjamin," *Australian Humanities Review*, 18: 2000.
Isocrates, "Against the Sophists," in *Isocrates I*, trans. D. C. Mirhady and Y. L. Too, Austin, TX: University of Texas Press, 2000.
James, L., "Seeing Is Believing But Words Tell No Lies: Captions versus Images in the *Libri Carolini* and Byzantine Iconoclasm," in A. McClanan and J. Johnson (eds.), *Negating the Image: Case Studies in Iconoclasm*, London: Ashgate, 2005.
James, W., *The Will to Believe*, New York: Dover, 1956.
James, W., *The Philosophy of William James*, New York: Modern Library, 1925.
James, W., *Pragmatism: A New Name for Some Old Ways of Thinking*, Indianapolis, IN: Hackett, 1981 [1907].
Jay, M., "Scopic Regimes of Modernity," in H. Foster (ed.), *Vision and Visuality*, New York: New Press, 1988.
Jay, M., *Downcast Eyes: The Denigration of Vision in Twentieth-Century French Thought*, Berkeley, CA: University of California Press, 1993.
Jennings, T., *Reading Derrida/Thinking Paul: On Justice*, Stanford, CA: Stanford University Press, 2005.
Johnson, S., *Interface Culture: How New Technology Transforms the Way we Create and Communicate*, New York: Basic Books, 1997.
Jones, C. A. (ed.), *Sensorium: Embodied Experience, Technology, and Contemporary Art*, Cambridge, MA: MIT Press, 2006.
Jones, O., Buckholtz, J., Schall, J., and Marois, R., "Brain Imaging for Legal Thinkers: A Guide for the Perplexed," *Stanford Technology Law Review*, 5, 2009
Joseph, G., "A Simplified Approach to Computer-Generated Evidence and Animations," *New York Law School Law Review* 43: 875–893, 1999–2000.
Kafka, F., *The Castle*, trans. M. Harman, New York: Schocken Books, 1998.
Kafka, F., "In the Penal Colony," *Metamorphosis, In the Penal Colony, and Other Stories: With Two New Stories*, trans. J. Neugroschel, New York: Scribner, 2000.
Kahan, D., "The Cognitively Illiberal State," *Stanford Law Review*, 60: 115–154, 2007.

Kahan, D., Hoffman, D. and Braman, D., "Whose Eyes Are You Going to Believe? *Scott v. Harris* and the Perils of Cognitive Illiberalism," *Harvard Law Review*, 122: 837–906, 2009.

Kant, *Critique of Practical Reason*, trans. Mary Gregor, Cambridge: Cambridge University Press, 1997.

Kantorowicz, E. H., *The King's Two Bodies: A Study in Mediaeval Political Theology*, Princeton, NJ: Princeton University Press, 1981.

Kassin, S. M. and Dunn, M. A., "Computer Animated Displays and the Jury: Facilitative and Prejudicial Effects," *Law and Human Behavior*, 21: 269–281, 1997.

Katz-Schiavone, S., Levenson, J. S., and Ackerman, A. R., "Myths and Facts about Sexual Violence: public perceptions and implications for prevention," *Journal of Criminal Justice and Popular Culture*, 15: 291–307, 2008.

Kennedy, D. and Bellau, M. C., "François Gény aux États-Unis," in C. Thomasset, J. Vanderlinden, and P. Jestaz (eds.), *François Gény, mythe et réalités: 1899–1999: centenaire de méthode d'interprétation et sources en droit privé positif: essai critique*, Québec: Yvon Blais, 2000.

Khan, U., "Having your Porn and Condemning it Too: A Case Study of a 'Kiddie Porn Exposé'," *Law, Culture and the Humanities*, 5: 391, 394, 2009.

Kibbey, A. M., *Theory of the Image: Capitalism, Contemporary Film, and Women*, Bloomington, IN: Indiana University Press, 2004.

Kilborne, B., *Disappearing Persons*, New York: State University of New York Press, 2002.

Kincaid, J. R., *Erotic Innocence: The Culture of Child Molesting*, Durham, NC: Duke University Press, 1998.

Klein, N., *The Shock Doctrine: The Rise of Disaster Capitalism*, New York: Picador, 2008.

Kligerman, E., *Sites of the Uncanny: Paul Celan, Specularity and the Visual Arts*, Berlin: De Gruyter, 2007.

Koepsell, D. R., *The Ontology of Cyberspace: Law, Philosophy, and the Future of Intellectual Property*, Peru, IL: Open Court, 2000.

Kolakowski, L., *The Presence of Myth*, Chicago: University of Chicago Press, 1989.

Korotkin, J. B. and Giovannotti, M. (eds.), *Neo-Baroque!* Milan: Charta, 2006.

Kronman, A., "Rhetoric," *University of Cincinnati Law Review*, 67: 677, 1999.

Kuhn, T., *The Structure of Scientific Revolutions*, Chicago: University of Chicago Press, 1996.

Kurzweil, R., *The Age of Spiritual Machines*, New York: Penguin Books, 2000.

Kurzweil, R., *The Singularity is Near: When Humans Transcend Biology*, New York: Penguin Books, 2006.

Lacan, J., *Quatre concepts fundamentaux de la psychoanalyse*, Paris: Editions du Seuil, 1979.

Lacoue-Labarthe, P., "Sublime Truth," in *Of the Sublime: Presence in Question*, trans. J. S. Librett, Albany, NY: State University of New York Press, 1993.

Langleben, D. D., Longhead, H. W., Bilker, W. B., Ruparel, K., Childress, A. R., Busch, S. I., and Gur, R. C., "Telling Truth from Lies in Individual Subjects with Fast Event-Related fMRI," *Human Brain Map*, 26: 262–272, 2005.

Lanza, R. and Berman, B., *Biocentrism: how life and consciousness are the keys to understanding the true nature of the universe*, Dallas, TX: BenBella Books, 2010.

Laplanche, J., *Essays on Otherness*, New York: Routledge, 1999.

Laplanche, J., *Vie et mort en psychanalyse*, Paris: Flammarion, 2001.
Latour, B., *Iconoclash: beyond the image wars in science, religion and art*, Cambridge, MA: MIT Press, 2002.
Lederer, F., "Changing Litigation with Science and Technology," *Emory Law Journal*, 43: 1095, 1994.
Lederer, F. I., "Courtroom Technology and its Educational Implications," *Virginia Education and Practice*, 8: 3, 1998.
Lee, A., "The *CSI* Effect: TV's Impact on the Future of Forensic Science," in Cambridge University (ed.), *The Triple Helix*, 7: 22–23, 2007.
Legendre, P., *Dominium Mundi: l'empire du management*, Paris: Mille et une nuits, 2007.
Leibniz, G. W., *Monadology and Other Philosophical Essays*, trans. P. Schrecker and A. M. Schrecker, New York: Bobbs-Merrill, 1965.
Leibniz, G. W., *Philosophical Essays*, Indianapolis, IN: Hackett, 1989.
Leiter, B., *Naturalizing Jurisprudence*, Oxford: Oxford University Press, 2007.
Levinas, E., *Totality and Infinity: An Essay on Exteriority*, trans. A. Lingus, Pittsburgh, PA: Duquesne University Press, 1969.
Levinas, E., *Ethics and Infinity*, Pittsburgh, PA: Duquesne University Press, 1985.
Levinas, E., *Nine Talmudic Readings*, Bloomington, IN: Indiana University Press, 1994.
Levinas, E., *Otherwise than Being, or, Beyond Essence*, trans. A. Lingis, Dordrecht: Kluwer, 1991; Pitsburgh, PA: Pittsburgh University Press, 1998.
Levinas, E., *Proper Names*, trans. M. Smith, Stanford, CA: Stanford University Press, 1996.
Li, W., *Enchantment and Disenchantment: Love and Illusion in Chinese Literature*, Princeton, NJ: Princeton University Press, 1993.
Lifton, R. J., *The Protean Self: Human Resilience in an Age of Fragmentation*, Chicago: University of Chicago Press, 1999.
Longinus, *On the Sublime*, trans. W. H. Fyfe, Cambridge, MA and London: Harvard University Press, 1995.
Lorenz, K., *On Aggression*, Orlando, FL: Harcourt Books, 1966.
Luntz, F., *Words that Work: It's Not What You Say, It's What People Hear*, New York: Hyperion, 2006.
Lyotard, J., "The Sublime and the Avant-Garde," in *The Inhuman: Reflections on Time*, Stanford, CA: Stanford University Press, 1988.
Madrigal, A., "Courtroom First: Brain Scan Used in Murder Sentencing," *Wired Science*, 23 November 2009.
Maiorino, G., *The Cornucopian Mind and the Baroque Unity of the Arts*, University Park, PA: Pennsylvania State University Press, 1990.
Malpas, J., *Heidegger's Topology: Being, Place, World*, Cambridge, MA: MIT Press, 2006.
Manderson, D., "Judgment," in A. Sarat (ed.), *Law and the Humanities*, Cambridge: Cambridge University Press, 2009.
Maravall, J. A., *Culture of the Baroque: Analysis of a Historical Structure*, Minneapolis, MN: University of Minnesota Press, 1986.
Marcus, R., "E-Discovery and Beyond," *Review of Litigation*, 25: 633, 2006.
Marks, D. F., "On the Relationship between Imagery, Body, and Mind," in P. J. Hampson, D. F. Marks and J. T. E. Richardson (eds.), *Imagery: Current Developments*, London: Routledge, 1990.

Marks, L. U., *The Skin of the Film*, Durham, NC: Duke University Press, 1999.
Marks, L. U., *Touch: Sensuous Theory and Multisensory Media*, Minneapolis, MN: University of Minnesota Press, 2002.
Marks, L. U., "Information, Secrets, and Enigmas: An Enfolding–Unfolding Aesthetics for Cinema," *Screen*, 50: 86–98, 2009.
Marks, L. U., *Enfoldment and Infinity: An Islamic Genealogy of New Media Art*, Cambridge, MA: MIT Press, 2010.
Massey, L., *Picturing Space, Displacing Bodies: anamorphosis in early modern theories of perspective*, University Park, PA: Pennsylvania State University Press, 2007.
Mazzeo, J. A., "Metaphysical Poetry and the Poetic of Correspondence," *Journal of the History of Ideas*, 14: 221–234, 1953.
Mazzotta, G., *The New Map of the World*, Princeton, NJ: Princeton University Press, 1999.
Mazzotta, G., *Cosmopoiesis: The Renaissance Experiment*, Toronto: University of Toronto Press, 2001.
McCabe, D. P. and Castel, A. D., "Seeing is Believing: The Effect of Brain Images on Judgments of Scientific Reasoning," *Cognition*, 107: 343–352, 2008.
McCusker, C., "Between Natural Law and Legal Positivism: Plato's Minos and the Nature of Law," *Yale Journal of Law and the Humanities*, 22: 83–104, 2010.
Merleau-Ponty, M. M., *The Visible and the Invisible*, trans. A. Lingis, Evanston, IL: Northwestern University Press, 1969.
Merleau-Ponty, M. M., *Phenomenology of Perception*, London: Routledge, 2008 [1962].
Michalski, S., *The Reformation and the Visual Arts*, London: Routledge, 1993.
Mill, J. S., *Autobiography of John Stewart Mill*, New York: Columbia University Press, 1960.
Mitchell, W. J. T., "What is an Image?" *New Literary History*, 15: 3, 1984.
Mitchell, W. J. T., *Iconology: Image, Text, Ideology*, Chicago: University of Chicago Press, 1987.
Mitchell, W. J. T., *What do Pictures Want?* Chicago: University of Chicago Press, 2005.
Mnookin, J. L., "The Image of Truth: Photographic Evidence and the Power of Analogy," *Yale Journal of Law and the Humanities*, 10: 1–74, 1998.
Mnookin, J. L. and West, N., "Theaters of Proof: Visual Evidence and the Law in *Call Northside 777*," *Yale Journal of Law and the Humanities*, 13: 329–390, 2001.
Mobbs, D., Lau, H. C., Jones, O. D., and Frith, C. D., "Law, Responsibility, and the Brain," *PLoS Biology*, 5(4): 693–700, 2007.
Modak-Truran, M. C., "A Pragmatic Justification of the Judicial Hunch," *University of Richmond Law Review*, 35: 55–89, 2001.
Mooney, M., *Vico in the Tradition of Rhetoric*, London: Routledge, 1995.
Morgan, D., *The Sacred Gaze*, Berkeley, CA: University of California Press, 2005.
Morley, S. (ed.), *The Sublime*, Cambridge, MA: MIT Press, 2010.
Muensterberger, W. (ed.), *Man and His Culture: Psychoanalytic Anthropology after "Totem and Taboo,"* New York: Taplinger, 1970.
Muller, J. P., *Beyond the Psychoanalytic Dyad: Developmental Semiotics in Freud, Peirce and Lacan*, New York: Routledge, 1996.
Murakami, H., *Hard-Boiled Wonderland and the End of the World*, New York: Vintage Books, 1993.

Murakami, T., *Superflat*, Tokyo: Madora Shuppan, 2000.
Murakami, T., *Little Boy: The Arts of Japan's Exploding Subculture*, New Haven, CT: Yale University Press, 2005.
Murdoch, I., *Metaphysics as a Guide to Morals*, New York: Penguin Books, 1993.
Murdoch, I., *The Sovereignty of the Good*, London: Routledge, 2002.
Murray, G., *Five Stages of Greek Religion*, New York: Doubleday, 1955.
Murray, T., *Digital Baroque: New Media Art and Cinematic Folds*, Minneapolis, MN: University of Minnesota Press, 2008.
Nancy, J., *The Experience of Freedom*, Stanford, CA: Stanford University Press, 1993.
Nasr, S. H., *Islamic Art and Spirituality*, Albany, NY: State University of New York Press, 1987.
Ndalianis, A., "Introduction. The Baroque and the Neo-Baroque," in *Neo-Baroque Aesthetics and Contemporary Entertainment*, Cambridge, MA: MIT Press, 2004.
Ndalianis, A., *Neo-Baroque Aesthetics and Contemporary Entertainment*, Cambridge, MA: MIT Press, 2004.
Nechvatal, J., "An Ecstasy of Excess," in *An Ecstasy of Excess*, Münchengladbach: Juni-Verlag, 1991.
Nichols, B., *Representing Reality*, Bloomington, IN: Indiana University Press, 1991.
Nietzsche, F., *On the Genealogy of Morals and Ecce Homo*, trans. R. J. Hollingdale, ed. W. Kaufmann, New York: Vintage, 1969.
Nietzsche, F., *On the Genealogy of Morality*, Indianapolis, IN: Hackett, 1998.
Nisbett, R. and Ross, L., *Human Inference: Strategies and Shortcomings of Social Judgment*, New York: Prentice-Hall, 1985.
Noonan, Jr, J. T., *Persons and Masks of the Law: Cardozo, Holmes, Jefferson, and Wythe as Makers of the Masks*, Berkeley, CA: University of California Press, 1976.
Olson, T., "Of Enchantment: The Passing of the Ordeals and the Rise of the Jury Trial," *Syracuse Law Review*, 50: 109–196, 2000.
Pascal, B., *Pensées*, New York: Penguin Books, 1995.
Perlin, M., " 'His Brain Has Been Mismanaged with Great Skill': How Will Jurors Respond to Neuroimaging Testimony in Insanity Defense Cases?" *Akron Law Review*, 42: 885–916, 2009.
Pisters, P., *The Matrix of Visual Culture: Working with Deleuze in Film Theory*, Stanford, CA: Stanford University Press, 2003.
Plato, *Symposium*, trans. A. Nehamas and P. Woodruff, Indianapolis, IN: Hackett, 1989.
Plato, *Phaedrus and Letters VII and VIII*, New York: Penguin Books, 1973.
Podlas, K., "The *CSI* Effect: Exposing the Media Myth," *Fordham Intellectual Property, Media and Entertainment Law Journal*, 16: 429–465, 2006.
Purgar, K., *The Neo-Baroque Subject*, Zagreb: Meandar Media, 2007.
Putnam, H., *Meaning and the Moral Sciences*, London: Routledge & Kegan Paul, 1978.
Quintilian, *Institutio Oratoria*, Cambridge, MA and London: Harvard University Press, 1976.
Rabinbach, A., *In the Shadow of Catastrophe*, Berkeley, CA: University of California Press, 2000.
Rajchman, J., *Constructions*, Cambridge, MA: MIT Press, 1998.
Rawls, J., "Overlapping Consensus," in S. Freeman (ed.), *Collected Papers*, Cambridge, MA: Harvard University Press, 1999.

Rawls, J., *A Theory of Justice*, Cambridge, MA: Harvard University Press, 2005.

Ricoeur, P., *Hermeneutics and the Human Sciences*, Cambridge: Cambridge University Press, 1981.

Ricoeur, P., "Between Rhetoric and Poetics," in A. O. Rorty (ed.), *Essays on Aristotle's "Rhetoric,"* Berkeley, CA: University of California Press, 1996.

Riegl, A., *Historical Grammar of the Visual Arts*, trans. J. E. Jung, New York: Zone Books, 2004.

Ries, A. and Trout, J., *Positioning: The Battle for Your Mind*, New York: McGraw-Hill, 1986.

Riley, P., *Leibniz' Universal Jurisprudence: Justice as Charity of the Wise*, Cambridge, MA: Harvard University Press, 1996.

Robin, C., *Fear: The History of a Political Idea*, Oxford: Oxford University Press, 2004.

Robins, K., *Into the Image: Culture and Politics in the Field of Vision*, London: Routledge, 1996.

Rodowick, D. N., *Gilles Deleuze's Time Machine*, Durham, NC: Duke University Press, 1997.

Rodowick, D. N., *Reading the Figural, or, Philosophy after the New Media*, Durham, NC: Duke University Press, 2001.

Rodowick, D. N., *The Virtual Life of Film*, Cambridge, MA: Harvard University Press, 2007.

Rorty, R., *Philosophy and the Mirror of Nature*, Princeton, NJ: Princeton University Press, 1979.

Rorty, R., "Foreword," in G. Vattimo, *Nihilism and Emancipation: Ethics, Politics, and Law*, New York: Columbia University Press, 2003.

Rosenzweig, F., *The Star of Redemption*, Boston, MA: Beacon Press, 1971.

Rosenzweig, F., *Understanding the Sick and the Healthy*, Cambridge, MA: Harvard University Press, 1999.

Sade, Marquis de, *Juliette*, trans. A. Wainhouse, New York: Grove Press, 1968.

Saleilles, R., *The Individualization of Punishment*, Boston: MA, Little Brown, 1911.

Sandel, M. J., *Democracy's Discontents: America in Search of a Public Philosophy*, Cambridge, MA: Belknap Press, 1996.

Santner, E., *On the Psychotheology of Everyday Life*, Chicago: University of Chicago Press, 2001.

Sarat, A., Douglas, L. and Umphrey, M. (eds.), *Law on the Screen*, Palo Alto, CA: Stanford University Press, 2005.

Sartre, J., *La Nausée*, Paris: Gallimard, 2002.

Scarry, E., *On Beauty and Being Just*, Princeton, NJ: Princeton University Press, 2001.

Schank, R. and Abelson, R., *Scripts, Plans, Goals, and Understanding: An Inquiry into Human Knowledge Structures*, Hillsdale, NJ: Erlbaum, 1977.

Schelling, F. J., *Philosophy and Religion*, Putnam, CT: Spring Publications, 1804.

Schelling, F. J., *Philosophical Investigations into the Essence of Human Freedom*, trans. J. Love and J. Schmidt, Albany, NY: State University of New York Press, 2006.

Scheper-Hughes, N. and Stein, H., "Child Abuse and the Unconscious in American Popular Culture," in N. Scheper-Hughes (ed.), *Child Survival: Anthropological Perspectives on the Treatment and Maltreatment of Children*, Boston MA: Reidel, 1987.

Schmitt, B. H. and Vrotsos, K., *There's No Business That's Not Show Business: Marketing in an Experience Culture*, Upper Saddle River, NJ: Prentice-Hall, 2004.

Schmitt, C., *Political Theology*, Cambridge, MA: MIT Press, 1985.

Schneider, M. A., *Culture and Enchantment*, Chicago: University of Chicago Press, 1993.

Schweitzer, N. J. and Saks, M. J., "The *CSI* Effect: Popular Fiction about Forensic Science Affects Public Expectations about Real Forensic Science," *Jurimetrics*, 47: 357–364, 2007.

Scott, S., *The Politics and Experience of Ritual Abuse: Beyond Disbelief*, Buckingham: Open University Press, 2001.

Seigel, J. E., *Rhetoric and Philosophy in Renaissance Humanism: The Union of Eloquence and Wisdom, Petrarch to Valla*, Princeton, NJ: Princeton University Press, 1968.

Seligman, A., Weller, R., Puett, M., and Simon, B., *Ritual and its Consequences: An Essay on the Limits of Sincerity*, Oxford: Oxford University Press, 2008.

Selznick, P., *The Communitarian Persuasion*, Baltimore, MD: Johns Hopkins University Press, 2002.

Seyhan, A., "Allegories of History: The Politics of Representation in Walter Benjamin," in D. Downing and S. Bazargan (eds.) *Image and Ideology in Modern/Postmodern Discourse*, Albany, NY: State University of New York Press, 1991.

Shakespeare, W., *The Merchant of Venice*, ed. B. Mowat and P. Westine, New York: Washington Square Press, 1992.

Sharp, A., *The English Levellers*, Cambridge: Cambridge University Press, 1998.

Sherwin, R. K., "Dialects and Dominance: A Study of Rhetorical Fields in the Law of Confessions," *University of Pennsylvania Law Review*, 136: 729–849, 1988.

Sherwin, R. K., "Law Frames: Historical Truth and Narrative Necessity in a Criminal Case," *Stanford Law Review*, 47: 39–83, 1994.

Sherwin, R. K., "The Narrative Construction of Legal Reality," *Vermont Law Review*, 18: 681–719, 1994.

Sherwin, R. K., *When Law Goes Pop: The Vanishing Line between Law and Popular Culture*, Chicago: University of Chicago Press, 2000.

Sherwin, R. K., "Law's Beatitude," *Cardozo Law Review*, 24: 683–704, 2003.

Sherwin, R. K., "Anti-Oedipus, Lynch: Initiatory Rites and the Ordeal of Justice," in A. Sarat, L. Douglas, and M. M. Umphrey (eds.), *Law on the Screen*, Stanford, CA: Stanford University Press, 2005.

Sherwin, R. K., "Law, Metaphysics, and the New Iconoclasm," *Law Text Culture*, 11: 70–105, 2007.

Sherwin, R. K., "Sublime Jurisprudence: On the Ethical Education of the Legal Imagination in our Time," *Chicago-Kent Law Review*, 83: 1157–1196, 2008.

Sherwin, R. K., "Visual Literacy in Action: Law in the Age of Images," in J. Elkins (ed.), *Visual Literacy*, London: Routledge, 2008.

Sherwin, R. K., "What Screen do you Have in Mind? Contesting the Visual Context of Law and Film Studies," in A. Sarat (ed.), *Studies in Law, Politics, and Society*, Bingley: JAI Press, 2009.

Sherwin, R. K., "Law's Screen Life," in A. Sarat (ed.), *Imagining Legality*, Tuscaloosa, AL: Alabama University Press, 2010.

Sherwin, R. K., "Constitutional Purgatory: Shades and Presences Inside the Courtroom," in D. Carpi and K. Stierstorfer (eds), *Law and the Image*, Berlin: De Gruyter, 2012.

Sherwin, R. K., Feigenson, N., and Spiesel, C., "Law in the Digital Age: How Visual Communication Technologies Are Transforming the Practice, Theory, and

Teaching of Law," *Boston University Journal of Science and Technology Law*, 12: 227–270, 2006.
Silbey, J., "Judges as Film Critics: New Approaches to Film Evidence," *University of Michigan Journal of Law Reform*, 37: 493–571, 2004.
Skrine, P. N., *The Baroque: Literature and Culture in Seventeenth Century Europe*, London: Methuen, 1978.
Smith, S., *Law's Quandary*, Cambridge, MA: Harvard University Press, 2004.
Smith, V., "Prototypes in the Courtroom: Lay Representations of Legal Concepts," *Journal of Personality and Social Psychology*, 61: 857–872, 1991.
Snead, O. C., "Neuroimaging and the 'Complexity' of Capital Punishment," *New York University Law Review*, 82: 1265–1338, 2007.
Sobchack, V., *Carnal Thoughts: Embodiment and Moving Image Culture*, Berkeley, CA: University of California Press, 2002.
Soleveitchik, J. B., *The Lonely Man of Faith*, New York: Three Leaves, 2006.
Sontag, S., *Styles of Radical Will*, New York: Picador, 2002.
Sontag, S., *Regarding the Pain of Others*, New York: Penguin Books, 2004.
Sorel, G., *Reflections on Violence*, New York: Peter Smith, 1941.
Spariosu, M. (ed.) *Mimesis in Contemporary Theory*, Vol. 1, *The Literary and Philosophical Debate*, Philadelphia: Benjamins, 1984.
Stachenfeld, A. J. and Nicholson, C. M., "Blurred Boundaries: An Analysis of the Close Relationship between Popular Culture and the Practice of Law," *University of San Francisco Law Review*, 30: 903–901, 1996.
Stern, J., *Denial: A Memoir of Terror*, New York: HarperCollins, 2010.
Stevens, W., "The Man with the Blue Guitar," in *The Collected Poetry of Wallace Stevens*, New York: Vintage, 1990.
Stone, G. P., *The Ethics of Nature in the Middle Ages: On Boccaccio's Poetaphysics*, Basingstoke: Macmillan, 1998.
Stone, J., *Province and Function of Law: Law as Logic Justice and Social Control: A Study in Jurisprudence*, Buffalo, NY: William S. Hein, 1946.
Struever, N., *The Language of History in the Renaissance: Rhetoric and Historical Consciousness in Florentine Humanism*, Princeton, NJ: Princeton University Press, 1970.
Supiot, A., *Homo Juridicus*, London: Verso, 2007.
Taussig, M. T., *Mimesis and Alterity: A Particular History of the Senses*, London: Routledge, 1993.
Taylor, D., *The Archive and the Repertoire: Performing Cultural Memory in the Americas*, Durham, NC: Duke University Press, 2003.
Toulmin, S., *Cosmopolis: The Hidden Agenda of Modernity*, Chicago: University of Chicago Press, 1990.
Trout, J. D., "Seduction without Cause: Uncovering Explanatory Neurophilia," *Trends in Cognitive Sciences*, 12: 281–282, 2008.
Turkle, S., *Simulation and its Discontents*, Cambridge, MA: MIT Press, 2009.
Turner, V., *The Ritual Process*, Ithaca, NY: Cornell University Press, 1969.
Turner, V., *Revelation and Divination in Ndembu Ritual*, Ithaca, NY: Cornell University Press, 1975.
Tyler, T. R., "Viewing *CSI* and the Threshold of Guilt: Managing Truth and Justice in Reality and Fiction," *Yale Law Journal*, 115: 1050–1085, 2006.

Unger, R. M., *False Necessity: Anti-Necessitarian Social Theory in the Service of Radical Democracy*, Cambridge: Cambridge University Press, 1987.

van Eck, C., *Classical Rhetoric and the Visual Arts in Early Modern Europe*, Cambridge and New York: Cambridge University Press, 2007.

Varela, F., *Ethical Know-How: Action, Wisdom, and Cognition*, Stanford, CA: Stanford University Press, 1999.

Varela, F., Thompson, J., and Rosh, E., *The Embodied Mind*, Cambridge, MA: MIT Press, 2001.

Vattimo, G., *Art's Claim to Truth*, trans. L. D'Isanto, ed. S. Zabala, New York: Columbia University Press, 2008.

Verene, D. P., *Vico's Science of Imagination*, Ithaca, NY: Cornell University Press, 1981.

Verene, D. P., *Philosophy and the Return to Self-knowledge*, New Haven, CT: Yale University Press, 1997.

Vico, G., *The New Science of Giambattista Vico*, trans. T. G. Bergin and M. H. Fisch, unabridged edn, Ithaca, NY: Cornell University Press, 1968.

Vico, G., *The Autobiography of Giambattista Vico*, Max Harold Fisch and Thomas Goddard Bergin (eds.), Ithaca: NY, Cornell University Press, 1970.

Vico, G., "The Academies and the Relation between Philosophy and Eloquence," trans. D. P. Verene, in *On the Study Methods of Our Time*, trans. E. Gianturco, Ithaca, NY: Cornell University Press, 1990.

Vidmar, N., "When All of Us Are Victims: Juror Prejudice and 'Terrorist' Trials," *Chicago–Kent Law Review*, 78: 1143–1178, 2003.

Wahl, J., *L'expérience métaphysique*, Paris: Flammarion, 1965.

Warhol, A., *The Philosophy of Andy Warhol: From A to B and Back Again*, San Diego, CA: Harvest Books, 1977.

Watt, G., *Equity Stirring: The Story of Justice beyond Law*, Oxford: Hart. 2009.

Weber, M., in G. Roth and C. Wittich (eds.), *Economy and Society*, Berkeley, CA: University of California Press, 1978.

Weil, S., *Waiting for God*, trans. E. Craufurd, New York: Harper Perennial, 1992.

Weisberg, D. S., Keil, F. C., Goodstein, J., Rawson, E., and Gray, J. R., "The Seductive Allure of Neuroscience Explanations," *Journal of Cognitive Neuroscience*, 20: 470–477, 2008.

Weiss, A. S., *Mirrors of Infinity: The French Formal Garden and Seventeenth-Century Meta-Physics*, New York: Princeton Architectural Press, 1995.

Welsh, A., *Strong Representations*, Baltimore, MD: Johns Hopkins University Press, 1995.

Whelan, D., "The Bloody Sunday Tribunal Video Simulation," in J. Elkins (ed.), *Visual Practices across the University*, Paderborn: Wilhelm Fink, 2007.

White, J. B., *The Legal Imagination*, abridged edn, Chicago: University of Chicago Press, 1985.

White, J. B., *The Edge of Meaning*, Chicago: University of Chicago Press, 2003.

Whitehead, A. N., *Modes of Thought*, New York: Capricorn Books, 1958.

Whitehead, A. N., *Process and Reality, 1927–28*, corrected edn, New York: Free Press, 1978.

Whitehead, A. N., *Science and the Modern World*, New York: Free Press, 1967 [1925].

Wölfflin, H., *Renaissance and Baroque*, trans. K. Simon, Ithaca, NY: Cornell University Press, 1967.
Wolosky, S., "A Reply to Vattimo," *Common Knowledge*, 9: 3, 2003.
Worringer, W., *Abstraction and Empathy*, Chicago: Ivan R. Dee, 1997.
Yates, F. A., *Giordano Bruno and the Hermetic Tradition*, Chicago: University of Chicago Press, 1991.
Young, A., *The Scene of Violence: Cinema, Crime, Affect*, New York: Routledge, 2010.
Zizek, S., *The Fright of Real Tears*, London: British Film Institute, 2001.

Index